*Charlotte and UNC Charlotte
Growing Up Together*

Charlotte and UNC Charlotte
Growing Up Together

KEN SANFORD

THE UNIVERSITY OF NORTH CAROLINA AT CHARLOTTE
Charlotte, North Carolina

Copyright © 1996 University of North Carolina at Charlotte

Suggested citation: Sanford, Kenneth J. Charlotte and UNC Charlotte: Growing Up Together.
DOI: https://doi.org/10.5149/9781469668550_Sanford

This work is licensed under a Creative Commons CC BY-NC 4.0 license. To view a copy of the license, visit http://creativecommons.org/licenses.

ISBN 978-1-4696-6854-3 (paperback: alk. paper)
ISBN 978-1-4696-6855-0 (ebook)

Library of Congress Cataloging-in-Publication Data
Sanford, J. Kenneth.
Charlotte and UNC Charlotte : growing up together / Ken Sanford.
p. cm.
Includes bibliographical references and index.
ISBN 1469668548
1. University of North Carolina at Charlotte—History.
2. Charlotte (N.C.)—History—20th century.
3. Community and college—North Carolina—Charlotte.
I. Title.
LD3950.s25   1996   96-17310
378.756'76—dc20   CIP

Unless otherwise noted, photos are courtesy of the UNC Charlotte Archives from the Special Collections of Atkins Library.

Design by Chris Crochetière
Produced by B. Williams & Associates, Durham, North Carolina

Published by J. Murrey Atkins Library at UNC Charlotte

Distributed by the University of North Carolina Press
www.uncpress.org

This book is dedicated to Bonnie Cone, our founder, and to the administrators, faculty, staff, and students of The University of North Carolina at Charlotte and to the citizens of the Charlotte region who helped light the lamp of learning to show the way for generations to come. It is dedicated as well to Alice for her great faith and courage.

Contents

Foreword by William Friday	ix
Preface by Doug Orr	xi
Introduction	xv
1. Charlotte Suffers an Education Gap	1
2. Charlotte Center Feeds a Hunger	15
3. Bonnie Cone Builds Charlotte College	33
4. Charlotte Campaigns for University Status	61
5. Colvard Plants Deep Roots	85
6. Becoming One of Sixteen Campuses	133
7. Fretwell Attracts National Notice	167
8. The University as Entrepreneur	197
9. Adapting to Charlotte's Pace	209
10. The University Wins National Ranking	221
11. After Friday, the Spangler Era	225
12. Woodward Comes to Bolster Support	241
13. Opening the Door to Doctoral Programs	267
14. An Infusion of New Blood	275
15. Footings for New Facilities	283
16. Out of Controversy, an Uptown Center	293
17. A Breakthrough on the Library	299
18. Approaching a Golden Year	303
19. Urban Wave Brightens Future	317
Appendix	329
Bibliography	337
Index	339

Foreword

IN THE course of educational and cultural advancement in the years following World War II, no single event will figure more prominently or have greater significance to the future of the Charlotte region than the establishment of the University of North Carolina at Charlotte.

Institutions rise out of the vision, hard work, uncommon devotion, and provision of reasonable resources by the people of a community and the state. And they rise and grow because of the splendid, uncompromising leader who moves among us to bring many forces and much enthusiasm into focus. Dr. Bonnie Cone was that leader, and our debt to her is as great as the guiding spirit in those early difficult and formative years.

The University of North Carolina at Charlotte had humble beginnings, as is true of most institutions. Once organized, however, it experienced unparalleled growth simply because the largest population center of the state did not have a strong public four-year program immediately available to its sons and daughters. Bonnie Cone understood this circumstance. She, along with a marvelous nucleus of dedicated faculty members, sustained by an unusually strong Board of Trustees, caused the university, happily situated on its farmland campus, to become the realized hopes and dreams of its founders. Through those formative years, the caring, guiding hand of Dr. Arnold K. King was ever present to insure essential academic relationships and standards so desired by everyone.

Thus we celebrate fifty years of growth and development, pausing to pay tribute and to give grateful thanks to our founders.

Living in such a dynamic region of America, this moment of reflection on the past necessarily requires attention to the future of this pioneering urban university and its enormous responsibility to its supporting constituency. Good teaching, appropriate research activity, and the kind and quality of public service the people of the state deserve constitute a worthy mandate for the next half century. Performed well, they augur well for the future of the Commonwealth.

These pages also record the influence and impact of the constructive leadership of Chancellor D. W. Colvard and Chancellor E. K. Fretwell Jr. The administration of Dr. James Woodward is now under way with the same energy, intelligence, and sense of mission of his predecessors.

Finally, it is good that this story has been written by Ken Sanford. This longtime and remarkable servant of the university has been a very important participant in the life and times of the place. His reporting is that of a loving and caring apostle, and I rejoice in his enthusiasm for the institution.

The University of North Carolina at Charlotte is one of the truly significant achievements of the people of the state during the last half of the twentieth century. For this enriching education and cultural blessing that already has meant so much to thousands of us, let us be grateful as we pause to celebrate our heritage and to gather our strength for the glorious days to come.

William Friday
Chapel Hill

Preface

IN AUGUST 1968, I was a freshly minted Ph.D. from UNC Chapel Hill and a very green and new administrative assistant to UNC Charlotte chancellor D. W. Colvard. It was the first day on the job, and the institution's senior administrative group—the executive staff—was conducting its weekly meeting. Among the weighty agenda items of the day was a memorandum to the chancellor from Dr. Harvey Murphy, Chair of the Department of Physical Education. It seemed that Dr. Murphy's athletic playing fields frequently were being invaded by cows from a contiguous pasture. To make matters worse, the intruders were leaving behind deposits that created hazardous footing for ongoing physical education activity.

As I listened to the discussion that followed—and Chancellor Colvard's past experience as Dean of Agriculture seemed unexpectedly appropriate—I wondered about this envisioned urban university I had just joined and reflected that it might be a long, winding cow path until the ultimate realization of a true university, connected to its metropolitan area. Perhaps not this century.

And yet two and a half decades later, and only fifty years since the embryo of a university called an "extension center" was created, a remarkable transformation has occurred, seemingly on fast forward, as UNC Charlotte has become one of the South's and the nation's preeminent urban universities.

Ken Sanford's account of this special university is worth reading on one level as an engaging account of one university's formative years during the second half of the twentieth century, and of the cast of individuals, decisions, and events that marked its progress and union with a city also experiencing its coming of age. But in a more universal sense, it chronicles the manner in which an American university created out of a cow pasture can address its urban dynamic and, in fact, reach out and envelop itself with that urban presence, and therefore be a model for building a contemporary university.

The eras of this story are appropriately categorized by the tenures of its four leaders: Bonnie Cone, of a persistence and a determination not to be denied her beloved dream of a full university created out of modest beginnings; D. W. Colvard, a man of the mountains and the farm who nevertheless defined the way in which this university could connect to an urbanizing society, who always insisted that growth and change could be anchored by an integrity of style and substance; E. K. Fretwell, a professor's son who brought national exposure to a regional university and remained steadfast to his father's calling by grounding and structuring the university with a solid base in the arts and sciences; and Jim Woodward, whose background at the University of Alabama at Birmingham was well suited to usher in the age of doctoral programs while understanding the need to galvanize the urban region in support of its university's mission.

I had the privilege of working with all of these gifted university leaders, each very different, but all emphasizing the critical importance of team-building for success in university-building. They would readily acknowledge, I am sure, that their UNC Charlotte eras were in reality the day-to-day stories of the faculty, staff, students, and trustees who could translate the work of the moment into the larger vision, coming to fruition each day. In essence, all these individuals were bound on two parallel tracks, or "two jobs," as we explained to candidates for new positions: today's agenda of teaching, research, and service, and the never-ending process of building a university. Most days, the ingredients for those roles included high energy, creativity, tolerance for frustration, openness to the free flow of discussion and ideas, and an abiding sense of humor.

And from the beginning, the personality of the university seemed to reflect that of its campus community—a "people's university" that was accessible and diverse, without a history of discrimination of any kind, often feisty, its face turned toward its many constituencies, and with a consistent honesty about itself. All were qualities that were good underpinnings for a university determined to make public service a true reality in carrying out its mission.

Appropriately, Ken Sanford's role as director of public information and publications was characterized by these traits, however difficult or sensitive the issue. They also influence a straightforward telling of the UNC Charlotte story in the following pages. For twenty-three years, I worked side by side with him and never ceased to be struck by the unflagging spirit and passion he brought to his task, and the special love he possessed for the university and its unique cast of characters. That honest affection, laced with anecdotal humor, gives this story a welcome human face. Additionally, his early training on a city newspaper staff was useful background to town-gown relationships, helping to launch a career later capstoned by an array of significant recognitions from his peers, including the prestigious Infinity Award of the Charlotte

Public Relations Society and induction into the North Carolina Public Relations Hall of Fame.

There will be other histories and stories about UNC Charlotte for future generations, but *Growing Up Together* will forever be one of a kind. For this is a university's story, from its birthing after a world war, through its sometimes struggling pastoral adolescence, to its maturation as a new kind of American university that has reflected the growing pains, achievements, and destinies of its city, region, and changing society.

Doug Orr
Asheville

Introduction

WRITING THE story of UNC Charlotte seemed inevitable for several reasons as my thirty-year career there progressed. First of all, as director of public information and publications (public relations), I had the privilege of working closely with all four chief executives—Bonnie Cone, D. W. Colvard, E. K. Fretwell Jr., and James H. Woodward.

Another reason was that I experienced the institution's entire history as a campus of the University of North Carolina, having first been employed in 1964, while it was still Charlotte College but as the campaign was building toward university status in 1965.

Also, from Bonnie Cone, who had been involved from day one, I learned firsthand much of what had transpired in the Charlotte Center and Charlotte College days—the first nineteen years. That gave me insights into the entire fifty-year history, although I had to construct those first nineteen years primarily from the Archives in Special Collections of the J. Murrey Atkins Library at UNC Charlotte. I am grateful to Robin Brabham, Madeleine Perez, Randy Penninger, and Cindy Ledbetter of Special Collections for their assistance. For her research assistance I am also grateful to Wanda Fisher of Academic Planning and Institutional Research.

Because I experienced a privilege that few have—watching a university develop from infancy to maturity over such a short time span—I felt some obligation to tell the story as an eyewitness.

A bad habit also helped somewhat. A packrat by nature, I had kept from the beginning the documents, drafts, and correspondence that have become source material for this book. I am grateful to the tolerance of my wife, Alice, toward my bringing home some three dozen boxes of those materials.

Also, I had the good fortune of meeting some of the characters in this story before I joined UNC Charlotte.

As a student at UNC Chapel Hill, I had an intriguing first meeting with

William C. Friday. At the time I was a staff member of the *Daily Tar Heel*, the student newspaper. Rolfe Neill, later publisher of the *Charlotte Observer*, was editor. He asked me to join him in a meeting with Friday on some issue, now forgotten. Friday was then assistant to Gordon Gray, president of the UNC system, and was shortly to become secretary of the system and, a brief time later, president.

In those days, we knew no distinction between the UNC system and the UNC Chapel Hill campus administration. Still, I knew that we had gone close to the top. I was somewhat shy for an aspiring journalist, but Neill had enough chutzpah to lean back in his chair and say, "Now, Bill . . . ," as he presented his questions.

As amazed as I was at Neill's brashness, I was equally amazed that Friday wasn't put off by it and dealt with us as adults rather than students.

After graduating and spending a couple of years in the army, I returned to Chapel Hill to work on a master's degree. Friday was an active Baptist layman and was speaker for a Baptist student retreat that I attended. Amazingly, he remembered me from my undergraduate days. That ability to recall names and faces of people all across North Carolina stood Friday in good stead through the years. My daughter, Jeannette, had the same privilege of meeting Friday the Baptist layman in 1995, when he invited the college youth of University Baptist Church in Chapel Hill to his home.

Friday had another important trait that helped him to succeed over thirty years and to become one of the most respected administrators in American higher education. He appreciated journalists and treated them with respect.

When I became an editorial writer for the *Winston-Salem Journal* and wrote about the UNC system, he called to learn who the author was, because the editorials were unsigned. He then wrote thank-you notes. Also, he sent Christmas cards to journalists with short personal notes. Later, when controversial issues threatened the UNC system, Friday was able to get his side of the issue illuminated by calling on some of the journalists he earlier had befriended. Clearly, he would have made a good public relations practitioner.

I met two other key players in the creation of UNC Charlotte during my editorial writing days. Governor Terry Sanford (no relation) was another public figure who understood the importance of communicating with journalists.

Sanford invited reporters and editors, including me, to the governor's mansion for briefings on key issues, mostly educational, during his term of office. Governor Sanford's assistant was Tom Lambeth, who had also worked on the *Daily Tar Heel* when I was there. Tom, later to become executive director of the Z. Smith Reynolds Foundation, was working beside me at the *Winston-Salem Journal* as we edited copy and wrote headlines one evening when he got a call from Governor Sanford to come to Raleigh to be his assistant.

Irving Carlyle was appointed by Governor Sanford to head a commission to study the issue of expanding the UNC system. A well-informed and intellectually curious attorney in Winston-Salem, Carlyle often called the editorial staff of the newspaper to suggest not only the topics for editorials but also the content.

A unique experience for me at the Winston-Salem newspaper likely led to my being employed at Charlotte College. Robert Campbell, editor of the editorial pages, decided it would be good for the writer dealing with the legislature to attend as much of the session as possible. So in 1963 I sat in on hearings, interviewed legislators, and heard discussions that included converting Charlotte College, Wilmington College, and Asheville-Biltmore College to four-year status and opening the door to eventual university status.

It took another connection to get me to Charlotte, however. From West Asheville Baptist Church, I had known Don Freeman and later met his wife, Ina. Don was a political science professor and Ina was a member of the library staff at Charlotte College. When I visited them in Charlotte in 1963, I learned that Bonnie Cone needed a public relations person to help in the campaign for university status.

After I communicated with Cone, she invited me to visit the campus. By then, Friday was engaged in discussions with Cone about the future of Charlotte College, and she asked him about me. Perhaps he put in a good word. Also, John Paul Lucas, a longtime supporter and adviser to Cone and a public relations officer for Duke Power Company, had visited with the *Winston-Salem Journal* editorial staff and thus knew me and also put in a good word.

But it was my experience at the legislature that probably convinced Cone. She never exactly offered the position, but as my interview progressed, she suddenly started talking as if I were her employee. I asked, "Does that mean you're offering me the job?" She said, "Yes." All that was left was for Alex Coffin, then a reporter for the *Charlotte News* and later a public relations practitioner and biographer of Charlotte mayors Stanford Brookshire and John Belk, to call and interview me and break the story, albeit a short one, that I was coming to Charlotte.

My lasting impression of Cone was shaped shortly after I arrived in Charlotte. My wife, Alice, and I invited Cone to dinner to show our appreciation for my joining her team.

When Cone and I arrived at my home, however, we discovered that my son, Tim, had a bad case of croup—the kind that sounds like a death rattle as the child struggles for breath. We had selected a pediatrician but had not yet visited him. He was Dr. Earle Spaugh, son of Bishop Herbert Spaugh, who, as chairman of the Charlotte School Board, played a role in building Charlotte College.

Cone called Dr. Spaugh, and he told her we should take Tim directly to

Presbyterian Hospital. Cone insisted that Alice accompany Tim and me and said that she would babysit our younger son, Scott. After Tim was placed in an oxygen tent and began breathing easily—in fact, began playing—Alice returned and relieved Cone. But neither of us could believe that the president of the college had babysat for us that night. I never met anyone who had a greater gift of relating to people one-on-one than Bonnie Cone.

In those early days, it was common practice for state colleges and universities to lobby the legislature, and Cone included me in trips to Raleigh to seek support for university status. Thus one of the greatest thrills of my thirty-year career happened at the beginning of my second year as I sat in the House gallery on March 2, 1965, as members passed legislation converting Charlotte College to the Fourth Campus of the University of North Carolina. There was no celebration on the floor, but it was all I could do to restrain myself from jumping up in the gallery and shouting, "Hurrah!"

Other high moments for me were being present for the elections and installations of Chancellors Colvard, Fretwell, and Woodward and for the inauguration of UNC president C. D. Spangler Jr., as well as for the first meeting of the Board of Governors of the UNC system on the tenth floor of the Dalton Tower on the UNC Charlotte campus. Almost as thrilling as passage of legislation creating UNC Charlotte was the moment when Chancellor Woodward relayed the message to the campus from a Board of Governors meeting in Boone on November 8, 1993, that the first Ph.D. degree programs for UNC Charlotte had been approved.

Touching personal occasions for me were the receptions given for me at my retirement.

I am grateful to the university's chief executives for including me in meetings of the executive staff as deliberations about the administration of the institution took place. My presence helped me understand those leaders and the university. Without my being kept informed, this book would not have been possible. Also, my access to them allowed me to put on the hats of Bonnie Cone, D. W. Colvard, E. K. Fretwell Jr., and James H. Woodward as I drafted speeches, reports, and statements for them over the years.

To all the faculty and staff members who cooperated with me in my news-gathering capacity and who included me in their coffee-table and lunch-table discussions over the years, I am particularly indebted. My life was thereby enriched immeasurably. Although Bob Gibson and Bill Steimer may have introduced jokes that were occasionally somewhat rowdy, the conversations, overall, were intellectually challenging and stimulating and about education, politics, religion, values, and the eternal verities.

My indebtedness extends to the skilled and dedicated journalists who lent understanding ears to my pleas for help in communicating the university's story to the public. From time to time, I had to counsel newcomers to UNC

Charlotte who came from a community where the media played an adversarial role. I told them that if they wanted to confront the media in Charlotte, the journalists would oblige them. But I also said that almost all the journalists were committed to the highest principles of truth and integrity, and they needed only to communicate with them, not combat them.

There are too many who assisted along the way for me to name them all, but I'll list some who worked with UNC Charlotte for the longest periods of time. That list would begin, interestingly, with the person who replaced me at UNC Charlotte—Jack Claiborne, whom I first met on a sidewalk along Franklin Street in Chapel Hill when we were both students. Then we met at Ft. Jackson, South Carolina, when we were serving in the army. I later worked with Claiborne in his various roles at the *Charlotte Observer* over most of my career. Tom Bradbury, later associate editor of the *Charlotte Observer*, began his associations with UNC Charlotte when he was a reporter for the *Charlotte News* and covered the arrival of D. W. Colvard on April 1, 1966.

Pam Kelley of the *Charlotte Observer* was perhaps the most dedicated reporter of higher education for the longest period of time during my tenure.

Another reporter who gave long service was Harold Warren of the *Observer*. We bounced his car across the fields that now are University Place but then were cow pastures. Even so, he was able to see with me the exciting "new town" that would develop there.

Many others from the print media covered the campus for varying periods of time. Almost all of them were helpful.

From the electronic media, there were numerous reporters and news and assignment editors, some of whom I did not deal with face-to-face but who nevertheless gave of their valuable time to hear my story "pitch" by telephone or fax.

Dozens of reporters covered stories within their special fields, whether it was business, politics, health, books, the arts, or other areas.

Some journalists moved on to the national media. They include Malcolm Scully, a senior editor with the *Chronicle of Higher Education*; Kathy Moore, a senior producer for CBS Evening News; John Cochran, chief White House correspondent for ABC News; and Sharon Cathey Houston, later an executive with NBC News Network, among others.

There were times of frustration with the news media, of course. In the early years, television news departments did cover the developing university as a hard news story. Later, as they became more competitive with each other, they covered the campus more often when there was crime or an accident or extreme controversy. Radio news coverage declined over the years to primarily a headline reading service. On the other hand, one of the best things the electronic media did for the university was to use faculty experts to give local illumination to national and international news developments.

In spite of some discouraging times, overall, the news media were understanding and supportive and fair. I am particularly indebted to editorial writers Claiborne, Bradbury, Jerry Shinn, and Jack Betts and to associate editor Ed Williams for interpreting the university editorially over the years.

Yes, there were times of stress. Around the same time I accompanied Chancellor Colvard to Raleigh and saw him experience "executive fatigue," I had my own bout with stress-induced illness. We were all trying to do everything that needed to be done in the early years, and our bodies protested. Thankfully, Sam Simono, head of the Counseling Center, suggested some relaxation techniques, taught by Steve Bondy, which helped me get through the following stressful years.

At times I was disappointed with historic state policies and politics that caused UNC Charlotte to remain last or next to last in funding per student and square feet of space per student. The other major times of personal discouragement were when I had to deal with the bureaucracy of the Office of State Personnel. A leading legislator once said that State Personnel was "broke and nobody knew how to fix it." That was my experience.

This disappointment led to frustration at our inability to communicate to the people of the state that assisting UNC Charlotte was in their own best self-interest. Tax revenues generated by the cash cow that is Charlotte have enabled North Carolina to make progress on many fronts. Why, then, could the citizens not see that to increase the flow of tax dollars from Charlotte, all they had to do was take their foot off the brakes for UNC Charlotte and let it fulfill its destiny of providing the educational assistance, the technological expertise, and the business support that would allow the region to compete more effectively in the global marketplace to which it had moved?

But a great debt is owed to the staff members in Public Relations who worked with me over the years and helped me survive the frustrations. The thing I miss most about them was my ability to hand to them a piece of my writing and ask them to critique it. They include Vivian Fogle, who worked with me for more than twenty years, and Sam Nixon, for nearly ten years. Others are Diana Nicholson and T. Wade Bruton. Among previous staff members who should be recognized are Garry Ballard, who returned to UNC Charlotte as alumni director after going to LSU as head of public relations, and Joe Bowles, Roy Beatty, B. J. Butler, Pilar Ramsey, Pam Taylor, Jane Nixon, Susan Jones, Sue Johnson, Josette Gourley Arvey, the late Carol Ostrowski, Gail Petrakis, and Bill Wright. Others include Steve Wilcox, a photography student in creative arts, and Max Street, a multitalented student.

There were many student interns who helped us and who I hope learned something about public relations in our office. Others in closely associated university departments who helped over the years were Harry Creemers, Mary Ellen Shuntich, Faye Jacques, Susan Piscitelli, Nancy Carter Stone, Betty Whalen, Diana Faison, Carla Wyatt, Sarah Lathrop, and Betty Stancil. Scotty

Williams, who worked with Vice Chancellors Bonnie Cone, Doug Orr, and Ed Kizer, was especially helpful to me over the years, as were the secretaries to the chancellors—Juanita Sims, Evelyn Whitley, and Rachel Freeman—and other members of that office. Donna Brady was helpful in providing information on trustees. I shared my first office on campus with Peggy Propst, then secretary to the academic dean and later to the academic vice chancellors. She retired in 1996 after thirty-two years of service.

I owe debts of gratitude to the vice chancellors to whom I reported: Bill Britt, Doug Orr, and Ed Kizer. Orr was especially encouraging as mentor, friend, and fellow folk music enthusiast. He had intended to coauthor this book with me, but the challenge of the presidency of Warren Wilson College was too great. As he left UNC Charlotte, he said, "Ken, you'll have to do the book by yourself." However, he has been immensely helpful and supportive in reviewing this manuscript and offering suggestions. I am grateful to Ed Kizer and Chancellor Jim Woodward for the financial arrangements that made this book possible.

Thanks go also to the chancellors' executive assistants over the years: Mark Tinkham, Julian Mason, Larry Owen, Orr, Ben Romine, Earl Backman, Bill Steimer, Hap Arnold, and James Dixon.

My public relations colleagues have also been great mentors and supporters in the Charlotte Public Relations Society, the North Carolina and Charlotte chapters of the Public Relations Society of America, the College News Association of the Carolinas, and the Council for the Advancement and Support of Education.

To the staff and volunteers at International House and its Council for International Visitors, I am indebted for their helping me share UNC Charlotte with the world. As a result of the international visitors that came our way, we were covered in international newspapers and magazines and even included in a doctoral dissertation by an Austrian scholar, Alexander Hohendanner. Through the council, I met VIP visitors from more than fifty countries of the world and was enabled to share UNC Charlotte and University Research Park with them.

The Charlotte Chamber of Commerce and the Charlotte Convention and Visitors Bureau allowed me to work on behalf of the city, and I am grateful. To the editors of the *Charlotte Observer* and the *Charlotte News*, I am appreciative of their allowing me to keep my editorial writing skills alive through my occasional columns and letters to the editor.

The saints of St. John's Baptist Church were always both my anchor and my beacon, and I am thankful.

In some ways, working at the university in the later years was like living in a city of 18,000 to 20,000. There were triumphs and tragedies. Some of the tragedies haunt me still.

Greater love hath no man: in 1966, poet Edwin Godsey of the English

Department died while unsuccessfully attempting to rescue one of his children, who had skated out onto thin ice on a frozen pond.

Walter Norem, my neighbor and faculty friend, helped Newton Barnette to launch the William States Lee College of Engineering, but Norem's tragic death in an Eastern Air Lines crash near Charlotte/Douglas International Airport denied him the opportunity to see the fulfillment of his dream. Thankfully, Barnette did live to enjoy retirement and to see the ascent of the engineering program before his death.

I was also diminished by those who died untimely natural deaths. Hugh McEniry never got to celebrate the academic accomplishments for which he laid the groundwork.

Jim Clay did live to see his dreams of the University Place and University City come true but did not get to retire and contemplate his successes. A son of the West Virginia hills, he left his mark on the urban landscape of Charlotte and on UNC Charlotte. Moreover, he gave Charlotteans an ability to see their community and region as they were. The James W. Clay Boulevard in University Place honors his genius, creativity, and entrepreneurial spirit.

Dean John B. Chase Jr., who had served since 1970, died in 1978, after helping build the College of Education. Dale Arvey, chairman of the Biology Department, traveled the world as an ornithologist, yet his ashes were scattered in the Van Landingham Glen following his untimely death.

John Wrigley, a history professor, had been sent as an outsider by Dean Schley Lyons of the College of Arts and Sciences to resolve conflicts in the areas of creative arts. Wrigley died before seeing his efforts completed, but he knew that progress had been made. Seth Ellis, for eleven years before his death in 1995, was able to enjoy reunion with his wife, JoAnne, from whom he was apart almost twenty years, and retired to enjoy his university successes and his associations with Rotary and the Masonic organizations. The English Department seemed to suffer more losses than any other—Margaret Bryan, Ann Newman, Darryl McCall, and James Hedges. Mary Denny, first chair of that department, did get to enjoy retirement and made a major contribution of land to the university. Robert Wallace, the second chair of the department, enjoyed retirement at the beach before his death.

On the other hand, the triumphs of members of the faculty and staff inspired and encouraged me over the years. In writing about the accomplishments of students, faculty, and staff, I was able to share their high moments with them.

It was subtle, but one moment when I knew that UNC Charlotte had arrived occurred in June 1993, when a delegation from the Town of Chapel Hill, Orange County, and the UNC Chapel Hill administration came to visit UNC Charlotte to find out why this campus was so successful at university-community relations.

Introduction | xxiii

The delegation wanted to learn how UNC Charlotte and the City of Charlotte worked together for economic development, technology transfer, and public-private ventures.

Mention of the university's role in economic development leads to my recalling some of the humorous events that occurred over the years.

Officials at UNC Charlotte often were visited by delegations from corporations considering relocating to the region. Once, when a drug company that manufactured condoms was deciding to locate a packaging facility in Charlotte, the president, in appreciation, sent campus officials a sample package of his goods, including some novelty and exotic varieties. Red-faced secretaries who opened the packages suggested that perhaps the executives should have to open some of their own mail on occasion.

Students had fun taking issue with the university's policy of naming residence halls for the state's governors when it came time to name one for James Holshouser, North Carolina's first Republican governor in the twentieth century. They complained the name was difficult to spell and pronounce, and further, they said, "If it has to have a name like that, why not name it Herlocker Dorm?" Herlocker was the proprietor of a nearby drive-in restaurant that served old-fashioned hamburgers. There were no complaints, however, when a campus apartment complex was named Martin Village for the second Republican governor of the century, James G. Martin.

Faculty members had their own variety of fun. In the early years, the faculty met as a committee of the whole, and the entire body was dragged through processes normally handled in committee. Once a fiery mathematics professor, Bill Perel, shouted to his colleagues, "If you don't agree with me, you are all a bunch of damned rat finks."

Professor Ben Hackney put the faculty committee-of-the-whole process in perspective and may have helped move it toward a representative form of governance after a lengthy, heated exchange over what symbol to use to indicate that some graduate courses also carried undergraduate credit. The particular proposal being considered called for use of the asterisk to designate the courses that carried both types of credit. After the prolonged meeting adjourned, Hackney went back to his office and distributed a little ditty to the faculty. It read:

> *Mary bought a pair of skates*
> *Upon the ice to frisk*
> *Wasn't she a silly fool*
> *Her little **

Dean Bob Snyder of Engineering rose at an opening convocation to introduce his new faculty, many of whom were internationals with hard-to-pronounce names. Engineering departments across the nation were having to employ international faculty members because of the dearth of Ph.D.-trained United States natives. On that occasion, Snyder introduced himself as dean of Foreign Languages.

Over the years, I also learned that teaching could be hazardous to one's health. Fortunately, none of the incidents proved seriously harmful. Dr. Wade Williams, a psychology professor and later a counselor in private practice, was teaching when a student jumped to the platform where he stood, yanked him to the floor, and started pounding him before being restrained.

Dr. John Wrigley, at the time chair of the history department, had the window of his office smashed by a pipe-wielding student who was angry over a grade. Wrigley later found an arrow stuck through his desk chair.

Drama professor Roland Reed had some anxious moments after finding one of his books, with a cover illustration of a Greek mask, symbolizing drama, pierced by a bullet.

Clashes of church and state occurred a couple of times, both involving the Reverend Joe Chambers, pastor of a conservative church. The first was when sex adviser Dr. Ruth Westheimer appeared as a campus speaker. Chambers brought a number of picketers to campus. Students then organized counterpicketers.

The second incident occurred during a student art exhibit. The mother of a student complained to Chambers that a student work of art was sacrilegious because it portrayed a penis among religious symbols. Chambers threatened to bring thousands of picketers to the campus. After a handful showed up and sang hymns, the protest ended.

The incident provided an educational experience, because hundreds of students who might never have been inside an art gallery visited the one in Rowe Building out of curiosity. It also gave Vice Chancellor Philip Dubois an opportunity to speak about the university's role in defending freedom of expression even when it was offensive. And it gave one wag an opportunity for humor: he dubbed the artwork "The Penis de Milo."

Some faculty members and students did the picketing when Dan Quayle brought his campaign for the U.S. vice presidency to the campus. They protested that the invitation implied that all the campus supported Quayle. The picketers played into Quayle's hands, however, because he used them as a ploy in his remarks.

All those experiences illustrate a major point: for a journalist/public relations practitioner, working at a university provides one of the most rewarding careers possible. A person in such a position is called upon to use everything he or she has ever learned. One day I would have to recall my freshman biology class, because I would be interviewing a botanist. Another day I would try to recall my physics class, because I was interviewing a professor concerning nanotechnology, which is about atomic-scale devices. On still other days, I would need some of my background in history, chemistry, political science, psychology, sociology, English literature, religious studies, and other subjects. There was rarely an unchallenging day.

I owe a particular debt of gratitude to those who read all or portions of my manuscript and made corrections and suggested important revisions: Douglas M. Orr Jr., Jack Claiborne, Harry H. (Hap) Arnold, Garry Ballard, Vivian Fogle, and Sam Nixon. Their help was invaluable in catching errors of fact and judgment.

I made one hazardous decision—to include as many names as possible. The story of UNC Charlotte, after all, is the story of people. It is likely that by including so many names, I may have unintentionally omitted names of key players, even those of good friends, and for that I apologize.

Above all, I am grateful for all who made my adventure at UNC Charlotte and in the greater Charlotte community such a pleasant and rewarding one.

Ken Sanford
Charlotte

*Charlotte and UNC Charlotte
Growing Up Together*

CHAPTER 1

Charlotte Suffers an Education Gap

THE FOLLOWING story is about a university born in 1946. It struggled through an austere childhood, then grew up over a span of fifty years to become a major state institution. It is also the story of a city that awakened after World War II to find that it needed a state-supported university if it were to compete and move into the top ranks of American cities. Like that of the university, the story of the city is also one of great success.

This is the story of a university born long after America's classic private universities, like Harvard and Yale. The University of North Carolina at Charlotte was born 150 years after its classic state university parent—the University of North Carolina at Chapel Hill, oldest of its kind in the nation. The Charlotte university's birth came almost sixty years after the creation of land-grant universities, like N.C. State University, and many years after the birth of state teachers' colleges, some of which later became regional universities.

UNC Charlotte was representative of a new kind of American university that was born shortly after World War II. The new universities' genealogy could be traced to the venerable European universities that developed in the great cities of that continent during the Middle Ages.

When America was being settled and for many years thereafter, educators deviated from the European model of placing universities in the heart of cities. Instead, American universities were usually placed in rural areas away from the distractions of city life—or, as humorist Grady Nutt put it, "twenty miles from the nearest known sin."

After World War II, both educators and city leaders realized that cities and universities needed each other. Cities needed the expertise that universities could bring, particularly as technology became a fact of economic life. Universities could benefit by being where the action was—in terms of economic development, societal changes, cultural and artistic opportunities, and population growth.

Along with UNC Charlotte came such other southern and southeastern metropolitan universities as the University of New Orleans, Georgia State University, the University of South Florida, Florida International University, the University of Central Florida, the University of Alabama at Birmingham, Virginia Commonwealth University, Old Dominion University, and George Mason University, among others. Some were born earlier than the 1940s and 1950s but were reorganized as metropolitan universities after the war.

Although UNC Charlotte's birth was like that of some of the other universities, the circumstances into which it was born were different from most. Many of the cities already contained large private universities, medical schools, or community colleges. When UNC Charlotte began as the Charlotte Center of the University of North Carolina, there were only three small private colleges in Mecklenburg County and no public college or university nearby in North Carolina.

In fact, Charlotte was a much more modest city nationally in 1946 than it would become fifty years later. Charlotte then had just passed the 100,000 mark in population. By 1996, the city had become the thirty-third largest city nationally, with a population of approximately 440,000 within its city limits. Its metropolitan area population had reached 1.3 million.

This is the story of how the university and the city grew up together. It is almost certain that without the other, neither would have become what it has.

Even into the 1980s, Charlotte was suffering an identity crisis. Nationally, it was often confused with other cities whose names began with the letters Ch, including Charlottesville, Virginia; Charleston, West Virginia; and Charleston, South Carolina. That problem was referred to as the "Ch factor."

Members of the Charlotte Public Relations Society organized a symposium on Charlotte's image. Their conclusion was that the city didn't have a bad image; it had *no* image.

Many of Charlotte's citizens were unaware of the city's true size or that its dimensions extended beyond the city limits. Neither were they aware of what a city its size should be offering in the way of amenities and services.

Things began to change when UNC Charlotte began recruiting outstanding faculty members with expertise in fields related to the city's needs and interests.

This account will show the impact of those faculty members on the city, ranging from that of the geographers who first accurately described Charlotte in the context of its greater region to that of the professors who described political realities. It will describe how the city's politics changed from power concentrated in a very closely knit power elite to representative governance following reports by faculty members on how district representation would work.

One of the threads of the story is the political climate of the State of

North Carolina. Charlotte was to some extent a victim of the political climate growing out of the settlement patterns of the state. Since their region was settled first, residents of eastern North Carolina obtained political power early and were not inclined to share it. As the state developed, eastern North Carolina retained an agricultural economy, and the Piedmont, in which Charlotte is located, developed an industrial economy. This situation created a mutual lack of understanding between the two regions. Pleas that Charlotte was sending an inordinate amount of taxes to Raleigh but getting little in return did not get a receptive hearing.

Leaders of eastern North Carolina disdainfully referred to the "Great State of Mecklenburg," implying that Charlotteans cared little for the rest of the state. There was some truth to that charge, because Charlotte had many of the internal problems of large cities that claimed attention and kept the city from being focused on statewide issues. Eastern counties also tended to keep their representatives in the legislature year after year, thus gaining power and influence through seniority. The political climate of Charlotte, on the other hand, was that of a volatile, rapidly growing city, creating constant turnover in the legislative representation.

In time UNC Charlotte's leaders helped the community to understand that it did have an important stake in what was happening in Raleigh, and as a result, Charlotte began to gain a better hearing in the legislature. At the same time, leaders elsewhere slowly began to understand that in helping UNC Charlotte and Charlotte they were helping the state and themselves.

As to the development of the city itself, this story will relate a professor's major role in halting the city's determined destruction of its historic landmarks and neighborhoods.

Another major thread of the story is the impact of the university on economic development. Charlotte was in danger of becoming a one-industry city, centered solely around banking and finance. The university's leadership in developing University Research Park helped create more than ten thousand jobs in technology-based businesses, thus diversifying the economy.

Moreover, UNC Charlotte helped reshape the map of Charlotte. When the university came upon the scene, residential and retail growth were concentrated in the southeastern corridor. Growth was moving headlong toward the South Carolina line, taking the tax base with it. Uptown Charlotte seemed destined to become the northern edge of the city. With help from city and county leadership, UNC Charlotte played an important role in developing University City, thus creating a new growth magnet in the northeast. Then development began to blossom in the Lake Norman area. Together University City and Lake Norman created double growth magnets, and that ultimately resulted in balanced growth in Mecklenburg County.

Thereafter the university's leadership role expanded to helping Charlotte and the surrounding cities and counties understand that they were not just self-sufficient entities but part of a greater city-state that was competing with other city-states around the world.

There were other university impacts on community and region. University professors moved out into political, social, religious, and cultural organizations and added to the community's understanding of its problems and opportunities, including schools, crime, transportation, economic development, and health and environmental issues.

It is doubtful that city leaders fully anticipated at the beginning the ramifications of having a major university in their midst. However, the coming of state-supported higher education to Charlotte set in motion a sequence of events that would forever change Charlotte and its greater region.

It wasn't for lack of trying that Charlotte had lacked a college until after World War II. In fact, Charlotte might have had the oldest state-supported institution in the nation had its earliest attempt succeeded. Indeed, Charlotte supplied some of the leadership that created the university at Chapel Hill.

Although Charlotte and Mecklenburg County were not North Carolina's most prominent locales at the time of the American Revolution, a tax-supported institution of higher education was founded there in 1771 under the name of Queens College. (It was not a predecessor of the city's current Queens College.) The college was up and running when word came that King George refused to grant a charter for it, apparently fearing that its Presbyterian supporters would foment further dissent from the Church of England and the British crown. His concern, of course, was justified: Mecklenburg became a hotbed of revolutionary fervor. The unchartered college's leaders then changed its name to Queen's Museum and later to Liberty Hall Academy. It closed when Lord Cornwallis invaded Charlotte in 1780.

According to William S. Powell in *The First State University*, four members of a committee to draft a constitution for North Carolina in 1776 were trustees of that early Queens College. Three were from Charlotte—Waightstill Avery, Hezekiah Alexander, and Robert Irwin. It was probably not by accident that the first state constitution included a provision that "all useful learning shall be duly encouraged and promoted in one or more universities."

The links between that first Queens College in Charlotte and the first state university went even deeper. Among the students at Charlotte's Queens College was William Richardson Davie of the Waxhaws, later to distinguish himself as a Revolutionary War hero and founder of the University of North Carolina at Chapel Hill.

During an 1820 meeting in Lincolnton of persons concerned about education in the region, there was an attempt to establish in the west an equivalent to the state-supported university in Chapel Hill. It was even chartered as Western College, but it never opened.

There was a hiatus in higher education in Charlotte for several years after the closing of Queens College, until the establishment of the Charlotte Female Academy in 1838. A Charlotte Male Academy was also operating at the time.

Over the years, three Presbyterian colleges were developed in Mecklenburg County—Davidson and Queens Colleges and Johnson C. Smith University. Local Presbyterians, who had had a hand in founding the short-lived, publicly supported Queens College in the 1770s, founded Davidson for men, which opened in 1837, and Queens for women, which opened in 1857. Northern Presbyterians founded Johnson C. Smith—for African Americans—in 1867. Although all three of the permanent colleges—Davidson, Queens, and Johnson C. Smith, were venerable institutions by the 1940s, all were committed to their long-established missions as small, traditional, liberal arts colleges. Davidson and Queens later adjusted their single-sex missions to become coeducational and, in the case of Queens, to offer adult and continuing education programs.

In the late 1880s, Charlotte had an opportunity to submit a bid for a land-grant college, the North Carolina College of Agricultural and Mechanic Arts, but it was outbid when a Raleigh farmer named Stanhope Pullen donated a tract of land for the campus. That institution became N.C. State University.

North Carolina Medical College, which had various links to Davidson College, was chartered in 1892 and operated as a distinguished medical institution until the costs of equipment and training for modern physicians proved too demanding for its board. The college closed in 1913. As late as 1946, Charlotte was contending for another medical college, a four-year medical school of the University of North Carolina. At that time, UNC Chapel Hill had a two-year medical school, and officials finally decided that it was better to expand there to keep all four years of the school together in one location.

The story of Elizabeth College reflects the support Charlotteans extended during these attempts to found lasting colleges. Local citizens raised $9,332 in cash, a sizable amount in 1896, as an inducement to the college to locate in Charlotte. The Highland Park Land and Improvement Company donated $3,600 and twenty acres of land for the campus, now the site of Presbyterian Hospital at Elizabeth Avenue and Hawthorne Lane. Elizabeth College operated as a woman's college and music conservatory until poor financing forced its closing on the eve of World War I.

Over the years following the American Revolution, Charlotte continued a sometimes slow but always continual march toward becoming North Carolina's largest city—a process that took until the 1930s. When Charlotte finally emerged as the state's largest city, the lack of a publicly supported university became even more obvious.

That was Charlotte in 1946, the state's largest city, and swept up in postwar euphoria. One of the most devastating wars in history had just ended, and the people of the city were adjusting to peacetime. After four years of rationing and sacrifice, they were eagerly seeking the things that had made for the good life before the war.

A *Charlotte Observer* advertisement from that year touted a new Oldsmobile with Hydramatic Drive that required no manual shifting of gears. Tires were finally available for the prewar automobiles badly in need of them. People had made do with the old cars, but they were in need of replacement, and the pent-up demand for new automobiles couldn't be met because of parts shortages and the difficulty of converting military assembly lines to civilian production. A news story estimated that production might reach 2,300,000 vehicles, as compared to the prewar production of 3,500,000 automobiles in 1939.

Not all the veterans had been able to return home immediately after the war. In the summer of 1946 ships were still returning to the nation's ports with veterans from the European and Pacific campaigns. Once the troops reached those ports, they quickly headed for hometowns like Charlotte.

In Charlotte, they found a city short on housing. Anything that provided shelter was pressed into service. Families shared quarters with relatives. Many of the veterans were returning with brides from abroad to set up housekeeping. Their GI Loans provided veterans with enough financial support to buy—if they could find available housing. Construction of new homes was proceeding so rapidly that the city was considering zoning policies to ensure some control over the process. Still, the demand couldn't be met. There were shortages of building materials because of the requirements the war had brought.

The State Travel Council met to decide how to accommodate people who once again wanted to vacation in the state despite the limited number of hotels and tourist cabins. The Hotel Charlotte and the William R. Barringer Hotel were booked up a week to ten days in advance. Charlotte Chamber of Commerce manager Clarence Kuester discouraged companies and associations from bringing conventions to the city because of lack of space to house them.

City leaders, looking ahead, were requesting additional air service. When a new Eastern Air Lines flight opened to Memphis, they celebrated with gifts to the first passengers.

New clothing was in short supply, but Sears announced plans to build a huge new store on North Tryon Street.

A Charlotte Hornets team was entertaining a war-weary community, but those Charlotte Hornets played baseball, not basketball. The city also was rooting for a professional football team, the Charlotte Clippers, who played in the minor Dixie League and went up against the NFL's Detroit Lions in an exhibition game in the fall of 1946.

A small advertisement in the *Charlotte Observer* announced that the Rev. Billy Frank Graham, a Charlotte native who grew up on a dairy farm where Park Road Shopping Center later was located and who had become national vice president of Youth for Christ, would be preaching on "Revival for Survival" at Bible Presbyterian Church. It would be a few years yet before that Billy Graham would achieve national and international fame with his worldwide preaching crusades.

Some other Charlotteans who would become prominent also were a few years away from fame. Charles Kuralt, later to become a popular television personality at CBS, was competing in the "My Favorite Hornet" contest with Jack Claiborne, later to become a *Charlotte Observer* associate editor and, still later, director of public relations at UNC Charlotte. Claiborne would win that one. Kuralt would come in second but later would win a national oratorical contest, "Who Speaks for Democracy?"

Kuralt was then a student at Alexander Graham Junior High School, along with C. D. Spangler Jr., later to become one of North Carolina's most prominent business leaders and president of the University of North Carolina system; Russell Robinson, later to become one of the state's most prominent attorneys and chairman of the UNC Charlotte Board of Trustees; and Alex McMillan, later to become a U.S. congressman from the state's Ninth District, which included Charlotte.

Two others who later would become prominent Charlotteans were attending elementary schools in nearby communities. Hugh McColl, who would become chairman of the board of NationsBank, was enrolled in Bennetsville, South Carolina, and Ed Crutchfield, who would become board chairman of First Union National Bank, was in school in Albemarle.

Bonnie Cone, a mathematics teacher who had left the Charlotte schools to teach at Duke University and earn her master's degree, had joined the war effort. She was finishing up her work with the Naval Ordnance Laboratory in Washington, D.C., and was eager to return to her teaching position at Charlotte Central High School. Little did she know that she would be teaching college courses as well, but it was that Bonnie Cone who would become founder of the University of North Carolina at Charlotte.

The veterans returning to Charlotte brought with them something else in addition to their GI home loans. They also had access to the GI Bill to further their educations. It would open a door that many had thought permanently closed—the door to a college education.

The availability of educational benefits, however, exposed a historic weakness of the Charlotte region. For all the momentum Charlotte had going for it after World War II, the lack of a state-supported institution of higher education was a potential shortcoming that could dampen the city's bright future. One question faced by the veterans, particularly those who were tied to Charlotte by family and other obligations, was this: where would they be able to use their GI Bill benefits?

At this time Charlotte's business leaders were becoming aware that they needed a better-educated workforce to handle increasingly technical jobs. Instead of cotton mills, the city now had factories making machinery for mills elsewhere. The war had brought sophisticated manufacturing to the city, even a rocket-building facility.

An awareness grew that Charlotte as a city trying to attract new businesses and industries was competing with other cities that already had public universities and community colleges.

Still, old social patterns persisted. For decades, the more affluent Charlotte families had sent their children away to UNC Chapel Hill, N.C. State, Davidson, Duke, or Wake Forest, and to a lesser extent to the several denominational colleges nearby. If the children were female, they often attended Woman's College of the University of North Carolina (now UNC Greensboro), which had a reputation as one of the best such institutions in the nation.

UNC Chapel Hill accepted females at the junior level only, with the exception of town residents. N.C. State was an institution for males. If a youth wanted to become a schoolteacher, he or she attended East Carolina, Western Carolina, or Appalachian State Teachers College. African American students attended the state's historically black institutions in Durham, Fayetteville, Greensboro, Winston-Salem, or Elizabeth City. Native American students attended Pembroke State College. All of this created a mindset in Charlotte that one "went away" to college—or didn't go at all.

So it was that at the time of the higher educational awakening that followed World War II, Charlotte found itself without a public institution of higher education, without a large private university with a broad array of programs, and without even a public community college. Yet returning veterans wanted to take advantage of the GI Bill, which opened college doors for the first time to people of modest economic means.

And as the veterans began obtaining college educations, youth who had been too young for military service during the war realized as they reached high school age that to compete with the newly educated veterans, they too would need a college education. Many of them, bound in place by family obligations or the need to retain current jobs, found access to college blocked by the ninety miles that separated Charlotte from the nearest state-supported university in North Carolina.

The returning veterans were to challenge and change the city's long-held mindset about where to attend college. The stage was set for public higher education in Charlotte.

In early 1946, Governor R. Gregg Cherry and other North Carolina leaders realized that the state soon would be flooded with returning World War II veterans eager to use GI Bill benefits for a college education. The governor and his aides conducted a quick study and estimated that fifteen thousand veterans would be unable to get into existing institutions.

On May 19, 1946, Governor Cherry called a conference of representatives of the Veterans Administration, the State Department of Public Instruction, and the state's two college conferences, one for institutions that were historically white and the other for those that were historically black. That session resulted in the creation of the Governor's Commission on Veterans Education; James E. Hillman, director of the Division of Professional Services of the North Carolina Department of Public Instruction, served as chairman, and Russell M. Grumman, director of the UNC Chapel Hill Extension Division, served as secretary. They prepared questionnaires for a more detailed study to assess the seriousness of the problem.

Responses were received from fifteen hundred veterans—not the fifteen thousand estimated—who said they could not find college accommodations. Even so, the committee considered the problem serious and recommended that educational centers be established by fall to provide for these students. The committee recommended that UNC Chapel Hill administer centers for white students at twelve locations and that African American centers be established at Asheville under the administration of North Carolina A&T College and at Wilmington under the administration of Fayetteville State College.

Some of the older universities did make extraordinary efforts to accommodate the returning veterans, thus easing the pressure somewhat. UNC Chapel Hill, for example, had emergency housing left from a World War II Navy training program and crammed students into those facilities. Quonset huts were scattered around the campus and served as temporary classrooms.

Initial white enrollment in the original twelve centers in the emergency college system, which included Charlotte, were: Albemarle, 46; Burlington, 48; Burnsville, 35; Charlotte, 278; Fayetteville, 66; Gastonia, 79; Goldsboro, 39; Greensboro, 57; Hendersonville, 58; Murphy, 45; Rocky Mount, 85; and Wilmington, 212. The total of 1,048 students was the size of a North Carolina liberal arts college. A planned Mt. Airy Center could not register the required 30 students and was not launched.

The North Carolina College Conference voted that all credits earned at the centers were transferable to a college or university in North Carolina on the same basis as if the work had been done in an established institution.

The Extension Division of the University of North Carolina at Chapel

Hill was designated the administrative unit with responsibility for the centers. As assistant director of the North Carolina College Centers, C. E. McIntosh was actually operations leader and became a somewhat accidental hero of the founding of UNC Charlotte, even though his intention was to close Charlotte and the other temporary centers after two years of operation. To his credit, while he led the centers, he gave them his full attention and his best administrative skills.

In 1964, William C. Friday, then president of the Consolidated University of North Carolina, wrote McIntosh, "The enrollment of students in 12 centers called attention in a dramatic way to the feasibility of making college instruction available in many parts of the state. The centers at Wilmington and Charlotte soon developed into community colleges and in 1963 became four-year colleges fully supported by the state. The memory of college centers persisted elsewhere and was doubtless a factor in stimulating the community college movement in the State."

The Charlotte Center was placed under the local administration of the Charlotte City Schools. Superintendent Harry P. Harding delegated the center's operation to Elmer H. Garinger, his associate.

Garinger was a well educated and respected public school administrator who demanded excellence. He had received his doctorate in education at Columbia University. In one of the many notable ironies of the founding of UNC Charlotte, Garinger studied at Columbia with Professor E. K. Fretwell Sr., father of E. K. Fretwell Jr., who would become the Charlotte university's second chancellor.

Garinger later became superintendent of schools. Not only did he play a role in launching the Charlotte Center; by the time Charlotte College later took its case to become a campus of the University of North Carolina system to the North Carolina General Assembly, Representative Elmer H. Garinger was also a member of the Mecklenburg delegation. A UNC Charlotte classroom building honors Garinger's role as a campus founder.

J. Murrey Atkins, chairman of the city school board, had responsibility for policy at the center. As president of R. S. Dickson and Company, a leading Charlotte investment firm, Atkins commanded the respect of the business community and used his considerable skills on behalf of the fledgling campus.

Atkins was born in Russellville, Kentucky, in 1906 while his father, Emmet D. Atkins, a Gastonia newspaperman, was there briefly to serve as interim president of Logan College for his father, who was president. J. Murrey Atkins married Judith Woods, and they had three children—J. Murrey Jr., who would become chairman of the UNC Charlotte Library Associates; Katharine; and Judith. Educated at Duke University, J. Murrey Atkins did graduate work at Harvard Law School and Columbia University. He began his career with

Charlotte school leader Elmer H. Garinger played a key role in the founding of UNC Charlotte. Portrait by Charles Tucker.

the Irving Trust Company in New York City and returned to Charlotte to head the Dickson firm.

Prominent in Charlotte's civic life, he served as a member of the city council and as member and chairman of the Charlotte School Board. Later he would become chairman of the Charlotte College Advisory Board, chairman of the Board of Trustees of the Charlotte Community College System, and finally chairman of the Charlotte College Board of Trustees before his death in 1963. UNC Charlotte honored his memory through the dedication of the library in his name on April 11, 1965.

Administrative leadership over all the centers was provided by Grumman; McIntosh; Charles W. Phillips, director of the Extension Division of Woman's College; and Edward Ruggles, director of the College Extension Division of N.C. State College.

As early as February 1946, Garinger had noted in a letter to J. W. Byers, superintendent of Asheville City Schools, that there was a possibility Charlotte might establish a junior college.

The *Charlotte Observer* reported on May 28, 1946, that there were plans to set up a junior college in Charlotte. That item was spotted by Charles Bernard, who had already been accepted as a Charlotte City Schools teacher. He said in a letter to Garinger that he would like to teach political science or history at the college if it should open.

Garinger told Bernard that the opening of the college depended on approval by the North Carolina State Department of Public Instruction and the North Carolina College Conference and the raising of $5,000 (outside of tuition) for operations. Garinger also told Bernard that some of the local teachers might want to be part of the college faculty, but he said the fact that Bernard was the only man in the group would make a difference. Apparently, schools were still suffering from the shortage of male teachers that the war had caused.

Bernard had attended the University of Tampa and received his B.A. and M.A. degrees from the University of Florida. He taught at Hillsboro, Tampa, Charlotte County, and Sebring High Schools in Florida before entering military service in 1942. At the time of his letter to Garinger, Bernard had entered graduate school in political science at UNC Chapel Hill and was on his way to Washington, D.C., to work at the Library of Congress and the State Department on his dissertation on world relations.

Garinger wrote to Grumman on his thoughts about who should direct the Charlotte Center. He said either Bernard or a teacher named Bonnie Cone would be an excellent choice. Of Bernard, Garinger said, he would have the advantage of being in Chapel Hill for the summer and consulting with people in the extension division. "The fact that he is a man might appeal to college boys," Garinger said; but one strike against Bernard, he noted, was that, unlike Cone, he was not from Charlotte.

In July, Garinger wrote Grumman that only a few girls had registered for the fall classes and that two-thirds of those registering were veterans. He complained about a for-profit school—Burton Institute—trying to enroll some of his prospective students, apparently in an attempt to obtain GI Bill benefits.

Gaining a temporary center was clearly not enough for Garinger in 1946. In a letter written July 16, 1946, Garinger told Mary Denny, whom he had recruited to become the college's first full-time instructor, "My intention is to make this junior college a permanent thing."

Had he known the obstacles ahead, Garinger might not have been as determined. But the fact that Garinger did have a vision of a permanent institution even before the Charlotte Center opened was crucial to the ultimate success of the venture, since the leadership at the state level envisioned only a temporary entity.

In June 1946, as the center was being contemplated, Garinger told Grumman that he believed he could place two hundred veterans in Charlotte. He acknowledged the difficulty of raising $5,000. But he said if he could operate a center under the sponsorship of the University of North Carolina, "I am confident the people in Charlotte would heartily approve, and I am convinced the University would be pleased with its experiment."

Reflecting the social climate of the time, Garinger reported to Grumman that "at the present moment, there has been no agitation from the Negroes, but that does not mean that we may not have later." Unfortunately, the state's college center plans for Charlotte initially did not include African American students. Not until the city school system took over administration of the Charlotte Center in 1949 was provision made for them.

By July, Garinger was convinced that Bernard was the right person to be director of the center and wrote to Grumman to that effect. Garinger said, "If he is appointed, he can do much of the drudgery that is to be done. . . . If he did teach one class and spent the rest of his time administering the school, I should say his salary should be at least $3,000 for the year." When Bernard received his appointment letter from Grumman on August 28, the salary was set at $2,750. Garinger told Grumman, "I am confident that our extension center will be a lusty institution, and we want to make it a credit to us and to you."

As students registered, and the Charlotte Center's total reached nearly 250, McIntosh wrote Garinger, "Your center seems assured beyond doubt."

CHAPTER 2

Charlotte Center Feeds a Hunger

THIS IS the story of the three-year existence of the Charlotte College Center of the University of North Carolina. In retrospect, it was the beginning of the history of a major university, but at the time its existence was so tenuous that only the true believers had much faith in its future. Yet the beginning in 1946 was a historic occasion for the City of Charlotte, which had tried a number of times, beginning in the colonial period, to establish a public institution of higher education.

The story of the center is also the story of the University of North Carolina at Charlotte's founder, Bonnie Ethel Cone, then a Charlotte Central High School teacher. She began with the center as a part-time instructor on day one, but her abilities already had so impressed the administrator in charge, Dr. Elmer Garinger, that when the directorship became open in the second year, she was his first choice to lead the Charlotte Center.

The Charlotte Center opened its doors to students in the Charlotte Central High School Building on Elizabeth Avenue on September 23, 1946, with two full-time employees—Director Charles Bernard and English teacher Mary Denny—and several part-time instructors, including Bonnie Cone. Cone had left Charlotte in 1943 to go to Duke University, but she said that she had promised Garinger she would return to Charlotte's city schools. She kept her promise: on August 9, 1946, the Charlotte Board of Education received a letter from the Naval Ordnance Laboratory of the U.S. Naval Gun Factory in Washington, D.C., stating that Miss Bonnie Cone had been employed since April 1945, doing analysis of highly classified mine-performance data. Her resignation had been accepted with regret, and the school board was told that it was lucky to be getting her back.

Thus it was that Bonnie Cone was available to become a part-time teacher in the Charlotte Center when it opened, along with teaching mathematics at Central High School. The employment policy was to have the UNC

Bonnie E. Cone was the inspiration behind developing Charlotte College into UNC Charlotte.

Extension Division employ the teachers and to have the university pay them. A high school teacher who was qualified—a master's degree was usually required—could teach one class in the center.

In that first year of the center, Bonnie Cone taught full time in the high school; this schedule included five classes and a senior home room. Additionally, she taught seven credit hours of Mathematics 101 and did testing for the Charlotte Center. "I coordinated my teaching with N.C. State College," she said. "I gave the same tests given at the Raleigh campus." Her additional testing duties were primarily for English and mathematics placement.

"Miss Bonnie," as she became known to thousands of students of Charlotte College and UNC Charlotte for some fifty years, may have had no inkling as a child that she would found a university, but she knew early that she would be a teacher. In her hometown of Lodge in the Low Country of South Carolina, a young Bonnie Ethel Cone organized school classes for the chickens pecking around the family home. In 1958 a *Charlotte Observer* reporter quoted Cone as saying that she "recited poetry and explained history to chickens who gobbled grain and ignored the mental menu she offered." Cone was quoted as saying, "I taught every little animal around in those fantastic years."

Cone later said the part about the chickens and animals was a bit exaggerated but the idea behind it was true: "I knew from the time I started to school that I wanted to be a teacher." Deciding to become a mathematics teacher came later. She finished high school too early to go on to college immediately, so she went back to high school to retake a course in geometry with a new teacher. "I got the same grade, but that time I saw the logic and reason behind it," Cone said. "It hit me that it wasn't the subject that made the difference—it was the teacher."

Cone majored in mathematics at Coker College, where she also had a scholarship grading mathematics papers. She was so good at her subject that when her teachers were absent, she was asked to substitute. She did become a schoolteacher—but later she became more: director of the Charlotte Center of the University of North Carolina, director of Charlotte College, president of Charlotte College, acting chancellor of UNC Charlotte, vice chancellor for student affairs and community relations of UNC Charlotte, liaison officer of the UNC Charlotte Foundation, and after her retirement from that final position, vice chancellor emerita and a lifelong advocate for the university.

After Coker, Cone taught at Lake View High School, beginning in 1928; McColl High School, beginning in 1933; and Gaffney High School, from 1937 to 1940. In her early teaching career, she lived with other teachers in "teacherages"—homes where they would be protected (and perhaps watched to be sure that they maintained good character).

To be hired to teach in Charlotte in those days, one had to have already established a reputation for excellence. Cone had built that reputation in her early assignments, and her work came to the attention of Dr. Elmer Garinger with the Charlotte City Schools in 1940. That ability later put her in a position to be selected by him for a leadership of the college center.

In her Charlotte College and UNC Charlotte days, Bonnie Cone always had the demeanor of a respected schoolteacher, and the appropriate response to her requests seemed to be, "Yes, ma'am." In her earliest years at the Charlotte Center of the University of North Carolina and Charlotte College, her students were predominantly male, and they gave her the respect due a dedicated and helpful schoolteacher. In fact, they dubbed themselves "Bonnie's Boys." In 1994, when the eighty-six-year-old Cone was given UNC Charlotte's Distinguished Service Award, a group of Bonnie's Boys raised over $100,000 toward the Bonnie E. Cone Distinguished Professorships for Teaching, named in her honor.

Some of her former students went on to fame and fortune. Reece Overcash, a member of the first class in 1946, who died in 1995, became chief executive of The Associates Corp., one of the nation's leading financial institutions, based in Dallas. He left UNC Charlotte the proceeds of a $250,000 insurance policy, which his family matched with more than $250,000, resulting in a scholarship fund worth $550,000. Another of Bonnie's Boys, Bill

Reece Overcash was one of "Bonnie's Boys" and later became chairman of The Associates Corp., a major national financial corporation.

Disher, transferred to Wake Forest University, where he was later named a distinguished alumnus and became chairman and chief executive of Lance, Inc. Ken Harris became a leading insurance executive and served as a mayor of Charlotte. Wyatt Bell went on to N.C. State University and later become president of J. N. Pease Associates, an architectural and engineering firm. Steve Mahaley went on to became a neurosurgeon and served at medical schools at Duke, UNC Chapel Hill, and the University of Alabama–Birmingham before his death. Jim Babb become president of Jefferson Pilot Communications and later Outlet Communications of Rhode Island. William L. Mills Jr., a wounded war hero from Cabarrus County, completed his work at the center and transferred to UNC Chapel Hill, where he attended law school; he became a prominent attorney in Concord before his death. Although most of Bonnie's Boys completed their educations at other institutions, the impact of Bonnie Cone, the center, and Charlotte College were so great that these students maintained a fierce loyalty to their first institution.

Many of Cone's students said that they had been headed toward mediocre futures until Cone inspired them and turned them around. Author William Styron, whom Cone taught at Duke University, later wrote of the influence Cone had on his life. Even into her Charlotte College and UNC Charlotte days, Cone continued that practice of inspiring students who weren't reaching their full potential.

Among those who credited her with turning them around was John Kilgo, a Charlotte newspaper reporter, editor, and radio and television commentator. Kilgo's relationship with Cone started in the fall of 1953. He had graduated from Central High School in June of that year and had gone to work at the *Charlotte News* as a copy boy at seventy-five cents an hour. His father had died in December of his senior year in high school, and with that loss, Kilgo said any thoughts of going to college had vanished. He planned to work his way into the newspaper business.

"Miss Cone showed up at the office one September afternoon, asked permission from my boss to speak to me, and the next thing I knew, I was in her car heading toward Central High School to register for classes at Charlotte College," Kilgo said. "I had no money, so Miss Cone paid the $75 quarterly fee for three classes," he said. "I paid her back weekly until we had settled up," Kilgo said. He added that Cone decided to get to know him because his brother, Jimmy, had attended school with her earlier. "Ironically, I won the first Bonnie Cone scholarship the next year," John Kilgo said.

After two years at Charlotte College, he transferred to UNC Chapel Hill to earn his four-year degree in journalism and return to his career at the *Charlotte News*. Over the years he continued to sing Cone's praises. "I've admired her since that first meeting in September 1953, and do feel that she is one of Charlotte's most important citizens ever," he said. On a videotaped presentation to her when she received the UNC Charlotte Distinguished Service Award, Kilgo said that when the next history of Charlotte is written, the name of Bonnie Cone ought to appear prominently in it.

Kilgo said that in his Charlotte College days, he worked from 7 A.M. until 3:30 P.M. at the *Charlotte News*, then caught a bus at the Square and arrived on campus about 3:45 P.M. He went to class from 4 to 7 P.M., then practiced with the Charlotte College basketball team at Piedmont Junior High from 8 until 11 P.M. "When I got tired, or discouraged, or just needed a dose of inspiration, I dropped by to see Miss Cone," Kilgo said. "I always felt better after being in her presence. She is an extraordinary lady," Kilgo added.

The late James J. Harris, an insurance company owner and son-in-law of North Carolina governor Cameron Morrison, asked Cone to have a word with his son Cameron in the late 1960s. The son went on to graduate from UNC Charlotte in 1968, and he built an insurance organization that equalled or surpassed that of his father.

Carolina Freight Carriers executive John L. (Buck) Fraley, a Charlotte College trustee, vice chairman of the UNC Charlotte Board of Trustees, and first chairman of the UNC Charlotte Board of Visitors, had Cone talk to his son John Jr. in the mid-1970s. The younger Fraley then graduated and became an executive in Carolina Freight and also succeeded his father on the UNC Charlotte Board of Trustees.

Cone was a short, dark-haired, open-faced woman who walked rapidly, with a determined forward tilt, and who had a way of asking for help that was difficult for even the most prominent people to ignore. "Now, Tom, we need your help," she would say to Tom Belk, one of the leading figures in the Belk Department Store family. "You won't let us down, will you?" Tom Belk and others approached in that way rarely did.

In an argument with a male protagonist, Cone would address him as "Sir," with such a bite it was startling to even the strongest. Cone didn't consider herself unusual even though she was a chief executive at a time when females were rarely seen in top management. And she knew how to be assertive even before the days of assertiveness training workshops for women. She could be tough when she had to. A coach, a professor, and a dean were among those she fired over the years.

She refused ever to admit things weren't going well. When asked how things were going on such occasions, her reply was "It's a pretty day" or "This too will pass." Of perfectionists, who often slowed the process too much to suit her, she would say, "In striving to make perfect, often we mar that which is good." Of people who gave her the most difficulty, the strongest condemnation she uttered was, "That booger."

Cone's hometown of Lodge, South Carolina, where she was born on June 22, 1907, to Charles Jefferson Cone and Addie Lavinia Harter Cone, had about two hundred residents when she was growing up. Her father was mayor, and she was proud of the fact that from one artesian well he was able to provide water to all of the town's residents. The mayoral job wasn't full time in a town that size. Her father also sold Hudson automobiles—with jump seats in the back. Along with the sales room, he had a garage for repairs.

Cone's hometown was named Lodge for the fact that one of the first buildings in town was the Masonic lodge. "We imagined mysterious things that went on in there," she said, "including that a goat was kept inside for rituals."

Bonnie was the youngest living child; a younger brother and sister died in infancy. Her two older brothers were sent to Carlisle School in Bamberg, where her father had gone as a young man. Bonnie and her sister went from the public schools to Coker College. Bonnie's personal choice for college was Winthrop, because it was a teacher's college. But the minister next door convinced her family that Winthrop was too large for such a timid little girl and that Coker would be better suited. Bonnie was in the last group of students admitted to Coker by examinations, which included one in Latin.

Later in her career, Cone felt that she did indeed have more opportunities at Coker. There she was president of the Math Club and of the YWCA and served on the student legislature. She did costuming for the drama club and was in the May Day programs—not as a queen but as a scarf dancer, twirling a large scarf to depict storms or rain. She excelled at athletics and was on the swimming, basketball, and field hockey teams and on crew. She didn't play tennis, she said, because in those days that was what girls who couldn't do anything else did. She and her classmates did sewing, mending, cooking, and ironing to raise money to build a boathouse for the college canoes.

The atmosphere was somewhat protective at the time. Girls were shipped (expelled) for smoking or playing cards. "If you went to town you had to wear a hat and gloves," Cone said.

As a child Cone longed to play the piano. She remembers pretending the windowsill was a keyboard and playing on it. When she was five, her father bought her a real piano. She took lessons from Miss Eugenia Fox, the only person in town who had studied piano in college.

When Miss Eugenia married and moved away, other parents asked if Bonnie could teach their children what she knew, so she became a young music teacher. At church, Cone played an old pump organ and later the piano. She took piano lessons again at Limestone College when she took a teaching job in Gaffney just before coming to Charlotte.

Her Charlotte friend Mrs. Ross Puett gave Cone a piano during her Charlotte College days. Cone enjoyed playing late at night or early in the morning—before or after strenuous days at the campus.

One of the few subjects Cone never wanted to discuss was romantic interludes in her life. "There ought to be some things off limits," she said. But then she went on to say, "The first valentine I ever got was from a young man who went into medicine, became a doctor, and came back and lived in a neighboring community in Colleton County. Oh, there were others, and my Daddy didn't particularly care for some of my friends. Some are still my friends." The Charlotte Center, Charlotte College, and UNC Charlotte obviously got more of Bonnie Cone because the institution, rather than one of those young men, was the object of her passion.

But the beginning of the center wasn't very glamorous. Charlotte Center classes started at 4 P.M. in Central High classrooms after the high school students were dismissed for the day. "We had a good faculty with very few exceptions," Cone said. She noted that C. A. (Pete) McKnight, editor of the *Charlotte Observer* and later a trustee of Charlotte College, taught Spanish. Miss Mary Denny taught English, Mrs. Frances Hoyle also taught Spanish, and Dr. Herbert Hechenbleikner taught biology.

The classrooms used were those on the high school building's third floor, because that's where the laboratories were and where the library was. Cone recalled that the center had to supplement equipment and provide its own supplies.

Cone also recalled that during that first year, she worked with Bernard in planning. "I had a full eighteen-hour day," she said. "There weren't any hours left for anything."

She describes the students as very eager to learn and very challenging to teach because of the experiences they brought with them. They were made up of 95 percent veterans and 95 percent men. There was only one female veteran, Isabell Bradford, who later transferred to UNC Chapel Hill and became an accountant. Cone believed the center opened up college opportunity to many students who never would have considered attending in earlier years. "In our first year, there were more graduates of Tech High attending than had gone to college from there in its twenty years of existence," she said.

In addition to the veterans, there were students who later would have been considered traditional college students. O. Ned Burgess Jr., who had graduated from Central High in May 1946, was an example of such a student. His enrollment at the Charlotte Center was accidental, and its opening came at exactly the right time for him. He played football for Central High at a time when the team was drawing 10,000 to 15,000 fans a game. Burgess said that the football coach at Davidson College was impressed with that success and offered him and several of his teammates scholarships. But after arriving for practice at Davidson, they discovered that the college wanted to become a football power, and the demands were far more than they bargained for. So they quit in the middle of August.

Only one player had covered his bases by applying to UNC Chapel Hill as well as Davidson. Burgess and some of the other players were faced with being left out in the cold, because all the colleges were jam-packed with returning veterans.

"Thank goodness for Charlie Bernard and the Charlotte Center," Burgess said. Burgess was particularly happy that the center was being promoted as the freshman class for UNC Chapel Hill. In terms of grades and status, he said, students felt everything was just the same as if they were at Chapel Hill.

Burgess said it was a smooth transition: having graduated from Central, it was just like going back for a thirteenth year. He said there was no downside to attending college where he had attended high school, because his classes began after the high school students were gone. "Some of us did try to get there before the high school senior girls left, however," Burgess added. The presence of much older veterans in the college did make a difference in the atmosphere, according to Burgess. He said those students related to Bernard very well, because he was a sort of college president, faculty adviser, and chaplain.

The only professor Burgess personally remembers who became a permanent Charlotte College and UNC Charlotte professor was Dr. Herbert Hechenbleikner, from whom he took botany and zoology. But Burgess said that Dr. Heck was rather low-key then and had not become the character he was to become later. He remembers Hechenbleikner as the first "doctor" professor he ever had.

Burgess assumed that the center was just a temporary solution. Most of his friends had plans to go on to Chapel Hill. But the Charlotte Center bailed out Burgess for his sophomore year just as it had for his freshman year.

He had decided sometime in his freshman year to be an optometrist and because he was planning to go to the Pennsylvania State College of Optometry, he didn't make arrangements to transfer to Chapel Hill. After visiting the Pennsylvania school, however, he discovered that nothing he had taken would transfer there, and it was a five-year program. "And when you are eighteen years old, six years out of your life seems like an eternity," he said.

So Burgess found himself stuck again without a college to attend. He came back to Charlotte and enrolled for the Charlotte Center's sophomore year, which had just been added. "My luck was either real bad or real good," he said.

After the second year, Burgess was back on track and entered Journalism School and finished with his UNC Chapel Hill class of 1950, except for one quarter he had to take in summer school. In majoring in journalism he returned to a childhood plan. Printer's ink was in his blood: his father and two uncles were printers, and he had been hanging around newspaper plants since he was a baby. Initially he worked for a chain of small newspapers, including those in Belmont and Mount Holly and the *Mecklenburg Times.* After three years he worked for WBTV as a public relations person, convincing newspapers in the region to run television schedules and columns—in essence, early television sections.

After seven years, Burgess bought and managed the *Yorkville Enquirer* and the *Clover Herald.* He sold the company in 1980 during a newspaper acquisition flurry and retired for two years and then did something he just enjoyed—working in the library at McClintock Junior High School in Charlotte—until his full retirement.

The Charlotte Center and its successor institutions served other members of the Burgess family as well. Ned's brother, Jimmy, attended and later became a financial vice president of a company in Chicago. Ned's wife, Nancy, took educational certification courses from UNC Charlotte, which enabled her "to spend twenty-seven fun-filled years as a teacher at Garinger High School." Ned Burgess even had a cousin born and raised in New York City who came down and attended Charlotte College. "It was the right school at the right time for me and a lot of other guys," Burgess concluded.

The story of the Burgess family is typical of the role the Charlotte Center and Charlotte College played for many local families in its early history. From the beginning, its leaders sought to create a real college, not just an extension center, with high standards. As in other colleges, the student body wanted student government and met as soon as October to arrange elections for student officers.

The cost of attending the center that first fall term in 1946 was sixty dollars per quarter for tuition, plus five dollars for registration and five dollars for a laboratory fee.

To promote social life for the students, Bernard and the Student Council arranged an open house that first year at the Charlotte Armory for the student body and the faculty and "sixty girls from Queens." And in an attempt to create an intellectual atmosphere and as close a tie as possible to UNC Chapel Hill, Bernard arranged assemblies to which he invited Chapel Hill professors as speakers.

In the academic arena, it is likely that a practice begun in 1946 set the tone for UNC Charlotte's high academic quality down through the years. The Charlotte College Center instructors met with academic coordinators from UNC Chapel Hill and N.C. State and used the same course outlines, the same textbooks, and often the same examinations used by professors at the senior institutions. But not everything went smoothly in the early months. Unfortunately, there were some misunderstandings arising from the shared use of the Charlotte Central High School facilities. "We had a very different type of young man," Cone said. "Most of the young men were just thrilled at the opportunity of coming back to college. Many of them were mature fellows who earlier had no thought that they would ever be able to get a college education."

Some of the high school teachers and students resented having to share their space with the college center, to the point of hiding the chalk and erasers. According to Cone, some teachers wrote across the whole board in

The old Central High School building was home to the Charlotte Center, Charlotte College, and later to Central Piedmont Community College.

small script and then posted a note saying, "Do not erase." However, some other teachers understood that Central High School was providing a much-needed public service, she said.

Garinger also had to notify Bernard that there was a problem with veterans' smoking in the building. "The students in the College Center should realize that continuance of the school depends upon the proper observation of the regulations and requirements of the local board of education as well as the university," he said—in other words, no smoking.

The first year came to a close on June 6, 1947, with no assurance that there would be another one. Bernard wrote to Garinger on July 30 that he had considered his advice about returning to graduate work at UNC Chapel Hill and had accepted a part-time instructorship in political science and was therefore submitting his resignation from the Charlotte Center with regret.

Garinger responded with thanks for Bernard's year of work and said, "I am expecting the state committee to give its approval for a second year."

Cone and Denny were teaching at Duke University in the summer of 1947 when they were visited by Garinger and Hillman, who represented the College Conference. Cone, Denny, and Garinger made their pitch to Hillman not only to continue the center for a second year but also to add sophomore work. They were successful.

Bernard's summertime resignation to return to graduate school presented a problem for opening the fall session in 1947, though. Garinger wrote to Bernard that he had previously told Cone he would offer the position to her if Bernard should resign. But he added that he was not sure she would accept. He quoted her as saying that a man was needed because the boys liked to have someone with whom they could talk. However, Garinger said he told Cone that if she did not accept, he would offer the position to Denny.

Bernard wrote Cone and said, "It will be a good job for you, Bonnie." He even recommended Annie Lee Sawyer as an assistant, and Sawyer did indeed become Cone's first secretary.

Cone said she took the directorship thinking, "I'll just have to keep it long enough for them to find somebody else. But I don't believe they really worked very hard to get anybody in the first place, and I know they certainly didn't seem to be working hard to relieve me of my tentative appointment."

Her beginning wasn't very auspicious. "When I got to duty (in mid-August), I found that all I had was one little tiny office—they called it the 'lost and found' area. It had three items of equipment. I had one homemade desk, probably no more than 24" by 36", that had no drawers, just one shelf. I had one beautiful two-drawer file which had been bought the year before, so it was nearly new, and one discarded Royal typewriter that had been owned by Charlotte Technical High School."

But by September 1, Cone had enrolled 228 students, 92 of whom were there for sophomore work. The center opened on schedule at 4 P.M. on September 27 with exercises in the auditorium of Central High School and a final total of 302 students enrolled. On opening day, they heard announcements about football tryouts, auditions for a male chorus, and instruction in dramatics.

After the year was under way, McIntosh said of Cone to a representative of the Duke University placement office, "I prophesy that she will operate a highly successful center this year and that she will reflect great credit upon your institution in so doing." Even so, it was clear that the administrators in Chapel Hill considered the centers nonpermanent. McIntosh wrote Cone to suggest that she add fluorescent lights to the classrooms being used. "We paid for four rooms last year, and we felt that if these fixtures were left in the building they would be of service after the college center program should cease to exist," he said.

The administrators in the central office, however, were helpful and enthusiastic about the centers. Bernard told Miss Cone that he would shortly become assistant to Roy Armstrong, director of admissions at UNC Chapel Hill, and that he would help expedite the transfer of the Charlotte Center students to that campus and that their records would be treated the same as those of regular UNC students. "I'll look after them on this end," he said.

Later Bernard wrote Cone, "You don't need me there to make any decisions now or later. I was confident that you would do a beautiful job, and you have merited all thoughts in that direction. Mr. Mac (McIntosh) is completely happy over the good job you are doing."

Things didn't go completely smoothly, however. For example, problems of communication and understanding grew out of hiring public school instructors to teach in a university system. At one point Cone urged that as full-time instructors, Mary Denny and Edyth Winningham should be paid at least $3,000, because even as public school teachers they would be paid $3,150 for high school work.

Cone even felt it necessary to complain about her own salary. She told McIntosh she had been told her salary would be $3,960 for nine months plus $200 extra for testing. "As a matter of fact, my salary for the nine months was less than that received by a G-12 high school teacher who taught one class in the college," she noted. After this complaint McIntosh settled her salary at $4,825, of which $665 was for summer school and $200 for testing.

Apparently Cone pushed persistently for things she believed the College Center should have. McIntosh lectured her about her not taking his decisions as official and being too impatient with him when he couldn't do something she wanted done. When she complained about needing smaller class sizes, he chided her, saying that finances would create trouble ahead.

One of the programs launched at the very beginning—athletics—did eventually create trouble. Arthur Deremer was the first Charlotte Center football coach. Before World War II he had played football for the Brooklyn Tigers, a team in the National League. Deremer came to Charlotte in 1946 to play center for the revived minor league professional football team, the Charlotte Clippers. He coached the Charlotte Center team on the side. Deremer wrote to other institutions in 1946 to try to schedule games. Mostly he scheduled the B teams of Clemson, Davidson, Catawba, Belmont Abbey, and Pembroke. All equipment and expenses had to be paid from gate receipts.

In January 1947, Bernard hired Howard Baker, an Erskine College graduate, as the first basketball coach. His team played the freshman teams of Davidson, Belmont Abbey, Burton Institute, and Navy of Charleston, and the industrial teams of Cramer Mills and Lance, Inc., plus some community teams. A softball team played mostly pickup games. Two students who wanted to participate in track were allowed to run in track meets at UNC Chapel Hill.

The returning veterans considered athletic teams necessary. Unfortunately, it wasn't long before the difficulties of running an athletics program on a shoestring became apparent.

In the fall of 1947, McIntosh complained about athletics taking students out of classes. He also said the teams should carry their own weight financially. His concerns resurfaced when the school's second football coach, Marion "Footsie" Woods, reported that creditors were pressing for payment for "football suits" and other expenses. So McIntosh told Cone, "Unless the interest in Charlotte is sufficient to pay for the expenses of equipping the team we

UNC Charlotte had a football team in its CCUNC days. The 1947 squad is shown here. Photo from CCUNC News.

do not feel that we are justified in taking student fees and applying them to athletics."

McIntosh admonished Coach Woods, "I cannot advise you nor the administration at Charlotte how to enlist greater interest.... But I hope you will exert every effort to have as large crowds as possible, both in football and basketball, for many people will be drawn to your center by its athletic accomplishments. You all know, of course, that with no athletic fund available it is necessary to make your program carry as much of the expenses as possible. I believe you will plan your basketball program with this financial necessity in mind"—a challenge that would make contemporary athletic directors shudder.

It was a challenge even in those days. Gate receipts at a 1948 basketball game with the Lenoir-Rhyne B team were $33.40, resulting in a net gain of $3.22 after expenses. There was a net loss of $3.75 when the team played Belmont Abbey. By April 1948, McIntosh wrote to Earl Crowe, captain of the baseball team, and told him that his office could no longer sponsor athletic teams.

McIntosh told Crowe that he had to discontinue Coach Woods at the end of the winter quarter and that the central office for the college centers was planning to make a loan to the Charlotte Center to help liquidate the cost of the football uniforms and equipment bought the previous fall but that the loan would have to be repaid. He noted that though Woods may have been a good coach, he lacked the ability to handle financial arrangements. Even so, McIntosh continued, a football coach should be considered for the next fall. A football coach was indeed hired for the fall of 1948, but Cone decided that Coach Carol Blackwell was not working out and dismissed him.

Just as the hiring of a football coach that late in the center's existence implied that the center would continue, almost all other programs were operated from the beginning of Bonnie Cone's leadership in 1947 as if the institution were to be permanent.

It was also clear that from her first year as director of the center, Cone considered it the beginning of a permanent college. In a 1947 letter in which she attempted to attract Professor George Abernathy of Davidson to teach part time, she said, "I hope that when the college center is taken over by the city, we shall have the privilege of having you teach the course for us." Abernathy responded that he had noted Garinger's efforts to lay the foundation for a municipal junior college and said, "There is no reason why a city like Charlotte should not have a strong junior college."

Another indication that the Charlotte leadership was thinking about a permanent institution was the establishment of the Advisory Committee—a move that would have been unusual if the institution were only temporary. Cone wrote to J. Murrey Atkins, a stockbroker and chairman of the city school board, on September 16, 1947, soon after her assumption of the leadership of the center, and told him she wanted an advisory board in order to encourage increased enrollment and a broader program. It would be an advisory committee made up of representatives of local "civic and educational organizations and other interested persons to help us in making our programs fit the needs of the community," she wrote. Cone invited prospects for the advisory committee to a dinner on November 12, 1947, and then to Memorial Stadium to see the center's football team play the Appalachian State University B team.

Comprising that first board were Atkins; P. H. Batte of the *Charlotte Observer*; Herbert Baxter, the city's mayor; Henry Belk Jr. of the mercantile family; George Everett of the U.S. Employment Office; Mrs. J. B. Ficklen of the American Association of University Women; Garinger; James H. Glenn of the schools commission; James J. Harris, an insurance executive and son-in-law of former governor Cameron Morrison; D. E. Henderson, U.S. district attorney, who later became a federal judge for the Western District of North Carolina; Clarence O. Kuester of the Charlotte Chamber of Commerce; Charlotte Mobley, president of the Altrusa Club; John Otts, principal of Central High, which the center used for its classrooms; Dr. Paul Sanger, physician; Chester Whelchel of the Jaycees; J. W. Wilson, superintendent of Mecklenburg County Schools; and Dick Young of the *Charlotte News*.

In her letter of invitation, Cone gave a status report on the center. With 304 students, she said, it was the largest of all the centers—indeed, in its second year of operations, larger than all the others combined. She acknowledged that the center faced an uncertain future. It was up to the executive committee of the North Carolina College Conference to determine whether the emergency caused by returning World War II veterans still existed and therefore whether there was a continuing need for the centers.

The only centers still operating in the second year (1947–48) were in Burnsville, Charlotte, Gastonia, and Greensboro. Wilmington leaders, in the second year of the centers, had taken over theirs as a city institution with support from a five-cent tax levy. Asheville-Biltmore was continuing as a junior college with the help of a yearly appropriation from the Asheville City Council.

In her update to the new advisory group, Cone told them of two possible ways to retain the Charlotte Center: either make it a permanent branch of the University of North Carolina or let the City of Charlotte and Mecklenburg County take over and administer the center to meet community needs for terminal courses as well as college transfer work.

In continuing correspondence with Jesse P. Bogue of the American Association of Junior Colleges, Garinger said he favored a tax levy similar to that in Wilmington to continue the center as a college.

By the end of 1947 and beginning of 1948, the UNC administrators seemed ambiguous about the centers. But some certainty about the issue emerged when the executive committee of the College Conference voted to continue the remaining centers for 1948–49. They agreed also to recommend that the centers be discontinued after 1948–49.

McIntosh wrote Cone, "One of the greatest delights I have had during the past 15 months is working with you and your faculty in the making of your center into the outstanding college center in the state," he said. Later he wrote, "This year we have only five centers and so far as we know, Charlotte is the only one which promises to be permanent."

While the uncertainty continued, Cone kept pressing for her needs. In January 1948, she asked McIntosh for a summer school session on behalf of many students who needed and had requested it. By March, she was told that she could operate a summer school.

Despite the fact that Charlotte was taking some ownership of its center, there was some disagreement over what to call it. J. Henry Highsmith of the State Department of Public Instruction reminded Cone that the center was not the creature of UNC.

McIntosh wrote Cone to complain about the use of the designation "CCUNC" for the Charlotte Center. He said that a newspaper headline, "UNC to Continue Sponsorship of College Center," was incorrect because UNC was only the administrator of the program. However, it should be noted that the practice of using this shorthand version, "CCUNC," continued until the institution became Charlotte College.

As further evidence that none of the uncertainty had deterred Cone, as early as March 1948, she was attempting to have the Charlotte Center admitted to the American Association of Junior Colleges even though it had no permanent or continuing status. Hillman of the State Department of Public Instruction told her he saw no advantage to be gained by this move and, further, that it was not customary for his department to give a "rating" to a school until it operated for a year under conditions appropriate for such a school.

At a spring 1948 meeting, the Charlotte Center's advisory committee asked Cone to notify the UNC Director of Extension that they wanted the university to take over the Charlotte Center and administer it as a permanent unit of the university system. At about the same time Cone wrote to Professor Cecil Johnson of UNC Chapel Hill asking him to participate in a discussion on a permanent junior college and telling him, "Many of our people would like to see a branch of the University located here."

The College Conference's move to close the centers meant that something had to be done quickly or the Charlotte Center would end. In January 1949, Cone notified McIntosh that a legislative bill was being prepared to enable the Charlotte school system to operate the Charlotte Center. She pointed out that she had never received a reply to the earlier request that the UNC system administer the college.

J. Murrey Atkins began working with school board attorney Brock Barkley in shaping the bill. In a prepared press release, Atkins announced that the city school board was also establishing a school for African American students, providing them with opportunities similar to those of the Charlotte Center.

That new institution was to be called Carver College and would be located at Second Ward High School. Later the name was changed to Mecklenburg College. Ultimately it would be merged with Central Industrial Education Center to become Central Piedmont Community College.

Dr. Garinger had seen no need for a center for African American students while the college centers were administered by the University of North Carolina. But apparently officials had now realized that the Charlotte City Schools would have to provide opportunity for African American students after the board took over the operation.

At the time, the segregationist "separate but equal" tradition prevailed. Carver College thus opened in September 1949, with sixty-two African American students. It offered liberal arts courses, a business program and a business and secretarial terminal program, cosmetology, adult education, and an accelerated high school program. The Supreme Court's *Brown v. Board of Education* decision, which opened the door to desegregation in public schools and also led to the desegregation of colleges, came five years later, in 1954.

By 1956, Carver College had 484 college-level students out of a total enrollment of 728; the remainder were in the terminal and high school completion programs. For a number of years it was led by director Edward H. Brown.

Charlotte now at last had in place the beginnings of its public higher education system, thanks to the foresight and wisdom of a group of dedicated local leaders. The stage was set for permanent institutions of public higher education in Charlotte.

CHAPTER 3

Bonnie Cone Builds Charlotte College

THE STORY of Charlotte College, like that of the Charlotte Center, is one of steady progress in spite of meager resources. It is also the story of Charlotteans like W. A. Kennedy asserting that it was time for the state to provide financial support for higher education in this community, which contributed the largest share of taxes to Raleigh and got nothing back for higher education.

This chapter recounts the story of people of vision—people who could see a state-supported university for Charlotte on the horizon even while Charlotte College operated in borrowed quarters in Central High School. It was also a time when state leaders like Luther Hodges, Terry Sanford, Frank Porter Graham, William C. Friday, and others began to pay attention to Charlotte's pleas and to understand that for the state as a whole to progress, its largest city had to have some type of higher educational institution.

For citizens of the community, the Charlotte College years were a time when they put their money where their mouths were in terms of supporting their institution. They not only voted to levy taxes on themselves at the city and county levels but approved a statewide bond issue as well.

The second chapter in the move toward a university for Charlotte began on April 4, 1949, when the North Carolina General Assembly ratified a bill creating the Charlotte Community College System, providing for Charlotte and Carver Colleges.

At the time, the North Carolina General Assembly met only every two years—in the odd-numbered years. Bonnie Cone said later that she didn't know what would have happened had the Charlotte Center been phased out in a year when the legislature was not in session. "If it had been an even-numbered year, we would have just died. There would have been no way out," she recalled.

Charlotte College was also fortunate to have J. Murrey Atkins's quiet but efficient leadership. He carried the ball in getting the legislation approved.

That would prove to be one of the easiest legislative quests Charlotteans ever undertook on behalf of Charlotte College. That was because the state was being asked to put little at risk in terms of future support. Under the legislation, the Charlotte Board of School Commissioners was authorized to use "surplus funds"—money from nontax sources—and no more than $5,000 each for Charlotte and Carver Colleges.

The legislation also authorized the county's Board of Elections to hold a referendum on levying a tax, not to exceed five cents on the $100 valuation. Also, the city school board could receive gift lands, buildings, equipment, money, or anything else of value for an endowment or operating funds for the Charlotte Community College system.

Even while the institution was still under the administration of the University of North Carolina, Cone got her wish to participate in a professional organization. In February 1949, she attended an American Association of Junior Colleges meeting in California. She had been in Lodge, South Carolina, during January, following the death of her father, and went from there to Chicago to travel with other junior college administrators to the convention.

They traveled by train, filling three cars and being assigned an extra dining car. Cone said the people she met on the train became longtime friends whom she consulted whenever she needed advice. The group then traveled around California visiting junior colleges that at the time were setting the pace for the rest of the nation.

While her center was temporary and administered by the University of North Carolina, Cone had made contacts with the junior college organization. She had also pushed for early accreditation. When told there would be a one-year wait, she pointed out that actually the institution had operated for three years, two of which had included the sophomore year of work.

In a letter to Henry Highsmith of the State Department of Public Instruction, she told him that Wilmington College, with only one previous year of freshman work and no sophomore work and with a much smaller enrollment, had been given a letter of assurance that it would be accredited at the end of its first year of independent operation.

Accreditation was an issue because under Charlotte College Center status, students could transfer with full credit to senior institutions. They could not do so if they transferred from a brand new unaccredited junior college. Cone explained that students wanting to transfer would face a handicap if accreditation were to be delayed until 1950. Finally, Hillman assured her in May 1949 that her institution could be issued a statement similar to that given Wilmington College if she furnished data certifying that the institution had operated by the principles of a junior college.

Cone was supported in her efforts by Jesse P. Bogue, executive director of the junior college association. A member of Bogue's staff, Mildred English, became acquainted with Charlotte College's efforts at that time, and a few years later she joined Bonnie Cone's staff.

Following the tentative letter of approval as an accredited institution, Hillman and Highsmith notified Cone on May 30, 1950, that Charlotte College "may now be recognized as a standard junior college as of the academic year 1949–50." In her letter of thanks to the two, Cone cited two students from the center who would be graduating Phi Beta Kappa from UNC Chapel Hill the following week—Joe Bookout and David Littlejohn. After graduating, Littlejohn returned to teach Spanish for Charlotte College for a time.

With accreditation settled, there was work to be done in administering the new junior college. Because the old advisory committee was rather large for a college board, an executive board was created in 1951. Its prominent members included Atkins as chairman; James Glenn; Dr. George Heaton, pastor of Myers Park Baptist Church; W. A. Kennedy, owner of textile-related companies; John Paul Lucas, a Duke Power public relations executive; Miss Charlotte Mobley; and Dick Young, a reporter for the *Charlotte News*. Cone was fond of saying that Young wrote the first story about the institution; it appeared in his newspaper in 1946.

Of all the board members, W. A. (Woody) Kennedy took his role on the executive board most seriously. Cone said that he even set aside a portion of his business office and called it his "college office." A native of Wilmington, Kennedy was the son of a Baptist minister and a teacher. Orphaned at an early age, he worked his way through preparatory school and N.C. State University. There he was editor of the college magazine and senior class poet.

During World War II Kennedy served in France with the 81st Division, and after the war he studied at the Sorbonne in Paris and married a French woman. After returning home to Charlotte, Kennedy sold textile machinery and organized his firms—WAK Industries, the W. A. Kennedy Company, and Kennedy Investment Company.

Kennedy understood better than almost any other Charlottean what the lack of a public college meant to the region, and about 1950, he launched a one-man campaign to gain equity in state funding, along with local support, for Charlotte College. Kennedy wrote Governor W. Kerr Scott about his dream for Charlotte, using terms that he thought Scott, a dairyman, would understand. He wrote, imagine that "you only had permanent pasture for 21 out of 100 cattle, the other 79 had to graze on old run-down broom sage [sedge] fields. It would be a predicament, would it not. . . . Certainly you would not fatten 21 of the 100 steers and let the other 79 wander around half starved, and yet that is exactly an analogous situation to our high school graduates up here in the Piedmont, particularly those graduates of our rural high schools."

W. A. Kennedy was the spiritual father of Charlotte College and an unflagging advocate for state support.

Kennedy enclosed a map showing the location of state-supported colleges and pointed out that Charlotte was completely overlooked in the center of a large section of North Carolina, and "yet we have thousands of high school graduates who cannot attend a state supported college here but who cannot afford to go off, as the average cost of room and board . . . is $490 a year."

Kennedy wrote U.S. Senator Frank Porter Graham, former president of the University of North Carolina, "It is most regrettable that such a thickly populated area as Charlotte and the Piedmont section has no state-supported college. We have made great progress in industrial development and in trade and commerce. We send more money to Raleigh than any other section of the state and yet our high school graduates are only going to college at the rate of one-third of the more favored counties, such as Wake, Durham, Orange and Guilford."

Added Kennedy, "The governor suggested that perhaps Davidson College might be expanded to accommodate as many as 2,000 students and that state support might be secured for a technical college." Kennedy said that he had talked with a number of "loyal Davidson men" and that "they see absolutely no chance whatsoever of Davidson expanding as it is not their desire to become a large college."

Graham wrote back to Kennedy that there were many constraints upon state dollars; but he continued, "You evince such enthusiasm, however, that I am impressed with your chances of success and I will be very happy to discuss the whole matter with you the next time we meet."

Even the *Daily Tar Heel*, the student newspaper of UNC Chapel Hill, drew Kennedy's attention when it wrote an editorial opposing a state-supported college in Charlotte. Kennedy responded to the article in a letter to the *Charlotte News* of October 4, 1950:

> We who see the need of and want a four-year state supported college for the Charlotte area do not ask for same because a million people live within a 50-mile radius of Charlotte. We do ask for this college because out of this one million population living in this area, there are some 5,000 . . . young men and women finishing high school each year and because only a maximum of some 1,500 out of this 5,000 go on to college. However, if the rate of college attendance of high school graduates in the Piedmont area could be raised to the high level of those more fortunately situated to state supported colleges and privately endowed colleges, our rate of college attendance would increase approximately 20 percent each year. That means 1,000 additional high school graduates would go to college each year if they had the same opportunity or the same available facilities as some other areas of our state.

Garinger was also conducting his own campaign on behalf of the college. He wrote to Governor W. Kerr Scott in 1951 that James B. Duke once considered Charlotte a potential site for Duke University. He also noted that many in Charlotte advocated a campus of UNC for the city. "Some of the states of the Far West and the Middle West have followed the practice of establishing branches at large population centers in the state. . . . The University must be brought to the people. Chapel Hill and Raleigh are too remote for a great many deserving men and women," Garinger added.

On April 13, 1951, the General Assembly passed an act permitting the Board of School Commissioners of the City of Charlotte to change Charlotte College from a two-year to a four-year college at its discretion. There was no immediate response in Charlotte, because leaders feared they would never gain state support if they accepted that offer and created a four-year city college.

In 1952, Kennedy began using comparative data to make his case. He said that with a population of 135,000, Charlotte had only 400 college students, or one student for each 338.2 residents. Raleigh, on the other hand, with a population of 66,100, had 6,183 students, or one for each 10.6 residents. Atlanta, with a population of 331,300, had 28,180 students, or one per 11.7 residents. Nashville's ratio, with a population of 74,900, was one student per 28.9 residents.

At times Kennedy's arguments on behalf of Charlotte College took on a caustic tone. On June 16, 1951, he wrote a letter to the *Charlotte Observer* complaining that the city and county had turned down a request for $50,000 for funding Charlotte College and that one official had said, "We ain't going to appropriate nothing." Kennedy noted that the honorables did appropriate $18,000 for an animal shelter. "Apparently the needs of stray animals is more important [to local government leaders] than the needs of our youth," Kennedy said. And at times Kennedy's ideas appeared to run counter to the interests of the college; or was it that he had a more global view of Charlotte's future? He wrote Cone in 1954 that he opposed plans to assess Charlotte property owners five cents on the $100 valuation for the operation of Charlotte and Carver Colleges. Instead, he wanted state appropriations.

So perhaps Kennedy understood that only the state budget could support the kind of institution Charlotte ultimately needed. "If the Charlotte Chamber, the Merchants Association and perhaps one or two women's clubs would get back of this, as they should, engage a full-time secretary or lobbyist for 12 months, also engage an assistant lobbyist from the eastern part of the state, then I fully believe Charlotte could secure a reasonable amount of financial aid from the State Legislature," Kennedy wrote. He later told the Advisory Board that he would support a tax of one cent per $100 valuation.

Before Charlotte College could be placed on sound financial footing, Charlotte leadership began pursuing a technical institute, realizing that it would be needed to help the city compete in industrial relocations. Visits were made to technical institutes in Cincinnati and Atlanta. N.C. State University chancellor J. W. Harrelson expressed some interest in establishing such an institute.

Kennedy strongly opposed having an institute under N.C. State, although he was a State alumnus. "Certainly as far as I am concerned," he wrote Miss Cone, "I would fight such a move to the last ditch although I do believe both Carolina and State would like to have our Charlotte efforts as part of their extension departments if they could get us under their thumbs."

He added, "An important city like Charlotte should have a state supported college and technical institute with a great deal of autonomy and on the same level as the other state supported colleges, working under and with the Commission on Higher Education but not using any of the other colleges as an intermediary." In such statements Kennedy was beginning to articulate a concept that was ultimately to prevail in the form of the University of North Carolina at Charlotte and Central Piedmont Community College.

In fact, Kennedy chided those who did not share his vision. At an executive committee meeting of the Charlotte Chamber of Commerce in June 1956, he said in his role as chairman of the chamber's College Subcommittee that the city was not aiming high enough and did not have the vision to go ahead on the scale required. He recommended going all-out for a full senior college.

An interesting footnote to Charlotte College's funding problems is that after a State Advisory Budget Commission visit in 1954 resulted in nothing being recommended for the college, Charlotte's leaders continued their efforts during the ensuing legislative session.

Near the end of the 1955 legislative session, the Joint Appropriations Committee supported a request for $150,000 for Charlotte College. That action took place on a Friday. By Monday, other colleges had rushed in with their own bills, and the legislature responded by appropriating only $10,800 for each community college system.

Still, all of this activity in Charlotte began to penetrate the thinking of the Raleigh bureaucracy. In the summer of 1956, Kennedy said he detected a feeling in Raleigh's Education Building that Charlotte would get a four-year college.

At about this time D. S. Coltrane, assistant director of the state budget, wrote to Kennedy that the Advisory Budget Commission had visited Wilmington and been favorably impressed. He expressed his belief that the commission would also be impressed with Charlotte and its need for state help with its community colleges, as well as the possibility of developing a four-year college.

Thus encouraged, Kennedy intensified his rhetoric. He used gimmicks to make his points. In July 1956, he wrote a select group of Charlotteans and attached to each letter a check for $1,000 but left it unsigned. He asked the recipients to imagine getting the check signed and taking it to the bank but getting back only $500 in cash. Then he made his point: "That's what's happening when you pay North Carolina taxes for the support of 12 colleges. One half goes to build and maintain dormitories. You could do it for $500 in the Charlotte area." He meant that commuting institutions wouldn't need dormitories.

He added, "The most undercolleged city in the South cannot afford to wait any longer." That reference to Charlotte as "undercolleged" apparently was taken from remarks made by D. Hiden Ramsey, chairman of the State Board of Higher Education. On April 7, 1956, Ramsey was quoted by the *Charlotte Observer* as saying, "I don't know of any city of comparable size and prospects that doesn't have more college facilities than the Queen City."

In 1956 Kennedy also began playing his "taxation without benefits" card. He took note that the legislature had recently appropriated $71 million for capital projects; 10 percent of those funds had come from Charlotte, which got none back. As early as 1949 he had asked in a letter, "Is the sole purpose of this area to be used for tax paying purposes only, or are we entitled to some of the benefits enjoyed by other parts of the state but paid for in large part by our citizens?"

That position didn't get a responsive hearing by politicians in the eastern part of the state, even among officials in Raleigh. Kennedy took notes on a conversation with George Ross, director of the Conservation and Development Board, in which he quoted Ross as saying he wished the Charlotte crowd would get behind a trade school proposal and forget the four-year college. It was even suggested to Kennedy that support of a college in Charlotte would require some diversion of funds from already-established institutions in other parts of the state—as if that were an unthinkable outcome.

Kennedy said a representative of the Raleigh Chamber of Commerce told him that Charlotte should drop the college idea for a few years "on account of the scarcity of building materials." Kennedy quoted Andy Monroe of Carolina Power & Light as saying he favored a trade school but not a college for Charlotte. Even William C. Pressly, president of Peace College in Raleigh, wrote, "My own personal feeling is that the state needs to do more for its present system before it enlarges and develops other centers." These comments caused Kennedy to conclude that representatives of Raleigh and perhaps other cities where colleges were then located would "oppose Charlotte's just demands."

He expressed a similar worry to G. S. McCarty of Carolina Annile & Extract Co., who had expressed interest in Charlotte College: "Our old established colleges, the last of which was founded in 1910, represent a certain amount of entrenched power, and they are not going to permit other colleges to be organized and receive state support if they can help it. Therefore I believe a certain amount of 'needling' might be helpful and result in gaining their encouragement in securing state support for the community colleges now located in Charlotte, Asheville and Wilmington."

To Governor William B. Umstead, Kennedy wrote on March 18, 1953, "It has been 43 years since the last state supported college was founded. Charlotte was a very small city at that time, and since Mecklenburg sends to Raleigh 10 percent of the state taxes, I must tell you that I feel Mecklenburg is being much discriminated against in the way of state supported college facilities." A reply to that letter came from Ed Rankin, the governor's assistant, who informed Kennedy that Umstead was recovering from a "mild heart attack." Governor Umstead died in 1954.

In 1953 Representative Phil Whitley of Wake County, who opposed support for Charlotte College, received a Kennedy letter that included this argument: "I do hope that you must realize that anything that assists the economic conditions of the youth here in the Piedmont section will also be of benefit to the entire state." And in a *Charlotte News* editorial of March 26, 1954, Kennedy said, "Our county of Mecklenburg pays nearly 11 percent of the total state taxes and receives less per capita from the state than almost any other county.

When it comes to state money, Mecklenburg seems to be simply on the sending end."

The *Charlotte News* itself could be pretty blunt. In an editorial published April 5, 1955, the *News* said, "For too long a political straitjacket has prevented any territorial expansion of higher education in North Carolina. It is time for that straitjacket to be removed. If it is not done soon, the state may tumble even farther down the educational ladder." Similarly, the *Charlotte Observer* argued on April 7, 1955, "The Piedmont area is well-developed and heavily populated. Its contribution to the state tax coffers has been largely overlooked in the development of the Greater University System."

Continuing to push his appeal for equity, Kennedy wrote to Carey Bostian, chancellor of N.C. State: "Personally I think that we have fine college setups at Chapel Hill, at Raleigh, at Greenville and other places, but if these colleges were the very best in the world, they would not serve many hundreds of young people in this section, as on account of economic conditions, they cannot go off to a boarding institution."

And some people were listening. Bostian replied that he had told the North Carolina Commission on Higher Education that the Charlotte area did need a state-supported college. "I believe that the state should provide a college for your area before continuing to expand some of the colleges already in existence," Bostian said. Lieutenant Governor H. Pat Taylor said the Board of Trustees of the university was considering establishment of a branch somewhere in western North Carolina.

In a June 1956 letter to Governor Luther Hodges, Kennedy reminded him that the General Assembly had passed legislation in 1951 allowing the Charlotte Board of School Commissioners to change Charlotte College from a two- to a four-year college. He told the governor that he and many others believed now was the time. In fact, a petition to that effect contained 1,132 signatures. However, Kennedy told the governor that many also feared that if Charlotte College were changed to a four-year institution under the school board, it might lose the state funding that had started flowing to the community colleges. Kennedy also updated the governor on the ratio of college students to the population as of 1956. His figures were: Raleigh, 1 to 12 residents; Greensboro, 1 to 13; and Charlotte, 1 to 156.

Governor Hodges suggested that Kennedy appeal to Dr. Harris Purks, director of the State Board of Higher Education. But the governor admitted he couldn't believe the ratio of college students was so low in Charlotte. As an economic-development governor, Hodges understood the necessity of access to higher education if the state were to progress. It was Hodges's support, for example, that moved the Research Triangle Park from just a concept by some academicians and dreamers to reality.

Continuing his drumbeat, Kennedy wrote to a supporter,

> For years Carolina and State have both tried to throw us a sop or bone here in Charlotte in the nature of an extension course in order to keep us quiet. I find absolutely no valid reason whatsoever why Charlotte should be satisfied with an extension department of either State or Carolina. Certainly Charlotte is the largest and most important city in North Carolina and one of the finest in the Southeast; and for that reason, I will continue my fight to see that we get first class consideration from the state directly and not via either State or Carolina.

Kennedy compared the timidity of Charlotteans on this issue to that of southern textile manufacturers of years earlier. He recalled that they once assumed they weren't capable of finishing textile goods in the South and thus sent their goods to New England for final finishing. Some Charlotteans, he said, thought that junior college work could be done in Charlotte but that students would have to be sent elsewhere for senior college work. "Junior colleges are for junior towns and cities," Kennedy said in disdain.

Kennedy's campaign was beginning to bear some fruit. In 1954 Hoyt Galvin, head of the Public Library of Charlotte and Mecklenburg County, wrote him that "single handed, you have managed to get Dave Coltrane and the Advisory Budget Commission to visit Charlotte College. That in itself is a sign that we might get some state assistance."

Galvin was a visionary about his own work, building the base for a library that in the 1990s would be named top library in the nation. Galvin also served the institution for a short time as interim librarian after it became UNC Charlotte. He died in 1995. Also, like some of the other Charlotteans of the time, Galvin apparently could see the future. He wrote to Kennedy in December 1954, "You know important officials from the University of North Carolina came to Charlotte, the day we were in Raleigh, to establish a graduate branch of the university here. With our foot thus in their door, we should be able eventually, to have Charlotte College become a full-fledged branch of the university system." That was indeed a visionary statement, coming just eight years after a temporary college center opened in Charlotte.

In 1955, Charlotte College got its first state appropriation—$11,000, which was just a token to be sure, but it was a significant foot in the door.

In 1956, Kennedy urged the city school board to take advantage of the enabling legislation of 1951 to make Charlotte College a four-year institution, but he got no positive response.

The irrepressible Kennedy spent his own money to mail out questionnaires about Charlotte College. They likely wouldn't pass the test of objectivity that social scientists use in preparing questionnaires. Kennedy's asked,

"Are you satisfied with the indifference and lassitude with which this tremendous problem has been approached in recent years?" Another question was, "Do you think we should continue to let matters roll along and wait for the legislature to provide funds for our assistance, which no doubt will mean another two- or three-year wait?" Then he asked, "Do you believe in a timid or bold approach to this problem?"

Douglas Aircraft executive and Charlotte College board member Sheldon P. Smith responded to the Kennedy questionnaire this way: "Recently in a trip to Greensboro, I was amazed to find that Greensboro supported seven four-year colleges. My only disappointment in coming to Charlotte was to find that there was no higher education available for those who wanted to improve themselves." Smith had moved to Charlotte to head Douglas Aircraft's missile-building facility.

David Coltrane, the state budget director, told Kennedy he thought he would come nearer getting state assistance for a junior and eventually a four-year college than for a community college. He suggested that the state might even adopt a policy of nonfunding for community colleges.

But Governor Hodges told Kennedy that Coltrane went too far and "led you astray in suggesting that you ought to consider a junior and/or senior college. It is far too early to consider things of that character, if at all, and I believe it would be much better if we went along with the thinking of the Board of Higher Education, with which I agree, and try to get something in the way of community colleges for those communities that are willing to do something for themselves, as Charlotte has indicated."

Such a letter from the governor didn't intimidate Kennedy, who replied he didn't think Coltrane should be censored and then restated the Charlotte case.

Meanwhile, Kennedy was not only addressing state support on behalf of his college project; he was seeking private philanthropy as well. He proposed that former governor and Mrs. Cameron Morrison give money for an institution to be named "Morrison College" and wondered if N.C. State College might support a Charlotte branch called "Morrison College." Chancellor J. W. Harrelson of N.C. State said his college was definitely interested in a campus in Charlotte but had no funds. The Morrisons were "not interested at this time."

But Kennedy didn't give up easily. He wrote Harrelson again in 1949, suggesting that he could get $1 million each from the Morrisons, the Belks, J. A. Jones, and perhaps others.

An influential State alumnus, George Hobson, who was Mecklenburg County Extension Agent, said he thought such a college would be unwise. He said N.C. State was growing by leaps and bounds and that a similar school in Charlotte would weaken State College, "and, of course, I would not be in favor of anything that would in any way hinder the growth and prestige of 'dear old State.'"

It's clear that Woody Kennedy's passion was largely responsible for moving Charlotte College toward university status. It's also clear that his enthusiasm and drive were shared by a small core of supporters. What's not clear is how much community understanding and enthusiasm existed.

Many of the community's leaders lacked concern because they could afford to send their own children away to college. The *Charlotte News* addressed this issue in an editorial published May 11, 1956:

> It will take a massive thrust of civic pride and resolution on Charlotte's part. Charlotte has never been short on pride, but with the chips down, it has often exhibited distressingly little interest in higher education in the past. Two years ago, six percent of the city's voters bothered to register for a special election to determine the fate of a proposed two-cent tax levy. . . . A whopping 94 per cent of the electorate was either too forgetful or too apathetic even to qualify as voters. Charlotte's resolve will have to be firmer and, if you will, more passionate in the future if it is to escape its undercolleged status.

In a letter to the *News*, Kennedy wrote that a prominent lawyer had told him "Charlotte has made great strides in things of a material nature but was far behind in cultural development. . . . In many respects, Charlotte is becoming the rival of Atlanta as a trading center, however, Charlotte is so far behind Atlanta in higher education facilities that the contrast is almost pitiful."

Most of Kennedy's ire was targeted at those elsewhere in the state who were insensitive to Charlotte's needs. On April 24, 1956, in a letter to the *Charlotte Observer*, he vented his frustration about Greensboro in particular: "I certainly wish that our editor friend up at 'The Greensboro Daily News' would stop being so antagonistic toward the Charlotte area's much needed and just aspirations toward a state supported college system." Then he noted that Greensboro got a total of $15.3 million for its two state institutions, "10 percent of which came from Mecklenburg taxpayers. . . . We need Greensboro's help not their hindrance."

Despite the frustrations, by 1957, enrollment at Charlotte College had grown to 492, larger than two of North Carolina's four-year colleges—Pembroke State College, which had 341 students, and Elizabeth City State College, which had 383—and almost as large as Fayetteville State College, which had 524. At that time enrollment at UNC Chapel Hill was 5,958 (with an additional 1,080 in health affairs), and at N.C. State, 5,600. Woman's College in Greensboro had 2,276; Appalachian, 1,814; East Carolina, 3,239; and Western Carolina, 1,154.

With that growth, attention turned toward finding permanent sites for Charlotte and Carver Colleges. In June 1956, the Charlotte Chamber of Commerce endorsed a plan to have Charlotte and Carver Colleges moved from their high school locations to new sites.

Site selection was another area in which Kennedy made a significant contribution to the development of Charlotte College. Even though W. S. Lupo of Sears, Roebuck & Co. was first chair of a site committee for college expansion, it was Kennedy who was the idea man.

Among his proposed sites, growing from the early explorations in 1952, were: the Governor Morrison Estate; the Naval Depot (a shell-loading facility later known as Arrowood Industrial Park); a site south of City Hall where slums could be razed; the Thompson Orphanage site; the Industrial Home on New Concord Highway; the Myers Park High School campus; the Van Matthews plot on Albemarle Road; the Veterans Hospital site on Albemarle Road; the Charlotte Sanatorium site; the Alexander Graham Building; the Central High site, which was at that time being used by the college; and the Armory Auditorium, later known as the Grady Cole Center.

Kennedy commented about the Industrial Home site, which was to become ultimately part of the campus and later the location of University Place, that "it is a beautiful location, but a little far out. Across the road is the County Home. It would have one particular advantage in that it reaches out toward Concord and Kannapolis, and no doubt we would secure political strength... from that area." It is intriguing that the eventual campus site was identified so early in the institution's history.

Kennedy's amazing foresight allowed him to envision an institution serving an entire region. He added, "A circle drawn on a 25-mile radius from this home not only takes in Charlotte, but runs through the cities of Gastonia and Monroe, taking in entirely, such towns as Belmont, Mount Holly, Concord, Kannapolis, Mooresville, Davidson and others."

That 1952 Kennedy statement refutes later comments from some journalists and civic leaders which implied that the college planners had sited the campus in an out-of-the-way location without giving much thought to the consequences and that moving the campus out of the uptown Charlotte area hurt its development.

When it became urgent a few years later that Charlotte College secure a permanent site, Kennedy notified Chairman Murrey Atkins in August 1957 that options had been placed on two hundred acres of property at an estimated cost of $650 an acre. This site was the County Home location identified earlier. He said that if the county would only let the college have an adjoining three hundred acres, the committee would be within striking distance of the number of acres recommended for the campus by a consultant. The committee was working to acquire at least six hundred acres, an amount that had been recommended by Dr. Stanton Leggett of Engelhardt, Engelhardt, and Leggett, a nationally known firm of educational consultants.

A site survey noted that 20,000 gallons of water per day could be supplied from wells, that water for fire protection could be drawn from a lake, and that sewage disposal could be handled by a plant that would discharge into a creek. Power could be supplied from a 13,000-volt line.

In addition to Kennedy, who had become chairman, other members of the site selection committee were banker G. Douglas Aitken, librarian Hoyt Galvin, and automobile dealer Ben Huntley.

The committee had identified seven sites as finalists, with offers of gifts and concessions on five sites and tentative offers on the other two. These included a plot of land on Providence Road, worth about $50,000. The committee said it considered the site too far out and not accessible for the great majority of people living in Mecklenburg and adjoining counties.

Another offer was a wooded site near the old Charlotte Coliseum later known as Independence Arena. It was valued at $400,000. It would have accommodated 1,000 students, but since 5,000 to 10,000 students were projected within ten years, it was considered inadequate. Additional land would have been bought at a dear price. Still, the committee admitted that it gave up that site reluctantly.

The third site was two hundred acres located seven miles from the Square. It was abandoned when the division highway engineer notified the committee that a "projected federal non-access highway" (later to be known as Interstate 85) would probably bisect the site and make at least one side inaccessible.

A "beautiful site way up in North Mecklenburg" also was offered. It was two hundred acres in an area where land was selling for $200 an acre. The downside was that it was fourteen miles from the Square, bordering on the Cabarrus County line, and it had only a three-mile secondary road leading into it. No network of highways provided access, although an interstate highway was projected to run near it.

Here's what the selection committee said about the site finally selected, which was to become the present campus: "It is considered by highway engineers as one of the most accessible points in Mecklenburg. The largest holder of real estate made a concession price of $400 per acre or $80,000 for the large tract. Other interested residents of the area have donated about $20,000 worth of property; and there are options on 240 acres plus an additional 10 acres as a gift."

In other words, the committee could obtain $250,000 worth of property for $151,000. All the surrounding landholders had agreed to enter into restricted agreements and impose land restrictions to assure orderly development and growth of the college community. A large water main ran to within three and a half miles of the site and could be extended later.

In its report, obviously written by Kennedy, the committee noted examples of institutions with too little land. Queens College was cited as having only twenty-five acres at the time. Also cited were Woman's College (later UNC Greensboro) and N.C. State. "The founding fathers simply did not envision their phenomenal growth and the advent of students having their own cars," the report said. The early problems of Meredith College, Duke University, and Wake Forest University, all of which later moved, were noted.

The report said, "The writer [Kennedy] along with groups of interested people—school officials, engineers, and laymen—have spent many hours and many Sundays traveling all over Mecklenburg in the quest of the best available site. We believe the proposed site on Highway 49 is the choice location in all of Mecklenburg."

That's the story of the site selection. Some later apocryphal stories didn't help communicate the true version. Years later Charlotte industrialist Oliver R. Rowe, with tongue in cheek, claimed the site was selected when he and Bonnie Cone traveled to the cow pasture in northeast Mecklenburg that was to become the campus. He said, "Miss Bonnie stood on a dried cow pie to get a good view of the countryside, scanned the horizon, and then declared, 'This is the place. This is the place.'"

On August 12, 1957, Hoyt Galvin of the site committee made a motion that the Construction Brick & Tile Company property on NC 49, adjoining the Mecklenburg County Home property, be acquired as the site for Charlotte College. The motion was seconded by automobile dealer Ben Huntley and was passed unanimously. Galvin also made a motion, which was approved, that the Advisory Board take steps to obtain three hundred or more acres of the County Home property.

As the site committee's final report described it, the site "affords beauty almost beyond belief. Standing in the center of the site, one appears to be standing on a high plateau overlooking distant mountains and valleys. The land rolls very gently and is well arranged with wooded areas and open lands."

In 1961, when the Kennedy Building was named for him, a trustee statement noted that Kennedy had purchased a key portion of the campus land through a personal loan and made provision in his will for the college to obtain it at the original purchase price.

The new campus retained very visible signs of its past—a silo and a big metal-covered barn. The barn itself presented unique challenges. Miss Cone wrote Biology Professor Herbert Hechenbleikner that a neighbor of the campus had called and asked for the privilege of cleaning out the old barn for the manure that it contained. Reflecting the years of penury the college had endured, Miss Cone asked Hechenbleikner, "Do you think that at this stage of the game we need to give away even the manure?" "Dr. Heck," as he became known to all, replied, "Let's keep it for our landscaping."

The year 1957, in addition to bringing the site selection decision, saw passage of a Community College Act, which established a type of community college that provided for college parallel work rather than the broad array of technical and terminal programs provided by the comprehensive community colleges established in 1963. Also, 1957 saw the beginning of daytime classes for Charlotte College and accreditation by the Southern Association of Colleges and Secondary Schools. Daytime classes at the Central High site were possible because a new Garinger High School was built, and some Central High School students were transferred there.

Momentum continued into 1958 with the two-cent tax levy on city property extended on a countywide basis. More significant was the passage of $975,000 in county bonds in 1960 to match $575,000 in state funds to pay for the campus site and begin construction of the first buildings.

Arthur H. Jones, chairman of the Education Committee of the Charlotte Chamber of Commerce, was looking into the future after those elections. He said, "They voted to make a dream of a future university come true, for some day it will be so." It took until the 1990s in the Woodward administration for another Jones insight to be understood. Jones said, "All we have to do now is to get a few more million dollars from the state authorities, convince the counties in the surrounding area that their members of the legislature should team up with ours in convincing Raleigh of our needs in the future." In between, Charlotte supporters seemed to lose sight of the need to build a political base with regional legislators.

On May 11, 1958, the Board of Trustees of the Charlotte Community College System took over responsibility for Charlotte College from the Charlotte City School Board.

The first chair of the new board was a familiar face—J. Murrey Atkins, president of R. S. Dickson and Company. The other members were John A. McRae, attorney; Dr. E. A. Beaty, a professor at Davidson; Robert L. Taylor, a special representative of Lincoln Life Insurance; John Paul Lucas, a public relations person for Duke Power Company; Addison H. Reese, then president of American Commercial Bank, a predecessor of NCNB and later NationsBank; Linn D. Garibaldi, president of North Carolina Telephone Company and Western Carolina Telephone Company; Oliver R. Rowe, executive vice president of R. H. Bouligny Company (later to become president and change the name to Rowe Corporation); Thomas M. Belk, executive vice president of Belk Stores Services; Cecil Prince, editor of the *Charlotte News*; Sheldon P. Smith, plant manager of Douglas Aircraft Company; and Dr. Thomas Watkins Sr., a dentist.

In 1959 came passage of a statewide bond issue of $1.5 million for capital improvements for community colleges. By 1960, the county passed its second bond issue, providing $975,000.

Bonnie Cone had continued to teach at least one class a year until 1958. She also was being recognized in her profession. She became president of the Southern Association of Junior Colleges, the first woman to hold that position, and was noted as "one of the few women administrative heads of co-educational colleges, private or community." Garinger remarked, "To me, Miss Cone is one of the very choice people in college education work, because she takes such a personal interest in all of her students."

Atkins was equally complimentary: "Miss Cone has provided the faith on which the college many times found its primary ability to exist. She has stuck with it and never even thought of giving up when sometimes the sledding seemed pretty hard. She hasn't stopped to gloat over the achievements or the distance the college has covered, but is always thinking about how much more we might be able to achieve the next period."

In addition to those pioneers named earlier—Mary Denny, Edyth Winningham, and Herbert Hechenbleikner—some of the notable faculty of the community college years included:

- LeGette Blythe, a noted writer and UNC Chapel Hill classmate of novelist Thomas Wolfe.
- Lucille Puette, chemistry teacher and former employee of Carolina Paper Board, the National Bureau of Standards, and Celanese, considered a right hand for Bonnie Cone. She left in 1952 to help her father with his company, Carolina Paper Board, and to marry Ed C. Giles.
- Rupert Gillett, associate editor of the *Charlotte Observer*, English teacher.
- Hughes Hoyle Jr., professor of mathematics and physics at Queens College, who taught mathematics at Charlotte College.
- David Littlejohn, Spanish teacher and a former student body president at Charlotte College.
- John A. Nattress, head of the Charlotte Technical Institute, by this time a unit of Charlotte College, and later to become the Central Industrial Education Center and ultimately Central Piedmont Community College.
- Robert D. Potter, chemistry teacher, an attorney who later became a Charlotte judge, known as "Maximum Bob" for his tough, lengthy sentences, notably exhibited later in the trial of televangelist Jim Bakker.
- Billy J. (Bill) Reid, a graduate of Charlotte College and Davidson College, who served as director of public relations and alumni affairs in

1959. Reid went on to become an executive with Rexham Corp. in Charlotte.
- Ann Vann (Mrs. Gordon Sweet), mathematics teacher. Her husband was a professor at Queens College and later an official of the Southern Association of Colleges and Schools.
- John G. Wheelock, a retired Illinois attorney, teacher of business law and economics.
- Harry Golden, editor of *The Carolina Israelite* and author of *Only in America, For Two Cents Plain,* and other books, teacher of Shakespeare at Charlotte College.

A report to the legislative Joint Appropriations Committee in 1959 detailed Charlotte College's progress. The passage of the two-cent countywide tax election in April 1958 qualified Charlotte and Carver Colleges as state community colleges and made them eligible for grants-in-aid. Passage of the countywide bond election in November 1958 qualified the colleges to receive state funds for classrooms, buildings, and equipment. Later college leaders suffered a disappointment in November 1961, when despite passage of a statewide bond issue in Mecklenburg, it was defeated statewide.

At this point, another spokesperson for Charlotte College and university status began to emerge—industrialist and board member Oliver Rowe. In a PTA speech in 1958, Rowe sold Charlotte College as an institution for "those that will forego the luxury of fraternity life, for those that can give up football and big-time athletics, for those who have a burning hunger for learning and will work and put forth as a personal effort to get an education." In his eloquence in advocating for lower-income students, he may have stereotyped the institution for a number of years as catering only to the poor. In presenting the college's budget request in 1959, he cited its objectives:

- to take a load off the senior colleges and universities in the freshman and sophomore years.
- to save the state considerable money by eliminating the need for many new dormitories. [That point was made so effectively that it came back to haunt UNC Charlotte years later when it sought its first residence halls.]
- to save citizens the cost of sending students away to college.
- to bring a college education within reach of thousands of "our deserving young people who cannot pay to go away to school."
- to teach at such a high level that students can transfer with ease.

Rowe disarmed legislators when he apologized for an initial campus building request that included $500,000 for gymnasiums and $360,000 for auditoriums "for two schools which up to this point do not own one square

Oliver Rowe became an eloquent advocate of Charlotte College and its transition to university status. Photo courtesy of the Rowe Corporation.

foot of classroom space nor the roof over their heads." In the revised buildings request, he said, "You will see that we propose to spend the money for only the things a young college really needs."

An information sheet again emphasized the Charlotte market. Within eighty-five miles of Charlotte College were more people than within a similar area around Atlanta, Jacksonville, Memphis, Birmingham, or Richmond.

As planning began for the first Charlotte College buildings on the new campus, Cone and her board members had to learn new skills—those of dealing with a state bureaucracy. A. G. Odell Jr. and Associates had been employed to begin design with the assistance of the New York consulting firm Engelhardt, Leggett and Cornell.

In May 1960, Frank Turner, state property officer, wrote to Addison Reese, citing the state law that gave him review and approval authority over building plans and specifications. Then W. W. Pierson, acting director of the State Board of Higher Education, wrote to Cone that his board also would review all plans.

A struggle began over aesthetics for the first campus buildings. Turner usually opposed architectural design features that provided any character for buildings. He and Cone battled at times over such items as the window treatment of the earliest buildings—Macy, Winningham, Barnard, Denny, and the King Building. Spartan as they were, those buildings would have been plain indeed if Cone had yielded, because those were the only distinctive architectural features. Later, the campus did have to yield on the window treatments for the Smith Engineering Building, resulting in a very plain appearance.

To her dismay, Cone learned that Odell also was in the process of designing a consolidated Presbyterian College, later to be called St. Andrews, in Laurinburg. Although Gouldie Odell wrote Cone that "all of us here in the office are most enthusiastic about Charlotte College, and we naturally have the utmost interest in its development since it is right here in our hometown," nevertheless there was a sameness to the two designs, and had UNC Charlotte not exploded in growth and St. Andrews remained static, the two would have been look-alike campuses.

Odell's master plan included what is now the center of the campus, including Atkins, Kennedy, Macy, Winningham, Barnard, Denny, King, Cone Center, and Smith Buildings. His first plan also included what later became Colvard and Reese Buildings and additions to Cone Center, but new architectural firms changed the character of those buildings.

A bell tower where the current Belk Bell Tower now stands was on the Odell plan but as a more traditional tower than the one later designed by Little and Associates. On a revised version of his first master plan, Odell showed a large lake downstream on Toby Creek from the current playing fields. That later plan had to be hidden away, because the lake covered land still owned by Trustee Thomas M. Belk that he had promised to give to the college but had not yet transferred. Belk was a bit offended that the college and the architect would take his gift for granted and show it under development before he had even transferred it.

Meanwhile, the consulting firm was making its enrollment projections. It forecast an enrollment of 1,400 in a two-year institution by 1965 or 2,400 in a four-year college. Further, the consultants suggested a planning figure of 4,000 students for the first master plan. They added that the master plan should also allow for development beyond the 4,000-student level.

In terms of curriculum, the consultants said the college would likely continue to strengthen science and engineering and would have a large enrollment in liberal arts. Terminal work was suggested in business. Nursing work in cooperation with local hospitals was recommended. Teacher training was recommended because of the local demand. The report urged continued evening programs and adult education.

Unlike some of Charlotte College's most enthusiastic boosters, the Engelhardt firm consultants suggested that it would not always remain a commuter institution: "It is possible that although the college is thought of as predominantly a commuting college, it may be necessary in the future to provide some dormitory space. Arbitrarily, it is suggested that dormitory locations for 240 men and 160 women be shown on the master plan."

Then the consultants issued a farsighted recommendation that took until 1995 to implement with the creation of UNC Charlotte's Uptown Campus at CityFair. The consultants said, "With the movement of the college to its new site, the desirability of continuing to operate programs in the downtown section of Charlotte remains. In our opinion, there should be continued a nucleus of college activities in downtown Charlotte closely related to the needs of people working in that area."

By this time, Bonnie Cone herself was becoming an even stronger voice of prophesy about Charlotte College. In 1959 the *Charlotte News* quoted her as saying, "Charlotte will have a university within the next 10 years." Indeed it did.

Professor Mary Denny joined in as well with what turned out to be a most unusual prediction for the time. She said, "It is my belief that when we add the third year, the junior class will be larger than the freshman class." That's precisely what happened and has happened since. UNC Charlotte's junior and senior classes have been larger than its freshman classes because of the transfer population. That has been so unusual in North Carolina that UNC Charlotte has gotten no funding credit for offering more upper-level courses than general college courses.

One of the most farsighted predictions came from Woody Kennedy himself in his 1957 letter to Tom Belk, telling him that the college would like his property adjoining the new campus site. Uncannily, Kennedy predicted, "When Charlotte College becomes a four-year institution and receives sufficient financial support from either taxes or private donations, the student enrollment may reach 12,000 to 15,000 within the next 15 to 25 years." UNC Charlotte reached an enrollment of 12,000 in 1987.

As well as things were going for Charlotte College by 1960, there were still occasional setbacks. Jack Claiborne, then a *Charlotte Observer* reporter, interviewed Major L. P. McLendon, chairman of the state Board of Higher Education for a story published June 17, 1960. McLendon told Claiborne that Charlotte College wasn't necessarily destined to become a four-year institution. When asked when it might become a four-year institution, McLendon replied, "We aren't sure that it ever will. That will be determined as the need arises, when enrollments increase and additional educational facilities in the area are needed."

Arthur Jones, chairman of the Education Committee of the Charlotte Chamber of Commerce, sent McLendon a telegram the day the article appeared. In it he said, "It is hoped that this morning's quotation regarding Charlotte College does not imply any change of attitude of your board which has been thus far greatly encouraging in our efforts to meet the area's most urgent need—the fullest development of Charlotte College."

Charles Reynolds of Spindale, a prominent N.C. State alumnus, didn't help the Charlotte mood when he responded to Jones's wire, "For selfish reasons, if for no other, I would like to see a fine four-year institution 70 miles from where I live and from where my business is located. I feel very strongly, however, that it is premature to consider a four-year institution for Charlotte at this time." The reasons he gave were that the community college system had only been established in 1957 and that ground had not yet been broken at the new site.

The first gathering of faculty and students on the new campus site took place at a picnic on Saturday, April 4, 1960. A note on a program for the day said, "It rained, so we served in the barn."

Groundbreaking for the first two buildings, later named Kennedy (for W. A. Kennedy) and Macy (for Pierre Macy, the first chairperson of foreign languages), took place at 11 A.M. on Monday, November 21, 1960. The contracts had been awarded on November 14, and contractors began work on November 18, even before the groundbreaking.

But some of the dreamers and planners would not live to see the realization of their hopes. Like the biblical Moses who led his people to the Promised Land but did not get to cross over himself, three key leaders of the

Bonnie Cone breaks ground for the new campus on NC 49 with the help of Addison H. Reese (left) and J. Murrey Atkins (right).

The first two buildings on the new campus. Kennedy (left) and Macy share space with an old barn in 1961. Photo by Bill Barley.

move to bring a campus of the University of North Carolina to Charlotte did not live to see the goal accomplished.

W. A. Kennedy died on May 11, 1958, the eve of his installation as a trustee of the Charlotte Community College System. In tribute to him, the *Charlotte News* said on May 13, "The College was his dream and his personal goal. He recognized earlier than some, the great need, but more important, he recognized the route Mecklenburgers must take to answer that need." At a memorial service to Kennedy, Trustee J. A. McRae proclaimed, "It is said that institutions are the lengthened shadows of great men. So Charlotte Community College, and its predecessors, is the lengthened shadow of 'Woody' Kennedy, who was a great businessman, a great civic leader and a great worker for education."

Trustee Cecil Prince, editor of the *Charlotte News* and author of several key editorials about Charlotte College, died on May 24, 1960, at the age of thirty-seven. The college was fortunate in that his replacement was C. A. McKnight, editor of the *Charlotte Observer*, who was to pick up the battle flag and carry it into the struggle for university status.

Nor did trustee chair J. Murrey Atkins, who had been involved with the institution since 1946, when it was the Charlotte Center of the University of North Carolina, get to see university status achieved. He died on December 2, 1963.

Cone and her other trustees pressed ahead with the business of building a campus, relocating and keeping an eye on the ultimate goal—university status.

In a 1960 speech, Cone referred to the college's founders as "Dr. Garinger and the Board of Education, Woody Kennedy and the Charlotte College Advisory Board, Cecil Prince and our own Board of Trustees, the Charlotte Chamber of Commerce, civic and professional organizations."

By now Oliver Rowe was really taking up the battle where Kennedy left off and developing his own techniques. In a speech given on August 17, 1959, to the Charlotte Engineers Club, he declared the age of the "hand" at an end. "Today we are truly entering the age of the 'mind,'" he declared, using the mill owner's terminology about how many hands were needed to get a job done. "And standing in the ranks of 'brain power' as the greatest contributors to industrial production—heads and shoulders above all the rest—are the engineers," Rowe said. Others made the comparison of old and new requirements for competition in a technological age as muscle power versus brain power.

Rowe added, "The greatest new potential for the education of engineers for this state lies in the proper development of Charlotte College." He then lamented that one thing was lacking—a great organization that understood the present need, like this group of 675 members. "I challenge you to make this the main project of your club," he concluded. It should be noted that N.C. State was continuing to operate a Charlotte Division in cooperation with Charlotte College, enrolling an average of sixty-one students each term in engineering courses.

At the September 29, 1959, meeting of the Charlotte College Board of Trustees, Cone and Tom Belk reported back from a Chamber of Commerce meeting that there was a move to put an engineering program under N.C. State rather than let the Charlotte College program expand. That did not happen.

But a breakthrough with implications for the future did occur at a meeting of the trustees on May 20, 1960: in reporting for a committee on the formation of a foundation for the community college system, B. W. Barnard recommended that a separate foundation be established for Charlotte College. The recommendation was approved at the July 5 meeting, and Addison Reese announced the first corporate donation of $2,500 from his bank, North Carolina National, a predecessor of NationsBank.

The first board of the foundation was named at the November meeting. It included Barnard, investor James G. Cannon, lawyer Robert Lassiter, banker

Carl G. McCraw, department store executive John M. Belk, banker Joe Robinson, developer Dwight Phillips, banker J. Scott Cramer, insurance executive James J. Harris, textile manufacturer W. H. Barnhardt, chemist C. W. Gilchrist, and banker Douglas Aitken, and there were three ex officio members: Atkins, John Paul Lucas, and Oliver Rowe. The board then elected Barnard as first chairman; Cannon as vice chairman; Cramer as secretary; and Belk as treasurer. An early scholarship fund was established through the foundation by Brycie Baber of Washington, D.C., a native of Charlotte, where she had lived until 1918.

Another sign of confidence in the future occurred when even before the first two buildings were completed, the Board of Trustees voted in August 1960 to begin preliminary planning for the second phase. Board members were able to proceed because Odell and Associates agreed not to charge for work done if an upcoming bond issue for the buildings failed. Addison Reese announced that bricks made in North Carolina would be used for building exteriors.

Academic planning also proceeded. After a recommendation from the faculty, the trustees approved a change from the quarter to the semester system, to begin September 1961.

Early in 1961, the trustees had to respond to complaints about the continued operation of dual colleges. Ernest Delaney, spokesman for a delegation of twenty-five, had appeared to ask the trustees to "use all available funds for construction of one community college, which should be open to all qualified students and that if it were deemed advisable to continue Carver College for the time being it be continued at Second Ward High School" rather than at a new campus off Beatties Ford Road, which had been purchased from businessman C. D. Spangler Sr.

Atkins appointed a committee of Lucas (the chairman), Thomas Belk, and C. A. McKnight. The committee reported that it was operating two colleges because the voters had approved taxes and bonds for two, that Charlotte and Carver were and would continue to be open to any qualified candidates, that race was not a factor in determining qualifications, and that the colleges had distinct purposes.

The committee report asserted, "Charlotte College will, in time, become a four-year, fully-accredited liberal arts institution with entrance requirements and academic standards equal to those of the Consolidated University of North Carolina." The other college was envisioned as not becoming four-year but as providing special technical and vocational training and preparation for employment in business and industry.

That differentiation set the stage for Carver (later known as Mecklenburg) College to later be merged with the Central Industrial Education Center, which remained at the old Central High School location when Charlotte

College moved to its new campus. The merged institutions were then transformed into Central Piedmont Community College after the state legislature passed the State Community College Act of 1963.

All these years, Bonnie Cone had been in every respect president of Charlotte College, but with the title of "director." On July 13, 1961, the trustees voted to name her president. Atkins indicated that the trustees would next seek an executive head for the system over both presidents. That never happened.

By this time, the total value of land, plant, and equipment at the new campus was placed at $3,062,819, of which Mecklenburg County contributed $2,138,319. Thus a college that had owned nothing a short time earlier now had tangible assets. The college library had grown from just some borrowed books to 19,400 volumes.

Trustees now began moving headlong toward the goal of four-year or university status. McKnight reported at the September 1961 meeting of the trustees that he, Lucas, and Reese had met with University of North Carolina officials and found them enthusiastic about the future of Charlotte College.

McKnight said he anticipated that Charlotte College would be a four-year institution by 1970, with an enrollment of five thousand students and a graduate school. He called on the trustees to seek broader state support, examine the adequacy of the present property, take a new look at the curriculum and the long-range administrative structure and budgeting. After that report, Atkins appointed a follow-up committee of McKnight (the chair), Dr. Beaty, Lucas, Rowe, and Belk.

By fall 1961, enrollment had climbed to 915, and Cone reported that from 1954 to 1960, given its increase of 247.4 percent, Charlotte College was the most rapidly growing college or university in the state. A completed long-range plan called for a building program to house 2,500 students by 1965 and to be expandable to a four-year institution with a student body of 10,000 by 1972. Not surprisingly, a weakness listed was the lack of full state financial support.

The plan said that the Charlotte area needed a four-year, state-supported college now, along with some graduate programs in the near future. It noted that students from a fifty-mile radius could commute almost as quickly as students from southern Mecklenburg County; as soon as the college moved to the new campus, enrollments from nearby counties jumped. In addition to the 270 acres of campus, the report stated, the available property next door was being preserved by the county.

As to curriculum, the plan suggested a broad one with engineering and the sciences, the liberal arts, and the humanities, plus special courses in business administration and finance.

As to governance, the plan suggested that the college could either be a four-year independent or a tax-supported institution, or a campus of the Consolidated University of North Carolina. Further, it recommended that if the college were state-supported, the local tax support should be transferred to any other community colleges that might be developed. This was to provide the financial base for Central Piedmont Community College.

Trustees voted at a May 8, 1962, meeting to request the addition of the junior year in 1963 and the senior year in 1964. That action brought to an end the early chapters in the history of the Charlotte region's struggle to gain a stake in North Carolina higher education. In 1962, events began to move rapidly toward four-year and university status for Charlotte College.

CHAPTER 4

Charlotte Campaigns for University Status

CHARLOTTE HAD to have a four-year college or a university campus; by 1961 that much had become clear, both in Charlotte and in Raleigh. The drive to achieve university status had united the greater Charlotte community. Already, advocates of a state-supported institution were raising their sights from obtaining a four-year college to creating a campus of the University of North Carolina system. The struggle to make Charlotte College the fourth campus of the university system proved that when Charlotte's legislative delegation was united in purpose and determined to win, it had great strength despite a reputation for divisiveness and weakness at other times.

The struggle also displayed the vision, determination, persuasiveness, and leadership ability of Bonnie Cone and clearly identified her as the founder of the University of North Carolina at Charlotte even though a number of others played important roles in the quest.

It was Charlotte's good fortune that Governor Terry Sanford came into office in 1961, determined to make improvements in education the hallmark of his administration. Expanding higher education opportunities to areas of the state not then served fit his vision for North Carolina.

The door to the future for Charlotte was opened in September 1961, when Governor Sanford appointed his Governor's Commission on Education Beyond the High School. The appointed group later became known as the Carlyle Commission for its chairman, Winston-Salem attorney Irving E. Carlyle.

Sanford, a tall veteran of World War II who, as a paratrooper, had jumped into France during the Allied invasion, spoke with a strong North Carolina accent but with Chapel Hill polish from his days there as an undergraduate and law student. Terry Sanford got his start as a Young Democrat and began his political life early and never left politics even when out of political office later as president of Duke University. In addition to politics, Sanford had a

North Carolina Governor Terry Sanford authorized a study of the expansion of the UNC system.

passion for education, apparently influenced by his mother, who had taught school for forty years. So his commitment was sincere and intense.

In his statement appointing the Carlyle Commission, Sanford personally cracked open the door a bit for Charlotte when he asked, what standards should be adopted in determining the need for the establishment of additional four-year colleges? Should the need for resources and facilities of higher education in the more populous areas be met by establishing additional branches of the university or by supporting existing four-year colleges in those areas?

Sanford also raised the issue of allocation of function among existing and future institutions. That question also should have favored Charlotte, since it lay in a region of the state without competing university functions.

Irving Carlyle was an ideal choice for chairman of the commission. A member of a prominent law firm, he had been president of the North Carolina Bar Association and had served in the legislature. Other prominent members of the commission included Bonnie Cone; William C. Friday, president of the Consolidated University of North Carolina; and Leo Jenkins, president of East Carolina.

The final report of the Carlyle Commission was sent to Governor Sanford on August 31, 1962. The door was opened even wider for Charlotte in the written report, although it didn't recommend immediate university status for Charlotte College. What it did recommend was that the junior year be instituted at Charlotte College in the fall of 1963 and the senior year in the fall of 1964.

The door-opening recommendation was that "the statutes be amended to authorize the Consolidated University Board of Trustees to establish additional campuses of the University under conditions prescribed by the Board, subject to applicable statutory procedures." As a "simple matter of economics," the report added, "the State now and for the foreseeable future can afford only one university, and that one should be the best that intelligent leadership can build with the means available."

Second, it suggested that new campuses of the Consolidated University should be established "only where there is a clear need for the types of programs (particularly in graduate and professional fields) that only a university should offer." Finally, it appeared that the recommendations favored Charlotte's gaining, in due time, true university status, with programs through the doctoral degree. The report recommended that "within the state system of higher education, only the institutions within the Consolidated University be authorized to award the doctor's degree."

Cone later said that there were some commission members who wanted very much to immediately recommend university status for Charlotte College. "But I remember President Friday's attitude was that this was a thing that would have to be recommended by the Board of Trustees, and I think he was right," she said.

Answering another concern of Charlotte leadership, the commission report recommended that a comprehensive community college system be established to include the two-year, university-parallel programs, adult education programs, and technical vocational programs. This paved the way for the establishment of Central Piedmont Community College as part of a fifty-eight-campus system.

The Charlotte College Board of Trustees had voted at its May 8, 1962, meeting to ask that Charlotte College be permitted to offer a junior year in 1963 and a senior year in 1964. But that wasn't enough to satisfy the trustees' hunger.

At a called meeting of the board on May 22, 1962, the trustees passed a resolution that said: (1) The college educational needs of the area in and around Charlotte can best be met by the establishment of a new campus of the University of North Carolina in Charlotte. (2) The university has the duty and responsibility to provide the young people of this area with a broad undergraduate curriculum, including engineering, business administration, arts and sciences, and other instruction needed in this populous and highly industrialized area of the state.

Their resolution stated, "The Trustees of the Charlotte Community College System also believe the present Charlotte College campus is the most logical site for this new institution. The assets of Charlotte College, including land, plant, furniture, equipment, and library books, are valued at more than $3 million, of which citizens of Mecklenburg have contributed over $2 million." It added, "In addition to the present 270 acres, contiguous acreage is readily available to provide a campus of from 1,000 to 1,200 acres. Moreover, the site of Charlotte College was deliberately selected for its accessibility to the 10 counties surrounding Mecklenburg."

The position statement was clarified further at a June 14, 1962, meeting of the trustees. They then said that their request for the establishment of a fourth campus of the University of North Carolina should not imply that they had any less interest in a continued broad comprehensive community college and industrial education center.

Again, the trustees made a commitment to high quality, saying, "The Trustees of Charlotte College would insist and confidently anticipate that the same high quality of instruction would be maintained in Charlotte that exists in the other branches of the University." They added that they would expect the new campus to develop by means of logical and orderly procedures.

Cone said that people of Charlotte who wanted a university almost universally wanted it to be part of the University of North Carolina. "We never did feel the way, may I say, like Leo [Jenkins] felt. He wanted a university [at East Carolina], but he did not want to be a part of the University of North Carolina," she said. "Now we knew and accepted the fact that to be a part of the University of North Carolina meant that we would certainly make tremendous gains. But we knew with this also would come controls."

University of North Carolina system officials moved to get out ahead of developments. Friday said that it became clear to him during the Carlyle Commission process that a fourth campus in Charlotte needed to be considered. C. A. (Pete) McKnight reported at the August 14, 1962, meeting of the Charlotte College board that Friday would have a special committee of the university board of trustees (which at that time comprised one hundred members) visit Charlotte College to investigate the need for extending the services of the university to other areas of the state.

Then officials of the North Carolina State Board of Higher Education, which at that time was the coordinating body for all higher education, announced that they would visit the campus on October 18, 1962.

Members of the House Higher Education Committee made it clear in early 1963 that any designation of additional campuses of the University of North Carolina would have to come to the legislature by way of a recommendation of the UNC trustees and the Board of Higher Education. At least that defined a path that Charlotte College supporters could follow.

In early 1963, trustees felt it necessary to restate that the purpose of a four-year institution for Charlotte should include engineering and business administration. The trustees said they "believe emphatically in the need for a university-type education program in this long-neglected, populous and heavily industrialized area of North Carolina."

When a legislator from New Hanover County wanted colleges at Wilmington and Asheville to have identical purposes to that of Charlotte College, a compromise had to be worked out that omitted specific mention of engineering and business administration in Charlotte's mission statement.

As a result, all three campuses got a statement which said that the primary purpose of the institutions should be to provide undergraduate instruction in the liberal arts and sciences, the training of teachers, and certain graduate, professional, and other undergraduate programs.

Being forced into the same mold as the other two colleges made Cone more determined than ever to differentiate Charlotte College as a more comprehensive institution, designed to serve the state's largest city and adjoining areas.

The 1963 North Carolina General Assembly officially moved Charlotte College forward when it approved four-year, state-supported status.

In the meantime, Cone and her colleagues were busy recruiting faculty members and expanding the curriculum as part of their push toward four-year status. Enrollment for the fall of 1962 reached 1,188, a 30 percent increase. To provide instruction for those students, Cone recruited a number of experienced senior college faculty members and some promising new ones.

She recruited Robert Wallace from the University of Alabama to head the English Department. Wallace was willing to leave that venerable institution because he had been registering students inside the gymnasium as Governor George Wallace (no relation) had stood in the door to bar entry to the first African American student. English Professor Seth Ellis also left Alabama, to teach first at Redlands University in California and then at UNC Charlotte. History Professor George Abernathy also came from Alabama. Some others, including Dr. Joseph Schlechta of the French Department and Bill Perel of mathematics, were recruited from Louisiana State University at New Orleans (now New Orleans University) following some faculty discontent there. Charlottean David Nixon came from N.C. State, where he had earned a doctorate in mathematics. Among the bright but unseasoned academicians hired by Cone was Dan Morrill, fresh from completing requirements for a history Ph.D. at Emory University.

When reports reached the administrative area that young Professor Morrill was teaching his class by standing on his desk and shouting, there was a feeling that a true university was taking shape.

To lead the mix of experienced and brand-new faculty members, Cone brought in Dr. S. J. McCoy, an experienced college dean.

By this time Cone had developed a strong recruiting pitch based on sharing her vision of the university to come. Few of the faculty and staff recruited in 1963 and 1964 would have come to the brand new four-year college without seeing through Cone's eyes the university that was to unfold.

Cone used that lure to recruit Sherman Burson and James Kuppers from Pfeiffer College to develop a chemistry program. Even so, Burson said he turned Cone down after a delicious barbecue meal at a genuine southern cafe—Herlocker's on US 29 at Mallard Creek. But Cone persisted and promised she would help him get a set of *Chemical Abstracts*. He was then convinced and joined the faculty, and Kuppers followed.

Those recruited in that way were never surprised as the university developed later into a midsized, then full-fledged, and, finally, a large state university. All had seen the picture of the future as painted by Bonnie Cone in 1963–64.

Cone took on her faculty and staff's problems as her own, but on the other hand, her whole life was wrapped up in the college, and she expected her staff to be as dedicated as she was. Thus a normal workday often went into the evening. Cone's secretary, Juanita Sims, could sometimes be found crying as she worked past 7 P.M., because she felt she should be home with her family. Yet she had a commitment to the college as well and was torn between the two loyalties.

That work ethic was to become contagious and carry over into UNC Charlotte days. Undoubtedly, it was responsible for the fact that UNC Charlotte developed rapidly despite inadequate staff and resources.

All the dedication and hard work that could be mustered was necessary in the first two years of operation as a four-year institution. For a new four-year college it was an ambitious offering of work toward the degrees of bachelor of arts in biology, business administration, chemistry, economics, English, French, Spanish, history, mathematics, political science, psychology, and sociology.

The bachelor of science degree was offered in accounting, biology, chemistry, and mathematics, and courses were available in nursing. The bachelor of science degree in engineering was offered in the electrical and mechanical fields. Also, the college continued offering some terminal two-year programs in business areas during its first two years as a four-year college. Courses in education were offered for certification requirements for elementary and secondary school teachers but without a major in education.

Enrollment in daytime classes increased and declined in the evening to the point that the college took on the appearance of a more traditional institution.

There were continuing reminders of the earliest beginnings as the college took shape. Some nostalgia had developed around the old barn in the center of the campus, but by mid-1963, it became clear that a contemporary university and a barn weren't compatible, and so trustees approved moving it in May. In the area later known as the Van Landingham Glen, small streams fed into concrete cooling tanks that had been used for milk cans when the area supported a dairy farm. A concrete silo stood near the later site of the McEniry Building. It lasted well into the UNC Charlotte era, and at one point Professor Herbert Hechenbleikner suggested turning it into an observatory, but that proved impractical and it was demolished. Other remaining vestiges of the farm were the woods and fields that were interspersed. The soil had become so thin on the site of the central campus that dirt berms later had to be constructed so that trees would grow there.

Preparations began for the official transfer of the institution from the

Board of Trustees of the Charlotte Community College System to the Charlotte College Board of Trustees, effective July 1, 1963. At that time, an old school bell was acquired from Elizabeth School. It was to be rung for many of UNC Charlotte's later historic milestones.

At its final meeting, the Charlotte Community College System board paid special tribute to Oliver Rowe of the Finance Committee, John Paul Lucas of the Education Committee, and Addison H. Reese of the Buildings and Grounds Committee for their leadership during the transition in status.

That old board met jointly with the new Board of Trustees on July 22, 1963. Members present from the new board were Atkins; Dr. E. A. Beaty, a Davidson College professor; Dr. Jesse B. Caldwell, a Gastonia physician; James H. Clark, an attorney; John H. Delaney; John L. (Buck) Fraley Sr., chief executive officer of Carolina Freight; Linn D. Garibaldi, head of a local telephone company; C. Frank Griffin, a Monroe attorney; Lucas, public relations officer for Duke Power Company; C. A. (Pete) McKnight, editor of the *Charlotte Observer*; Reese, chief executive of NCNB; Rowe, president of Bouligny Company; Sheldon P. Smith, plant manager for Douglas Aircraft's missile factory; Robert L. Taylor, an insurance executive; Mrs. A. W. Thomas Jr., a Concord businesswoman and later a member of the North Carolina General Assembly; and C. H. Wentz, a Salisbury businessman. Absent were Thomas M. Belk of Belk Stores Services and Thomas Watkins Sr. Atkins was named chairman of the reconstituted board at the September 24 meeting.

At that same meeting, Kenneth Batchelor, who had been a budget analyst for the Board of Higher Education and had conferred with Cone on several occasions, was named chief business officer for Charlotte College.

Because of Atkins's illness, he served only two months, and Addison Reese was named chair of the trustees at the November 11, 1963, meeting. At that meeting the board also voted to request the B.S. degree in nursing (approved in April 1964 by the Board of Higher Education), approved plans for another classroom building, and purchased 123 acres of land at $123,325, increasing the campus from 270 to 393 acres.

Atkins's death on December 2, 1963, ended his long-term guidance and leadership of Charlotte College. Beginning in 1949, when the Charlotte Board of Education took direct responsibility for the college, through 1958 when he became chairman of the Board of Trustees of the Charlotte Community College System, and through July 1963, when he became chairman of the Charlotte College Board of Trustees, Atkins had been one of the major players in developing the institution. A resolution in Atkins's memory at the January 14, 1964, meeting of the trustees stated, "As this college moves ahead toward the full university status which was always the dream of Murrey Atkins, we pledge in his memory our dedication to the high goals of academic excellence and intellectual integrity he set for this great institution."

A major step toward that higher status was taken when UNC president

Bill Friday named an Advisory Council on Educational Policy on January 8, 1964, with a major charge to consider expansion of the university to new campuses and geographical areas of the state.

Friday began his activist role in the history of UNC Charlotte at this point. Having grown up in Dallas in nearby Gaston County, Friday knew the territory. Friday's father was a successful textile equipment salesman and a leader in the Dallas community.

Young Bill Friday was a good athlete. He and John L. (Buck) Fraley, who was to become a Charlotte College and later UNC Charlotte trustee and founding chair of the Board of Visitors, played American Legion baseball together in Gaston County.

After attending Wake Forest College for a year, Friday transferred to N.C. State College to attend Textile School—a plan no doubt influenced by his father. At State, Friday became active in campus life. After graduation, he worked briefly in textiles, then returned to the student affairs office at State to work until he entered the U.S. Navy.

After his discharge, Friday entered law school at UNC Chapel Hill. But instead of entering a law practice upon graduation, Friday again was drawn to student affairs work—this time at the Chapel Hill campus.

His position there led to his role in administration with the three-campus UNC system, where he became secretary in the Gordon Gray administration and later president after Gray's resignation to serve in Washington as President Dwight Eisenhower's assistant secretary of defense for international affairs.

Friday's people skills undoubtedly helped see him through his early crises. Expansion of the university system to include UNC Charlotte might even be considered a crisis for Friday because of the ripple effect it had, which led to the ultimate restructuring of all of higher education. Friday would say, however, that the creation of UNC Charlotte in his home region was one of his proudest accomplishments.

Once the issue of expansion moved to the top of the UNC system agenda, momentum accelerated. Arthur Tuttle, director of planning for the university system, notified Cone that 1,000 to 1,500 acres should be available for a university campus. "An area less than 1,000 acres is in my opinion too small for the size of the institution you probably will become," he said.

Friday's UNC Advisory Council toured the campus on February 12, 1964, and had lunch with the trustees, administrative staff, faculty representatives, and representatives of education, government, business, and industry in the Charlotte region.

Friday told the group the university needed answers to these questions: Is there a need for educational services for this area that cannot be performed by a four-year college? Under its statutory definition, are there university-allocated functions that should be performed in this area? If new programs are needed here, how soon must they be established?

On the heels of the visit by the University Advisory Council, the North Carolina Board of Higher Education held its biennial visit on the campus on February 28, 1964. In addition to board members and staff, the group included presidents of state-supported colleges and several private colleges. At that visit, William C. Archie, director of the board, said it would conduct its own study of the needs for higher education in the region.

In response to those meetings, on May 12, 1964, Charlotte College's trustees restated that

> the Trustees of Charlotte College wish to formally endorse and reaffirm the request of the Board of Trustees of The Charlotte Community College System that Charlotte College become a campus of the University of North Carolina. Therefore, the Trustees of Charlotte College hereby request that the trustees of the University of North Carolina approve Charlotte College as the fourth campus of the university and recommend to the General Assembly that adequate financing be made available for this purpose.

As a statement of local support, the trustees added that "for 17 years the citizens of Charlotte-Mecklenburg and 10 surrounding counties have given time, money and encouragement to the development of Charlotte College. They went to the polls four times to vote upon themselves taxes."

A major breakthrough was the commitment by the Mecklenburg County Commissioners to contribute 520 acres of land adjacent to the campus. The final transfer of land actually comprised five hundred acres, because the County Commissioners decided to retain a small tract from the old County Home property. The smaller tract later would become the site of University Hospital, a campus of Carolinas Medical Center, and still later the site for the University City branch of the Public Library of Charlotte-Mecklenburg.

The trustees in a statement said that four-year status for Charlotte College, "though welcome, was too little and too late." They then stated their true goal: "The Charlotte area needs an institution of university scope, an institution of equal quality and prestige with three present campuses of the University of North Carolina. . . . This urbanized, industrialized area depends to a large extent on a more highly educated and highly skilled manpower pool than do many sections of the state. . . . Graduate training is needed in the arts, sciences, business administration, teacher education, and engineering."

Charlotte College trustees apparently knew how much was too much to request; by this time, the issue of establishing a medical school at East Carolina had arisen. It was clear then and has remained clear to independent observers that an additional medical school should have been placed in the state's largest city. Outside consultants confirmed that. The emergence over three decades of Carolinas Medical Center, which has essentially everything but a medical school, reaffirms that Charlotte would have been an appropriate site. However, the decision ultimately was made in the political arena that a medical school would be placed in Pitt County at East Carolina University, and it has prospered there.

At the time, Charlotte's leaders had yet to be given the university campus the region so desperately needed and deserved. The trustees stated in a November 1964 resolution, "It is recognized that to develop a medical center would require from 10 to 15 years and the expenditure of a large sum of money. Therefore, any discussion of a medical center is not for today or tomorrow, but for the next decade."

The community was not to be denied in its bid for a campus of the University of North Carolina. Because of the intense political pressures for expanding the university system, the University of North Carolina Board of Trustees needed some help in knowing how to respond. On July 8, 1963, the executive committee of the Board of Trustees authorized President Friday to conduct a study and submit a report.

That authorization resulted in "A Study of the Need for an Additional Campus of the University of North Carolina to be Located at Charlotte College." Arnold K. King was elected vice president for institutional studies and designated the principal staff officer to the board's Advisory Council on Educational Policy, and in those capacities he led the study of Charlotte College and Mecklenburg County's needs. King personally played the major role in conducting the study and writing the report.

King was a trusted aide to Friday. At age sixty-two, he had already been involved with UNC as student, professor, graduate school dean, and head of the summer school. Perhaps because Friday became president of the university at such an early age, over his years in office he called on several advisers well past retirement age to give him advice and historical perspective.

King was one of those advisers, and he went on to serve the university a total of more than sixty years. When UNC Charlotte dedicated the King Building on April 9, 1982, King was eighty years of age and still an active part of the UNC General Administration. On that occasion, Friday acknowledged King's longevity with a story about his administrative staff's discussing what they were going to do on an upcoming holiday. Friday said, "When we asked Arnold what he planned to do, he said, 'I think I'll go see Mama.'" Indeed, the eighty-year-old King did plan to go see his hundred-year-old mother.

On that occasion Friday also talked about King's integrity. He said that when King was dean of the graduate school he received a call from Bob Jones, the fundamentalist head of a Bible college in Greenville, S.C. The minister wanted one of his graduates admitted at Chapel Hill. King said he had reviewed the student's record, and she wasn't admissible. "But God told me you should admit her," Jones is reported to have said to King, who himself was a devout and active Methodist layman. King replied, "Well, when I also hear from God, I will admit her."

King himself was a great storyteller, perhaps reflecting his mountain boyhood in the Brevard-Hendersonville area. During the inevitable waiting period before university meetings began, he told stories like the one about the first paved road near his home in Brevard. He said the road was being paved past the home of Mary Jane Jenkins, a very fertile woman who had borne thirteen children, when a neighbor came running into her home, yelling breathlessly, "Miss Mary Jane, one of your younguns has got out in the road and got hisself all covered over with tar." To which Mary Jane replied, "Oh, lawsy mercy, I reckon it would be easier just to have another one as to clean that one up."

King's good humor saw him through events that otherwise might have been contentious. He had dark hair that thinned only late in life, and he walked with a vigor that belied his true age. The twinkle in his eye and his mischievous smile might have belonged to a young boy. Until the time of his death, he took an annual vacation trip west, traveling by automobile.

So it was a vigorous King who launched the Charlotte area study. After the February 12, 1964, visit to Charlotte College, the advisory council, led by King, issued a report with the following conclusions: that a new campus would be an asset to the state as it grew, and particularly in the Charlotte region; that a large institution would develop in Charlotte anyway; that an early decision should be made as to whether it would be a campus of the university or separate; that the leadership of the area was ambitious for Charlotte College and wanted it to become a university campus; that it would be fairly easy to merge a young and flexible institution; that it shouldn't happen at the expense of existing campuses; that graduate and professional programs should be added only after a strong undergraduate program was developed and a strong faculty assembled; that it shouldn't remain a commuting campus indefinitely; that a new campus of the university should have identical administrative structures to existing campuses; and that close liaison should be maintained with trustees and administrators at Charlotte College on such matters as faculty, buildings, land acquisition, and budgets as the study progresses.

Following that report, King was assigned to develop a procedure and follow it to carry out a formal study. On March 26, he began the study in earnest, meeting with trustees, faculty members, and administrators. Later, Friday said that it was clear what the outcome would be even as King launched the study. He and King knew that the UNC system had to have a presence in Charlotte. Friday said the reasons for certainty were that it was the most populous area, that there was a core group of financial, corporate, and management leaders emerging with enormous energy, and that, besides, no one could explain why a state-supported institution had not yet emerged in the region.

Until the arrival of D. W. Colvard as the school's first chancellor in April 1966, King became a "shadow chancellor," working closely with Bonnie Cone and helping her understand university policy and procedure as the study and, ultimately, the merger proceeded. He provided liaison on evaluating the library, selecting faculty, working with the budget (although he said he didn't carry a satchel of funds with him), planning construction, and developing the academic program.

University staff came down from Chapel Hill for important meetings, such as one with Board of Higher Education staff on planning future buildings and another with the Advisory Budget Commission on appropriations.

King reviewed all the records of Charlotte College as well as faculty credentials. Outside the campus, King studied population growth projections and other data that could be expected to impact a new university.

Next, King developed some assumptions about a new campus. He proposed that a transfer of assets from Charlotte College trustees to UNC system trustees without any reservations would be required; that the level of financial support would be commensurate with that of other campuses of the university (unfortunately, this assumption apparently carried reservations as far as the university administration and the legislature were concerned); that a development campaign would be necessary; that admission standards would be comparable to existing campuses; that employment standards and teaching and work loads for faculty and administrators would be the same as at existing campuses; that undergraduate programs would have standards comparable to existing campuses while graduate and professional programs were being planned; that new programs would not be undertaken until adequate financing was assured; and that residential facilities would be provided as rapidly as possible in order to serve the entire state and attract students with a wide range of interests.

The King study sought to answer the three pertinent questions: Was there a need for an additional university campus? Was the Mecklenburg County area the appropriate location? And was Charlotte College suitable as the nucleus of the new campus?

He answered the question as to need by pointing out that with projections for growth, student enrollment in the United States would have grown by 3,500 percent in seventy-five years and that North Carolina's growth rate would have exceeded the national average.

King noted that the three UNC campuses had grown from 12,681 students in 1954 to 24,772 in 1964, an increase of more than 95 percent. He also addressed North Carolina's underenrollment of college students compared to the national average and indicated that part of the problem was lack of accessibility to colleges.

In addressing the Mecklenburg area's suitability for a new campus, King noted that nationally, new campuses in recent years had been located in or near metropolitan areas to serve commuting students, to relate to a hospitable intellectual climate, to take advantage of cultural and infrastructure resources, and to serve expanding populations in those areas.

Also, King noted that a university would become an economic asset,

Eugene Payne cartoon in the Charlotte Observer *makes the point that a campus in Charlotte is the missing piece of the state's education puzzle. Reprinted with permission from the* Charlotte Observer.

attracting desirable industries and new population. He cited Charlotte's population of 226,000 as the state's largest and noted that it had grown over 100 percent between 1940 and 1960. He noted as well the Metropolitan Statistical Area population of 350,000, which placed the city eighty-second in the nation. (That MSA population had reached 1.3 million, and Charlotte's city-limits population 440,000, by 1995.)

Charlotte's other educational resources were assessed but were little changed in 1964 from what they had been in 1946. King noted that Davidson had 1,000 students, Queens 675, and Johnson C. Smith 940. Central Piedmont was in its infancy and enrolled only 220 college-parallel students plus a large number of technical-program students.

Charlotte College already had an enrollment of 1,414. Within a fifty-mile radius King cited five other senior colleges and four junior colleges, all church-related, totaling an enrollment of 5,200 students, many of them from beyond the region's and state's borders.

Eugene Payne cartoon in the Charlotte Observer *of July 1, 1965, celebrates Bonnie Cone's success in lifting Charlotte College to university status. Reprinted with permission from the* Charlotte Observer.

Additionally, he pointed out that a community college had just begun in Gaston County that would merge with Gaston Technical Institute to form Gaston College. It was clear from that report that Charlotte was likely still the most undercolleged city of its size in the nation, almost twenty years after that complaint was first made.

As to whether Charlotte College could become the nucleus of a new campus, King reported that existing facilities and those provided for by the 1963 General Assembly would bring their value to $7,738,803, including the value of land. The facilities, he reported, were planned for university functions. One serious deficiency he noted was the lack of city water and sewer service.

King believed that Charlotte College could now be more selective in its admissions, since Central Piedmont and Gaston Colleges were present and had open-door admissions policies. Charlotte College had raised its average Scholastic Aptitude Test scores from 787 in the fall of 1962, when it was a two-year institution, to 926 in 1964, after it attained four-year status.

The library was found to be stocked with a well-selected collection. However, King noted that the collection of 40,000 volumes would have to be expanded rapidly to 200,000 volumes within a ten-year period. (It should be noted that no financing plan was put in place to help the institution meet that goal; in contrast, several new metropolitan campuses in other states, notably Florida, had had 100,000 volumes in place at their opening.)

Charlotte College's early-stage development was seen as an advantage in converting it to university status. Of the faculty, the report stated that it was small and had a high proportion of the total in the lower ranks, that it was doing an adequate job of undergraduate teaching and was led by some competent scholars and had no hard and fast rules governing academic tenure.

"Taking all of the factors into consideration, it is reasonable to conclude that the faculty would be an asset in continuing the undergraduate program," the report said. The average salary was $7,600. The study said that higher salaries would be essential for attracting and holding university faculty.

The administration was lean. King noted that in addition to the president there were a business manager, an academic dean, a dean of student affairs, the director of admissions and registration, the director of student personnel, and the public relations officer.

The Charlotte College Foundation was one of the most valuable assets of the young Charlotte College, King noted. It had received a large gift of a factory and land from the Celanese Corporation (later Hoechst Celanese), valued at $1,140,000. Annual income of $45,000 helped to supplement the salaries of faculty in engineering and the sciences. Since 1961, the foundation had received a total of $1,225,148.

The operating budget was found to be too limited if the institution were to operate at a university level. King said that the institution would need additional funds to offer the baccalaureate program in nursing that had already been approved. Also, he said the faculty-student ratio would have to be lowered from eighteen-to-one to allow the campus to operate at a university level. (It later was lowered to sixteen-to-one.) Also suggested were obtaining additional funds for the library and increasing the average salaries.

In his conclusion, King said the answers to the three major questions were all affirmative. "It is therefore recommended that the Board of Trustees of the University, subject to the provisions of General Statute 116-2.1, take appropriate action to make Charlotte College the fourth campus of the University of North Carolina," the report concluded.

Thus the King report became the pivotal document on which approval was based to give Charlotte its university at last. Even so, much hard work remained before Charlotteans could celebrate.

The full University of North Carolina Board of Trustees approved the recommendations on November 16, 1964, and forwarded their endorsement to the State Board of Higher Education. According to King in his book *The Multicampus University of North Carolina Comes of Age, 1956–1986*, debate was lively at the trustees meeting: one member opposed the recommendation, saying the university should "not expand and acquire quantity and lose quality."

The State Board of Higher Education unanimously approved the recommendations for making Charlotte College the fourth campus of the University of North Carolina on January 15, 1965, and forwarded its endorsement to the legislature.

At that point Charlotte's quest for a university campus officially entered the political arena. The Mecklenburg delegation to the General Assembly was criticized as being too divided by partisan politics and too naive to win anything in a legislature controlled by powerful and entrenched politicians from eastern North Carolina, where politics was a way of life.

Yet Mecklenburg's delegates were to prove critics wrong and to demonstrate that when the stakes for Mecklenburg were high enough, the delegation would pull together and prevail. In fact, in 1964–65, the Mecklenburg delegation went about the task of getting the necessary votes with a vengeance. Bills to create the fourth campus were introduced in both houses on February 9, 1965. Representative James Vogler, as head of the delegation, introduced the bill in the House.

Senator Irwin (Ike) Belk of the prominent mercantile family set about to ensure the outcome by getting the signature of every senator on the bill as a sponsor. He got every signature but one. In fact, the forty-nine signatures on his bill to create the fourth campus was another serendipitous reason for calling UNC Charlotte teams "The Forty-Niners."

But Belk's strategy had a backfire effect as well. The one missing signature was that of Senator Thomas J. White, the powerful representative of Kinston. Senator White said he wasn't sure that he was for or against the legislation but he wanted to look at the fiscal side of the issue first.

White didn't like being singled out as a lone opponent. White grew up in Concord in the Charlotte metro area and said that his family owned some property in the UNC Charlotte area. But when he moved to Kinston to practice law, he became a confirmed Easterner with a grudge of unknown origin against Charlotte and the Piedmont area.

He also enjoyed holding positions of power. As chairman of the committee to oversee construction of a new building for the General Assembly in the early 1960s, he tolerated no questioning of his decisions by reporters, editors, or even state officials.

Some years later White repeated that pattern when he was chairman of a committee overseeing construction of the North Carolina Museum of Art. Criticism by members of the news media only hardened his disdain for them.

A strange twist to this story occurred a couple of years after the successful campaign to create UNC Charlotte. Senator White was chairman of the Advisory Budget Commission, which was to pay a visit to hear of the new university's needs. Bonnie Cone was acting chancellor, and White was reported not to like women in high public places. The senator had also become incensed about a *Charlotte Observer* feature on eastern North Carolina. He thought the feature was demeaning to his adopted region.

The senator instructed Cone to post the full-page feature on a big poster board and bring it and display it prominently at the hearing of the Advisory Budget Commission on the UNC Charlotte campus. He instructed that it have a headline above it that said, "Scurrilous Attack on Eastern North Carolina."

Cone became distraught over this demand, feeling that White was willing to wreck her institution's chances at an objective hearing of its urgent budget needs simply in order to vent his own anger, likely in front of a *Charlotte Observer* reporter.

The feature was mounted on a board and taken to the meeting. Cone decided that she would at least keep it covered until the moment White called for it. Strangely, he never did. Thus the only cost of the episode was the anguish caused to Cone.

Realizing that the incident needed to be recorded for posterity, a staff member wrote a description of the episode and placed it, along with the poster, in the UNC Charlotte archives.

Charlotte College's advocates had one major stroke of good political fortune. Dan K. Moore, a gubernatorial candidate from Canton in the western North Carolina mountains, endorsed the move to create the fourth campus. Possibly he felt the need for political support in the Charlotte area. At any rate, Charlotteans were lucky that although many faculty members at Charlotte College and the UNC campuses had strongly supported Moore's opponent, Richardson Preyer, Moore still supported the transition to university status. In his legislative address on February 4, 1965, Moore said, "I strongly recommend that the fourth campus of the university be located at Charlotte as proposed by the university trustees and approved by the State Board of Higher Education."

Bonnie Cone became a strong lobbyist in the campaign. Later, when asked if she considered herself a lobbyist during that period, she asked—a bit tongue-in-cheek—"Is that what you call it? Lobbying, is that what I was involved in?" Cone said, however, that it wasn't just Charlotte people working. "This was a university and a state project by now. We met with the delegations of the ten surrounding counties and tried to inform them the best we could." It appeared that the Charlotte measure had smooth sailing.

On February 16, both the Senate and House Higher Education Committees held a joint hearing and sent the bill to the floor of both houses. The legislation passed easily in the Senate on February 24. Perhaps Belk's work was worth the risk of irritating Senator White after all.

On the eve of the key vote in the House, the effort somehow hit a snag hidden beneath the water. Cone said she was in the legislative building on a Thursday—"you might say I was there politicking—I don't know—I was there doing my work. I thought I was doing work that needed to be done, making contacts that needed to be made with our own delegation and others."

While there Cone got word that two people needed to see her. One was a representative of Governor Moore and the other a representative of President Friday. Governor Moore wanted the legislation withdrawn and had Friday's concurrence. The governor's lieutenants had heard from legislative leaders that there weren't enough votes, and he didn't want to lose his first big battle in the legislature. So the governor felt that the legislation should be withdrawn for two years, until the next session.

"This was pretty much of a shock to me," Cone said, "because the two gentlemen asked me to inform my delegation. When I informed them they were shocked, because Representative Jim Vogler was sure and the other legislators from our delegation were sure that they had the support needed to pass it in the House." She added that members of the delegation were "just as provoked as they could be." Representative Vogler called the governor and said he was sure he had the votes but that if the governor's reading were otherwise, he would like to postpone action until the next Tuesday to check his count. The governor agreed, and one of the busiest weekends ever was in store.

It was later said that Bonnie Cone drove up stock in AT&T substantially that weekend. She called everyone she knew with legislative connections, as did other Charlotte College trustees and supporters. "We had not just the Mecklenburg delegation, there were several people from throughout the state who worked with us," she said. "We knew we could determine that we had the support we thought we had, but then we had one additional thing we had to do: after it was determined that we did have the votes to pass it in the House, we had to be sure that the governor was persuaded to let the bill be taken to the House," Cone said. It was the belief of the Mecklenburg delegation that to convince the governor they had to have someone who had supported Governor Moore in his election.

"But every single soul seemed to be in Florida fishing," she said. "I didn't give up—I just kept trying to find somebody who could speak to the governor and whose voice could be heard by the governor."

She had been calling from her apartment but realized she needed to go to the campus to continue her efforts. "I worked Sunday afternoon and Sunday evening, and it was getting very late Sunday night, and I still hadn't found anybody and in checking with different people they would give me different names," she said. Finally, she said, "If I remember correctly, it was in the neighborhood of eleven o'clock Sunday night when somebody said, 'Oh, the man you ought to get is George Broadrick. George supported the governor, and you ought to get him.'"

Cone said that at the time she didn't know George Broadrick. "But when you are that close to getting legislative approval for a university in Charlotte, you put your pride in your pocket, and you go and try to get the help you need," she said.

She hoped Mrs. Broadrick would be a kind soul and let her speak to Broadrick at that hour. Broadrick himself answered the telephone. After hearing Cone's plea, he said, "Yes, Miss Bonnie, I'll be glad to go see the governor." Cone offered to get him a chartered plane or put him on a commercial flight, but Broadrick got to Raleigh on his own.

Broadrick was a private, courtly man, of whom Alex MacFadyen of First Citizens Bank said, "I don't know of a man more respected and well liked than George Broadrick." A native of Fort Valley, Georgia, Broadrick had a distinguished military career as a decorated captain in the Army Air Corps in World War II. He later was recalled to serve in the Korean War. After attending Young Harris College, Broadrick graduated from Mercer University, where he majored in economics. He began his banking career at C&S Bank in Georgia and then joined First Citizens Bank in Smithfield in 1954.

In 1960, Broadrick moved to Charlotte to open an office for First Citizens. Later he would become president of the bank. After he retired in 1987, he would continue to serve as a member of the Board of Directors and chairman of the executive committee.

When he moved to Charlotte in 1960, Broadrick quickly entered civic life, serving as president of the Chamber of Commerce. For his service to the community, he was named *Charlotte News* Man of the Year in 1970.

This then was the George Broadrick who had been recommended to Cone and who would prove to be the right person to resolve her crisis. Broadrick told Cone that he would meet with the governor on Monday and with her on Monday night. He said he would be standing at the left-hand side of the front door of the Hotel Sir Walter.

When she got there at 7 P.M., indeed, there was Broadrick. He told her, "The governor is with us, Miss Bonnie." Cone recalls, "That was the most glorious word I ever heard."

Later, the main drive to the administrative area of the UNC Charlotte campus leading to Reese and Colvard Buildings would bear the name Broadrick Boulevard in recognition of his role. Still later, in his role as district highway commissioner, Broadrick would come to UNC Charlotte's aid again by helping get approval for Harris Boulevard to serve University Research Park.

After meeting Broadrick, Cone went upstairs to meet with her delegation and with R. D. McMillan, chair of the House Higher Education Committee. They then knew they had the votes, had the governor's support, and would win.

"That walk I took around the block that night was about the freest air I had breathed in many days," Cone said. "It was really a wonderful feeling to know that what we had been working for all those years was not going to be thwarted, but indeed it was going to be possible for us to get the institution here which we knew would make it possible for us to serve better the people of this area of North Carolina and the state itself."

Tuesday, March 2, Cone said, "was the longest day I ever lived." The House convened at noon. She believed it wise to stay in her hotel room so she would be available if needed. It was 2:30 or 3 P.M. when the vote finally came. "Finally the call came that said, 'It's passed on the third reading, and it's passed,'" Cone said.

Cone immediately called Addison Reese, her board chair, to tell him. Then she called her secretary, Juanita Sims, to tell her. But Sims had already heard. She held out the telephone to pick up sound from the campus and said to Cone, "The bell is ringing. It's ringing once for each member of the delegation and twice for you." A victory celebration had been planned in front of Atkins Library, since officials had had some confidence in the outcome. Professor Loy Witherspoon, who also served as campus chaplain, came out and delivered a prayer of thanksgiving.

Still another celebration was planned, unknown to Cone and her assistants, who had been in Raleigh for the legislative vote. Ken Batchelor, the business manager, and I had been in Raleigh with Cone. She had a speech the next day in Red Springs and talked of getting a ride there and letting us drive her car on to Charlotte.

As we prepared to return home, we were sort of drained of energy by the tension of the campaign, particularly the last few days, and the emotion of victory. So the three of us were relatively silent on the way home by way of US 64 and NC 49 through the Uwharrie Mountains.

The silence was broken early only by a brief disagreement over whether to eat supper before leaving the N.C. State area of Raleigh. Batchelor's hunger won out.

As we reached the town of Harrisburg in Cabarrus County near the campus, they wondered whether anyone would be left on campus by the time they got there, which was about 7:30 P.M. The campus seemed darker than usual.

Perhaps someone had cut off the street lights to heighten the element of surprise. Cone said later she did remember seeing in the headlights that the Charlotte College sign had been covered over with a University of North Carolina at Charlotte sign.

As they drove onto the campus, a student stepped out of the darkness with a flashlight and told the driver to follow him. He did so and was directed to park in the breezeway between Denny and Garinger Buildings. Suddenly lights came on everywhere and a shout went up.

A student stepped forward and placed a bouquet of red roses in Cone's arms. Her eyes glistened with tears. Then she was instructed to follow the crowd to the student center, where music was playing and students were dancing, and a gala impromptu celebration ensued.

March 2, 1965, was a momentous occasion, but strangely, Arnold King, in his liaison role, said it shouldn't be celebrated as the university's victory day. He said March 3 was the official day, because that was the day the clerk of the legislature officially enrolled the bill in the records. But to anyone who witnessed the passage and the celebration on March 2, that has to be the highlighted day.

March 3 did, however, bring the realization that the campus was still Charlotte College until the official transition day of July 1, 1965. There was time to graduate the first, last, and only four-year class of Charlotte College on June 6. Students were given the option of graduating at that time or waiting and getting a diploma that said "The University of North Carolina at Charlotte." That permission diminished the size of the class to twenty graduates, but nevertheless, it was a historic occasion.

On June 17, the Charlotte College Trustees approved a resolution transferring title to the campus and its facilities to the hundred-person University of North Carolina Board of Trustees.

Representatives of State Archives came to make certain that important Charlotte College records were preserved in the library. Charlotte College

Trustees signed over the deed on June 30, 1965, and Charlotte College was officially no more.

Major preparations had begun soon after March 2 for celebrating the official transition in style on July 1, 1965. It was considered such an important occasion for the city that the Chamber of Commerce provided funds and assistance in preparing a beautiful souvenir program, with gold stamping and a tassel, and help in arranging the program and speakers for the day.

John Paul Lucas, longtime member of the old advisory board and advocate for the college, presided as chairman of the chamber's Convocation Committee. The 581st U.S. Air Force Band performed the National Anthem. Bishop Earl G. Hunt Jr. of the Western North Carolina Conference of the Methodist Church gave the invocation.

Brodie Griffith, publisher of the *Charlotte News* and president of the chamber, introduced special guests. Bonnie Cone gave brief remarks. Addison Reese, chair of the Charlotte College Trustees, presented the deed to the campus to Governor Dan K. Moore, who was also serving in his capacity as chairman of the Board of Trustees of the University of North Carolina.

As principal speaker, the governor reviewed the early struggles of Charlotte College, commended Bonnie Cone, and referred to an "exciting vision of this institution's future greatness as a full partner in the Consolidated University of North Carolina." He said he believed the creation of a new campus

The first, last, and only graduating class of Charlotte College as a four-year, state-supported institution poses in spring 1965.

Governor Dan K. Moore rings the campus bell on July 1, 1965, to celebrate the creation of UNC Charlotte.

was in keeping with the plan for the Consolidated University carved out by Governor O. Max Gardner and the 1931 General Assembly.

Moore noted that the new campus would begin the biennium with a budget of $3.2 million to upgrade positions, acquire materials, and add the bachelor's degree in nursing. He indicated that capital improvements would be forthcoming to strengthen the institution.

The most memorable photographs of the day were of Governor Moore ringing the same campus bell that had rung out on March 2 and posing with Acting Chancellor Bonnie Cone. It was an end to an era but, more important, a promising new beginning.

CHAPTER 5

Colvard Plants Deep Roots

AFTER THE celebration of university status on July 1, 1965, was over, reality set in. The name at the front of the campus on Highway 49 had been changed from Charlotte College to the University of North Carolina at Charlotte. That didn't change daily routines, but it did open the door for pundits who kidded about an "instant university."

The task of taking what was a university in name only and making it a real one still lay ahead. Bonnie Cone was lauded for her accomplishments in bringing the campus to university status, but local trustees as well as administrators in the Consolidated University offices wondered whether the campus needed a leader who had already headed a university.

The challenge for UNC president William C. Friday was to bring in an experienced chancellor who knew how to build and administer a major university and at the same time keep Bonnie Cone as part of the team because of her enormous reservoir of goodwill and her skills in human relations. It was heartbreaking for many of Cone's supporters that she was not to continue as the university's chief executive. But unlike Woody Kennedy, Murrey Atkins, and Cecil Prince, she did get to cross over into the Promised Land and participate significantly in the building of a great university. It wasn't too difficult for Friday to identify the new leader; Friday already knew him very well and had great confidence in him. It took a bit more effort to convince Cone that she was wanted and needed to help build the new university.

Once the new chancellor, Dean Wallace Colvard, arrived, however, he discovered that in expending tremendous energy in gaining university status, Charlotte College's leaders had failed to assure adequate funding for a university campus. In fact, it might have been impossible to do that and achieve a positive vote for the transition at the same time.

A formula determined that UNC Charlotte would have an adequate number of faculty members for the students enrolled and that they would be paid the going rate for those in similar institutions. In the early years, Colvard also got significant funding for construction of new buildings. The shortfall was in establishing administrative and support-staff positions. No formula existed to insure that the new university had adequate staffing.

The story of the early years of building UNC Charlotte is therefore a continuation of the account of Charlotte's struggle for adequate funding from the legislature. Sometimes the administrative staff was so lean that overwork and stress took a toll on those who tried to do all that was required to build a new campus. Faculty members volunteered or were pressed into service to accomplish many administrative tasks in the early years.

At the time of transition to university status on July 1, 1965, however, the new chancellor had not even been identified, and Cone was asked by Friday to continue leading the institution as acting chancellor. A. K. King was asked to continue in his role as liaison officer from the University of North Carolina administration to the campus. With those issues settled, the campus ended the spring semester of 1965 as Charlotte College and opened the fall semester of 1965 as the University of North Carolina at Charlotte.

Several rather mundane tasks presented themselves. For example, the new university needed new school colors, because the Charlotte College colors were baby blue and white, the same as UNC Chapel Hill's. Choosing new colors was a rather easy task. A committee considered the colors of the other existing campuses. Colors already taken were the blue and white at Chapel Hill, red and white at N.C. State, and gold and white at UNC Greensboro. White was a unifying color for the other three campuses, and the committee believed that it would be good to continue that tradition. Green seemed a logical choice, then, for the other color.

A new campus needed a university seal for embossing official documents and, early in its history, for use as a logo. A committee for that purpose was chaired by Maud Gatewood, the first head of the art program at UNC Charlotte, and she strongly influenced the final design. Gatewood later left UNC Charlotte to return to her painting full time, and she became one of North Carolina's leading artists. She returned to campus sometime later to spend a year as a distinguished visiting artist.

As a result of Gatewood's influence, the seal was somewhat nontraditional. A stylized pine cone symbolized founder Bonnie Cone as well as North Carolina, the land of the longleaf pine. A tuliplike representation was taken from the most significant architectural feature at the time—the arches at the entrance to the W. A. Kennedy Building. The date, 1946, commemorated the founding.

Later, as seals fell out of favor as college symbols, UNC Charlotte turned to designers for logos, and the seal was reserved for use only on official documents.

Professor Edyth Winningham was the founder in 1965 of the University Forum. Photo by Tommy Estridge.

As Cone contemplated other necessary changes, Professor Edyth Winningham told her there was something else a new institution ought to have. "If we are to be a real university," she said, "We must have a forum to which we can bring distinguished speakers to help us examine the great issues of the day." Cone gave her blessing, and for years the University Forum brought together members of the faculty, the student body, and the community to plan one of the most significant events of the year. The intent was that both sides of controversial issues be examined. Among distinguished speakers who participated in the Forum over the years were Henry Kissinger, Buckminster Fuller, Herman Kahn, Ralph Nader, Carl Rowan, Maggie Kuhn, Charles Kuralt, and Elizabeth Sewell.

The first Forum helped set the tone for the new university. It was titled "The University and the Development of the Modern City." Speakers were Noah Langdale, president of Georgia State University in Atlanta; Daniel R. Grant, a political scientist at Vanderbilt University and an expert on the governance of metropolitan areas; Leo Molinaro, executive vice president of the West Philadelphia Corp., an urban redevelopment organization; and James W. Rouse, a Maryland developer and planner of the new city of Columbia, Maryland.

This Forum was held March 2, 1966, to celebrate the first anniversary of the passage of legislation creating UNC Charlotte. The event also helped UNC Charlotte cast itself in the role of an urban- or metropolitan-oriented university. In later years it also helped set the stage for the development of University Place, Charlotte's "new town," and Rouse was invited back to a planning session for it.

Langdale said in his address, "There is no city in the world which can claim that title unless that city possesses the impulse, the stimulation, that fly in the ointment that a campus can bring to such a metropolis or city." Precisely what UNC Charlotte's founders wanted it to be in Charlotte. Prophetically, the annual report for the year said, "The Forum may become significant as the forerunner of urban affairs activities on the Charlotte campus."

Although he didn't attend that first Forum, Chancellor-elect D. W. Colvard was contacted about it and had input into the planning. He invited John Osman, a senior staff member at the Brookings Institution, to observe the Forum, because he had heard him, as a speaker in another setting, talk about the need for institutions that responded to the nation's urban needs.

In a bit of serendipity, Osman met John Paul Lucas at the Forum. Their conversation later led to a series of seminars called the Piedmont Urban Conference, funded by Lucas's Duke Power Company. The Piedmont Urban Conference played a significant role in helping Charlotte and the surrounding communities discover that they comprised one of the nation's largest urban regions, centered around the city of Charlotte.

Lucas presented satellite photographs of the Piedmont area of North and South Carolina which showed indisputably that the Piedmont Urban Crescent was a real urban region, similar to the one that ran from Boston down to New York City and on down to Washington, D.C., or the one extending from Los Angeles down to San Diego.

Many of UNC Charlotte's young professors attended those sessions and were influenced as they helped shape the academic future of the campus. Indeed, the most important tasks of the new university were organizing the academic program and acquiring faculty members.

New degrees in accounting and economics were added in that first year to respond to community needs.

For fall semester 1965, there were 90 full-time faculty members, of whom 13 were professors, 15 associate professors, 30 assistant professors, and 32 instructors. Even for so young a faculty, there was evidence of quality at that early date: Professor George Abernathy received a prestigious American Philosophical Society Research Grant, Professor John O. P. Hall was elected president of Labor Historians, and several others were elected to state and regional academic organizations.

Several faculty members brought continuing research projects with them, and others launched their research during the year and obtained National Science Foundation and other research grants. Several books were in preparation. The English Department invited poet James Dickey to campus to read from his works.

Enrollment for fall 1965 was 1,815, an increase of 20 percent over fall 1964. Overall, the year marked an auspicious beginning for the infant university.

While Bonnie Cone and her associates worked with A. K. King to put the infant university on its feet, the Board of Trustees of the Consolidated University had designated a search committee to seek a chancellor. According to King, the committee members were directed to make a national search. The chairman was Thomas Leath of Rockingham, and members were Irwin Belk, Elise Wilson, Henry Foscue, and Thomas McKnight. There was no representative from the fledgling campus, which caused a bit of resentment on the part of some faculty members, although many others felt the institution was too new for faculty to contribute much to the process.

As the search began, there were advocates for Bonnie Cone to become the first chancellor. But King later said in his book about the multicampus university system that the search committee as it proceeded "came to the conclusion that if the university at Charlotte was to achieve true university status, it would have to have an experienced university president." Members of the old Charlotte College Board of Trustees might have contributed to that thinking as well.

C. A. (Pete) McKnight shared some years later the trustees' belief that Cone was just too used to dealing with people one-on-one and wasn't accustomed to delegating, a skill that would be required to handle the more demanding responsibilities of a major university. She would have spread herself too thin trying to do everything, he feared.

McKnight also said Cone's administrative strength lay in resolving crises and that she sometimes allowed an event to reach the crisis stage so that she could resolve it at that point. On the other hand, McKnight said it was a tribute to Cone that she had brought the institution to university status. He said that there were two types of institution builders, dreamer-planners and administrators, and that Cone was the former.

Friday shared with his associates that the decision not to select Cone was one of the most distressing of his career. Cone was revered in the community and appreciated for her unrelenting drive toward university status. Based on what the trustees and the community leadership told him, however, Friday believed that to get off to a fast start, the new university would need as its chancellor someone who already had headed a university.

Dean Wallace Colvard at the time had that qualification as president of Mississippi State University. Growing up in the North Carolina mountains and attending Berea College in the Kentucky mountains had helped shape the

Dean W. Colvard became the first chancellor of UNC Charlotte in 1966. Photo by Hord Studio.

character of the man. As a youth in Grassy Creek in Ashe County, Colvard had developed the native virtues of honesty, integrity, hard work, and respect for other people. Friday said, "The state has no finer public servant than Dean Colvard. He is clean, honest and the most sincere man you'll ever meet."

Colvard grew up on a family farm of seventy acres, which produced poultry and eggs, some cattle, and fruit and vegetables. In addition to farming, his father, W. P. Colvard, also was a county commissioner, a magistrate, and later a county surveyor, positions that brought in some additional income. Dean Colvard's mother, Mary Elizabeth Shepherd Colvard, kept the home and lived to the advanced age of 102; she died in December 1994.

From his father, Colvard acquired an understanding of mathematics and was a better-than-average student in his school years. His family lived so close to the Virginia state line that the school he attended was called the Virginia-Carolina School, and the two states divided responsibility for it. Through Future Farmers of America, Colvard was exposed to Virginia Tech and the idea of college. He would be the first in his family to obtain a college education.

He attended Berea College, one of the nation's leading work-study institutions, dedicated to educating mountain boys and girls. There he was successful both in the classroom and in his work assignments. Those included making cheese in the college creamery, working in the business office, and assisting in zoology, preparing specimens for laboratory sessions. It was there, in the college chapel, that he met his future wife, Martha, whom he married in July 1939.

Because of his success at Berea, when he graduated Colvard was employed at Brevard College, which was establishing a work-study program similar to Berea's. There he taught and supervised work-study students. One of his projects was to build a rock wall around the campus. Colvard was invited back to the campus in 1993, to celebrate the designation of that rock wall as a national historic site.

After two years at Brevard, Colvard returned to college for his master's degree in endocrinology at the University of Missouri. There he learned that North Carolina was looking for a superintendent for a research station at Swannanoa, just outside Asheville, and he returned to North Carolina to take the position.

When World War II began, the research station's land was taken for an Army general hospital. That station was then replaced with two sites, one at Waynesville and one at Laurel Springs. Colvard lived in Waynesville and traveled between the two sites.

His work impressed administrators at N.C. State, who were then building a strong School of Agriculture. They brought Colvard to the campus, where he began teaching in 1947. He became head of the animal science program in 1948, and his mentors urged him to return to graduate school to earn a doctorate. By this time, Colvard's interest had shifted to economics, and he entered Purdue University for his Ph.D. work and received that degree in 1950.

From head of his department at N.C. State, Colvard was promoted in 1953 to dean of agriculture and thus became Dean Dean Colvard. Dean of agriculture was an important and prestigious state position in those days, because N.C. State through its extension program had strong advocates in all one hundred counties.

At N.C. State, Colvard had the distinction of teaching two young men who would become future governors of North Carolina—Robert W. Scott and James B. Hunt Jr. An indication of his integrity is the fact that although both governors said that they highly respected him, Colvard never went to them to ask for special favors.

Later some observers wondered how a person like Colvard, with an agricultural background, could become a successful chancellor of an urban-oriented university. There was no mystery behind it. Colvard concluded that a university could serve the needs of an urban constituency and do related research in much the same way that an agricultural school served the needs of farmers and rural people. This would serve as an introduction to his deep commitment to public service on the part of UNC Charlotte.

Likely, it was Mississippi State University at Starkville, Mississippi, that prepared Colvard for the work he would have to do in Charlotte, Friday said. But Friday said that he always felt in his heart that Colvard would be drawn back to North Carolina. At the time Colvard went to Mississippi State in 1960, according to Dr. Louis Wise, who was later to become a vice president there, "Mississippi State was basically a cow college." He meant that not in a derogatory way but in the sense that the institution was narrow in focus and not keeping up with the times. Colvard launched a major private fund-raising campaign, made the institution truly coeducational, and strengthened graduate education and research.

Perhaps his most visible accomplishments related to desegregation. Colvard stood firm when Mississippi State's basketball team received an invitation to the 1963 NCAA tournament, which meant it would face teams that included African American players. There was an unwritten rule in Mississippi that state institutions would not play teams with African American players. Politicians in Mississippi threatened Colvard and put intense pressure on him to reject the NCAA bid. Having received indications that he might be arrested, Colvard slipped out of the state. The coach and the team left the campus on separate airplanes and thus did play in the tournament but unfortunately lost to Loyola of Chicago.

In 1965 Colvard also led the university in admitting the first African American student, in a peaceful fashion, without the sort of violence that had accompanied the desegregation of the University of Mississippi in 1962. Colvard accomplished those missions despite opposition and lack of support from the state's governor, Ross Barnett. Some in Mississippi thought the specter of Barnett having another term in office might have convinced Colvard that it was best to leave.

Thus there was little surprise in the state that he left, but there was great surprise that he went to a fledgling campus rather than to a major state university. Colvard admits that he was drawn back to North Carolina by a love for his native state and a feeling that he had not completed his work back home. He knew there was a chance in Charlotte to build something that would positively affect his entire home state.

Colvard said that Friday had first broached the subject of the chancellorship in Charlotte after tracking him down on July 24, 1964, while he was vacationing at Carolina Beach.

Friday had reached Colvard by calling his office at Mississippi State and finding that he could be contacted in an emergency by way of a telephone at the beach cottage next door to the one where the Colvard family was vacationing. Colvard said that Friday inquired as to whether he would be interested in putting his name in the hopper for chancellor of the new campus being planned in Charlotte. The way Friday put it was, "I asked Dean if he were ready to come home." Colvard said he responded that he would put his name on the list and would be glad to discuss the position with trustees should they wish.

"It was understood that there was no commitment on either side," Colvard said. He added that this had been "no emergency call, but a most interesting vacation interruption."

Friday said he called Colvard because the two had been friends from the days when Friday was assistant to Gordon Gray, then president of the UNC system. He said he watched Colvard develop Chinqua-Penn, a 4-H camp operated by N.C. State, and had appreciated his leadership in restructuring the whole extension service. He said it was a case of a very strong friendship. Whatever Friday's motivation for contacting Colvard even before Charlotte College became UNC Charlotte, he had observed Colvard up close and in action on several occasions.

Colvard had been approached about becoming the dean of agriculture at Ohio State University. That was a similar position to the one he held at N.C. State but at a much larger university. His friends, however, including Friday and some leading trustees, encouraged him to pass up that position and convinced him that something better lay in store. That better position turned out to be the presidency of Mississippi State University.

Even as the process to convert Charlotte College to UNC Charlotte unfolded, Colvard was having to make difficult choices. He was approached about the presidency of Auburn University and about positions at Florida State, Iowa State, and the University of Missouri. Regarding UNC Charlotte's potential opening, he said he feared he would be faced with a "bird in the bush versus a bird in the hand" situation.

In the meantime, the people at Mississippi were making it difficult for him to contemplate leaving. The directors of the Mississippi State Foundation presented him with a check for $5,000 as a token of their appreciation for his work for the university and the foundation.

During a meeting in North Carolina in December 1964, Colvard had lunch with Friday, who told him he really was interested in his coming to Charlotte. But overtures continued from elsewhere as the legislative process continued in North Carolina. Colvard said he was frustrated at delays in North Carolina, but he later learned about the intense, distracting activity concerning the state's Speaker Ban Law. Several intervening crises kept the matter on the burner, but without final resolution, until Friday clarified Cone's continuing position and made Colvard a firm offer on January 22, 1966.

Colvard first visited the UNC Charlotte campus in the late fall of 1965. He and Martha met first with Bonnie Cone, who insisted on giving them a tour of the campus even though it was closed because of an eight-inch snowstorm.

Cone drove them onto campus, but her car became stuck in the snow.

While she went to call for help, Colvard got the car unstuck and blew the horn for her to return to the car. He had not yet been elected chancellor, but Cone said to him that she believed he would be a good one because of his ability to get things unstuck.

Colvard's election as chancellor took place on January 28, 1966—barely. On the day of the election, North Carolina was almost immobilized by a major snowstorm that arrived during the night. The UNC Board of Trustees began gathering in the old State Capitol for their monthly meeting at which Colvard was to be elected. Time for the opening of the meeting at 10 A.M. came and went, and some wondered what was happening. The Colvards were appropriately out of sight in a room in the Capitol. Finally, word came that there was no quorum because of the storm.

Governor Dan K. Moore, who was then the presiding officer over the hundred-person board, had telephone calls made to trustees who hadn't shown up. Finally, when only one person was lacking for the quorum, the governor dispatched a Highway Patrol car to Burlington to pick up trustee Reid Maynard, who was just recovering from an illness, and bring him to the meeting. That mission was successful, and Colvard was elected in the early afternoon after a few hours' delay.

Back on campus a few days later, a reception was planned so that faculty, students, and staff could meet the new chancellor. Once again, a snowstorm struck, and faculty slipped and slid their way onto the campus to meet a man well acquainted with snow from his mountain days but a bit weary of it during his early going at UNC Charlotte.

By the time Colvard began his official duties on April 1, 1966, things were much sunnier, but there was no chancellor's residence. Colvard and his wife, Martha, had to find temporary quarters. They rented a home near Cotswold owned by Elizabeth Prince, who had lived there with her late husband, Cecil Prince. He was the former editor of the *Charlotte News*, a strong Charlotte College advocate editorially and an articulate board member.

Tom Bradbury, then a young reporter for the *Charlotte News*, was assigned to cover Colvard's every move that April day. Bradbury began the day at the house, then moved to the campus, and ended it at the house as Colvard continued unpacking in the evening. Bradbury later was to become associate editor of the *Charlotte Observer* and to continue following the progress of UNC Charlotte over more than thirty years.

Colvard's election had raised the question of what role Bonnie Cone would play—if any. Many of her supporters, still upset by the decision not to appoint her chancellor, began working to find her a college presidency elsewhere or perhaps a government position. There were feelers from other institutions, and she discussed her options with other organizations.

Ultimately she went with her heart. UNC Charlotte was so much a part of her that she couldn't abandon it now. She agreed to accept the newly created position of vice chancellor for student affairs and community relations. When questioned about her relationship with Colvard, she said, "He's my chancellor now."

Colvard was required to submit his first annual report for the year 1965–66 in July, although he had been aboard only three months. In it he said of Cone, "This is to ascribe due credit to Dr. Bonnie Cone, who served as president of Charlotte College and acting chancellor of the University and to members of faculty and staff who have worked with her." He continued, "The writer is sensitively aware of the dedication, the purpose and the educational statesmanship displayed by those responsible for bringing the institution into being."

Although his first convocation address and his official installation address were some months away, Colvard revealed some of his thinking about the new university in that annual report. He said, for example, "Already there is evidence that one of its hallmarks will be its interaction with the metropolitan community in which it is located."

He also listed some of his goals: upgrading faculty salaries, adding to the library holdings, identifying leaders in several disciplines, planning residential facilities on campus, adding offerings in the liberal arts and establishing professional programs, building adequate physical facilities, adding graduate programs (with an emphasis on training for teachers), and improving the beauty of the campus. He noted that there was a consensus that a new university was in the making.

Clearly Colvard fit the mold of Charlotte leaders at the time and easily slipped into the social order. He was a Presbyterian and Rotarian, and members of the Belk family sponsored his membership in the old-line Charlotte Country Club, where he golfed with Mayor Stan Brookshire, businessman-philanthropist Harry Dalton, and Dr. Monroe Gilmour.

Colvard, like Cone, had an ability to paint a vision so that members of the campus community didn't focus too much on the reality of a still somewhat spartan campus. In fact, it was so spartan that security was provided by a night watchman who also delivered campus mail in a grocery cart. But the fact that progress was being made kept hopes high.

But until this point, William Frank (Hutch) Hutchison, the physical plant director, sometimes had to haul overflow from the sewage treatment plant to another location in a truck he dubbed the "honey wagon." During the year, a treatment plant addition was built to relieve that problem.

Occasionally, cows from the adjacent property got through their fence and onto the athletic playing fields, and Hutch had to drive them home and clean the field so that students could participate in their physical education classes without slipping in the manure.

Besides his official role of keeping the young university's buildings in working order, Hutch played the important side role of campus character, keeping faculty and staff loose with his humor and pranks. When new psychology instructor George Windholz bought his first car, a VW Beetle, he asked Hutch for advice about maintenance. Hutch told him the first thing he needed to do with winter coming on was to get the air in his tires changed from summer air to winter air. When Windholz showed up at nearby Newell Gulf Station and made that request, the owner said, "Aw, hell, Hutch must have sent you."

When the first campus tennis courts were completed, Doug Orr, assistant to Colvard, and Spanish professor Ed Hopper were trying them out, one after the other. As they played, they noted that Hutch drove up in a truck, apparently to watch them. After a bit, they noticed that Hutch and the truck were gone. But they noticed something more startling. Across the new tennis court a large black snake was slithering toward them. They were sure it was another prank.

On the other hand, Hutch was loyal to his faculty too. When he attended a community league softball game in which a UNC Charlotte faculty team was competing, he razzed the umpire so badly on behalf of his friends that he was ejected from the stands.

Professors also used humor in dealing with the lack of amenities on campus. At one point in the early days, three departments were sharing space in close quarters. A professor from one of the departments asked that the administration allow the design of a new logo to be placed on a locational sign. He suggested that to represent the three—physical education, geology, and psychology—it should depict a jock, a rock, and a nut.

It wasn't just campus humor that lifted morale. Campus physical improvements began to help. The first campus parking lot was paved, saving shoe leather for faculty and staff who earlier had to traverse a gravel lot. The downside was that the paving marked the beginning of parking fees for students, faculty, and staff, because the state required that the cost of lots and parking decks be self-liquidating.

An administration building was completed, later to be named for A. K. King, as was an addition to the student center, later to be named for Cone. The student center addition was critical, because UNC Charlotte at that point was totally a commuting campus, and students needed space in which to study and relax between classes.

Having succeeded at Mississippi State in increasing the level of private giving, Colvard didn't waste time in importing his program to UNC Charlotte. The UNC Charlotte Foundation adapted his Patrons of Excellence program almost immediately.

Under that plan, individuals, corporations, or foundations became

The campus begins to take shape by 1966, with the Cone Center (left), the Denny Building (far right), and Hechenbleikner Lake (center).

Patrons of Excellence by pledging a minimum of $10,000 each over a ten-year period. The goal was to produce $100,000 a year.

The Patrons program was officially launched November 4, 1966, with a formal dinner honoring Governor Dan K. Moore for his support of the university and attended by U.S. Senator B. Everett Jordan and other government and business and civic leaders as well as prospective donors.

The foundation hired retired Charlotte banker Bascom Weaver "Barney" Barnard, a mountain man (he grew up near the towns of Barnardsville and Weaverville) to implement the program. An ideal choice, Barnard knew most of the key members of the business community in Charlotte well and had a wonderful sense of humor. Barnard pledged his own $10,000 to the university, wrote himself a thank-you letter, had one of the Patrons plaques inscribed with his name, and then presented it to himself at a foundation meeting.

The program enjoyed early success. During 1966–67, some seventy Patrons pledges were made, for a total of $1 million; several of them were for more than the minimum $10,000. Among the major gifts were $100,000 each from Mrs. Charles H. Stone, the Dickson Foundation, Inc., the American Credit Foundation, and the Belk interests—family, foundation, and company.

The Belk gift was for a bell tower. An early master plan by the firm of

The Belk Tower is topped out as the first high-rise structure on campus. Photo by Hank Daniel.

Charlotte architect A. G. Odell included a bell tower, but it was depicted as an open, square structure. Colvard believed that the campus needed a structure with some height to it, because the existing campus buildings were only two or three stories high. He said that he wanted something to symbolize the university's "upward reach toward excellence."

Architects for Little, Lee & Associates found that to construct a tower with any height, given the limited budget, they would have to be creative. The solution was to design a tower 147 feet high. It was created by stacking twenty circular, hollow, seven-foot sections of white concrete aggregate material. That column sat atop a seven-foot base of brown brick. It housed a 183-bell electronic carillon, which could be played manually or programmed to play automatically.

The tower was dedicated in 1970 to William Henry Belk, patriarch of the Belk family and founder of the mercantile empire, in a ceremony attended by North Carolina governor Robert W. Scott.

Because of the tower's phallic appearance, the university had to withstand some kidding, and over the years, some students felt compelled to call attention to the obvious. Other critics said it looked like a rocket on a launch pad.

Another design feature had to be explained. There was a second hump at the base of the tower. Rumors were that a second tower was to have been constructed there. Actually, it was just a feature to allow a hatch and entrance to be built for access to the inside of the tower so that it could be serviced.

The tower did fit its contemporary campus setting. At night, when lighted, the design was dramatic and certainly distinctive.

Another major contributor, Miss Alice Tate of New York City, began her gifts at about the same time, with the guidance and assistance of her Charlotte attorney, Thomas Lockhart.

Her first gift was an irrevocable trust, valued at the time at $275,000, and designated for scholarships for African American students—the Tate Culbertson Scholarships.

Later, she established an endowment of $100,000 to create the Frank Porter Graham Professorship in Black Studies, first filled by Bertha Maxwell. It was of course named for the legendary president of the UNC system, who was an early advocate of desegregation.

Tate was a Charlottean who moved to New York as a young woman to pursue a career in opera; she appeared in a number of productions there. A niece of North Carolina governor Thomas M. Holt (in office from 1891 to 1893), she had always carried a burden of guilt about the mistreatment of African Americans. Tate also apparently carried guilt from childhood about her fellow Southerners' lack of understanding of religions other than Protestant Christianity. She studied Eastern religions and Judaism. She contributed to the Atkins Library from her collection of Eastern literature, and her later bequests to UNC Charlotte provided for a collection of Judaica and Hebraica and for the establishment of the Rabbi Isaac Swift Distinguished Professorship in Judaic Studies.

When Tate died some years later, her funeral request created a bit of a problem. She wanted it conducted by a rabbi. However, she had never actually converted to the Jewish religion, and mainstream rabbis could not conduct her funeral. UNC Charlotte professor Loy Witherspoon used his knowledge of the religious community to find a person who would comply with Tate's last wishes.

Another indication of Tate's complex personality was her gift of beautifully bound and illustrated East Asian books, including some erotica, to the library. That wasn't the library's only gift of erotica. The widow of a Davidson College professor discovered after his death that among the many books in his personal library were a number that she believed were not suitable for her to give to a Presbyterian college because of religious constraints.

However, they were rare examples of late-nineteenth-century and early-twentieth-century erotica, and she felt they should be preserved. UNC Charlotte accepted her offer, believing that in an institution dedicated to free exchange of ideas there was room even for erotica. Chemistry professor Robert Gibson referred to it as the "rare, rare book collection."

A Colvard friendship from his N.C. State days led to a more traditional library gift. Jule Surtman, then president of Charlotte Ford Tractor Company in Charlotte, had become friends with Colvard when consulting him about agricultural conditions in the state. Surtman had moved up the ladder in the Firestone organization and left it to come to Charlotte to seek success on his own but needed to learn something about local conditions—information that Colvard provided.

When Colvard moved to Charlotte, they renewed the friendship and Surtman provided $50,000 to help build the library collection in business administration. As a result, the fifth floor of the Dalton Tower of the library was named for Surtman. Other gifts would follow. Following Surtman's death, his daughters would create a distinguished professorship honoring him.

The flow of many other private gifts gave the university a needed boost in those early years. But Colvard's most significant endeavors were in building an academic structure.

He found that James Wahab, then acting academic dean, was not temperamentally suited to working with him, so an early goal and challenge was to find a chief academic administrator. Because Wahab had clashed with some key faculty leaders, Colvard was afraid he might have to replace him before he found his new leader and would be left without an academic administrator in place.

Colvard called a friend, C. O. Cathey, a dean at UNC Chapel Hill, about his problem. Cathey suggested that Colvard already had a good person in Julian Mason of the English faculty, a classic type of scholar in the liberal arts. So Colvard made Mason his assistant, believing that he could become a liaison to the faculty in a transitional period.

As Colvard pursued his search for a permanent academic leader, he endured his first major crisis. In his search, he had similar objectives to those for which he had made Mason his assistant. He wanted a scholar and administrator out of the liberal arts to complement his own strengths in the sciences and economics.

The name of W. Hugh McEniry, dean and chief academic administrator at Stetson University, soon caught Colvard's attention. McEniry had served a term as president of the Southern Association of Colleges and Schools. From everyone he asked, Colvard got the same strong recommendation: "Hire him." Colvard made the offer but McEniry said no. That made Colvard more determined than ever, and he went back with stronger offers and finally got a yes after about the third refusal.

Then Colvard looked for funds to meet McEniry's salary requirements. He found there were none. There was no help from the UNC system, although Colvard said he assumed there would be no problem.

When he went to President Friday, whom he had kept informed of his search, Colvard said that Friday wondered aloud if the funds were in the budget. Colvard said Friday called Ed Rankin, then assistant to Governor Moore. Rankin checked and said that no, there was no such position funded in the budget.

Colvard then said he couldn't operate that way, having worked a year and a half to get McEniry. He asked whether he had to go back and tell McEniry he couldn't come. Friday put Colvard on the telephone with Rankin. Colvard told Rankin he wanted to talk to Governor Moore. Rankin told him Governor Moore was out of town, and Colvard said he wanted to talk to him wherever he was. "If I can't do that," Colvard said, "I'm going to resign and call a press conference and tell why." Colvard said that Rankin then said, "Well, we can work that out. We can upgrade the position that's there." The crisis was resolved.

But that was the way Colvard learned that he had no budgeted support for top-level leaders. In his first budget request in 1967, he asked for five key people at salaries above the others on campus so that he could put some leaders in place. None of those positions was granted. The only top leader who came in a budget line was one in architecture when that program was established some time later.

When Friday remarked that the creation of UNC Charlotte was one of his proudest accomplishments, some faculty members asked why he hadn't provided greater financial support as the campus struggled to establish itself. Looking back, Colvard said he believed Friday was as fair as he was able to be to the new campus and supported it in getting substantial early capital appropriations.

Friday himself said that he pushed as hard as he could. There was not much money at the time, he said. He also was dealing with a political reality where the mindset was that UNC Charlotte was just another four-year college—nothing more. Leaders in other regions could not see the future of Charlotte and UNC Charlotte as clearly as it could be seen in Mecklenburg County. Nobody outside the region believed the campus and the city would grow as fast as they did, Friday said. He also said that some resentment was expressed toward him for the support he did give the new campus. Friday said some critics felt that the campus should remain a day school, and he well remembered what a breakthrough it was when architect Leslie Boney of Wilmington designed the first dormitories for the campus. "I feel we did fairly well by Charlotte," Friday said. "Once we got past some of the political problems, it took off."

Colvard hastened to add that Friday was a good supporter but that it would have helped to have had some supplemental money and some planning funds at the beginning. The commitment made to him when he was appointed, Colvard said, was that UNC Charlotte would become a full-fledged university and a brother or sister to the other three campuses over time. But he said he discovered he had basically the Charlotte College budget with just a little adjustment for enrollment increase.

As a result, Colvard had to create leadership positions the best way he could—by transforming faculty positions into academic administrator positions and enhancing the salaries in whatever way possible. But there were no line-item deanships or other such positions. Given those constraints, Colvard was fairly successful anyway.

In going about his task of building a structure, he made one unfortunate statement, one that was perhaps misinterpreted but nevertheless created some resentment. He said that he was going to have to recruit a faculty of "university quality." Perhaps because they had been through such tumultuous but lean times, faculty already on board felt that was a slap at their qualifications and a denial of their commitment and sacrifices. They pointed out that they joined the institution to become university faculty members—not to remain forever Charlotte College faculty members.

Later events would prove that Colvard did not make the statement in a derogatory way. He selected some of his first deans from the ranks of the Charlotte College faculty: Newton Barnette in engineering and Edith Brocker in nursing. Other Charlotte College faculty members served as department chairs: Sherman Burson in chemistry, Robert Wallace in English, Harvey Murphy in health and physical education, Robert Rieke in history, Joseph Schell in mathematics, Loy Witherspoon in philosophy and religion, and Louis Diamant in psychology.

Still other Charlotte College staff members served as directors of academic support units: Joseph Boykin in the library; David Nixon in the computer center; Robert Grogan in admissions; Donald MacKay as dean of students; and Mildred English in placement.

Indeed, there was some ambivalence on the part of a few of the early faculty as to whether they really came to the campus to build a full-fledged university or liked UNC Charlotte the way it was, as a small institution.

As UNC Charlotte moved closer to research and graduate work and an emphasis on publications, creative work, and public service, some faculty members began to say that they came to a campus that they believed was committed, as the first and highest priority, to teaching. Their implication was that they therefore should not be evaluated for promotion, tenure, and salary increases using university-level criteria.

But however resentfully some faculty members reacted to Colvard's statement, it didn't cause a deep rift, and he pressed forward.

At the first university commencement in 1966, UNC Charlotte degrees were awarded to eighty-one graduates, including some who could have graduated from Charlotte College but chose to delay their graduation and receive a UNC Charlotte diploma instead.

Colvard's strongest commitment in July 1966, as he began his first full academic year, was to some serious planning. He believed that although members of the Charlotte community had been working toward university status almost from the beginning, energies were consumed in just getting there, and there had been no opportunity to plan much beyond achieving their goal.

The first major step was to bring back Odell Associates, Inc., creator of the first master plan, to do an updated master plan for physical development. That plan was intended to anticipate a campus for 20,000 students. Colvard said he didn't want it to be overly specific, because he didn't want to tie the hands of future planners.

What the plan did do was to establish several principles. Among those were keeping automobiles and trucks out of the central campus and providing parking in perimeter areas. The central campus was to be relatively compact, with walking distances kept at a minimum.

The plan indicated that the central campus might remain that or become one of several cluster colleges later on. Housing was to be kept close to the central campus and related to dining halls and recreational spaces. Space was to be reserved for lakes, wooded areas, and gardens, "with the conviction that a pleasant environment is more conducive to work and study."

The latter goal was realized more quickly than many would have expected because of a friendship developed by Dr. Heck (Professor Herbert Hechenbleikner). He was fascinated by stockbroker Ralph Van Landingham's development of rhododendron gardens around his home on The Plaza near uptown Charlotte.

Dr. Heck began to assist Van Landingham with his project. That friendship led Van Landingham to begin contributions that in turn led to the establishment of the Van Landingham Glen on campus. Later it was described as one of the leading rhododendron gardens in the Southeast. Still later, using Van Landingham's gift funds, Dr. Heck developed the Susie Harwood Garden, a more formal ornamental garden named for Van Landingham's mother.

Van Landingham's health began to fail as he was helping Dr. Heck develop the glen. The garden patron then realized that after his death, the gar-

Herbert Hechenbleikner accepts a plaque honoring his development of the campus gardens and landscaping. Photo by Susan Jones.

dens on The Plaza might not be maintained. In his will he left the house and gardens to the university but included a provision that should it be appropriate, the university could sell the property and apply the proceeds to development of the on-campus gardens. After struggling to maintain what was becoming a white elephant, the university did sell the property on The Plaza.

Only later was it discovered that because Dr. Heck didn't quite trust university administrators, he had encouraged Van Landingham to leave his funds in a trust to be administered by an independent, three-person board. For years Dr. Heck had nagged the physical plant staff over adequate water for his gardens and over campus construction that he believed encroached on them.

Another friendship of Dr. Heck's led to the development of the McMillan Greenhouse complex. He had worked with the McMillans (the former Dorothy Schoenith and Dr. Thomas McMillan) in their cultivation of an orchid collection. Early in the development of the campus, they provided a small greenhouse and an orchid collection for the Biology Department. Despite the failure of the heating system and the loss of a number of orchids during a severe cold spell, the McMillans maintained their interest in the campus botanical developments—even after they moved to Hawaii.

(Their orchid house in Hawaii was featured as a set for the television series *Magnum P.I.*)

Their continued interest led to their contribution of funds to build a new campus greenhouse, a facility with various temperature zones. It featured orchids, carnivorous plants, cactuses, and a tropical rain forest and was dedicated as an attraction for off-campus visitors as well as a teaching facility.

Dr. Heck's other major contribution to the campus was in the early landscaping. Primarily, he took a naturalist's approach. If an exotic plant struck his fancy, however, he didn't hesitate to use it. He even planted a California redwood tree near where the Rowe Building later stood.

To create the lake at the front campus, later named for him, Dr. Heck took advantage of the contributed services of a school that trained students to use heavy earth-moving equipment. He used student assistants to help clear the lake bed of trees and brush, then followed an Odell plan to make the dam the main entrance road to the campus.

The magic of water added to the ambience of the campus. Dr. Heck had left a little island out in the middle and planted some cypress trees at the west end. He brought in a pair of swans, which graced the lake until construction began on the Rowe Building. Suddenly the swans disappeared. Dr. Heck was so upset that he chartered a small plane and flew over the lakes and ponds of the county in a vain attempt to find them. He never replaced them. Instead, the duck and Canada goose population expanded rapidly. One goose even evidenced intellectual curiosity. After automatic door openers were installed at the entrance to the library to aid students in wheelchairs, a goose wandered up, stepped on the pad that signaled the doors to open, and waddled inside. On learning this trick, the goose daily visited the library until it was removed to a farm pond some distance away.

Dr. Heck, a hands-on gardener with a Harvard Ph.D., wore a goatee befitting his Austrian ancestral homeland. A visiting reporter came to the campus one day and, spotting Dr. Heck grubbing in a flowerbed, remarked, "I'll be damned. That's the first workman I ever saw with a goatee."

Even after his formal retirement from the faculty and well into his seventies, Dr. Heck continued to work almost daily, rain or shine, in the campus gardens—digging, grubbing, weeding, planting, or whatever it took to maintain their beauty.

Dr. Heck invited the campus community to his home for a picnic in the late 1960s. When the faculty and staff and their families had gathered, he went to his basement and brought out Oscar, who then held the record as the oldest rattlesnake living in captivity. "A real professor," new staff members thought of a man who would keep such a pet.

Even all those activities don't tell the full story of Dr. Heck. There was

Dr. Heck the dedicated professor of biology and geology, and Dr. Heck the first chairman of the Biology Department. His enthusiasm for his subjects was so contagious that his courses were the highlight of the college careers of many students. Many recalled, years later, the excitement of joining him on field trips into swamps or up mountain slopes. An early student named Larry Mellichamp was inspired, obtained his Ph.D. in horticulture from the University of Michigan, and returned to the campus as a professor and took up where Dr. Heck left off, developing the botanical gardens.

There was also Dr. Heck the benefactor. His family had owned a large tract of land in fast-developing southeast Charlotte, near Fairview and Carmel Roads. As a result of developing that land, Dr. Heck was able to contribute generously to UNC Charlotte and to Belmont Abbey College.

In implementing the overall physical plan for the campus, Colvard was fortunate in fairly generous early capital appropriations and authorizations for buildings. These included the first two dormitories to house one thousand students, an adjacent cafeteria, the gymnasium, the Dalton Tower addition to the Atkins Library, and the Rowe Building for the arts.

To help UNC Charlotte get off to a fair start with its dormitories, the legislature appropriated the campus's first and only funds for housing—half the amount required. The UNC Charlotte appeal, which was accepted, was that older campuses spread the cost of new dormitories over old dormitories, which had long since been paid off but were still bringing in revenue.

If UNC Charlotte students had been required to carry the entire cost of amortizing the new dormitories, their rentals would have been far higher than those on competing campuses. Later construction of residence halls had to be amortized by student rentals. Also, the cafeteria was to be amortized with part of the cost of student meals.

One of the early public relations problems for the campus came from private college supporters who, to make their case for their own survival, would ask, "Why should the state continue to appropriate money to build dormitories on state campuses when we've got empty ones?" Well, the state wasn't appropriating money for dormitories (with the exception of the onetime start-up fund for UNC Charlotte). In fact, even later, taxpayers probably were unaware that state appropriations rarely went to build dormitories, cafeterias, parking lots and decks, bookstores, and student centers on state university campuses. These structures were amortized by user fees, just as a homeowner built a home with financing from a mortgage.

Colvard also saw a need to buy small tracts of land that were integral to the campus but still in private hands. To obtain those tracts, he used some state appropriations, plus some gifts and backing from the UNC Charlotte Foundation, which held some tracts until they could be purchased.

The most important aspect of preparing the new university for its future, however, was in academic planning. Shortly after he arrived on campus, Colvard received funds from President Friday to tour four urban-oriented universities to gain ideas for the Charlotte campus. The visits included the University of Illinois at Chicago Circle, the St. Louis campus of the University of Missouri, the Oakland University campus at Rochester, Michigan, and the University of Southern Illinois at Edwardsville. Those visits helped orient Colvard to the special needs of campuses in urban settings with large numbers of commuting students.

Colvard's own goals for the campus became more evident in his installation address on March 3, 1967, the second anniversary of approval of university status. He announced forthrightly, "We at Charlotte do not claim yet to have become a fully developed university." But he promised, "Let me now make very clear that we intend to build here, and are daily striving to build here, not only a fully developed university, but as soon as possible a great university; and in doing this we believe we reflect the spirit of the Latin motto adopted by the people of this great state in 1893: 'Esse Quam Videri'—To Be Rather Than to Seem."

Among the major points he made in his address were that UNC Charlotte would commit to some pattern of emphasis on urban affairs, that there would be a continuing education component, and that there would be an international component.

In that address Colvard also emphasized the need to maintain the personal touch. He said that UNC Charlotte didn't want to presume to be that which it was not but that it did seek the opportunity to progress reasonably toward true university status.

As to the academic organization, Colvard said that he would build a strong college of arts and sciences and strengthen the departments of engineering, business, and nursing. He added that teacher education would likely be the first area to offer graduate degrees and that other professional areas would be given consideration based on demand.

As Colvard organized his administration, he set a precedent that was later followed by other campuses of the university system—that of placing major divisions under vice chancellors. Hugh McEniry became vice chancellor for academic affairs in 1967, and, of course, Bonnie Cone had been named vice chancellor for student affairs and community relations in 1965.

The business affairs position was upgraded from business manager with the appointment in 1969 of Silas M. Vaughn as director of administration after Ken Batchelor left to become business manager at West Georgia College; then, in 1971, that position was changed to vice chancellor for business affairs.

The vice chancellor for development position was created in 1972 and filled by William M. Britt. Later, the vice chancellor for research and public service position was created and filled by Douglas M. Orr Jr., who had served as assistant to Colvard as well as a professor in the Geography Department and later, following the retirement of Cone, vice chancellor for student affairs.

Colvard found that this beginning organizational structure still left a gap between the levels of vice chancellor and departmental chairperson. Department heads began working together in a council for academic planning, and out of those sessions came a recommendation for creation of several academic divisions. These were: business administration and economics, education, engineering, humanities, mathematics and natural sciences, nursing, and social and behavioral sciences.

Hindsight would prove that Colvard's earlier concept of a college of arts and sciences might have been a better structure than having that area divided into three units: humanities, mathematics and natural sciences, and social and behavioral sciences. It probably wasn't all bad to begin with, because it put leadership closer to the faculty of departments as they were beginning to develop and expand. But many members of arts and sciences divisions felt that, divided, they didn't have the clout to compete with the professional colleges for equal consideration when it came time to allocate positions, raises, equipment, and other amenities of university life.

In 1970, the university felt the impact of outside forces in determining its curriculum and structure. N.C. State University's School of Design, which included architecture, had grown as large as was considered desirable. Yet the architectural firms of the state said they couldn't find enough new architects. With the support of N.C. State and the architectural community, a new program was requested for UNC Charlotte. There were reports also that some architects felt that N.C. State was relegating architecture to second-class status in a program that included design.

The new program for UNC Charlotte was approved in 1970, and architecture was added as a division. Also in 1970, the Academic Council recommended further refinement of academic administration, and the divisions became eight colleges headed by deans.

Newton H. Barnette became dean of engineering, having joined Charlotte College in 1964. Before that he had been Westinghouse Professor of Electrical Engineering at Georgia Tech.

Allan V. Palmer served as dean of business administration. He joined UNC Charlotte from Old Dominion University in Norfolk, where he was professor and director of graduate studies. William Wubben, an economics professor, had led the program earlier.

John B. Chase Jr. was dean of education. He came to UNC Charlotte in 1969 to replace Philip Vairo, who first headed the teacher education program but left when he felt he couldn't get the commitment he wanted to the kind of program he envisioned. He later became president of a college in Connecticut. Chase, whose mother was a member of the North Carolina House of

Representatives, came to UNC Charlotte from UNC Chapel Hill, where he was assistant to the provost, professor of education, and chairman of teacher education.

William S. Mathis was dean of humanities, having come to UNC Charlotte from Hope College in 1967 to head the department of fine arts.

Norman W. Schul was dean of social and behavioral sciences, chairman of geography and earth sciences, and head of the Urban Institute. He came to UNC Charlotte in 1967 from UNC Greensboro.

Robert G. Anderson was dean of architecture, having come to UNC Charlotte from the chairmanship of architecture at the University of Miami (Florida) to launch the new program. His father, Dr. D. B. Anderson, was a vice president in the UNC system.

Philip Hildreth was dean of mathematics and natural sciences and distinguished professor of biology. He came to UNC Charlotte in 1967 from the Lawrence Radiation Laboratory of the University of California at Berkeley, where he was a genetics researcher.

Edith Brocker was dean of nursing. She came to UNC Charlotte in 1965 from Duke University, where she was assistant dean and director of undergraduate studies in nursing.

Another key academic administrator, although he didn't hold the rank of dean, was Seth Ellis, who had joined the English faculty in 1963 and was awarded the first NCNB Award for Excellence in Teaching in 1968. He was

Seth Ellis, the first winner in 1968 of the NationsBank Award for Excellence in Teaching.

assistant to the vice chancellor for academic affairs and director of summer sessions and evening programs. Later his duties were expanded to include continuing education.

Under Colvard, departments were allowed a great deal of freedom to create their own structures; they could be as innovative as they wished. Several departments took advantage of this freedom and created avant-garde programs.

In engineering, instead of the traditional names, civil engineering was called "urban and environmental engineering"; electrical was called "engineering analysis and design"; and mechanical was called "engineering science, mechanics, and materials."

Education was called the College of Human Development and Learning. It adapted some of the trendy educational innovations of the day. In fact, faculty critics referred to it as the "touchy-feely school of education" when they observed blindfolded students leading other students across the campus.

When the College of Business Administration planned its first master's degree program, the decision was to call it a "master of management" degree.

Perhaps the departments within the arts—visual, music, dance, and theater—were the most experimental. All were under the umbrella of "creative arts." William Mathis developed a program without grades, in which students only had to show progress, not make passing grades, to complete the program. Critics pointed out that arts students were allowed too much latitude in selecting courses outside the arts and could graduate without a complete understanding of liberal learning because they could avoid the electives required in most other programs.

In contrast, many academic units on campus were as traditional as those in the oldest state universities. The chemists, for example, were sticklers for standards relating to the number of class-days and hours in a semester, and they were firm in their opposition to grade inflation.

A lesson learned from the experiments was that a university that itself has not become well established and where faculty have the insecurities that come with youth does not have the luxury of a great deal of innovation.

Students came to the university looking for electrical engineering, for example, not engineering analysis and design. Likewise, employers came to the campus to hire a civil engineer, not an urban and environmental engineer. Or prospective students came to the campus asking why there was no school of education, when actually there was—under another name.

In the arts, students who were not completely self-motivated and who were not very sophisticated could not easily design their own curriculums and discipline themselves to get a full liberal education. In business, UNC Charlotte was graduating its first master's degree students with the master of management degree when all the business world at the time was clamoring for M.B.A.'s. So in time, the nontraditional programs had to become more traditional to survive.

Some of the innovations did stick. Newton Barnette, for example, led the development of an engineering technology program, an ideal fit for a university that had an earlier history as a two-year college. The engineering technology program was built on the base of students' two-year technology degrees from community colleges. It opened a door to students who otherwise would not have gone on to four-year institutions. It also provided a type of hands-on technical expertise needed by businesses and industries, which didn't always need a professional engineer for every technological task.

Another positive result of the freedom of program design was that it led to an entrepreneurial approach to education. Academic units were not inhibited by a hundred years or so of tradition. If resources were not readily available, many departments found a way. For example, the geography department did outside work in map-making and urban planning for clients. This enabled the department to acquire state-of-the-art equipment, including sophisticated computers.

UNC Charlotte's friendly attitude toward two-year institutions was a major boon as it developed. The engineering technology program was one example. So was the criminal justice program in its earliest years. Another evidence of UNC Charlotte's affinity for two-year institutions was a training program for presidents of the rapidly expanding two-year institutions; this program was conducted for the first several years after university status was gained. It was coordinated by Bonnie Cone and Professor Ben Hackney of education.

Still another example of the university's appreciation of the two-year institutions was its receptiveness to enrollment applications from transfer students. This sent a strong message that UNC Charlotte "hadn't gotten above its raising." Soon a prediction made earlier by Mary Denny came true: UNC Charlotte's junior class was larger than its freshman class because of transfer students.

The rapid growth and development of North Carolina's community college system to fifty-eight campuses paralleled UNC Charlotte's own progress. At first UNC Charlotte was by far the most open to those institutions, but as other campuses of the university observed what was happening and when their enrollments plateaued, they also became more accommodating.

UNC Charlotte also benefited from the fact that the state's largest community college, Central Piedmont, was a neighbor, as were Gaston, Stanly, Rowan-Cabarrus, Mitchell, and others from nearby counties. UNC Charlotte also shared a common heritage with Central Piedmont, both having used the Elizabeth Avenue site of the old Central High School as a campus.

There were many successes and some false starts, but the overall trend of the campus was rapidly upward. Shortly after Colvard's arrival, he got a call from a friend at Mississippi State asking how things were going. "Wonderful," Colvard said. "I don't have a football team, and I don't have an alumni association." Lack of a football team likely was a continuing blessing, although some disputed that opinion. (Colvard later lamented not having a mature alumni association, however, for the fund-raising and advocacy such groups provide.) And it wasn't that Colvard didn't have an appreciation for the role of athletics in a university. After all, the way he handled Mississippi State's playing an integrated basketball team strengthened his hand at that university and paved the way for the later integration of that campus.

UNC Charlotte's athletic heritage, of course, went back to 1946, the first year of operation as the Charlotte Center of UNC. After the football team was disbanded and the uniforms sold, the institution continued fielding basketball teams with part-time coaches. The teams carried the nickname "The Owls," after the institution's early history as a night school.

In 1962, Charlotte College had landed a very competent part-time basketball coach in Irving Edelman, a scholarly public school teacher, later a principal, who earned a Ph.D. later in life. The team was practicing at Piedmont Junior High School and playing its games at Garinger High School. It competed in the Dixie Athletic Conference with schools like the College of Charleston, St. Andrews, and N.C. Methodist. Charlotte College even won the Sun Coast Tournament in St. Petersburg, Florida, its first tournament victory.

As a next step in moving the athletic program to a higher level, in 1965 Dr. Harvey Murphy was employed to begin a physical education program. He was given the extra responsibility of coaching basketball. Of course, his primary interest was as a scholar in physical education. But he gave the best he had to a basketball program built with nonscholarship athletes. It wasn't easy. Once, because some of the young faculty members wanted to make a clear statement that academic standards had been raised, Murphy suddenly found half his basketball team on academic probation. This left him with five players and no help in the event a player fouled out. Murphy was quoted in *Sports Illustrated* as saying, "This could have a negative impact on team morale."

He did get some help when players such as Nick Stavrakas, who later earned his Ph.D. in mathematics and returned to UNC Charlotte as a professor, walked on for the team. In fact, three players on Murphy's early teams— Stavrakas, Lane Hurley, and Danny Coggins—were to earn Ph.D. degrees, a claim not many coaches can make.

It could even be said that on one occasion Murphy risked his hide for the program. His team was playing a game in a public school gymnasium at nearby Harrisburg when a scuffle broke out on the court. A player on the opposing team, a giant compared to most of the other players, had been declared ineligible and was sitting on the bench as an assistant to his coach.

When the pushing match broke out, Murphy, who insisted on good sportsmanship, rushed onto the floor to separate the players. The would-be assistant coach misinterpreted Murphy's move as an attempt to participate. Murphy, short of stature in comparison even to his own players, was grabbed by the seat of his pants by the gigantic assistant, lifted into the air, and then skimmed across the floor like a stone tossed across the face of a stream. Murphy said he had floor burns for some time afterward.

Without the full athletic staffs of major programs, colleges in the league in which Murphy's team played could make mistakes. Once the UNC Charlotte team piled into vans and headed across the state to an opponent's campus, only to pull up to a darkened and locked gym. That team had changed its schedule without informing Murphy.

Those early teams were exemplified by player Ben Basinger, who never entered a game thinking the 49ers were going to lose, even though some of the competition was playing at a much higher level. Sometimes that spirit carried the team to victory despite the odds. The early fans were exemplified by professors Burt Wayne of engineering, Jim Matthews of biology, Tom Turner of accounting, and Ben Hackney of education, and staff members Mildred En-glish, Juanita Sims, and Scotty Williams, who rarely missed a game.

Professor Murphy had a sound philosophical approach to athletics. He noted that 50 percent of teams will win and 50 percent will lose—unless it's a sport that allows tie games.

Not many coaches and certainly very few fans ever seem to accept that fundamental "Murphy's law." Murphy also observed that fans attach themselves to a particular team for the most illogical reasons—a North Carolina native pulling for a team in California, for example.

Some UNC Charlotte faculty purists liked the idea of a low-key athletic program, saying that some of the best universities, like Harvard and the University of Chicago, thrived with such programs. Colvard knew that UNC Charlotte's peer institutions had a different attitude, however, and that to obtain visibility and a rallying point for his academic programs, he needed to plan toward a higher level of competition. So the athletic program was added to the planning table.

In the meantime, Murphy went about the task of building the physical education program. Among his projects were stress testing and body fat measurements. A number of faculty members participated. To resolve their various problems, Murphy suggested that they begin jogging. Several who began then continued until later in life, including Sam Simono, Ben Hackney, George Antonelli, Doug Orr, John Robbins, David Goldfield, Fowler Bush, Ed Perzel, Tom Turner, Bob Reimer, and others. In fact, some attributed their exercise program to saving their lives. Antonelli, later a member of the UNC General Administration staff, believed he wouldn't have survived his overweight condition and his smoking had he not taken up an exercise program. Robbins, later a resident of Virginia, survived liver surgery and credited his continuing survival to his running.

As he added athletics to the table, Colvard continued to put major emphasis on planning. Even with the physical plant plan prepared by the Odell firm and the planning visits he had made to other urban-oriented institutions, Colvard still felt the need for a formal overall planning process. He believed he needed outside expertise to bring objectivity and insights to the process. To get that help, in early 1968 he presented grant proposals to the Z. Smith Reynolds and the Mary Reynolds Babcock Foundations for funds to assist with planning. He was successful.

To guide the planning process thus funded, Colvard brought to the campus one of the nation's distinguished leaders in higher education, Dr. Paul A. Miller, as director of university planning studies and distinguished professor of education. Miller had been provost at Michigan State University, president of West Virginia University, and, most recently before coming to UNC Charlotte, assistant secretary for education of the U.S. Department of Health, Education, and Welfare in the administration of President Lyndon Johnson.

With Miller the campus received a benefit in addition to his leadership of the planning process. Miller became a mentor for several young faculty members and assisted their maturation process. Young professors had the opportunity to sit at the feet of an academic leader who had wrestled with issues of higher education at the highest levels.

Unfortunately, Miller's tenure at UNC Charlotte was brief. He was approached about several university presidencies and accepted the one at Rochester Institute of Technology. Miller was replaced by Dr. James E. Heald, who had been head of the Office of Planning and Development and professor of educational administration at Michigan State University. Illness cut short his stay at UNC Charlotte, but he added yet another dimension.

Planning during that stage of the university's development involved sending teams of faculty and staff members to other universities, consulting with local professional groups related to the proposed curriculum, developing a model of the proposed new program, and then bringing scholars in the field to the campus to evaluate the plan and prepare a written response.

All of that activity gave the young UNC Charlotte faculty a sense of connectedness to the rest of the academic world and allowed them to measure themselves against some of the nation's best. Undoubtedly the process moved UNC Charlotte forward much more rapidly than would have been expected for so young an institution.

A strong work ethic established by the example of both Cone and Colvard was another asset to the young university. It was contagious and was passed on as new faculty and staff joined the university. That work ethic allowed the university to compensate for the lack of resources and support staff. UNC Charlotte was lean in staff from its earliest days and emphasized productivity before that became a national obsession. In fact, Cone's personal work ethic and expectation for her staff was so strong that Colvard found when he arrived that he had to tell them that they could go home at the end of the normal work day.

Colvard expressed some regret that young faculty members not only had to develop as teachers and researchers but also had to serve on various committees to help create the university's administrative structures and processes. For most, however, that was not a negative factor. Many faculty members came to the university and remained precisely because of the opportunity to help build it. Several later noted that they could have gone to a well-established university, but there they merely would have taught their classes and conducted their own research without the opportunity to feel that they had a role in creating an institution.

They understood the moral of the oft-told inspirational story about the visitor to a work site who asked two workmen what they were doing. The first workman replied, "I'm cutting stone." The second replied, "I'm building a cathedral." Many of the UNC Charlotte faculty understood that they were building a cathedral for learning.

Yet the challenge of so much to do, so little time, and so few resources exacted a toll. In 1969, Colvard, Cone, and I went to Raleigh for "discussions" with the area legislative delegation. (Actually it was lobbying, which was permitted at that time.) The three were preparing for a dinner at the Hotel Sir Walter.

Cone went to her room, and Colvard was working in his room on the evening's plans. He and I were joined by Rudy Pate, who at the time was assistant to President Friday and was assisting in negotiations with the legislators, and planning continued. Suddenly, in the midst of the conversations, Colvard began a strange pattern of behavior. He began asking the same question over and over: "Is everything ready for tonight?" Each time we patiently answered, "Yes." Pate signaled that we should leave the room. Outside we conferred and called in Cone.

At first we feared that Colvard had suffered a stroke. Pate called a friend who was head of the health center at N.C. State, where Pate earlier had been head of public relations, and asked his advice. The friend suggested that Colvard be taken immediately to the university hospital at Chapel Hill. Pate called Friday, who arranged for the hospital to admit Colvard and reserved rooms for Cone and me at the Carolina Inn.

In the meantime, another strange thing happened. Pate asked Colvard if he would like him to call Colvard's wife, Martha. When Pate called her and began talking, Colvard said he would like to talk to her. Colvard told her that the others felt he should go to the hospital for a checkup. During that conversation, Colvard's behavior returned entirely to normal.

Pate then volunteered to meet with the legislative delegation while the others took Colvard to Chapel Hill and had him admitted for tests. The next day, the other two returned to Charlotte to await word of Colvard's health, fearing what the diagnosis might be. But after a complete battery of tests that showed nothing but did give Colvard a few day's rest, the doctors concluded that he had suffered only "executive fatigue." Apparently he had experienced a stress overload. His mind and body had said, "We can't take any more." All of us were very much relieved when nothing serious was discovered, and shortly thereafter Colvard returned to his normal routine but learned to pace himself better. Doctors did, however, discover an ulcer, which Colvard blamed on the stress of the intense battery of tests he underwent.

Pressures didn't ease a great deal for Colvard, but he did learn to deal with them. While he was recuperating from his illness, the restiveness of African American students had grown stronger. The students were presenting their demands at campuses across the country. While Colvard was out of the office recuperating, the students picketed the administration building at UNC Charlotte and presented their demands to Doug Orr, who was then Colvard's assistant. Vice Chancellors McEniry and Cone then met with the students to discuss their concerns. The demands were essentially identical to those presented at UNC Chapel Hill and other campuses.

One symbolic demand was that a black flag be flown on the campus flagpole. Orr and other officials conferred with state officials and learned that no flag could be flown above the American flag but that others could be flown lower on the same pole. It was agreed that the black flag would be hoisted for a day. Meanwhile, opposition developed to the flag plan, particularly from some veterans on campus, and there was a bit of tension when the flag was raised. However, negotiations with the student leaders prevented any serious problems.

One of the students involved in making the demands was Ben Chavis, who was to become a national civil rights leader. He was the first African American student to major in chemistry at UNC Charlotte. He also helped organize the Black Student Union and was elected to the number two campuswide position as head of the program board. Later he described himself as having been a student militant during his UNC Charlotte days. Chavis also became active in civil rights activities in the greater Charlotte community, and he said those activities led to his being shadowed by Charlotte and Mecklenburg County police whenever he left the campus.

It wasn't enough for Chavis and his associates that UNC Charlotte had made the transition in 1964 to four-year, state-supported status and in 1965 to university status as a desegregated campus. Even though there were no out-

Ben Chavis (right) returned in 1994 to speak at a University Forum and here attends an uptown reception in his honor with Chancellor Jim Woodward and alumna Stephanie Counts. Photo by Wade Bruton.

ward signs of discrimination, African American students said that vestiges of a segregated society persisted. Their complaints related to the lack of African American faculty and staff and the lack of a curriculum that related to their history.

Apparently the students also were unaware of Colvard's history in relation to civil rights in Mississippi, where at that time it required courage to advocate desegregation. Colvard's being away recovering at the time was taken by the students as an attempt to avoid hearing their demands. They posted a sign that said, "Colvard has Blackitis."

The university did respond to and meet many of the demands. Later Chavis said he and his fellow students learned that if you get what you demand, you have to follow through. Out of their demands grew the African American and African Studies Department.

Chavis gave Bonnie Cone credit for helping him keep his militancy within bounds. He also gave credit to Sherman Burson, then chairman of his chemistry department, for helping him keep his stances in perspective. To demonstrate his militancy, Chavis wore a fifty-caliber machine-gun bullet on a chain around his neck. One day he said that Burson, a dedicated Quaker, came into class wearing a hand grenade around his neck. Chavis responded, "Doc, I think I get the point." Despite the lack of African American role models in those early days, Chavis said, some white faculty went out of their way to serve as mentors for him.

Chavis also credited his UNC Charlotte days with shaping his later civil rights career. He said that Professor Loy Witherspoon turned him toward the ministry even though he was majoring in chemistry. Witherspoon challenged him, he said, by making him think for himself. Chavis found that he was able to debate his professor about some of the profound questions of existence.

But those were heady times. Protests were beginning to grow over the war in Vietnam, and civil rights activities were at a peak. After his graduation from UNC Charlotte, Chavis was convicted as part of the "Wilmington 10" over charges of burning a store during civil rights protests in that city. He served prison time, but his conviction was overturned and he was given a gubernatorial pardon. He later earned a doctoral degree. He subsequently became head of the national NAACP but resigned during a controversy over management of that organization. Chavis continued his civil rights activities in other organizations and in 1995 served as a co-organizer of the Million Man March on Washington.

Several of Chavis's fellow African American students of that era also went on to successful careers—Humphrey Cummings as an attorney and civic leader in Charlotte, Dr. Ron Caldwell as an Asheville physician, T. J. Reddy as a Charlotte poet and artist, and Harold Pully as a minister in New England.

Unlike some universities, where violence was the legacy of the activist antiwar and civil rights movements, UNC Charlotte may have actually grown stronger, because both administrators and protesters dealt with the issues in a fair and rational manner.

In addition to working on academic matters, civil rights, and human relations, the administration was able to do something about developing the physical plant. The General Administration and the 1967 legislature had been good to the university, providing funding for the Dalton library tower, the Rowe Arts Building, and the Belk gymnasium, and granting approval to build residence halls and a cafeteria plus add improvements to the grounds.

The university was fortunate that the federal government, in an attempt to respond to the explosion of growth on college campuses, provided partial funding for several projects, including the library addition, the Rowe Building, and renovation of the Kennedy Building. A federal grant for the gymnasium had been received the previous year.

All of these projects improved the quality of student life. Having residential students was an enriching experience. The gymnasium allowed for much-expanded intramural and athletic activity—although the campus responded with laughter when a professor said he really would like to use the gym for an exercise program but that it was too far to walk from his office on the east side of the campus. The library tower expansion was essential in providing study space, especially for commuting students, as well as shelving space for the growing book collection.

UNC Charlotte accomplished one statewide breakthrough: the construction of air-conditioned residence halls, a first for state-supported institutions. That move was to prove beneficial to summer school and summer activities of all kinds. Because no air-conditioned dormitories had been built before, property control and budget officials in Raleigh objected to plans to do so at Charlotte. Colvard said he knew they had the power to argue against the air-conditioning on some technical grounds, but only the legislature could absolutely prohibit the air-conditioning. He said the officials tried to use cost to defeat him on the issue. When the buildings' bids came in under budget even with air-conditioning, the case was won, and UNC Charlotte got the first air-conditioned dormitories in the state. High-rise dormitories without air-conditioning continued to be built even later at some campuses.

Of course, something was sacrificed to bring the high-rise, air-conditioned dormitories in under budget. They were rather spartan, poured-in-place concrete buildings. Ed Crutchfield, chairman of the board and chief executive officer of First Union Corp. and a UNC Charlotte trustee in the 1990s, complained that they looked like buildings seen in Eastern European countries. If Crutchfield saw them when they were first completed, he did indeed see the raw concrete look of Eastern European architecture. Architect Boney had said they would be attractive that way. He was wrong. They really looked drab and gray. When it rained, and they turned dark, they were almost depressing in appearance. Cream-colored paint did brighten them somewhat.

Aesthetics aside, the buildings did make it possible for UNC Charlotte to become a residential campus almost instantly; they provided housing for two thousand students. Certainly by 1969–70, student life had changed. With the completion of even the first residence halls, some six hundred students had moved in and, for the first time, brought twenty-four-hour life to the university. That event, of course, required putting in place residence counselors and residence advisers and governance procedures for the residence halls.

There was even some pioneering in opening the first residence halls. When they opened, landscaping had not been completed, and students and parents had to move in across boardwalks to avoid the mud. The first high-rise became a forerunner of coeducational dormitories: men and women had to move in on alternate floors because the second high-rise was not ready in time for the campus opening. Female students protested that they didn't want to give up their privacy by living in coed dorms. At any rate, on-campus living had arrived. UNC Charlotte kept its "commuter school" label for a while longer, but it no longer fit.

Even given the roadblocks in Raleigh, Colvard said that UNC Charlotte was able to build a campus faster than had ever been done before. He gave

Friday much of the credit, saying he had provided a "hunting license" that allowed UNC Charlotte to go to the legislature with its needs. Colvard felt that Friday wasn't always able to deliver on everything, because, as is often the case, bureaucrats within the university administration sometimes lacked the same vision of what the new campus would mean to the system.

Felix Joyner, a former Kentucky state budget official, was a jolly elf at times. Once in a casual conversation, it was pointed out to Joyner that UNC Charlotte was suffering by having the lowest space per student in the system. His response was that Charlotte was relatively well-off because all its space was new, whereas some older institutions were using many old buildings. True, but space was space was space, and when you were out of space, any old building would do.

At the same time, every administrator over the years at UNC Charlotte willingly accepted the concept of having and maintaining one of the nation's premier state universities at Chapel Hill as the flagship campus and even of supporting the concept to include N.C. State. What was frustrating was that many systemwide officials seemed to lack a basic understanding that the entire state would benefit from having a full-fledged metropolitan university in its largest city. On occasion there seemed to be even a lack of awareness of the model of the urban-oriented or metropolitan university that was developing across the nation.

UNC Charlotte administrators perceived that every campus in the system was to be measured by the historic, classic model of the earliest state universities.

A kind of inside-the-beltway mentality seemed to be growing in Chapel Hill. In fact, a warning about that mindset had been sounded around 1971, when the decision was made to keep the General Administration in Chapel Hill, where it had been since consolidation in the 1930s. Some had advocated moving the administrative headquarters to Raleigh. Others even suggested that it be located at Asheboro, since that city lay at the center of the state.

On the other hand, the argument for keeping the administrative headquarters in Chapel Hill—and it had validity—was that the headquarters would serve as a daily reminder to that staff that it served real students and real faculty and staff and was not there just to shuffle paperwork.

Indeed, in some ways the presence in Chapel Hill of the system's administrative headquarters was more of a detriment to UNC Chapel Hill than to outlying campuses in Charlotte, Greensboro, and elsewhere. Staff of the UNC Chapel Hill News Bureau often lamented that when a systemwide problem developed, the public often linked it with the Chapel Hill campus rather than the system as a whole.

Overall, membership in the university system was a positive for UNC Charlotte as it developed. That membership gave the institution instant recognition. Being one of the campuses of a system that carried the UNC name was especially important in the early years.

Even when all four-year institutions were merged into the university system, in 1972, there was little added recognition benefit for campuses such as Appalachian State, Pembroke State, Elizabeth City State, Western Carolina, and the other institutions that did not carry the UNC tag. Only by reading the fine print would a layperson know that those campuses were part of UNC.

The name UNC was better known than Charlotte College. In the 1960s, even the City of Charlotte was not well known outside North Carolina. Still, some in Charlotte were concerned that the name "the University of North Carolina at Charlotte" would convey to the lay public that the institution was a branch campus, not a freestanding entity in a system in which UNC Chapel Hill, N.C. State, and UNC Greensboro were also freestanding. Part of the problem for Charlotte was its proximity to South Carolina, where campuses such as USC at Spartanburg were indeed branches of the Columbia campus.

To give the Charlotte campus a distinctive identity, the administration turned to Jack Pentes, whose professional design firm agreed to take on the identity program as a pro bono project. Joe Sonderman, then with that firm, was the designer of the first logo. The result was a stylized "UNCC" in a relatively heavy block form. It worked well for a number of years, conveying instant recognition locally and regionally. Later, the consensus was that it didn't mean much outside the region. Another logo was designed to address that problem.

A related identity problem developed in time. It began when Central Piedmont Community College began using the acronym "CPCC." Others in the community college and technical system adopted that style. For example, Guilford Technical Community College became "GTCC."

Thus concern arose that the last two letters, "CC," would cause UNCC to be lumped with all those with a similar acronym. To create the block logo, the institution had stopped using the original hyphen in "UNC-C." But continued use of the hyphen would have prevented the developing problem.

The block-letter design was UNC Charlotte's first logo.

When the switch was made to the block logo, some students even developed a bumper sticker that said, "I lost my hyphen at UNCC." At the time, UNC Charlotte was in good company in using a block type logo. NCNB, later to become NationsBank, used a similar style.

Changing logos, seals, mascots, and other symbols is difficult to accomplish at a university campus. It took until the 1980s for UNC Charlotte to make the next change. Names and logos alone don't make a campus distinctive. One thing that did set UNC Charlotte apart was its active role in creating the environment around itself, particularly in the development of University Research Park, adjacent to its campus.

Although University Research Park was the result of joint efforts by the Charlotte Chamber of Commerce, Addison Reese of NCNB and other bankers, and UNC Charlotte, the community and region were especially fortunate that Colvard was chancellor and was present in the planning.

Colvard had played a role in the development of Research Triangle Park while he was dean of agriculture at N.C. State University. He served on the original Research Triangle Committee, made up of three officials from each of the three Triangle universities—Duke, N.C. State, and UNC Chapel Hill.

Thus he had the background to help with planning for a research park in Charlotte, but even with his experience, it was an enormous leap of faith for Charlotte to begin planning a research park just a year after UNC Charlotte became a campus of the university.

It was clear that the concept could work, based on the experience of Research Triangle Park, which by then was ten years old. But there was Charlotte, building on a connection to just one university, and an infant one at that, when the other park was built on the base of three well-established and internationally known universities.

Had Charlotte not moved forward when it did, however, University Research Park might never have developed even after UNC Charlotte gained maturity as a university. Attempts later to build research parks elsewhere in the nation became so competitive that one expert in the field said in the early 1980s, "If you don't already have one, it's too late to start now." Based on the number of parks around the nation that existed in name only, he was right. Years later, there were still dreamers out there who hoped that one day a major tenant would want to locate in "You-Name-It State University Research Park."

The other amazing aspect of University Research Park is that it was almost totally an entrepreneurial venture. There were no state start-up funds. The park was begun with borrowed money put up by Charlotte's major banks for the purchase of the first tracts of land.

The original concept was that University Research Park would link UNC Charlotte and Davidson. Once again, though, Davidson officials indicated that they were sticking with their mission of maintaining a small but excellent liberal arts college. Participation in a research park venture didn't fit that profile, and Davidson opted out. Had it participated, Davidson would have been a beneficiary of part of the endowment created by the park. The college's withdrawal from planning left UNC Charlotte as the sole beneficiary of the park.

Whatever assets had been created and left over after the park was totally built out were to become part of UNC Charlotte's endowment. At one point in the early 1990s, Rusty Goode, president of University Research Park, estimated that if the unsold land and other assets were liquidated, UNC Charlotte might benefit at that point in the amount of about $30 million, a sizable addition to an endowment.

With the exception of a few hundred thousand dollars it accepted for special needs, UNC Charlotte administrators encouraged the park board to plow back funds generated by sale of appreciated land. Those funds were used to expand and improve the infrastructure, thereby enhancing the park's appeal for future occupants.

Of course, Colvard was not the only visionary in creating University Research Park. W. T. Harris, a cofounder of the Harris Teeter grocery chain, was president of the Charlotte Chamber of Commerce at the time. His appointment of John Paul Lucas as head of the committee to develop the chamber's program of work led to planning for University Research Park and a second major concept, the development of University City around the campus.

Another whose vision came to the fore again was Reese of NCNB, who had been chairman of the Charlotte College Board of Trustees and was then on the Consolidated University Board of Trustees. His leadership was enough to bring on board the other major banks in loaning funds for the purchase of the first tracts of land for University Research Park. The firm of J. N. Pease Associates created the first master plan for the park's infrastructure.

The first occupants of the park also should be considered farsighted, given that the area was rather rural at the outset. They were Collins & Aikman, Allstate Insurance, and Reeves Brothers. Collins & Aikman broke ground first, on January 11, 1968.

Both Collins & Aikman and Reeves Brothers used portions of their facilities for research functions. During a later recession, Reeves Brothers vacated its park facility and moved its research function back into its manufacturing plants.

Here a discussion of terminology is appropriate. Some critics took issue with using the term "research park," because companies within the park engaged in a wide variety of activities, ranging from pure research to applied research to light manufacturing to data processing and headquarters office functions. Actually, though, University Research Park was much like others that used the terminology.

A French visitor said his nation had found a more appropriate term for such entities as Research Triangle Park and University Research Park—"TechnoPark." Certainly most such parks were technology driven. To call them research parks was perhaps misleading. An expert on the subject said that there was not enough pure research going on in the world to fill up even one major research park. But, of course, University Research Park couldn't afford to abandon the term "research park" while it remained in such vogue around the nation.

The establishment of the research park and some crises on campus brought the City of Charlotte and Mecklenburg County together to solve one critical problem. The growing campus and its demand for water began to exceed the capacity of the wells and storage tanks that had served adequately during the first few years. More than once the campus had to be closed as the tanks were drained dry. Colvard said he learned from that experience that "a lack of water will close a campus quicker than a lack of educational sophistication."

The arrival of city water was such a momentous occasion that Colvard called for a celebration. The result was a "wetting ceremony" in which two students, Earleen Mabry and Dwayne Spitzer, posed as bride and groom. Earleen, a very attractive and popular campus leader, represented Charlotte, and Dwayne, a student leader from Concord, represented Mecklenburg. They symbolized the coming together of city and county. Food service manager Loren Haus, an imposing figure dressed in lederhosen, gave the bride away. Student president Bill Billups conducted the ceremony that united the two. Among the witnesses to the ceremony was Jim Martin, then chairman of Mecklenburg County Commissioners, who played a role in working out arrangements with the city to provide the water. He later would become a U.S. congressman and then North Carolina governor.

Having obtained city water service, the campus received sewer service in 1969–70, when a new treatment plant was built with the aid of partial financial support from the university. That service proved to be another wedge in opening the door to development in the University City area.

Until then, development in Charlotte-Mecklenburg had been one-dimensional, following sewage lines southward out Providence and Carmel and Park Roads toward the South Carolina line. A ridge just south of the UNC Charlotte campus divided drainage, with streams on the other side of that ridge flowing south. Streams north of the ridge flowed northward, and until a sewage treatment facility was built across the ridge there could be little development. A city bond issue allowed the construction of a large water tank near the ridge so that it could feed lines running to the campus and the research park and later to residential developments. Bonds also allowed for the Mallard Creek Treatment Plant, which processed sewage using the northward-flowing streams.

Solving the water and sewer problem was as important to the research park as to the campus. Another urgent need in building the research park was roads. The state of North Carolina had a policy of building them into a major corporation's new site as a locational incentive. The area that was to become University City was fairly well served by four-lane, north-south arteries—US 29 and NC 49—with I-85 and, somewhat later, I-77 on the way. What was needed was an east-west road, intersecting with all the above north-south routes.

Park supporters turned to George Broadrick of First Citizens Bank, who had first helped out in getting legislation approved to create UNC Charlotte. Broadrick had by then become district highway commissioner, and his help led to the building of Harris Boulevard, named for W. T. Harris. Thus the University City area acquired that much-needed major east-west artery, although four-laning of the entire route was not completed until 1995.

An early initiative growing out of planning for University Research Park led to the first University City Plan, as envisioned by Chamber of Commerce leaders. William E. McIntyre was director of the Charlotte-Mecklenburg Planning Commission at the time. He could envision what was ultimately to happen—a satellite city springing up around the university, providing most urban amenities.

A fairly restrictive plan was drawn. In that early version, drawn by planner Dick Hauersperger, a "town center" was to be developed across from UNC Charlotte. It was envisioned to be what University Place was later to become, a mixed-use center for shopping, entertainment, dining, and social gatherings.

A pedestrian overpass would have allowed students to get to and from campus without dodging traffic on busy NC 49. The area was zoned for high-density residential and restrictive "institutional" development, which only allowed such uses as churches, YMCAs, libraries, schools, and similar organizations.

That portion of the plan may have been too restrictive. Later critics felt that some enterprises that catered to students—pubs, delis, bookstores, and other types of hangouts—should have been allowed to locate in closer proximity to where students lived, in order to create a more supportive atmosphere.

The restrictive zoning did, however, protect the community from undesirable developments and preserved the area for a time when critical economic mass would be achieved. In other communities that once had student-friendly streets—like Raleigh's Hillsborough Street, across from N.C. State

University, and to some extent Chapel Hill's Franklin Street—there were up and down cycles in quality.

Leadership in those communities had to intervene to prevent serious deterioration. On the other hand, Tate Street at UNC Greensboro was improved to become almost an integral part of the campus, with enterprises of fairly high quality.

In Charlotte, the vision of a University City was created early, and University Research Park and other projects in the area had rather auspicious beginnings. Yet to bloom into reality, such visionary plans had to await financial feasibility, which was not to come until the 1970s.

The boom was earlier to arrive on the campus itself. Enrollment began to grow rapidly, with a 17 percent increase in 1968. In back-to-back years, 1969 and 1970, student enrollment didn't just increase, it exploded, exceeding 31 percent annually for both years. Likely that was the fastest growth experienced by any university in the nation at the time. At about this time, UNC Charlotte was also surpassing other institutions in terms of visibility in the local media. It was inevitable, of course, because of the growing size and complexity of UNC Charlotte's offerings.

That required a bit of adjustment, but relations among UNC Charlotte and other local institutions were cordial and cooperative. In fact, Vice Chancellor Hugh McEniry took the lead in organizing the Charlotte Area Educational Consortium to make it easier for students at area colleges to take courses at other campuses when they were not available at the home institution. UNC Charlotte was on the receiving end of many of those students because of its greater variety of offerings, but in the early years its students were able to participate in Army ROTC at Davidson College only through the consortium arrangement.

Some of UNC Charlotte's rapid growth could be attributed merely to the filling of the vacuum in higher education that had long existed in Charlotte. But some growth was also generated by recognition in the media.

UNC Charlotte was achieving many "firsts"—the first graduate courses, the first residence halls, the first architecture students, and many others. Most of those led to media coverage, thus gaining exposure for the campus not only in Charlotte but throughout the region. In addition, faculty and students were beginning to achieve personal recognitions, so there were opportunities to herald those accomplishments.

In the late 1960s, for the first time, the community realized that the rosy predictions, made over a period of twenty years, about a real university in Charlotte would become actuality. They could witness it for themselves as the buildings rose and a full-blown campus took shape.

As the university developed, it began to organize the usual campus activities and even to experience a bit of controversy. In 1966 an attempt was made to award an honorary degree to Governor Dan K. Moore to recognize his role in creating UNC Charlotte. Unfortunately, his campaign for the governorship had been very divisive, and many of the faculty members had supported his opponent, Richardson Preyer.

Faculty members refused to approve the degree for Moore. Later, the trustees would in turn refuse the first faculty request to award an honorary degree to controversial author Harry Golden, an early advocate of desegregation. When the degree was rejected, faculty members organized a Harry Golden Day. Some years later, an honorary degree was awarded to Golden, and one of the first two high-rise residence halls was named for Governor Moore.

Because of the controversy, honorary degrees were held in abeyance until 1968. That year, the university issued its first two honorary degrees to Frank Porter Graham, former president of the Consolidated University of North Carolina, and to Addison Reese, chairman of the Charlotte College Board of Trustees at the time of transition to UNC Charlotte. In recognizing Graham, the young campus linked itself to the long history of the University of North Carolina. Unfortunately, by the time of the presentation, Graham had grown ill. His physician sat just off-stage at the commencement ceremony to keep watch on his patient.

It probably took until 1968 for the campus to have the feel of a real university community, particularly in terms of student life. By then a critical mass of student leadership had developed. Volatile times nationally and internationally created intellectual foment.

The war in Vietnam was heating up, with resulting protests, particularly on campuses. African American students were actively pressing their concerns. The real world of crime intruded when a murder-suicide, stemming from a perceived love triangle, took place on the front campus. The campus had its first "hippie" student in John Hostetter, who wore long hair before it was "cool." He drew a large crowd to the campus lake when he announced that he would walk on water. He didn't, but students were nevertheless exposed to a very creative personality.

Campus speakers in 1968 included Henry Kissinger and Senator Barry Goldwater. UNC Charlotte history Professors Dan Morrill and Ed Perzel drew a little local heat when they spoofed the Mecklenburg Declaration of Independence, a document whose authenticity had already been challenged by historians. Another historian, Professor John Robbins, a strong opponent of the war in Vietnam, was becoming active in city politics.

Students created a mystery organization called EMFC, which some took to mean the "Earleen Mabry Fan Club," in recognition of a very active and attractive student. Whatever the meaning, the letters "EMFC" popped up all over campus. Overall, 1968 was a vintage year.

By this point, the city of Charlotte was becoming a financial center, with NCNB beginning the acquisitions that would lead it toward its current status as NationsBank, and with First Union beginning its successful expansions. Thus it became UNC Charlotte's good fortune that one of its first quantifiable measures of quality came in accounting.

Faculty members had said from the beginning that the campus had good students, and professors were providing added value to those who enrolled. In 1967, under the leadership of Chairman Thomas Turner, the accounting program produced its first graduates.

From the beginning, UNC Charlotte accounting graduates performed well on the state CPA examination, and soon they were ranking either first, second, or third. The accounting graduates also began getting top jobs, such as those at what were then the "Big Eight" firms. One of the first graduates, Gary Baucom, was successful early on and eventually became president of Squires Homes, Inc., one of the area's leading home builders. Baucom served as an early president of the Alumni Association and launched a tradition of Alumni Association leadership by accounting alumni. All that success got the attention of the Charlotte business community.

Again, in many ways 1969–70 was a breakthrough year. The master of arts in education degree was approved in English, history, and mathematics, along with a master of education degree for elementary school teachers. By the end of the year, two hundred graduate students had enrolled, removing any doubt that there was a demand for graduate education in Charlotte. The master of management degree (later to become the MBA degree) was also approved, to begin with the fall semester of 1970.

Courses in engineering technology began in September 1969, majors in German and art were launched, and planning was well advanced for majors in religion and music. Planning was continuing for degrees in physical education and fine arts.

Colvard declared that the undergraduate program was being rounded out. Planning was under way for master's degree programs in chemistry, biology, geography, English, history, and mathematics—remarkable activity for an institution that was only five years old as a university.

The campus administration began providing incentives for faculty research projects, using funds from the UNC Charlotte Foundation that covered grants for twenty-seven projects. In addition, a number of faculty members began applying for and receiving grants from such agencies as the National Science Foundation, the National Institutes of Health, and U.S. military branches.

During 1969–70, an event took place that was to give UNC Charlotte much of its public identity. That was the launching of the Urban Institute. Colvard had seen the need for such an entity growing out of his experience with schools of agriculture. He envisioned an organization that would do research and problem-solving for urban communities in ways similar to services provided to rural communities by the agricultural extension services of land-grant universities.

When Colvard took his proposal to the UNC General Administration, however, the chancellors at UNC Chapel Hill and N.C. State weren't willing to allow him to claim the new mission all by himself. They applied for and received funding for their own versions of the Urban Institute. The result essentially was that the funding Colvard anticipated was split three ways. Still, it was a major forward thrust for UNC Charlotte, and ultimately the institutes at the other campuses developed along different paths from that taken by UNC Charlotte.

One of the earmarks of the Urban Institute at UNC Charlotte was its ability to leverage its state appropriation into soft money in terms of grants, along with contracts to do specific projects, and thus create a much larger entity. Beginning with about $250,000 in appropriations, the institute built a budget of about $800,000.

It was a year of significant Greek activity; four men's and four women's social fraternities were organized. Three of the men's groups affiliated with national fraternities—Chi Phi, Kappa Sigma, and Kappa Alpha Psi. The others would affiliate later.

Because of student unrest nationwide, a retreat was held for faculty and student leadership at Chinqua-Penn Plantation, resulting in more student involvement in university affairs.

An innovative new university constitution was created under the leadership of Professor Newton Barnette and then ratified. Previously there had been a separate faculty constitution and student constitution, as was the case at most institutions. This one combined faculty and students into one governing body. It responded to the student concerns of the time—that they help control their destinies.

Unfortunately, the times were such that because of restiveness over the war in Vietnam and civil rights issues, students were not disposed to grapple with the mundane but essential issues of curriculum reviews, scheduling, course approvals, and such other issues necessary to the building of a university. Instead, some of them tended to disrupt and obstruct.

Some advances were made on substantive issues, but the new document was short-lived, and the university had to return to a more traditional Faculty Council, while the students returned to their own student government organization.

One early dream in the area of student affairs was only partially realized. Cone had begun having meetings with Charlotte clergy sometime before the transition to university status. They wanted their denominations to have access to students as the new university developed.

The discussions, along with the need for a chairperson of philosophy and religion, led Cone to invite Loy Witherspoon to return to Charlotte as a professor of philosophy and religion and as campus chaplain in the fall of 1964. Witherspoon had been associate minister of Myers Park Methodist Church in Charlotte before going to Dakota Wesleyan College as a professor.

After his arrival, Witherspoon and Cone formed a plan to create an ecumenical ministry to students and to build a center that would provide a gathering place for students of all faiths and offices for ministers of those faiths. That skirted the legal thicket of church and state issues. Their concept was that the ecumenical ministry and facility would prevent the construction of competing religious centers around the periphery of the campus. The ecumenical ministry was established with the formation in 1967–68 of the United Religious Ministry, which brought together those religious organizations seeking to reach UNC Charlotte students. North Carolina Baptists then assigned the first full-time campus minister, the Reverend Quentin Perreault.

Formation of the United Religious Ministry organization did stop plans by Baptists and Presbyterians to build off-campus ministry centers. But that might have been unfortunate, given that a building for all the faiths never materialized. Space was so short on campus that denominational houses just off campus would have provided much-needed meeting places.

Builder Dwight L. Phillips contributed to the UNC Charlotte Foundation what he believed would be challenge money for constructing such a center. However, no major fund-raising effort followed that would have put together sufficient funds for a building. Eventually, with permission from Phillips's family, his money was used to build outdoor athletic facilities on the campus in an effort to put the funds to work for a needed purpose.

The programming aspects of the United Religious Ministry worked quite well, however. The chaplains from the various faiths were laudatory over the years, noting that the program allowed them to work closely together in serving students rather than competing with each other.

Meanwhile, in 1970 the Alumni Association began maturing and taking on some of the expected roles—soliciting funds and making plans for alumni activities—under the leadership of its president, Gary Baucom. Still, the association was a long way from providing significant advocacy and financial support to the university at that point, just five years after university status had been attained.

By fall 1969, enrollment had reached 3,085, a wide array of undergraduate programs was in place, graduate work had begun, and UNC Charlotte had residential students. The future looked exceedingly bright.

But at about this point, the past came back to haunt the institution. UNC Charlotte had distanced itself from Asheville-Biltmore and Wilmington Colleges. But advocates for those campuses retained a mindset they held when the Carlyle Commission was discussing the future of higher education and considering expansion of the UNC system to geographic areas not then served. The other campus advocates looked at UNC Charlotte as merely getting a jump on their own ambitions. They recalled strategy sessions in which they and Charlotte College advocates had first sought state funding support together.

In his biography of Bill Friday, however, William A. Link pointed out, "Expansion to Charlotte was no more at issue in the Carlyle Commission than was expansion of the community college system. The real question was whether—and how—Asheville and Wilmington might also be added to the system."

Link suggests that Friday held deep-seated reservations about adding the two campuses and that he preferred making them colleges of the University of North Carolina. But the powerful political coalition of East and West brought UNC Asheville and UNC Wilmington into a six-campus UNC system in 1969, four years after UNC Charlotte's admission.

Colvard believed that attitudes toward UNC Charlotte changed overnight. Until 1969, the Charlotte campus was seen as advancing toward full partnership with the three original campuses of the university; at the admission of the two new campuses, UNC Charlotte was dropped back into a package with them.

In fact, the official UNC system history, included in the catalogs of the sixteen campuses, makes no reference to 1965; instead it says, "By 1969, three additional campuses had joined the University through legislative action: the University of North Carolina at Charlotte, the University of North Carolina at Asheville, and the University of North Carolina at Wilmington."

More significant was what expansion did to the other institutions outside the UNC system. Their administrators and supporters were unable to view the admission of UNC Charlotte, in the state's largest city and most populous region, as urgent and necessary for the future economic health of the entire state. Instead, they saw through competitive eyes a campus of 1,800 students jumping out ahead of their own institutions, many of which had been in existence at least seventy-five years and were already offering education through the master's degree.

The competitive struggle led those campuses to seek elevation to university status, but outside the UNC system. East Carolina College, Appalachian State Teachers College, Western Carolina State Teachers College, and North Carolina Agricultural and Technical College all were elevated to regional university status in 1967. Three had been former teachers colleges but began expanding their curricula during the enrollment boom of the 1960s. North Carolina A&T had the distinction of being a land-grant institution, historically serving African American students.

By 1969, the entire existing hierarchy had collapsed, and the remaining four-year colleges also were elevated to university status—Elizabeth City State, Fayetteville State, Winston-Salem State, North Carolina Central, and Pembroke State. Only the North Carolina School of the Arts remained undesignated as a university.

Even more alarming was that in this complete collapse of control over higher education, the legislature granted all of those regional universities the right to establish doctoral programs. They were then under the supervision of the State Board of Higher Education, and there was at least a safety clause that approval of doctoral programs would be subject to that board. Also, the addition of doctoral programs could not take place before 1972.

Five of the nine regional universities thus created were offering the master's degree—Appalachian, East Carolina, A&T, N.C. Central, and Western Carolina. The four others—Elizabeth City, Fayetteville State, Pembroke State, and Winston-Salem State—were offering only the bachelor's degree. The School of the Arts, then in a category by itself, offered the bachelor's degree and also had a program for secondary school students preparing for performing careers.

It was clear that intervention of some sort was needed. As the external turmoil increased, UNC Charlotte continued its steady progress. Colvard said in his 1970–71 annual report that as debate continued about structure, the people at UNC Charlotte concluded that their task was to do a good job of the primary assignment: teaching students.

In 1970–71, E. Daymond Turner was named the first director of graduate studies, a position that later became a deanship. Research grants began to grow; a total of $394,415 was recorded that year. Under the leadership of Librarian Joseph Boykin, construction was well under way on the Dalton Tower addition to the library, along with the largest expansion to date of the book collection. All indicated progress in university-level activities. Facilities completed included the new Rowe Arts Building.

By fall 1970, enrollment had reached 4,068, including 414 graduate students. About a thousand of the students lived in the new residence halls. The one-to-four ratio of students in residence on campus was equivalent to that of many major universities in urban settings—about the same as that at N.C. State, for example. The significance of this statistic was that UNC Charlotte could no longer be legitimately called a commuter school, although it took awhile for that perception to change. Like many other events of those early years, the arrival of a critical mass of residential students marked a turning point in the development of UNC Charlotte.

Still, in spite of Colvard's statement that UNC Charlotte was proceeding with the business at hand, the issue of the structure of the system cast a shadow over it and all other campuses and would eventually have to be addressed.

CHAPTER 6

Becoming One of Sixteen Campuses

IT IS rare for a new university campus to share in historic milestones of a system of much older and larger campuses, but UNC Charlotte had that privilege as the tumult within North Carolina higher education resulted in a totally new structure in the early 1970s.

An expanding universe is the theme of this chapter. It details the expansion of the University of North Carolina from six campuses to sixteen. All state-supported institutions offering four or more years of college work now were incorporated into one system. Chancellor D. W. Colvard and his faculty and staff had to adapt to a different environment, but ultimately they would thrive within it.

It is also the story of athletic glory: UNC Charlotte's basketball team became Cinderella and reached the Big Dance.

Above all, this chapter holds the story of successes by Colvard, UNC Charlotte's first chancellor.

Herein also is the story of a governor who played a major role in sorting out the confused higher education puzzle that emerged as the 1970s began. Governor Robert W. Scott was alarmed that all sixteen state-supported institutions of higher education made equal claim to the state's tax dollars and to their right to offer Ph.D. degrees or whatever programs they wished.

The solution worked out under Scott's leadership—to restructure all campuses in the state into one system—may have been the hallmark of his administration, but it is not likely that he fully understood the challenge when he took office in January 1969. Still, his inaugural words set a tone for the way he was to approach the higher education crisis. He said, "Let the timid, the fainthearted, the foot-draggers, the 'do-nothings' be forewarned. We are going to make progress during this administration."

The son of Governor W. Kerr Scott and nephew of influential state senator Ralph Scott, Robert Scott inherited the family propensity for blunt speaking. They also had in common their roots in farming in the Haw River area.

Kerr Scott was the "good roads" governor who campaigned to pave dirt roads so that farmers could get their crops to market. He also took a great deal of heat from conservatives for appointing UNC system president Frank Porter Graham to the U.S. Senate.

Even after Graham's bitter, unsuccessful campaign for election to a full U.S. Senate term, Scott said that he would appoint him all over again if he had the opportunity. Kerr's brother, Ralph Scott, exercised power beyond his position in the legislature by the force of his personality and insights. Much of his influence was used to improve social programs. He told his colleagues there, "If you don't have much sense, you've got to learn to use your head."

It was out of that family tradition of courage and independence that young Bob Scott took the oath as governor. In his message to the General Assembly, Scott endorsed expansion of higher education, an activity that actually contributed to the uproar over governance. He supported adding UNC Asheville and UNC Wilmington to the UNC system, aiding the historically black institutions, and studying the feasibility of providing state assistance to students at private colleges and universities.

Scott soon became fully aware of the explosive situation in higher education, and on December 13, 1970, he called together at the executive mansion a group of trustees of the senior institutions and the Board of Higher Education. He said the heart of the problem was the lack of a statewide planning and coordinating body.

Coordination of higher education in the state had simply evolved over the years since the 1930s. The first effort was the creation of the Consolidated University of North Carolina in the Great Depression year of 1931. This move brought together UNC Chapel Hill, N.C. State College, and Woman's College in Greensboro. It eliminated some duplication; for example, engineering was moved out of Chapel Hill to N.C. State. It allocated functions. N.C. State was given agriculture, engineering, forestry, architecture, textiles, education, and basic studies. UNC Chapel Hill was allocated liberal arts, professional schools, education, and traditional graduate studies. UNC Greensboro was given home economics, elementary education, and liberal arts.

The next oversight body was created in 1955 as the result of recommendations by a commission headed by Victor Bryant, a powerful longtime UNC system trustee. Out of that commission's recommendations came the Board of Higher Education, an organization that had somewhat limited powers but was charged with overseeing all state-supported institutions of higher education.

During the rapid enrollment growth of the 1960s, programs were added rapidly to the existing campuses, then to the three new campuses. Also begun were specialized programs like water resources research, highway safety research, marine sciences, urban affairs programs, environmental studies, educational television, and nuclear research, among others.

At the time UNC Charlotte was added to the UNC system in 1965, and Asheville and Wilmington in 1969, the six campuses were governed by the hundred-person, legislatively appointed UNC Board of Trustees. Of course, appointing a board of that size provided plenty of opportunities for officials to respond to many political obligations, but a fifteen-member executive committee had to serve as the real power structure of the UNC system. At times there were complaints that the structure relegated the hundred-person board to a role as rubber stamp for Friday and the executive committee.

By fall 1970, restructuring moved to the top of Governor Scott's agenda as he contemplated the lobbying under way by sixteen campuses, all bent on becoming or remaining major universities. He and Friday began discussing the form of a restructured system, only to find that they weren't understanding each other. Throughout the discussions, Friday was clearly intent on preserving the excellence that had been attained in the earlier three-campus Consolidated University. Once the forces of expansion were unleashed, however, he realized that some kind of restructuring was essential.

To resolve the problem, Scott appointed the Governor's Study Committee on Structure and Organization of Higher Education, headed by former state senator Lindsay Warren Jr. of Goldsboro. That committee released its report on May 25, 1971.

The governor then spoke to the General Assembly about the committee's recommendations. The outcome of restructuring partly results from the fact that Scott was an N.C. State alumnus. He showed no deference to UNC Chapel Hill; in fact, he showed hostility and spoke some of the harshest criticisms of the Chapel Hill campus ever to come from a governor. "Let us be honest," he said. "When the Consolidated University leadership speaks of the 'University of North Carolina,' it is harking to the sound of Tar Heel voices—it has reference to the campus at Chapel Hill."

He went on to cite a rigid pecking order. "The agendas, the length of discussions, indeed the attitudes, reflect the fact that most of the attention is given to the campus at Chapel Hill, with the Raleigh campus following close behind but definitely in second place," Scott said. "These two are the older brothers of the university family," he added. "The university at Greensboro is the oldest sister, who is to be admired and protected but is not expected to say or do much and should be subservient to the oldest members of the family," Scott said.

He added, "The campuses at Charlotte, Asheville, and Wilmington are newcomers who have been married into the family. They are, therefore, to be heard, considered, and protected but are not and never will be part of the inner circle—the original three. They are the in-laws of the university. All other institutions in the state are outside the family."

In a report to the Warren committee, Friday gave a more positive report on the University of North Carolina system and the role of its individual institutions. He cited allocation of function that allowed the different campuses to develop strengths in different areas.

UNC Charlotte was being allowed to emphasize urban concerns to serve the needs of the one-fifth of the state's population that lived within commuting distance, he said. He also called attention to plans to cap the enrollments at Chapel Hill and N.C. State and to allow major growth at the newer campuses.

Friday also defended the UNC system's internal controls over the addition of new programs, particularly doctoral programs. "The University of North Carolina at Charlotte, though growing rapidly in size and excellence," he said, "cannot and will not propose any doctoral program until work at the master's level, which has just begun, has developed and has established its graduate productivity at a high quality level." It had also been publicly stated that Asheville and Wilmington would not add doctoral programs in the foreseeable future, Friday indicated.

The majority report of the Warren committee recommended that the two-part system of higher education be replaced by a new statewide planning and coordinating agency to be called "the Board of Regents of the University of North Carolina." A minority recommended that no change be made other than to revise the powers of the Board of Higher Education. The majority report would have allowed each campus to be governed by its own board of trustees but would have significantly strengthened the regents' role as a coordinating body.

To critics who warned of a "deconsolidation" of the university system, Scott asked them to support "reconsolidation" of the entire sixteen campuses. Among those critics were the presidents of the alumni associations of the six campuses of the Consolidated University. Following their attendance at the system's board meeting on May 24, 1971, they issued a statement declaring firm opposition to "dismantling" the Consolidated University.

It was considered too late in the regular legislative session to deal with the restructuring issue, so in October 1971, legislators were called back to deal with the Warren report. In the interim, the governor and legislators did a lot of rethinking about the Warren committee report. There were also various lobbying efforts by institutional supporters. These activities resulted in a revised plan. The plan resulted in a University of North Carolina system incorporating all sixteen campuses under the thirty-two-member Board of Governors. That board, in turn, delegated certain powers to the thirteen-member boards of trustees on each of the sixteen campuses.

The biographer of William C. Friday, William A. Link, said that Friday withdrew from the political part of the fray for fear that a more active role would make the Consolidated University a target. He also suggested that Friday took personally the governor's attacks on the University of North Carolina at Chapel Hill. Link said, however, that Friday worked furiously in the background for UNC positions during the legislative battle.

The resulting restructuring preserved the flagship campuses and favored the UNC approach to management and leadership of higher education in the state. Through his own actions, Friday emerged stronger than ever. And as a stronger Bill Friday appeared, the next question was about who would be the president of the restructured UNC system. Friday emerged as the obvious choice and was pressed to name Cameron West, the former executive director of the Board of Higher Education, as his top associate. The historically African American institutions asked to have Chancellor Marion Thorpe of Elizabeth City State University named to the second spot. Friday named neither.

The rejection of Cameron West essentially marked the end of the struggle between the UNC system forces and the newly merged campuses outside the system, who favored West because they thought he would represent their interests. West was named a vice president for planning in the UNC General Administration but remained there only for a relatively short time.

William C. Friday became the head of the restructured 16-campus UNC system in 1972.

The Bill Friday who emerged was considered more powerful than ever. In fact, on occasions when he was encouraged to run for governor or senator, pundits would invariably ask, "Why should he step down?" Friday himself would later say he had the best job in the state. With Friday as leader, the new structure was ready to be implemented.

The historic first meeting of the new University of North Carolina Board of Governors took place July 7, 1972, on the tenth floor of the Dalton Tower of Atkins Library on the UNC Charlotte campus. Governor Bob Scott presided, as former chair of both the UNC Board of Trustees and the Board of Higher Education and new interim chair of the Board of Governors until the end of December 1972. The first members of the University of North Carolina Board of Governors were sworn in and conducted business at the UNC Charlotte meeting.

That meeting was followed the same day by the first meeting of the new UNC Charlotte Board of Trustees. Many at UNC Charlotte had felt somewhat underrepresented on the hundred-person UNC Board of Trustees, even though leading Charlotteans such as Addison Reese, C. C. Cameron, and Irwin Belk were on it. Those who had been dissatisfied thus were pleased to have their own board again.

Governor Robert W. Scott (left) presides at the historic first meeting of Board of Governors on UNC Charlotte campus in 1972.

Addison Reese, who was serving as chairman of the Charlotte College Board of Trustees at the time it transferred authority to the UNC Board of Trustees, became chair of the new UNC Charlotte Board. At this stage in UNC Charlotte's history, the tall, intent banker was probably the institution's most influential community leader.

Reese had come down from Baltimore to head American Commercial Bank, which he turned into North Carolina National Bank and then NCNB. He contributed his services to UNC Charlotte at a time when he was laying the groundwork for the growth and expansion of NCNB. His legacy ultimately became NationsBank, which would later rank among the nation's three, four, or five largest banks, with headquarters in Charlotte. Reese's ambitions for his bank were similar to his ambitions for UNC Charlotte. So bank board chairman and campus were a good fit.

Reese had maintained close contact and strongly supported the Charlotte campus even while serving seven years on the UNC board. During that period, Reese exerted his influence and leadership primarily through service on the UNC Charlotte Foundation board. For example, in 1968 he and his bank had established the NCNB Award for Excellence in Teaching.

As the process of appointing members to the UNC system Board of Governors began, not all who wished to sit on that board could be accommodated. Those who weren't appointed were assigned to one of the boards of the sixteen campuses. Some were deeply disappointed not to be directly affiliated with the UNC Chapel Hill campus or the Board of Governors.

Another impact of the reassignments was that administrators at some of the other campuses of the system were to complain that they got political appointees, while UNC Charlotte got movers and shakers from the business world.

Indeed, UNC Charlotte found itself with a very strong board, a tradition that continued over the years. In addition to Reese, it included N. K. Dickerson, a Monroe contractor, as vice chair; Betty Dorton Thomas of Concord, a member of the Charlotte College board at transition time, as secretary; Thomas Belk of the Charlotte mercantile family; C. C. Cameron, chief executive of First Union Bank; Frank H. Crowell, a hospital administrator from Lincolnton; Edwin Duncan Sr., chief executive of Northwestern Bank, of Sparta; James A. Hardison Jr., a banker from Wadesboro; Amos N. Johnson of Garland; Thomas H. Leath, a Rockingham attorney and chair of the search committee that had recommended Colvard as the first chancellor; Patrick R. Spangler, a contractor from Shelby; and John B. Stedman, chief executive of Republic Bank of Charlotte. In addition, UNC Charlotte's student government president, Roland Gentry, served as an ex officio member, and Juanita Sims, secretary to the chancellor, served as assistant secretary.

Interesting sidelights to that first board were that Betty Dorton Thomas was the daughter of Dr. J. S. Dorton, who headed the state fair in Raleigh for many years and who had owned property near the UNC Charlotte campus where a fair had been held many years earlier. Her brother, Sib Dorton, was a member of the UNC General Administration. Patrick Spangler was a relative of C. D. Spangler Jr., who would later become president of the UNC system.

Several terms expired right away, and the 1973 board changed somewhat, with members Belk, Cameron, Crowell, Dickerson, Hardison, Leath, and Reese continuing. New members were Mrs. Mary Jarrett Adair of Newton; F. Douglas Biddy, an alumnus, of Durham; Dr. William Bluford, a retired African American educator from Johnson C. Smith University in Charlotte; John L. Fraley Sr. of Cherryville, who had been a member of the Charlotte College Board at transition; Margaret King, a leader of the Republican Party in Mecklenburg County, a cousin of the distinguished North Carolina novelist Reynolds Price, and the new secretary of the board; and Richard B. Butterfield, a student from Canada, as the ex officio member from student government. Again it was a powerful board.

Dickerson was an interesting trustee to observe. He brought great expertise from the business world, but it was in the hardnosed area of contracting, primarily road building. He didn't quite approve of tenure for professors and the various layers of appeal open when they had a grievance. He often said, "I feel if you don't like the way they are performing, just fire them. That's the way we do it in the business world." Dickerson was strongly committed to UNC Charlotte, however, and overall was an effective trustee. Often he brought a needed real-world perspective to the proceedings. Fraley would later be replaced on the board by his son, John L. Fraley Jr., an alumnus.

With restructuring and new boards in place, UNC Charlotte was poised to move toward its appropriate role as a full-fledged university in the state's largest city, the only state university in the populous Southern Piedmont region.

In 1965, UNC Charlotte had been poised to become a coequal partner to UNC Chapel Hill, N.C. State, and UNC Greensboro in a four-campus system. The addition of UNC Asheville and UNC Wilmington in 1969 tended to position UNC Charlotte as just one of the three new campuses. Now UNC Charlotte was perceived by some as just one of sixteen campuses.

Friday later viewed the situation differently. He said he believed UNC Charlotte fared better as one of sixteen campuses than it would have fared among the three original campuses, where it would always have been seen as the newcomer. It ultimately emerged as the fourth largest of sixteen rather than the smallest and newest of four.

While all of the maneuvering was taking place at the state level, the vision on campus among faculty, administrators, and students of a major metropolitan university never wavered. They determined that they would just work harder so that destiny could not be denied.

The hunger of the Charlotte region for graduate work is illustrated by the rapid growth of the programs at UNC Charlotte. In May 1970, one master's degree was awarded; in May 1971, 23 were awarded; and in May 1972, 116 were awarded. Enrollment in graduate programs had grown to five hundred by fall 1971.

Its dedication to regional needs began to make UNC Charlotte indispensable to the leadership of Charlotte and Mecklenburg and surrounding cities and counties. An early revelation of the substantial impact UNC Charlotte would have on the region came by way of the *Metrolina Atlas* (1972), edited by Professors James W. Clay and Douglas M. Orr Jr. and published by the University of North Carolina Press, with chapters written by a number of faculty members. The first really major project of the UNC Charlotte Urban Institute, under the leadership of Norman Schul, the atlas became an invaluable tool to Charlotte area business, civic, and governmental leaders.

A book review in *North Carolina Magazine* in August 1972 said, "The book represents a star in the crown of the youthful University of North Carolina at Charlotte and its recently created Institute for Urban Studies and Community Service." The reviewer added, "One of the principal arguments for the establishment of an urban public university at Charlotte in 1965 was the service such an institution could provide for that largest metropolitan and economic region of North Carolina. In the project which produced 'Metrolina Atlas,' the university and the institute have acquitted themselves admirably."

With chapters on the region's history, environment, population, industry, transportation and utilities, communication, trade and finance, politics, education, and cultural amenities, the atlas provided area citizens with graphic evidence that a major metropolitan region was developing around the central city of Charlotte. Until the advent of the atlas, many citizens of Charlotte referred to the city as a town and failed to understand its ranking among major American cities. The *Atlas*'s publication marked a breakthrough and paved the way for "regionalism" as an approach to planning for Charlotte-Mecklenburg and the surrounding counties.

As a result of the information provided by the *Atlas*, those who marketed Charlotte were able to attract new business and industry based on the true demographics of the region. This kind of information also was to lead ultimately to the acquisition of two professional teams, the NBA Charlotte Hornets and the NFL Carolina Panthers.

Publication of the *Atlas* enhanced the images of the Urban Institute and the Department of Geography, which provided much of the technical expertise for producing the maps and graphs that made the book such a dramatic and useful tool.

The *Metrolina Atlas* was followed in 1975 by the *North Carolina Atlas*, edited by Clay, Orr, and Al Stuart, and again comprising contributions by UNC Charlotte professors as well as experts from other institutions. Governor James Holshouser wrote the foreword. Rod Cockshutt, then Sunday editor of the *News and Observer* of Raleigh, said in a review, "Now we have the 'North Carolina Atlas,' which applied the same format techniques to the entire state that the 'Metrolina Atlas' did to the Charlotte area. The result is a triumph, the creation of a reference work on nearly all aspects of life in North Carolina. Not only is the book crammed with useful statistical information and detail. It is also a joy to behold and read."

Another professor beginning to affect the Charlotte area's understanding of its political dynamics was Schley Lyons, who in 1972 published a study called "Citizen Attitudes and Metropolitan Government: City-County Consolidation in Charlotte." That study was important on several occasions over the years as Charlotte and Mecklenburg County studied the issue of consolidation. Lyons also launched a long-running series of summer workshops for teachers, the Robert A. Taft Institute, which provided insights on America's two-party system of government. As a result of these activities, Lyons began to be called frequently by members of the news media to interpret political trends and events. His impartial and dispassionate insights helped citizens of the community understand political issues, adding to the perspective provided by the news media. Later Lyons was called on by reporters from national networks and newspapers to interpret North Carolina political races of nationwide interest.

Another political scientist, Ted Arrington, made an impact with a different style. His colleagues noted that Arrington was the master of the "pithy quote."

Academic programs also had an impact on the community. At its beginning, a new program in criminal justice functioned much like the engineering technology program in that it took graduates of community college criminal justice programs and gave them the final two years toward a bachelor's degree. Later the program was adjusted to allow students to begin the program in the freshman year at UNC Charlotte as well. As crime became an increasing concern of citizens, faculty members in criminal justice helped provide needed insights.

To provide students with a leadership and experiential learning opportunity similar to that offered by Outward Bound programs, Vice Chancellor Orr led in establishing the Venture program. It offered physical challenges such as rock climbing, ropes courses, canoeing and whitewater rafting, and hiking to help create self-confidence and team-building skills. This was the first adaptive program of Outward Bound. Several university administrators, including Orr, Hoyle Martin of Continuing Education, and Sam Simono of the Counseling Center, participated in an Outward Bound experience to understand the new program. Dot Jackson, a columnist for the *Charlotte Observer*, also went along with my encouragement. Unfortunately, she injured an ankle in swinging over an obstacle on a rope.

In addition to academic and organized student activities, there were informal programs. Students may not have been aware of their opportunities, but their ability to attend live public addresses by major national figures was greater in the early 1970s than would be the case in the 1980s and 1990s. The escalating fees charged by prominent figures put them out of reach in the later years.

Among those appearing on campus in 1972–73 were U.S. Senator Robert Dole, later to become a candidate for the U.S. presidency; U.S. Senator George McGovern, who had already lost a presidential bid; U.S. Secretary of Agriculture Earl Butz, who later had to resign that post because he told an imprudent joke; Dick Gregory, an African American comedian and Vietnam War opponent; CBS correspondent Charles Kuralt, a Charlottean; Elizabeth Sewell, poet; Raymond Hull, coauthor of *The Peter Principle*; and Eliot Wigginton, editor of the *Foxfire Book* series.

High-caliber entertainers that later would have been financially out of the university's reach, including Jimmy Buffett and Gordon Lightfoot, appeared on campus in the Rathskeller. Comedian Steve Martin, then little known, appeared and led a snake dance out the door of the Rathskeller and across the campus. Another comedian who appeared and later achieved success was Robin Williams. It helped UNC Charlotte, of course, that these entertainers had not yet become superstars.

These big-name speakers and talented entertainers helped to give a collegiate atmosphere to the campus, which continued its steady growth. An enrollment milestone was reached in the fall of 1972: just seven years after attaining university status, the campus passed the 5,000 student mark.

By now the campus had been in existence long enough to experience some resignations and retirements. Changes in leadership positions in 1972–73 included the appointment of Hoyle Martin as coordinator for extension and continuing education. Martin later left the university to lead the city housing authority, become a city council member, and, in 1995, run for mayor of Charlotte.

Dr. William A. Davis Jr. was appointed the first director of the Brocker Health Center, but he died in an airplane crash a short time later. Louis W. Moelchert Jr. was appointed vice chancellor for business affairs to replace

Silas M. Vaughn, who became president of Montreat-Anderson College. After a brief stay, Moelchert moved to the University of Richmond as vice president for business.

Marinell Jernigan became dean of nursing to replace the retiring Edith Brocker, who had organized the college. The Department of Philosophy and Religion was divided into two departments; James D. (Bill) Shoemaker became the first chairperson of philosophy, and Loy Witherspoon, who had headed the combined department, became chairperson of the newly renamed Department of Religious Studies.

Because the level of salaries allocated didn't allow Colvard to bring in many senior administrators or professors, he created an apprenticeship program of his own by bringing bright young people into his office as his executive assistants. After two or three years they were placed in key positions in the university.

Larry Owen came to the campus from Kentucky state government in the early years. He later assisted Paul Miller during the planning project and then moved to the Urban Institute before leaving to take a position in the administration of Governor Jim Hunt and later as business manager of the UNC Center for Public Television.

Julian Mason left the office to serve for a number of years as chairman of the English Department and as a strong advocate for Atkins Library's expansion in the general book collection as well as in the acquisition of rare books and artifacts. He continued as a productive scholar as well, particularly in the works of Phillis Wheatley, the first published African American poet in the United States.

Douglas M. Orr Jr. became vice chancellor for student affairs and later vice chancellor for research and public service. He also continued his scholarship through the Geography Department, contributing to the several atlases produced there. One of his most significant accomplishments was his work with James W. Clay in creating University Place.

Benjamin Romine left the chancellor's office to head what was later known as the Office of Academic Planning and Institutional Research. He later left the university to open a private practice in counseling.

Earl Backman, a political scientist, became the first director of the International Studies Program. He made a major contribution to the area by alerting Charlotte to the fact that it was becoming an international city with a booming population of internationals, including leaders of the growing number of international business firms, refugees from places like Eastern Europe and Vietnam, and immigrants. He and his assistant, Marian Beane, organized the first International Festival on the campus in 1975. For the first time, longtime Charlotte residents had an opportunity to rub shoulders with members of the growing international community and sample their cultures.

The colorful festival drew to the campus members of forty or so international communities; they showcased the foods, dance, art, music, costumes, and other aspects of their native lands. Backman later left to become a dean at Northern Arizona University.

William Steimer continued to wear the dual hats of university attorney and executive assistant to the chancellor during the Colvard years, but later he would give up the assistant's role to concentrate on the university attorney role as the campus became a more litigious place. Steimer had to handle cases ranging from tort claims for damaged pantyhose to charges involving failure to obtain reappointment, promotion, or tenure, and sexual and racial harassment. Steimer, who was tall and, at the time, heavyset (later on, through a diet and exercise regime he became a slender shadow of his former self), also habitually defused any tension with somewhat self-deprecating lawyer jokes.

Colvard understood the importance of keeping the public information officer informed so that I could in turn keep the campus community and the public informed. He said he learned the importance of that policy at Mississippi State University during some tumultuous events there. Thus he had me sit in on executive staff meetings and attend retreats.

Another Colvard management-teaching technique was to take the vice chancellors, the deans, and other members of the executive staff on summer planning retreats around the state, with stops at other North Carolina university campuses. Those visits provided insights and understanding important to the management team at a developing institution. It also provided insights into different management styles.

At East Carolina, the group was welcomed to the chancellor's residence, then occupied by Leo Jenkins. It was not surprising that his home was something of a shrine. The hallway walls were covered with photographs of Jenkins posing with every major dignitary who visited that campus. A sitting room was decorated with student-produced portraits and busts of Jenkins. Perhaps that type of personality was essential to Jenkins's success in using political campaigning to uplift a campus that had been disdained by the old-line universities.

On the other hand, on the grounds of the chancellor's home at Western Carolina in Cullowhee, the group was introduced to Chancellor Cotton Robinson's hounds. The group knew Robinson's brother, Jay Robinson, as superintendent of Charlotte-Mecklenburg Schools and later as a vice president in the UNC system. Both men had retained some of the twang of their mountain speech—they had grown up in the shadow of Mount Mitchell.

The retreats also provided insights into the dynamics of UNC Charlotte personalities in a way that was not apparent in formal meetings back on campus. At a retreat at the Grove Park Inn in Asheville, one dean became so upset with his own representation of his college's interests that he shut himself up in his room. Another overindulged at a social hour and rendered himself ineffective during the following session. At a retreat in Boone, a participant fell asleep in a very comfortable but tilting chair and toppled over backward with a noisy crash that revitalized a drowsy afternoon session.

Even though her reluctant retirement in spring 1973 created a major leadership change, Bonnie Cone assured some continuity by not severing her ties. It was clear that she was not ready to retire, but President Friday had already approved for her one additional year beyond the traditional sixty-five-year retirement age for senior executives of the university. Cone continued her service to the university as liaison officer between the UNC Charlotte Foundation and the campus. In that capacity she continued courting potential donors and soliciting new ones.

That retirement did allow the university to acknowledge her role as its founder and to honor her with the naming of the Cone University Center—an appropriate tribute, given her commitment to students. At the time of the naming, it was announced that Cone Center would be enlarged to make it at the time the largest building on campus; a 40,000-square-foot addition would soon expand it to almost 100,000 square feet. At the dedication of the Bonnie E. Cone University Center on June 29, 1973, Governor Jim Holshouser, who gave the dedicatory address, declared it "Bonnie Cone Day" in the State of North Carolina.

Cone's retirement set the stage for Doug Orr to succeed her and to commit his career toward administration—combined with a strong mix of teaching, research and publishing, and public service. By 1973–74, Colvard was again concerned about planning. Pressure on the university to provide programs was building. In 1972, the university received 340 unsolicited requests for graduate study in areas not currently served.

Even though the library had grown to 163,000 volumes by 1973, that was not sufficient for a campus of the size and complexity of UNC Charlotte. The nursing program had grown from seven students in 1965 to 270 and the faculty from one director to 13 faculty members.

Physical plant expansion was continuing in 1972–73. In addition to two high-rise residence halls, housing a total of a thousand students, construction was under way on two more, to house another thousand. Preparation was also under way for the $2 million expansion of the Cone University Center. Those projects were to be paid for from student rentals and fees.

After planning it for some time, the university received approval from the 1973 legislature for an earth and life science building to cost $4.6 million. Various other small projects, such as roads and landscaping, also were under way.

Colvard was pushing the planning for a high-rise office-classroom building as well, because the shortage of classroom space would continue even after the earth and life sciences building was completed. Colvard believed that the campus should make a statement with a tall building—a tower of learning. However, that plan was later amended to include three low-rise buildings, because such a tall building presented the problems of obtaining adequate financing in any one session of the legislature and of transporting students up and down elevators between classes.

To help with physical plant planning, the Texas firm of Caudill, Rowlett and Scott (CRS) was engaged. Felix Joyner, vice president for business affairs in the UNC General Administration, provided a special allocation to cover the cost. That firm's planning process required also that the university's colleges and other units do an academic master plan, because those requirements would drive the physical master plan.

Department chairs met for planning in a three-day retreat just across the river, in a Gastonia motel. There was much joking about that, since the deans, vice chancellors, and chancellor met for their retreat in a much swankier spot—the Broyhill Center at Boone. To facilitate their planning, the chairs had the assistance of Fred Foulkes of the Graduate School of Business at Harvard. Getting away from the telephones assisted both groups in taking stock of how far the university had come in a short time and where it might go next.

Another aspect of planning had to do with compiling a new tenure document, which was required because of the merger of the sixteen campuses into one system. William Keast, chair of the Commission on Academic Tenure in Higher Education, was brought to the campus as a consultant on that document.

From those planning tasks, the academic community then had to turn toward preparing the Five-Year Plan requested by the newly restructured UNC General Administration.

Among the goals stemming from the academic planning were such objectives as encouraging intellectual learning rather than skills development, expanding community involvement, establishing research programs, orienting programs toward an urbanizing society, and making programs international.

Physical plant plans arising from the CRS plan were the establishment of people places on campus; the construction of an urban-type campus in a rural setting to maximize space use, efficiency, and energy and land conservation; and the creation of a campus appearance like that of a small city ringed by forests, lakes, fields, and streams. The plan suggested a ceremonial entrance to give visitors a sense of arrival. Vehicular and pedestrian traffic were to be separated.

While all the planning activities were taking place, growth was still exploding. From the high of 31 percent for a couple of years, it was down to about 19 percent in the fall of 1973, but in raw numbers, the enrollment grew from 5,159 in 1972 to 6,123 in the fall of 1973. The addition of a thousand students meant, in essence, that UNC Charlotte added the equivalent of a small, private liberal arts college in one year.

The university was able to initiate new master's degrees in biology, chemistry, and geography in the fall of 1973.

All of the academic planning might have been a highlight for Vice Chancellor Hugh McEniry. He had set a high standard for academic administration at UNC Charlotte. His integrity was almost universally respected, even by those who disagreed with him.

His insistence upon a strong liberal arts core for the university stood it in good stead as the professional colleges began to grow and wield a great deal of influence in succeeding years. Leaders in the professional areas might have reshaped the institution into an institute of technology or some other structure if not for the strong university base built under McEniry's leadership.

McEniry and his wife, Mary, never quite lost their "small liberal arts institution" approach, having moved to Charlotte from Florida's Stetson University. McEniry organized a social time with students during which he engaged them in educational, literary, philosophical, and even religious debate. (He was a dedicated Baptist layman.) Those sessions had a lasting impact on the participants, including R. T. Smith, later to become a published poet at Auburn University, and Bud Stewart, later to become a contractor in Charlotte.

Hugh and Mary built a home on several acres of land north of the city in an area that was then relatively undeveloped but later lay in the midst of a building boom. It became their refuge from campus pressures and the bustle of urban life.

Through McEniry's encouragement, the university adopted a statement of university values that embodied his belief in the worth of each person as an individual. It said, "In its relationship with students, faculty and staff members, alumni and the public, the university treats each person as an individual, respecting differences and guaranteeing individual rights of citizenship." He firmly believed these words.

McEniry's academic leadership was widely recognized off campus—in the Charlotte area, through his influence on the structure of the Charlotte Area Educational Consortium. Around the state it was recognized because of his impact on the North Carolina Association of Colleges and Universities, which later annually honored outstanding North Carolina leaders in higher education by presenting them with the Hugh McEniry Award. Winners included Colvard, Cone, and Friday.

Tragically, McEniry was not to see his efforts at UNC Charlotte come to full fruition. After restructuring, a new chancellor at Western Carolina had clashed so severely with his faculty that Friday had to remove him to the General Administration building until he could relocate out of state. Then, in

September 1973, Friday appointed McEniry as acting chancellor of Western Carolina to calm the troubled waters there. Colvard asked, "Why take someone from UNC Charlotte when the campus is already so shorthanded?" Friday replied that McEniry was the best he could find anywhere to perform the task at hand.

The stress at Western Carolina apparently proved too great for McEniry, who had suffered a mild heart condition shortly after arriving in Charlotte. After moving to Cullowhee he suffered a serious heart attack and had to undergo rehabilitation.

Meanwhile, Philip Hildreth, distinguished professor of biology and dean of the College of Science and Mathematics, was appointed acting vice chancellor at UNC Charlotte, and Sherman Burson, the Charles H. Stone Professor of Chemistry and chair of that department, was named acting dean to replace Hildreth.

McEniry returned to work at UNC Charlotte in March, but he suffered another heart attack and died on March 15, 1974. To fill the gap left by McEniry's death, Colvard appointed Hildreth to the position of vice chancellor for academic affairs. But just as he did when he appointed Paul Miller during an earlier critical juncture, Colvard felt that he needed another seasoned university veteran to help during the continuing planning process.

Colvard found the new leader in Frank Graves Dickey and appointed him the university's first provost. Dickey brought outstanding credentials as a former president of the University of Kentucky and was executive director of the National Commission on Accrediting at the time of his appointment at UNC Charlotte. He had also served as executive director of the Southern Association of Colleges and Schools. As in the case of Paul Miller, the presence of Frank Dickey instilled confidence in a still-young faculty and reassured them that despite the loss of McEniry, the campus would still have connections to the greater academic world. Dickey served in a similar way as a mentor, advising and encouraging developing professors.

Unfortunately, the role of provost had not been fully defined before Dickey's appointment. He found relatively little to do except to be a mentor, and as a result he grew somewhat restless. Officially, Dickey was to coordinate the activities of the offices of academic affairs and student affairs. But in reality, Colvard continued as the overall administrator of the campus, Hildreth assumed the day-to-day academic leadership, and Doug Orr directed student affairs. Some activities directly under academic affairs—the Computer Center, the Research and Contracts Office, and the library—were placed under the provost's office. But most of those programs had a life of their own under their directors, and Dickey found little need for daily oversight.

But Dickey, like Miller, was an invaluable asset to a young and rapidly developing campus. Other senior leaders had limited time to meet with and advise individual young faculty members. Dickey, a tall man with graying hair, a wide smile, and a firm handshake, welcomed all to his office and patiently shared what things were like in the outside academic community. His walls were covered with an impressive accumulation of plaques and photographs from his own illustrious career.

Even with the most impressive of credentials, not all administrators appointed in the early years lived up to their potential, perhaps through no fault of their own but through a mismatch of talents and position. One such leader was James L. Cox, who was appointed director of the Urban Institute in 1974 in order to allow Norman Schul to devote full time to his position as dean of the College of Social and Behavioral Sciences. Cox came to the university from a position as executive director of the Council of University Institutes for Urban Affairs, and his leadership should have helped place UNC Charlotte's Urban Institute in the forefront of such organizations nationally.

UNC Charlotte's Urban Institute, however, had been conceived as an applied organization, helping solve the urban problems of its region, in much the same way that UNC Chapel Hill's Institute of Government had solved the governmental problems of cities and counties across the state. Cox's vision, however, was of an academic unit, teaching courses in urban subjects and preparing students for careers in the field. The misfit between long-held vision and Cox's individual concepts led to his departure after only a short time.

As a result of taking the university's pulse during the planning process and seeing the continued climb in enrollment to 6,656, Colvard declared at the tenth convocation address in the fall of 1974, "It seems an appropriate time to declare that we are no longer an emerging university. Though not yet fully developed, we are a university in fact." Events bore out Colvard's assessment as the institution began to act more and more like a university. The year 1973–74 again saw distinguished speakers visit the campus—U.S. Representative Morris K. Udall of Arizona; author and television producer Rod Serling; Dr. Sam Keen, consulting editor for *Psychology Today*; Immanuel Velikovsky, author of *Worlds in Collision*; and Senator Mark Hatfield of Oregon.

At the 1974 commencement, the university awarded an honorary doctorate to Senator Sam Ervin Jr., a North Carolina son who was best known nationally for his role in the Watergate hearings, which led to the resignation of President Richard Nixon. The June 3, 1974, issue of *Time* magazine used this excerpt from the honorary degree citation: "When it seemed there was little integrity left, his statesmanship captured the nation's imagination."

In 1975, the university quietly acknowledged its tenth anniversary with the publication of a ten-year report. The introduction asked, "In an age when the distinction between past, present and future becomes blurred, is it possible that an institution can become a university in a mere 10 years? We believe that we can document one such transition in these pages—the coming of age of the University of North Carolina at Charlotte."

Other universities in metropolitan settings had also developed rapidly in the post–World War II era, but the number of such institutions was a relatively small percentage of the total of three thousand or so colleges and universities in the nation.

An outward stamp of approval on the quality achieved in such a short period of time was the national accreditation of individual programs. During 1974–75, accreditation was obtained for professional engineering and engineering technology by the Engineers' Council for Professional Development, and in nursing by the National League for Nursing.

Another milestone was achieved when the College of Architecture graduated its first class with the Bachelor of Arts in Architecture degree at the May 1975 commencement and accepted its first students for the Bachelor of Architecture degree—a fifth-year program. Even so early in its history, the College of Architecture had become a highly selective program within the overall university admissions program. For the fall of 1974, it accepted only sixty-two students from more than three hundred applicants. Moreover, its applicants were somewhat evenly spread from over the nation, whereas the majority of the overall institutional applicants were from the region and the state despite a growing out-of-state applicant pool.

The university launched its first attempt at an off-campus center on the campus of Queens College and enrolled some two hundred students in eight classes. Unfortunately, that action and some discussion about purchasing Queens College dormitories to accommodate UNC Charlotte's exploding enrollment for a time had a chilling effect on relations with that institution. Queens College was struggling at the time, with enrollment losses, a reduction in its faculty, and other cost-saving moves. Those events came at a time of dire predictions for the future of most small, private liberal arts colleges.

UNC Charlotte's initiatives may have helped save Queens, however. The college had powerful friends among the community's leadership elite, and there was some resentment that the upstart university would be making overtures toward this venerable Myers Park institution. Friends of Queens College thus grew determined that they would save the college. As a result, the Queens trustees brought in an aggressive new president, Billy Wireman, who set about saving it by creating an innovative evening and continuing education program and adding computer training and ultimately a graduate business program. With some leverage from those moves, Wireman also was able to save the institution's small, liberal arts component.

As UNC Charlotte withdrew the off-campus center at Queens, it discovered how difficult it would be to reestablish such a center. Not until 1995 did the university succeed in launching a full-fledged center in CityFair in the center city of Charlotte, even though during the intervening years there were attempts at the old Mutual Savings and Loan Building and at the old Federal Reserve Building. Part of the problem was the General Administration's reluctance to approve and support off-campus centers, even though they are a common component of many metropolitan universities. Other UNC system institutions also offer their programs at off-campus locations. Unless they are officially sanctioned by the UNC General Administration, though, the full cost of instruction and operation has to be charged to the students; the state subsidies available for on-campus instruction are not provided.

In another important arena, UNC Charlotte did extend its influence off-campus. It was out front in library networking and later in computerizing its card catalog and otherwise using computer technology to track acquisitions and manage information about the collection. Under the leadership of librarian Joe Boykin, the Atkins Library was linked to the Southeastern Library Network and through it to the Ohio College Library Center (OCLC), a national library network. Those links enabled UNC Charlotte scholars to tap into library resources across the nation and later around the world. Catalogues of distant libraries could be searched, and in many cases books and manuscripts from those collections could be borrowed. It was fortunate for a young university with developing researchers that these opportunities opened so early in the university's history. And the library crossed another milestone in its book collection in 1974–75, reaching 207,536 volumes. Boykin's leadership in library technology later led to his being lured away by Clemson University.

Even with all the progress noted, it was sad commentary on society that the way colleges and universities came to the attention of a great mass of people only marginally interested in higher education was through athletics. By the mid-1970s, Colvard had acted on his vision of the role athletics would play at the new university.

Colvard understood the impact sports could have as a rallying point for the student body and the alumni, yet he was determined that he would not allow the distortion to a developing university that football could create, given its requirements for huge investments in cash and administrative attention. Colvard's conclusion was that basketball should be the centerpiece of an athletic program at UNC Charlotte because of the sport's visibility in North Carolina and because of his own experiences with basketball at N.C. State and Mississippi State. Coach Everett Case at N.C. State had made basketball the North Carolina mania after arriving from Indiana, which had a strong basketball tradition. And it was Colvard's courage at Mississippi State in sending his team to play against an integrated team in the NCAA playoffs that brought him national acclaim.

To build the program at UNC Charlotte, in 1969 Colvard hired Bill Foster to develop it from the non-scholarship-athlete base established by Harvey Murphy. Colvard asked Murphy to continue coaching for a year while Foster organized and recruited a team. The athletic program was accepted as a member of the NCAA beginning with the 1970–71 season.

Foster was a tall, lean man with dark curly hair and an "aw, shucks" personality that belied the inner drive and competitiveness that burned within and gnawed at his innards. A native of Hemingway, South Carolina, Foster attended Wingate College and graduated cum laude from Carson-Newman College, starting at forward for both schools. After an injury he began his coaching as an assistant at Carson-Newman.

Foster returned to South Carolina to coach at Marion High School, where he compiled a 42–21 record. He left high school coaching to earn a master's degree at the University of Tennessee. His college coaching began at Shorter College, where he had one of the most successful programs among small colleges, compiling a record of 110–31. His teams averaged twenty-two victories a season against six losses. He left Shorter in 1969 to become an assistant at The Citadel, where he remained until coming to UNC Charlotte.

Coach Foster enjoyed almost immediate success. His records in his first two seasons were 15–8 and 14–11. He had an ability to find high-quality players that had been overlooked by top teams. One of his first stars was Robert Earl Blue III of Concord. Blue was a wonderful pure shooter. Foster said he had never seen a better one. The factor that caused Blue to be overlooked by the major teams, even with a scoring average of 26.5 points, was that he was, frankly, skinny.

Looking at Blue, one recalled the story former Wake Forest University coach Bones McKinney told on himself, about how he turned to basketball because when he went out for football, the coach saw him standing sideways, and McKinney's body was so thin the coach was afraid McKinney would cut somebody if he put him in a game.

Foster put Blue on all kinds of weight-gain programs, with little success. Still, though, Blue was able to put the basketball in the hoop, and remarkably, he withstood the pounding he took from much heavier players. Foster had a high-quality player, Norris Day, left from the nonscholarship team, and he also recruited a good guard in Rick Dobson of Greer, South Carolina.

One of Foster's players of that era—Jon Heath—had seemingly great potential but lacked consistency. Occasionally Heath would steal the ball on one end of the court and take a few strides to score on the other end. In one of the blowout games, with a point margin of thirty or so, Heath made one of his famous steals, dribbled to the other end of the court, and slam-dunked the ball to a thunderous roar from the crowd. At the time, dunking the ball had been ruled illegal by the NCAA. Referees assessed the required technical fouls, and Coach Foster lifted a towel in front of his face to hide his laughter.

WAYS Radio, then number one in the Charlotte market and owned by Sis and Stan Kaplan, decided to give the new university a boost: they assigned a broadcast team of alumnus John Kilgo, later a Carolina Panthers analyst, and Jay Thomas, later to move to Hollywood and achieve national fame in the television series "Love and War," to cover the 49ers in the early years. Kilgo did play-by-play announcing, while Thomas provided color. Thomas made irreverent comments about the cheerleaders or attractive female fans, or noted that State Representative Jim McDuffie had just arrived—"somebody must have been passing out free tickets." McDuffie had begun his political career as a gadfly at city council meetings. He gained attention by such stunts as dropping chicken feathers at a meeting to protest littering by trucks carrying chickens to market through city streets. After serving on the city council, McDuffie was elected to the North Carolina General Assembly. The legislator was also a dedicated UNC Charlotte basketball fan and often showed up for the games.

Doing sports information in those early days was a labor of love, primarily offered by student assistants. Two student assistants from the Murphy-Foster era went on to some level of fame. Larry Keith became a writer and later editorial projects director with *Sports Illustrated* after transferring to the journalism school at UNC Chapel Hill. Bob Rathbun became a television commentator for ACC and other basketball games. Joe Bowles and Roy Beatty of the Public Information and Publications Office, who helped out in sports information in the early days, went on to prominent public relations positions.

The team Foster built was so capable against the competition he was able to schedule that he spoiled the UNC Charlotte fans. Blowouts with a twenty-, thirty-, or forty-point margin of victory were common. The problem was that most of the victims were relatively unknown in Charlotte, and that made it hard for the team to gain respect. Gradually Foster did add competitive teams, including Marshall, Oklahoma, and N.C. State, and occasionally the 49ers gave them close games, except for N.C. State, which would only play UNC Charlotte in Raleigh.

In 1973–74, Foster's team compiled a 22–4 record. That was a playoff-quality record, but there was no bid. The next year, the record improved to 23–3, surely qualifying the team for a postseason bid—but again there was none. At that time Foster didn't have the political connections in the basketball world to get help in getting a bid. UNC Charlotte was too new as a university to have the necessary connections, so those great seasons ended in disappointment. The frustration left Foster open to an invitation to coach at Clemson University, where football had long overshadowed basketball. Still, Clemson was in the Atlantic Coast Conference, and Foster knew that if he produced at Clemson, he would gain the respect due him. He did attain considerable success there and later at the University of Miami and at Virginia Tech, reaching the 500-victory mark by 1996.

Before he left UNC Charlotte, however, Foster had continued mining the region for players with potential that had been overlooked by major programs. When he departed for Clemson, Foster left behind a team that would go on to athletic glory. The starting five were Cedric Maxwell of Kinston, who would later become All-American and ultimately win the MVP award in the NBA playoffs for the Boston Celtics; Melvin Watkins of Reidsville, later UNC Charlotte head coach; Kevin King of Lakewood, New Jersey, later a corrections officer for the State of North Carolina; Lew Massey of Pineville, nephew of UNC Chapel Hill basketball star Walter Davis; and Bob Ball of Tucker, Georgia. UNC Charlotte was the only university to offer Maxwell a full scholarship; East Carolina had offered him a half scholarship.

The reserves were Jeff Gruber of Cary; Henry Caldwell of Columbia, South Carolina; Ken Angel of Florence, Kentucky; Don Pearce of Greensboro; and Sheldon Shipman of Salisbury, later to become a minister. David Taylor was sports information director.

These players were the gift Foster left to his successor, Lee Rose. The selection of Rose was a fortunate happenstance of timing in which Provost Frank Dickey played a major role. He was filling in for Colvard while the chancellor toured China with a delegation from the American Association of Colleges and Universities (AASCU), which incidentally included E. K. Fretwell Jr., then president of State University of New York College at Buffalo and later to become UNC Charlotte chancellor.

Dickey appointed Orr head of a search committee to find a new coach quickly to avoid losing recruits. When Adolph Rupp of Kentucky was contacted for suggestions for the position, he responded with one name—Lee Rose, coach at Transylvania College, in Lexington, Kentucky. Rupp had overlooked Rose the high school basketball player but highly respected Rose the coach.

With that recommendation, Dickey took advantage of an opportunity to restructure the athletic reporting lines for Rose. For whatever reason, Foster had bridled at having to report to the vice chancellor for development. So Dickey agreed to a change: Rose would report, instead, to the vice chancellor for student affairs.

Rose cut a handsome figure as coach. At age thirty-nine, he had prematurely white hair that made him distinctive and perhaps made him appear to his players as more mature than his age would indicate. But the new coach brought with him a bit of a chip on his shoulder that coaching at UNC Charlotte wouldn't help.

After serving as an assistant coach at Transylvania and at the University of Cincinnati, Rose returned to Lexington as coach at his alma mater. In eight years there, his record was 160–57, with an average of twenty wins a season. His teams appeared in six postseason tournaments. Even with all that success, however, he was still a distant number two to UK in Lexington. Still, his record positioned him for the challenge with the aspiring UNC Charlotte Division I program.

Rose wasn't immediately impressed with the team Bill Foster left him. He commented that he would do the best with what he had until he could build a program.

One would have thought that Rose would have become used to being overshadowed and overlooked from his Lexington days. Even so, he was irritated with the attention UNC Chapel Hill and other ACC teams from other states received in his own new city. The talented team that he inherited began to win and continued winning, beating impressive teams like Eastern Kentucky, Florida, Vanderbilt, and Centenary, and narrowly lost to N.C. State during the regular season. Rose's team compiled a 21–5 record. Again there was no NCAA bid, but Rose appealed to the NIT to give his team a chance, and with Rupp's help, he succeeded.

The magic really began at the NIT in Madison Square Garden in New York City. That blasé city found something it liked in the upstart UNC Charlotte team and adopted it. UNC Charlotte, which hadn't really been discovered even by sports reporters and editors back home in Charlotte, was suddenly known on the streets of the Big Apple. People there and in the television audience imitated Cedric Maxwell's "pretend" free throw, practiced just as he stepped to the line. As the referee held the ball before handing it to Maxwell, the player took three pretend dribbles, lofted the pretend ball and flipped it toward the basket. When he got the real ball, Maxwell hit a high percentage of shots. With his long arms reaching up to snare rebounds, Maxwell was constantly being hacked and stepping to the line—and making his shots. He broke the NIT's record for free throw conversions.

The 49er team hadn't made preparations to spend a full week in New York City, and the players had left their books behind. When they kept winning, a box of books, take-home exams, and other necessities were sent on a bus taking more fans to the city. The 49ers defeated San Francisco 79–74 and Oregon 79–72. Suddenly they were face to face with an in-state team that gave them no respect—N.C. State. But this time the 49ers pulled out the victory 80–79, leaving Coach Stormin' Norman Sloan living up to his nickname. Back on campus, Bob Gwaltney, a former N.C. State administrator who had recently taken a position at UNC Charlotte, had his office rolled with toilet paper. Enterprising students were selling bumper stickers with the score the next day. Having faith, they had had the stickers prepared with all but the score, and the printer had opened up at midnight in order to have them ready for sale the next day.

The UNC Charlotte pep band hadn't planned on spending a week in New York and had run out of money. Back home, citizens of Charlotte took up a collection to keep the band there. Bob Alander, a retired *Charlotte Observer* executive who was serving as director of the UNC Charlotte Foundation, got his pinochle club to chip in with the pot from its lunchtime game.

Finally the 49ers were in the 1976 NIT final game against one of the biggest names in basketball, the Kentucky Wildcats. Perhaps the legend was too much for the Cinderella team or for the coach who had grown up in the legend's shadow. Anyway, UNC Charlotte lost in the final seconds, 67–71, after leading for much of the game. But UNC Charlotte had been discovered, and there was consolation in the fact that Cedric Maxwell was named MVP of the tournament, with 109 points, 46 rebounds, and 47 of 53 free throws. Maxwell also became UNC Charlotte's first All-American.

Back home Charlotteans celebrated as if the home team had won. Radio stations were called and informed of the team's arrival time. As the team members arrived in Charlotte, they were obviously stunned to be greeted as returning heroes. At the time it was the biggest crowd ever to gather at the airport. Thousands filled the old airport terminal to catch a glimpse of the team and shout their praises.

The UNC Charlotte trip to the NIT paid off big in academic terms. Because a recession had prevented funding through the usual pay-as-you-go process, the legislature had approved a bond issue to go before voters for construction of buildings at the sixteen campuses. UNC Charlotte's share was $6 million. Dean of Students Dennis Rash, later to join NationsBank, headed the campus bond campaign. He had banners painted with the slogan "Back the Bonds." As the UNC Charlotte team progressed through the latter part of the season and then through the NIT, television cameras showed students racing around the court in Charlotte and at Madison Square Garden waving large "Back the Bonds" banners. Fans from New York and from the other teams must have been puzzled.

In fact, not only the Charlotte region but the entire state benefited from UNC Charlotte's trip to the NIT. The bonds' 72 percent winning margin in Mecklenburg County, with its large population base, helped carry the issue statewide. How did it happen? An editorial in the *Charlotte News* gives some insight:

> Strong ties, both real and perceived, already existed between the institution and the community.... As if on cue, a group of unknown basketball players emerged who reflected the mood and aspirations of the institution. Cedric "Cornbread" Maxwell and his cohorts gave the institution a vehicle of the highest caliber. A handful of genuine folk heroes were born, but more importantly the institution gained

an outlet for its message. . . . In the 72 percent winning margin in Mecklenburg, though, there is another message. It is that the community and its institution are remarkably well met.

A *Charlotte Observer* editorial quoted a UNC Charlotte official as saying, "It's a funny thing, but without changing a course listed in our catalog, we've suddenly become a first-rate university in people's minds. We've been one all along, of course, but it took the basketball thing to get the public's attention." And a professor summed it up in a short note to Coach Lee Rose: "Thanks for solving our identity problem."

The NIT trip may have had more tangible impact on the academic enterprise because of the bond issue, but in terms of national attention, the trip to the NIT was nothing compared to the season of 1976–77. To the starters of the NIT team, Rose added Chad Kinch from New Jersey.

Even with the NIT success behind it, UNC Charlotte was still an upstart in basketball-crazy North Carolina, which considered any team outside the ACC subpar. UNC Charlotte was playing in a newly formed league called the Sunbelt Conference. But the 49ers just kept on winning; they lost only three games. There was no denying the team a trip to the NCAA Tournament this time, but in spite of one of the nation's best records, the team was considered a long shot going into the tournament, and again it needed Rupp's help.

Sports Illustrated said, "Every time Rose tried to tell somebody that his team was legitimate or that star Center Cedric Maxwell was 'the best player, pound for pound, in the country,' the press yawned and checked the radio for the latest ACC results. Hush, hush, sweet Charlotte." But the team finally got its bid, and many UNC Charlotte fans packed into buses, cars, or whatever mode of transportation they could find to attend the first-round game at Indiana University against Central Michigan, thinking perhaps it would be their first and only chance to see UNC Charlotte in an NCAA Tournament game. A very nervous team barely survived that first round.

But UNC Charlotte found the Kentucky arena in Lexington to their liking for the Mideast regional. First they beat an outstanding big-name team— Syracuse—81–59. Coach Rose responded to a strong press by having his center, Cedric Maxwell, bring the basketball up the court. It was learned that even the administrators in General Administration in Chapel Hill were watching on television, when President Friday said at a meeting, "But don't let Maxwell bring the ball up court; it makes us too nervous." Actually, it was good strategy. Maxwell, with his long arms, could dribble the ball close to the floor, and he was difficult to guard.

Up next was Michigan, the number-one team in the nation, with much-heralded center Phil Hubbard. One of the highlights of the game was when UNC Charlotte freshman Chad Kinch moved down the baseline with the ball, rose above Hubbard, and executed a beautiful slam-dunk, drawing a foul.

All-American Cedric Maxwell scores as UNC Charlotte defeats number-one-ranked Michigan on the way to the NCAA Final Four in 1977.

Sports Illustrated said, "The final score was Charlotte 75, Michigan 68, Experts, 0." So it was that a team only six years into NCAA Division I was in the Final Four—a true Cinderella story. Nervous Charlotteans contemplated the chances of UNC Charlotte at last facing UNC Chapel Hill, already a basketball legend.

But it was not to be. UNC Charlotte lost to Marquette on a disputed final-second call. In another small-world irony, Marquette's coach, Al McGuire, had coached just across the river from Charlotte, at Belmont Abbey College, before rising to coaching stardom. McGuire and his team ended up dispatching UNC Chapel Hill for the national championship.

Back home, Charlotteans received UNC Charlotte as if the team had won the national championship. Again a sea of people greeted the team at the airport. The sight so startled the pilot of the airplane that brought them home that he took off on the next leg of his flight without waiting for the team's luggage to be unloaded. The team and its coaches rode triumphantly down Tryon Street to the Square in convertibles as ticker-tape showered down on them. Noting the coverage the newspapers gave the team during its winning

The 1977 UNC Charlotte Final Four Team. Front (from left): Chad Kinch, Jeff Gruber, Lew Massey, Todd Crowley, Melvin Watkins, Henry Caldwell, Lee Whitfield, Jerry Winston, Head Coach Lee Rose. Back (from left): Asst. Coach Everett Bass, Dave Maas, Phil Scott, Bruce Stapleton, Cedric Maxwell, Greg Spain, Ken Angel, Mike Hester, Kevin King, Asst. Coach Mike Pratt.

run, sports columnist Ron Green compared the headlines with those appropriate to the "second coming."

UNC Charlotte's reign as Cinderella had opened opportunities for visibility for the young university. News media across the country wanted to know about the home campus of the 49ers. A highlight was the visit to the campus by a crew from ABC Television to do a profile on UNC Charlotte and the community. As Pete McKnight, editor of the *Charlotte Observer*, observed, "Bonnie Cone and Dean Colvard worked their tails off to get their university recognition, but it took 10 skinny kids in short pants running up and down the basketball court to actually get that recognition."

Preparing UNC Charlotte for the long haul in athletics, Orr, Rose, Professor Tom Turner, and Dick Bowers, athletic director at the University of South Florida, led in the formation of the Sunbelt Conference. Their choice of former Duke University coach Vic Bubas to serve as commissioner gave the conference instant credibility.

The problem with such a rapid rise to the top in a sport is fans' expectation that the team will stay there. That didn't happen with UNC Charlotte. The knock on Lee Rose was that he was a fantastic floor coach and strategist but that he couldn't recruit. He didn't successfully replace Cedric Maxwell and some of his other star players, and his team was bounced from the next year's Sunbelt Conference Tournament.

In the meantime, the chip on Rose's shoulder about not getting the respect he deserved grew heavier. So he left to coach at Purdue. Although Purdue had a strong basketball tradition, it too played in a shadow—the combined shadow of Indiana and Notre Dame. But Rose took the Purdue team his predecessor had recruited and, in a strange twist of fate, led that team in his first year to the NIT and in his second year to the Final Four. Quite a coaching accomplishment.

It was late in the season when Rose resigned to go to Purdue, and to keep from losing the recruits who had already been contacted, Vice Chancellor Doug Orr elevated Rose's assistant, Mike Pratt, a former University of Kentucky star, to the head coaching position. At the same time, Clyde Walker, who had been athletic director at the University of Kansas, was appointed UNC Charlotte's athletic director, thus splitting the combined positions of men's basketball coach and athletic director, which Bill Foster and Lee Rose had held.

Meanwhile, a women's basketball coach, Judy Rose, an alumna of Winthrop and the University of Tennessee, had been appointed and was achieving early success, the beginning of a move toward equity in women's sports. The first scholarships were provided for women athletes in 1977–78.

In contrast to the meteoric flash of men's basketball, the rest of the university continued on a steadier climb upward. By the fall of 1976, the Colleges of Architecture, Business Administration, and Nursing began to restrict their enrollments in an attempt to maintain quality controls. They raised entrance requirements for their programs above the general requirements for the institution as a whole.

In the mid-1970s, UNC Charlotte professors began to affect the greater Charlotte community, whether or not it was aware of what was happening; they began shaking up the establishment and changing forever the face of politics and business-as-usual. Both the city council and the board of county commissioners were homogeneous bodies, elected at large and comprised of people from the same neighborhoods and, at one point, even from the same church. But because of the growth of the city, citizens became restive at seeing such a concentration of power. They began to vote against bond issues and even to oppose issues considered in the best interests of the community.

A document by Professor William J. (Bill) McCoy of the Department of Political Science helped to change all that. It was titled "Electoral Districting Alternatives for Charlotte and Mecklenburg County." It served as the basis for the community's approval of district representation. After districts were established, voter confidence in elected officials was restored and airport improvement bonds were approved, as were a number of civic improvement bonds in subsequent elections. McCoy's involvement also set the stage for the important role he was to play some years later in making the Urban Institute a vehicle of support for the governmental agencies of the Southern Piedmont counties and in helping those counties understand the nature of regionalism and the need for cooperation rather than competition.

Professor Dan Morrill of the Department of History got the community's attention by shouting that it was about to destroy all vestiges of its past by razing historic buildings in the name of progress. Sadly, by the time Morrill stepped forward, many treasures were already gone. He did, however, save a number of other buildings after becoming director of the Charlotte-Mecklenburg Historic Landmarks Commission. In fact, Morrill helped establish the commission. In that role he led the restoration of a number of buildings and preservation of others by adaptive use. Morrill was something of an actor and used his dramatic voice and presence to command attention at speaking engagements or in television appearances.

Dennis Rash left his position as dean of students to head the NCNB Community Development Corp., one of whose major projects was to continue developing Charlotte's Fourth Ward uptown neighborhood—a project initiated by Rash and Ben Romine while they were still at the university. The two deserve major credit for helping revitalize uptown Charlotte. Rash would later marry Betty Chafin Rash, who had worked in the Urban Institute and then as associate dean of students. Betty Chafin Rash ran for the city council and was elected and became mayor pro tem. She later became a public affairs consultant in Charlotte.

Professor Jim Matthews of the Biology Department stepped forward to help the region preserve its natural heritage. Others who helped in that effort were Professors Larry Barden and Larry Mellichamp, two of Matthews's colleagues in the Biology Department. Matthews and his fellow professors and students tramped through forests, swamps, and ponds, spotting rare and endangered plants and calling attention to their presence. Matthews even joined hands with colleague Tom Daggy in Biology at Davidson College to preserve a rare plant habitat on the Rocky River in Stanly County. They raised money and put up some of their own to purchase the tract on Morgan's Bluff, a cliff that contained plants normally found in the Midwest.

Professor Harold Josephson of the History Department picked up the torch of internationalism by leading what under Earl Backman had been designated the nation's most successful statewide Great Decisions Program. In 1977, for Josephson's work, the program received its second Foreign Policy Association's Outstanding Program Award. On the strength of his leadership of Great Decisions, Josephson was later invited to head the Foreign Policy Association, a position that would help prepare him for his later role as associate vice chancellor for international programs at UNC Charlotte, taking to a higher level the program launched by Backman. Josephson took a two-year leave of absence and then returned to Charlotte.

Another professor making an impact on the community, and perhaps ahead of his time, was Edward L. Walls, an authority on hospital financing. He consulted with hospitals in the region and elsewhere on cost containment, well before the issue moved to the front burner of national attention.

A number of deanship changes occurred between 1976 and 1978. Robert Anderson of architecture, Allan Palmer of business administration, Newton Barnette of engineering, and Marinell Jernigan of nursing returned to the classroom. Dean John B. Chase Jr. of education died. They were replaced by Charles Hight in architecture, Richard Neel in business administration, Robert Snyder in engineering, Louise Schlachter in nursing, and H. William (Bill) Heller in education.

Enrollment growth provided some new positions and some relief to overburdened administrative staffs. The first full-time alumni director position was established; alumna Susan Piscitelli filled it, and with the support of the elected alumni president, Kit Ward Davis, began moving the association toward a more active role. Until that point, the director of public information had worn the alumni hat as an add-on assignment. Charles F. (Chuck) Lynch, who had been associate dean and director of the residence life program, was named dean of students to replace Rash. Jackie Simpson replaced Lynch.

In 1977, the time came for UNC Charlotte to change banks, so to speak. Addison Reese of NCNB (later NationsBank) had been the university's premier community leader since 1957, when he was first named to the advisory board of Charlotte College. But in 1977 Reese gave up the board chairmanship to C. C. (Cliff) Cameron, the chief executive of "the other bank," First Union. Even as he did, Reese accepted the chairmanship of the UNC Charlotte Foundation, which he had helped create and had supported personally and through his bank. Unfortunately, though, a terminal illness began sapping Reese's strength. He died on September 1, 1977. At Reese's death, Colvard said, "He had more impact on the development of the University of North Carolina at Charlotte than any other lay person." Colvard also noted that even when UNC Charlotte was without a local board in the period from 1965 to 1972, as chairman of the foundation, Reese had served in an advisory role somewhat comparable to that of a trustee.

The university had honored Reese as one of the first two recipients of an honorary degree. His citation included this praise: "A man of vision, he foresaw a university of excellence where those of less vision saw only a struggling community college. Schooled in the complex tradition of banking, he learned much of the world of higher education." When the new administration building was completed, the trustees moved the name "Reese Building" from the two-story building that had been the administration building to the new five-story facility.

Cameron shared many of Reese's qualities. He dedicated himself outside his banking responsibilities to making UNC Charlotte a true university. Like Reese, while he served as the UNC Charlotte board chair Cameron was also laying the foundation for the major national bank that was to emerge from the First Union of that day. Undoubtedly, UNC Charlotte owes part of the credit to its fast rise among North Carolina universities to the inspiration and drive of board chairs Reese and Cameron.

Like Reese, Cameron was tall, slender, and driven. Before joining First Union, Cameron had headed Cameron-Brown, a mortgage company in Raleigh. His genial exterior in that setting belied the competitiveness that become evident when he moved to Charlotte. Reports of his ascendancy at First Union tell of a power struggle in which Cameron, whose mortgage firm was acquired by First Union, ousted the existing leadership at the bank and took a firm grip on the reins. Cameron's entry into banking was somewhat unusual in that he had studied engineering during his college days at LSU.

As competitive as NCNB and First Union were, the two bankers Reese and Cameron put those issues aside to unite in building UNC Charlotte. As Cameron took over the leadership of the UNC Charlotte Board, two other board changes of note were occurring. Thomas I. Storrs of NCNB, later to serve as board chair himself, was coming on board, along with Meredith Spangler, wife of C. D. Spangler Jr., who would later become president of the University of North Carolina system. Meredith Spangler had earned a master's degree at UNC Charlotte.

Other personnel changes taking place in the period 1976–78 included that of the chancellorship. In January 1977, Colvard wrote President Friday of his plan to retire by December 1978. Because his sixty-fifth birthday would fall on July 10, 1978, Colvard, under university policy, could have remained to the end of that academic year (June 30, 1978), but he chose the earlier date and said he would step aside any time after July 1, 1978, if a successor could be found by then. By the time of his retirement, Colvard would have been employed in education for more than forty-three years, all but six of which were served in North Carolina.

Trustee chair Cliff Cameron organized and headed the search committee to find a successor to Colvard. What he heard from faculty members with regard to what they wanted in a new chancellor was a person who could gain the institution some recognition in the national higher education community. By the late 1970s, professors believed they had quickly built a high-quality institution that the world should know about.

As Colvard began winding down his UNC Charlotte career, he continued his planning process. At a retreat at Valle Crucis, and at a later one at Montreat that included the executive staff and the deans, a consensus began to develop about needed changes in the administrative structure. A majority of the leadership believed that the young university included too many colleges.

Particularly those in the humanities, science and mathematics, and social and behavioral sciences believed that they would fare better if the three colleges representing them were consolidated.

Colvard acknowledged that there might be merit in the suggestions, but he declined to make any changes so close to his retirement. His reasoning was that his successor at least ought to have the opportunity to study such a significant restructuring. There were suggestions for changes at the vice chancellor level as well, but again Colvard deferred to his successor.

What kind of report card did Colvard earn during his thirteen years of leadership? His record is fairly easy to detail. At his first commencement, in 1966, a total of eighty-two degrees was awarded. At his final commencement, in 1978, the total was 1,606, including more than two hundred master's degrees. More than 10,500 had been added to the Alumni Association rolls over those years. The university had achieved its regional accreditation from the Southern Association of Colleges and Schools and national accreditation for the programs in nursing, chemistry, and engineering. University enrollment had grown from 1,700 to 8,705.

As Colvard urged in his installation address, the university had developed an urban orientation, and the Urban Institute was a growing enterprise. Faculty members had become not only involved in but often the leaders in community issues. The university had developed an international dimension through the International Studies Program. The campus had developed a competitive athletic program—without football.

Orr said that Colvard's major legacy was that the mountain man generated rapid growth without compromising quality. Even in the dramatic development of the athletic program, Orr said, there was no compromise in integrity.

Another major Colvard accomplishment was the launching of a solid development program, based on the Patrons of Excellence concept he brought with him from Mississippi State University. It was fitting that some of Charlotte's leading citizens, particularly Edwin Jones and Bill Barnhardt, raised substantial funds to honor D. W. and Martha Colvard with the Colvard Scholarships for Merit.

Colvard began his UNC Charlotte years at a campus of eight relatively small buildings; by the time he stepped aside, the value of physical facilities totaled $54.5 million, including four ten-story residence halls and a twelve-story library tower addition.

Along with William McIntyre and Dick Hauersperger of the City-County Planning Commission, Colvard planted the seed for the creation of University City. And University Research Park, of which he was one of the founders, was ready to explode with growth: IBM had just taken an option on a sizable tract of land. In terms of Colvard's role in establishing University Research

Park, it is significant that IBM announced in June of 1978, his final year as chancellor, that it would exercise its option and build a large facility in the park. That announcement would set in motion the major growth of the park during Fretwell's tenure as chancellor, but the park's beginning and the arrival of its major catalyst took place on Colvard's watch.

Usually all business and with a somewhat serious demeanor, Colvard left the campus with something to laugh about—an unplanned part of his farewell roast that left the campus and the community in stitches. As Colvard arrived simultaneously with some of Charlotte's leading citizens at the Cone Center, where the roast was to occur, several guests joined him on the elevator to the top floor. Midway, the elevator stopped and got stuck between floors. Efforts by campus security and physical plant staff to free the group failed.

Time wore on, and the other guests were seated in the Lucas Room for the banquet. Radio personality Ty Boyd presided but was running short of material. Television and newspaper reporters had gathered for the occasion. Soon everyone sensed that something was amiss. When they learned about the stuck elevator, reporters and photographers rushed to the scene. By then the Newell Rescue Squad had forced the elevator door partially open—enough so that photographers got a great shot of an anxious Colvard and his friends, with their heads visible just above the level of the second floor of Cone Center. Eventually they all were freed, and the roast proceeded—anticlimactically.

A few good shots were fired at the retiring chancellor. Alf Cannon, former president of Queens College, jibed that Colvard, with his early agricultural background, had tried to grow grass and trees on the central part of the campus, only to give up because of the thin soil. He then concluded, Cannon said, that the best thing to do was just to cover the entire central campus in buildings and sidewalks. Indeed, Colvard had done his best to turn the patch of old farm fields, wooded areas, and ponds into a real university campus and did a pretty good job of it.

If Bonnie Cone is UNC Charlotte's founder, Colvard should be considered its builder.

CHAPTER 7

Fretwell Attracts National Notice

THE FRETWELL years are about UNC Charlotte's becoming connected to the greater academic community nationally and internationally. It is also the story of the university's gaining recognition for the quality of programs it had attained by the decade of the 1980s. Recognitions included being ranked in national magazines, winning an award from a national educational association, and having faculty and students win awards for individual accomplishments.

After fifteen years, there was some looking back and reflecting during the Fretwell years. Board of Trustees chair Cliff Cameron would tell a university magazine writer that for a time he had felt that the institution was looked at as that little Charlotte university that grew out of a high school. But he said that he perceived its image shift to that of an institution emerging as one of the top universities in the state system.

Likewise, this chapter is the story of UNC Charlotte's leadership in the building of University Place and University City, thus helping to balance Charlotte-Mecklenburg's growth. During this period UNC Charlotte would move from being isolated in a relatively undeveloped part of the county to being the anchor of a new urban core that would later become an integral part of the City of Charlotte.

During the Fretwell years many faculty members would rise to prominence in their academic disciplines and in the greater Charlotte community. Regional attention would be gained through the production of additional atlases and other publications and through the establishment of WFAE, a public radio station covering twenty counties with its FM signal.

Unfortunately, as in the earlier years, these would be times of continuing struggles to obtain adequate resources to build the major university the Charlotte region required.

Turning to the story of E. K. Fretwell Jr.'s arrival, it was snow—a relatively rare phenomenon in Charlotte—that may have helped in bringing him to UNC Charlotte. Odd that snow played a role in Fretwell's selection, just as it did in delaying the election of D. W. Colvard as the first UNC Charlotte chancellor. This time the snow was in Buffalo, New York, not Charlotte. The great Buffalo blizzards of 1977 didn't cause Fretwell to determine that he wanted to move to Charlotte, but it did cause him to consider offers from warmer or less snowy climes. When he learned about the opening in Charlotte through his many higher education contacts, Fretwell allowed his name to be placed in nomination. His credentials found favor with the search committee, headed by C. C. Cameron, chair of the UNC Charlotte Board of Trustees and chief executive officer of First Union.

Fretwell was then invited to meet with the committee in Chicago. He had requested that location because he could leave Buffalo after work, fly to Chicago, meet the committee, and return to work on the first flight the next morning. His day had been long when he got to the Chicago hotel, and he dropped into its restaurant for dinner. Near his table he noticed a very congenial group. As he looked closer, he spotted a face that had become familiar from a brochure sent to him from UNC Charlotte. It was that of Dean Sherman Burson. Actually, it was the ever-present Burson bowtie that first caught Fretwell's attention.

Fretwell thought to himself that the committee might be embarrassed later when they realized he had been nearby, particularly if they said something about the search that could be overheard. So he decided to go over and introduce himself. The committee invited him to join them then rather than wait for the appointed hour. The interview went well, and it was followed by a one-on-one session with Cameron. Fretwell left for Buffalo feeling good about prospects in Charlotte.

The process continued to go smoothly, and Fretwell was elected by the UNC Board of Governors. He arrived in Charlotte to take up his duties during a warm spell over the winter holidays, as 1978 ended and 1979 began. He even got in a game of tennis on New Year's Day, then met the faculty, staff, and students on January 2. The next day, however, he discovered the fickleness of the area's weather: a snow and ice storm developed. But he received a warm reception from faculty members, who felt that Fretwell was the answer to their prayers for a chancellor well connected in higher education circles—someone who could help them make connections.

It soon became apparent that few college presidents or chancellors at the time were better connected than Fretwell. By then, he had been president of State University of New York College at Buffalo for eleven years over a period of rapid growth. Even though "Buff State," as it was popularly known, was perhaps not the city's most prestigious university—that distinction probably belonged to the State University of New York at Buffalo—Fretwell himself had earned a national and international reputation in higher education administration.

Fretwell had already served as national president of the American Association for Higher Education, president and board chair of the Middle States Association of Colleges and Secondary Schools (the equivalent of the Southern Association of Colleges and Schools), commissioner of the Education Commission of the States, chair of the board of the Carnegie Foundation for the Advancement of Teaching, and a member of the American Council on Education Commission on Plans and Objectives for Higher Education. An alumnus of Wesleyan University, he had received an M.A. in teaching from Harvard University and a Ph.D. from Columbia University. He held an honorary doctorate from the Technical University of Wroclaw (Poland).

He had worked as a part-time correspondent for the Associated Press; as a staff writer for the American Red Cross; as vice consul in the American Embassy in Prague, Czechoslovakia; as a public school teacher in Brookline, Massachusetts; as a high school and community college teacher in Evanston, Illinois; as administrative secretary for the John Hay Fellowships in the John Hay Whitney Foundation; as assistant and associate professor and assistant to the dean of Teachers College of Columbia University; as assistant commissioner for higher education in New York; and as university dean for academic development at the City University of New York.

Through Fretwell's special assignments he had established contacts with some of the top people in higher education at the time. He was consultant to President Dwight Eisenhower's Commission on Education Beyond the High School and assistant to Dr. James B. Conant in the preparation of the book *The Education of American Teachers.*

Moreover, after his arrival Fretwell was to give UNC Charlotte an even greater connection to the national higher education establishment as president of the American Association of State Colleges and Universities. That position was followed by his being elected chair of the American Council on Education.

On the local front, however, some wondered how Fretwell, as a New Yorker, would relate to Charlotteans, particularly the old-line leadership. Although he spent much of his youth in New York City, Fretwell's father had grown up in Missouri, and the family retained some of the heartland culture. In fact, Fretwell traced the family ancestry to southwestern Virginia, near the North Carolina line, just above Rockingham County. Moreover, E. K. Fretwell was extremely adaptable, and as a result he fit in rather well.

Cameron said that through Fretwell's Buffalo State trustees, members of the UNC Charlotte search committee learned that he got along well in his local community in spite of the fact that he had a great deal of college competition in Buffalo. Like Colvard, Fretwell was a Presbyterian and a Rotarian, and those activities opened many doors. He also was active in the Boy Scouts, as his father had been before him.

Fretwell also brought with him some links to Charlotte. He had toured China with D. W. Colvard shortly after President Richard Nixon opened the doors to that nation. After he arrived in Charlotte, Fretwell made it a point to visit with Dr. Elmer Garinger. It turned out that Garinger had studied with Fretwell's father, who at the time was a professor at Columbia University. Through that linkage, Fretwell had a tie back to the very beginning of UNC Charlotte. As superintendent of Charlotte City Schools, Garinger had had responsibility for the Charlotte Center and Charlotte College.

The new chancellor brought with him something else that immediately commanded attention—his height. At 6 feet 7, with a full head of curly black hair, Fretwell usually stood out in a meeting room—unless it were full of basketball players. At the time of his arrival, he bore a resemblance to the great American novelist Thomas Wolfe, a native of Asheville and a tall man himself. There is some validity to the old saw that tall people command attention just by virtue of their height; but in Fretwell's case it was just an added attribute for a warm, outgoing, intelligent, inquisitive, optimistic man with a gift of gab. Mention any topic in conversation and Fretwell could plunge right in and add insights and information, especially if the topic were railroads. Then his companions might learn more about trains than they wanted to know. Fretwell was an addicted rail buff. He rarely missed an opportunity to ride a train wherever he traveled. Abroad, he sought out rare old railway lines and climbed aboard. Whenever possible, he rode up in the cab with the engineer. In his speeches, he rarely missed an opportunity to use a railroad metaphor in relation to higher education.

The private Fretwell was a family man whose wife, Dorrie, required her own identity and career rather than just being a chancellor's wife, lost in the tall shadow of her husband. Shortly after their arrival, Dorrie enrolled in UNC Charlotte's graduate school to earn a master's degree in psychology with a concentration in counseling. Thereafter she entered a counseling practice. His wife's status as a student was useful to Fretwell in at least two illustrations in public speeches. One was a joke—"It's been rumored that your chancellor is sleeping with a student, and it's true."

The other he used when he received complaints about North Carolina's tough out-of-state-tuition policy. Under North Carolina law, out-of-state students had to pay a much higher tuition for at least a year, even if they had become bona fide residents of the state. At gatherings of parents, someone inevitably complained that they had taken a job in North Carolina and moved the family to the state but still had to pay as if they were living out of state. Fretwell could legitimately say, "I know how you feel; I'm paying out-of-state tuition for my wife, Dorrie."

Mrs. Fretwell attributed her husband's height to the length of his legs. Which brings up another element of the Fretwell lifestyle—walking. With his long legs, Fretwell took long, quick strides and thus covered a lot of ground. When UNC Charlotte's Human Resources Office began a walking-for-health program, Fretwell often was one of the top participants in terms of miles covered.

He also took long strides, figuratively, in plunging right into the campus agenda. But another Fretwell characteristic was caution. On his desk when he arrived were recommendations from two retreats concerning administrative restructuring, but Fretwell bided his time. He later said that he understood the perils inherent in making changes too quickly or in installing one's own friends and colleagues from a previous institution.

Also, it was clear that Fretwell basically agreed with the overall commitments being made and the direction being taken at UNC Charlotte. In an interview with Harold Warren, Carol Collyar, and Laura King of the *Charlotte Observer* in April, after his arrival in Charlotte, Fretwell was asked why he had come to the city. He replied, "I can sum it up in a single sentence: Here there is an opportunity for the university and city to go forward together." He added that he had felt a "calling" to come to Charlotte.

Fretwell also was realistic. He told the interviewers, "The senior institutions [in the UNC system] have been around a long time. UNCC is a new kid on the block. This means we've got to go out to the world a little hungrier. We're going to have to be like Avis—try harder and be smarter and hopefully luckier."

Fretwell plunged right in, outlining his UNC Charlotte vision in his installation ceremony, on April 6, 1979. He acknowledged his institution's university system heritage, asserting, "The signal honor of establishing the first state university in the brand new republic of the United States goes to the University of North Carolina, created in 1789, and offering its first instruction in 1795, some two decades before the opening of Mr. Jefferson's University of Virginia in Charlottesville."

But at the same occasion, Governor Jim Hunt set UNC Charlotte apart from older institutions, declaring, "This university is at a jumping-off point. It must continue to grow. It has a special role different from other institutions in the state."

In his address, Fretwell called on UNC Charlotte to prepare students to move beyond the level of minimum competence to excellence and commitment and to find ways to measure the achievement of such goals; to help students gain maturity, allowing them to participate in their own learning process; to provide a reasonable variety of choices by reappraising the general education requirements for graduation; to develop honors work; to expand opportunities to enroll, particularly for minority students and women (who soon became, by a slight margin, the majority gender at UNC Charlotte); and to push academic decision-making down as close to the individual departments as possible.

The new chancellor also posed some questions: How can the university serve the world of research and scholarship and at the same time provide public service to the greater Charlotte region? How can it bring scholars together across disciplinary lines? How can it make membership in the sixteen-campus system a positive experience? How can it manage its growth to keep from spinning out of control? And how can it continue self-examination for quality control?

His installation contained an embarrassing moment for the public information office and comic relief for the audience. A medallion had been struck for the new chancellor, but a miscommunication involving the office, the vendor, and the manufacturer had caused the chain to be too short. The manufacturer was late in delivering the medallion, so there was no time to spot the error. In fact, Norm Manning, representing the vendor who was providing the medallion, had to pick the piece up at the airport and drive it straight to the Charlotte Coliseum (later called Independence Arena) just in time for its use.

As President Bill Friday took the medallion from its box and started to drape it over Fretwell's head, the chain's shortness became obvious. Friday was determined to make it work, though, and the audience had a good laugh

Stubborn medallion in place, Chancellor E. K. Fretwell, Jr. (left) and President William C. Friday share a laugh at Fretwell's installation in 1979. Photo by Gail Petrakis.

and photographers a good photo opportunity as the tight chain and medallion were forced down over Fretwell's head.

Since one of the expectations of Fretwell was that the institution should become better known nationally, he was given a bit of good fortune early in his tenure. At the time of Fretwell's installation, a young anthropologist named Russell Ciochon, who had recently joined the faculty, and his colleague Donald Savage of the University of California at Berkeley made a dramatic joint announcement. They displayed fossils that they claimed were of an early ancestor of apes and man, indicating that human beings might have originated in Burma rather than in Africa. The announcement was covered by *Time* and *Newsweek*, the *New York Times*, the *Washington Post*, ABC Television, and radio stations around the nation and in Canada, as well as by local and regional media.

The announcement also exposed some academic in-fighting. Some members of the Department of Sociology and Anthropology denounced Ciochon and Savage for publicity-seeking and one-upmanship and for going public in the early stages of research to gain funding support.

For Ciochon the episode was enough to launch a bigger career. He moved on to the Smithsonian Institution. For UNC Charlotte, it was an opportunity to have its name presented nationwide, alongside a major research university, in a breakthrough announcement.

Another professor, James Oliver of the Biology Department, who became a long-term key faculty member and later headed the biotechnology program, made national, regional, and local news that year. The media covered his research on a potentially deadly bacterium found in salt water along the eastern coast of the United States. This organism posed a particular hazard to persons with liver disease who went swimming at the coast or who ate raw seafood.

The early Fretwell months were mostly business as usual—but they were also marked by solid academic activity of a high quality. In his first annual report for 1978–79, which covered only the first six months of his tenure, Fretwell said, "The incoming chancellor's experiences here beginning Jan. 1, 1979, have confirmed his assessment of the Charlotte campus as a place of great potential and momentum. UNCC has continued its rapid development as a comprehensive university with a sound academic program and a growing involvement of its faculty and administration in national higher education organizations and in service to the surrounding community and the state."

Maturing faculty members were beginning to make a national impact with their research and publications. Among the results were books by Gary Ferraro of Sociology, Jack Evett of Civil Engineering, Cheng Liu of Engineering Technology, Paul Escott of History (two books), Belinda McCarthy and

David Hirschel of Criminal Justice, and James W. Clay and Gerald Ingalls of Geography. Also, poet Robert Waters Gray of the English Department had begun editing the *Southern Poetry Review*.

Something that portended well for the future was that the Office of Academic Grants and Contracts crossed the $1 million threshold in funding from outside sources to support faculty research and publications. Much of the expanding faculty research and publication activity could only be accomplished when supported by outside grants and contracts.

As Fretwell came aboard, the door was opening a bit wider for graduate studies. Master's degree programs were authorized in special education, music, psychology, criminal justice, metropolitan and community planning, engineering, and nursing.

The College of Nursing began responding to community needs by creating the Pathways Program, which allowed nurses who had obtained RN standing to take the courses required for a B.S. degree in nursing without too great a disruption in their family and professional lives.

When Fretwell arrived, enrollment was 8,705, including 1,268 graduate students. That was only 2.4 percent over the previous year, a figure lower than the prevailing average annual growth rate of about 4 percent. Speculation about reasons for the slower growth included the facts that there was a long waiting list of students who couldn't be accommodated in residence halls and thus went elsewhere, and that five academic programs had raised admission standards higher than those for the campus overall.

Sometimes in those days the university administration, faculty, and staff were so anxious to serve all the needs they identified that they began programs before they had adequate staff or resources. This was the case with the Evening Program Information Center (EPIC), which was aimed at older and nontraditional students. Such students needed support, including encouragement and advising and counseling about such matters as financial aid. But the program didn't have the staffing and support for the long haul and didn't last long. It would take until 1995 for the university to reestablish an evening services program, this one called OASES.

A mixed windfall for Fretwell was the state's allocation of $323,000 in "catchup" funds for the library, which had entered university status with only Charlotte College resources. Unfortunately, this sum, the last in a series of catchup allocations totaling $1.2 million, didn't go far enough. Campus officials continued to stress to the UNC system's General Administration that because of rapid enrollment growth, the UNC Charlotte library's ratio of volumes per student remained the lowest among the sixteen campuses.

Presiding over his first UNC Charlotte commencement on May 12, Fretwell had the opportunity to honor his two predecessors and acknowledge their institution-building leadership. On the recommendation of the faculty and with the approval of the Board of Trustees, he bestowed on Bonnie Cone and D. W. Colvard honorary doctoral degrees, the highest awards the university could offer.

Cone already had a building—the Cone Center—named in her honor, so trustees moved to pay a similar tribute to Colvard. When a $6 million, 130,000-square-foot classroom-office building was completed, it was dedicated and named in honor of Colvard with the participation of Governor Jim Hunt. At Colvard's request, the portrait of him that was hung in the new building included his wife, Martha.

Attempts to reach out to the community originated with students, faculty, and administrators alike. The idea for establishing a public radio station originated with students, but it succeeded so well that a professional staff had to be acquired later to manage it. Well before Fretwell's arrival, UNC Charlotte and Davidson College had been working toward getting public radio stations on the air. Davidson, under the leadership of Public Relations Director Earl (Buck) Lawrimore, won the race when UNC Charlotte's application became more complex because of the university's desire for National Public Radio affiliation and Corporation for Public Broadcasting funding. UNC Charlotte's 10-watt station even had to go off the air for several months as the conversion to 100,000 watts took place. The UNC Charlotte license was finally approved, and on June 29, 1981, the station went on the air at full power as WFAE-FM.

The bid for a station cost UNC Charlotte five state-supported staff positions—jobs that the university had to transfer to WFAE to meet federal funding matching requirements. But Vice Chancellor Doug Orr believed the dividend on the investment was the university's increased outreach to the region. He was to become the station's most ardent supporter and advocate. Through its radio station, UNC Charlotte gained a great deal of positive attention.

WFAE-FM had begun on campus as a student-operated station on carrier current, which used campus power lines to carry the radio signal to the residence halls. The students later moved to broadcasting at 10 watts of power. After he graduated, Robert (Bo) Pittman, a Charlotte student leader of the project, struggled to maintain the low-power operation and worked toward the day when the university would have a full-fledged public operation. Pittman left UNC Charlotte when he was employed to help put a station on the air at the University of Alabama at Tuscaloosa, just before he could realize his dream of seeing WFAE on the air at 100,000 watts. He was replaced by Jennifer Roth, a public radio veteran. Pittman later returned to Charlotte to work for Jefferson Pilot Broadcasting and still later to head his own firm, called BDC, Inc.

The first few years were heady for the station and the university. Local reporters and editors became very supportive of the station's in-depth national news programs. That paid off in endorsements when it came time for on-the-air fund-raisers. After organizing the first successful on-air fund-raising drives, alumna Kit Ward Davis, a Charlottean, was recruited away by WUNC-FM in Chapel Hill.

A Charlotte student, Kathy Merritt, began doing a local in-depth news program, and she continued the show after her graduation. Ultimately her staff expanded to three reporters, including herself. WFAE was the only radio station in the market doing extended local radio news coverage, and the station and its reporters were to win numerous state and national awards for outstanding news coverage.

The station's smooth jazz segments, created by alumnus Paul Stribling of Charlotte, caught on, and a decision was made to give up classical music segments to Davidson's WDAV in the belief that there wasn't a big enough audience for that music to split it between two stations.

Two of the station's early staff members—Barry Gordemer, an alumnus from Charlotte, and Jean Inaba—moved up to positions with National Public Radio.

WFAE even spawned a national and international program when a young exchange student, Fiona Ritchie, arrived from Scotland. She had been recruited to UNC Charlotte by Professor Nace Toner of the Psychology Department, with whom she did some research projects.

Ritchie volunteered at the radio station and quickly became a favorite because of her bubbly personality and a delightful Scottish accent. When she asked to try out a program of her own by playing and commenting on some of the Celtic music she brought with her, station manager Jennifer Roth said, "Well, we'll give it a try, but I don't know how the public will react to your accent."

The resulting program, "The Thistle and Shamrock," caught on so quickly that WFAE syndicated it, and stations around the country and then finally around the world picked it up. By 1995, it had become one of the most popular music programs on public radio and was carried by more than three hundred stations around the world. Credits on air were still given to its founding at WFAE. Ritchie herself became known all over the world.

During a budget crisis in the late 1980s and early 1990s, the legislature and the UNC General Administration looked for places to cut funding. Jay Robinson, a former superintendent of Charlotte-Mecklenburg Schools who had gone to Chapel Hill as General Administration vice president and lobbyist for the UNC system, felt that state support for WFAE and other public radio stations affiliated with the university campuses was expendable. He believed these stations served elitist audiences. That may have reflected his response to the Chapel Hill station's classical music format, but it didn't describe the Charlotte station and its listeners.

By 1991, when state funding began to be withdrawn, WFAE and UNC Charlotte had grown up and matured together, mutually benefiting from the relationship. When funding was withdrawn, it was considered unfair to WFAE and its station manager, Roger Sarow, who had arrived in 1989, to continue to saddle them with state controls without any benefits. WFAE was given its independence on April 12, 1993, but with an agreement to continue a close working relationship with UNC Charlotte.

In addition to launching the radio station, UNC Charlotte administrators explored other ways to improve relationships with the community. Trustees were asked to give their thoughts in an article in the winter 1980 issue of the university magazine.

Trustee chair Cliff Cameron, who said he already perceived an improvement in the university's image, also made some predictions for the future, including this one: "A downtown grassroots operation that will move into a center city campus eventually." He also expected the university to develop closer ties to the business community.

In terms of expectations for growth, Cameron said he could see enrollment at 15,000 to 20,000 students. A program he said he expected to see added was law. Actually, the UNC Charlotte trustees did request a law school. A study was conducted by the UNC General Administration, but it said that no additional law school was needed in North Carolina. Almost immediately, though, Campbell University announced the establishment of a law school.

Trustee Kathleen Crosby, who was an associate superintendent of Charlotte-Mecklenburg Schools and a leader in the African American community, praised the university's efforts so far to improve relations with the black community but said, "I would like to see more of an honest hard-nosed effort to serve the needs of the total community." She called for the university to help students get jobs.

Liz Hair, a leader in the Democratic Party and former chair of the Board of Elections and the Board of County Commissioners, called for the university to develop specific areas of expertise and outstanding programs, but not to overlook the liberal arts.

Student president Karen Popp of Mooresville said, "If students leave being proud, other people will see UNCC in a better light." She commended the athletic slogan, "Great Teams Begin with Great Fans." Popp later studied at Oxford, then studied law and joined the U.S. Justice Department.

Buck Fraley, then an executive of Carolina Freight Carriers, cited his twenty-year involvement, beginning as a trustee of Charlotte College, and said the only changes he foresaw were moves toward excellence.

Thomas Storrs, then chief executive officer of NCNB, said he saw rapid growth in the area around the university. Prophetically, he said, "I think the real concern for the school and for the community is the management of this development to insure that it is compatible with the role and environment of the University."

In terms of athletics, Cameron said he visualized UNC Charlotte as predominately a basketball school. "I don't see us in football," he said. "It shouldn't even be considered." Fraley added that football was too expensive, but Howard Haworth, a furniture manufacturing executive and later a member of Governor Jim Martin's administrative team, said he was not opposed to launching football someday.

Turning from that look to the future, Fretwell found he had to deal with the present, and as the spring semester ended in 1980, he acted on the restructuring recommendations that were on his desk when he arrived and that he had been studying and amending. The major thrust of his changes was to merge the individual Colleges of Humanities, Social and Behavioral Sciences, and Science and Mathematics into one College of Arts and Sciences. The change meant that Deans Norman Schul and William Mathis were given other assignments. Mathis returned to the Department of Music as a professor. Schul became acting chair of Criminal Justice and later headed Experiential Learning, which included Cooperative Education, and finally served as director of the cooperative education program within the William States Lee College of Engineering.

Faculty members jokingly called this occasion Black Friday, Bloody Friday, or the May Day Massacre, because Fretwell called a meeting on a Friday in May to make his announcements, made them, and left the room and the city without further comment or response. The changes marked the continued ascendancy of Sherman Burson, the mild-mannered Quaker who had been recruited by Bonnie Cone to build a chemistry department. Burson had later become dean of the College of Science and Mathematics and now was named dean of the new College of Arts and Sciences.

Because Arts and Sciences had become the largest college, his friends jokingly called him "Super Dean." Burson's wry wit occasionally contained a barb as well. He dubbed Robert Snyder of the College of Engineering "the Aggressor Dean" because of his assertive style in seeking resources for his college.

Since the death of Hugh McEniry, Philip Hildreth had served as vice chancellor for academic affairs. Fretwell replaced him, on an interim basis, with Dean Robert Snyder of engineering. Some deans, department chairs, and faculty members had complained that Hildreth was too kind and gentle to make some tough decisions that needed to be made. Hildreth thereafter spent some time bringing himself up to date in his field and returned to the Biology Department as Distinguished Professor of Biology and Genetics.

During his interim assignment, Snyder quickly earned a reputation as a tough administrator. He removed Joseph Schell as chair of the Department of

Mathematics after the two engaged in a dispute over procedures for registration on the floor of the gymnasium. On the other hand, Snyder then appointed Schell to guide the development of computer science and the university's computer-oriented relationships with business and industry.

In 1981, James H. Werntz of the University of Minnesota, where he headed the Center for Educational Development and University College, was named vice chancellor for academic affairs. Werntz's unit at Minnesota was essentially an experimental college where he worked on the improvement of instruction for the entire system. A native of Wilmington, Delaware, and a physicist, Werntz had received his undergraduate degree at Oberlin College and his M.S. and Ph.D. at the University of Wisconsin at Madison.

Fretwell believed that Werntz, because of his analytical approach, would provide a good balance to his own intuitive approach. However, some of the people who had complained about Hildreth's softness now complained that Werntz was too tough. Werntz led intensive studies of the division. These included the processes governing curriculum development and approval, salary increases and promotions, budget development, and expansion of off-campus instruction.

The Division of Academic Affairs was given additional staff with the appointment of Barbara Goodnight, former chair of Sociology and Anthropology, as interim associate vice chancellor (with the "interim" later removed) and Harold Clarke, former dean of admissions and registration, as

The Fretwell Team in 1981 (from left): Leo Ells, Doug Orr, E. K. Fretwell, Jr., Bill Britt, Bob Albright, Jim Werntz. Photo by Sue Johnson.

Barbara Goodnight, associate vice chancellor for academic affairs, 1982. Photo by Sue Johnson.

assistant vice chancellor. By removing the "interim" part of her title of associate vice chancellor, Fretwell later made Goodnight the highest-ranking female administrator on campus. She also gave the Academic Affairs administration a sense of continuity and a corporate memory because of the experience she had gained since 1967.

Academic Affairs changes also included David Nixon's resignation as director of the Computing Center to return to full-time teaching in the Mathematics Department. He had directed the center since its beginning in 1966 and through several generations of mainframe computers. Robert Blackmun was appointed as his replacement.

A key appointment was that of Raymond Frankle, director of library services at Stockton State College in New Jersey, as director of the library. The value of the Frankle appointment later doubled when he attracted to the campus a former colleague, Bil Stahl, an expert on the use of computer technology in library applications. Stahl's expertise was to prove essential later when UNC Charlotte was linked, first through the Microelectronics Center of North Carolina's microwave communications network and still later through the North Carolina Information Superhighway, to other universities and data sources worldwide.

Another part of the restructuring was the creation of a new Division of

Research and Public Service, which included the Office of Continuing Education and Extension, the Institute for Urban Studies and Community Service, the Center for International Studies, the Office of Research Grants and Contracts, the public radio station, the Office of Public Information and Publications, and Intercollegiate Athletics. The intent was to bring together in a major organization all of the units that were involved in community outreach. This was an extension of Colvard's vision of the university as the provider of advice and service to an urbanizing region. Fretwell bought the concept and added his own endorsement, raising community outreach to a level unprecedented in the UNC system. Doug Orr, previously vice chancellor for student affairs, was appointed the new division's vice chancellor

In the creation of the new Division of Research and Public Service, the significance of revitalizing the Institute for Urban Studies and Community Service was not immediately apparent, but it soon would be. James W. Clay, professor of geography, was named its director. Later Colvard was to say that Fretwell saw the role of the Urban Institute as he originally had envisioned it and that the leadership of Clay made the vision a reality.

Clay had created an entrepreneurial Geography Department that became adept at producing publications such as the atlases of the Charlotte area, North Carolina, and the South. It was also a department with an affinity for the work of the Urban Institute, which would shortly turn to the task of creating University Place and later to helping create an understanding of regionalism in Charlotte-Mecklenburg and surrounding cities and counties.

Charles F. (Chuck) Lynch, dean of students, in one of the several temporary assignments to the position before he was finally appointed to it, was named interim vice chancellor for student affairs. A native of New York State, Lynch came to UNC Charlotte from the University of Miami, where he had worked in the campus housing program. He began his UNC Charlotte career as first director of housing and residence life.

Robert Albright was appointed vice chancellor for student affairs in 1981, to fill the position on a permanent basis. Albright thus became the first African American appointed to a top-level administrative position. A native of Philadelphia, Albright received his A.B. degree in history from Lincoln University, his M.A. from Tufts University, and the Ph.D. from Kent State University. He came to UNC Charlotte from a position as special assistant to the assistant secretary for postsecondary education in the U.S. Department of Education. Earlier he had been director of the Moton Consortium on Admissions and Financial Aid and, before that, vice president for student affairs at Lincoln University.

He immediately made a positive impact on UNC Charlotte and the Charlotte community, and it soon became clear that UNC Charlotte would not be able to keep him any length of time. The trustees of Johnson C. Smith University took notice and named Albright president in 1983, after he served two years at UNC Charlotte.

The Fretwell appointments of Albright and Goodnight diversified the top administrative ranks and marked a point of maturity for the institution.

There was also growth in diversity in the student population. By 1980, UNC Charlotte had a sizable population of international students, including a large contingent of Iranians sent by the Shah of Iran to obtain an education to help modernize their country. Unfortunately for modernization, the revolution back home disrupted the Shah's plans.

The Iranian Revolution and the taking of American hostages created a crisis involving the nearly one hundred students from that country on the UNC Charlotte campus. As events unfolded, sidewalk confrontations between Iranian and U.S. students result in heated shouting matches and almost erupted into violence.

Marian Beane, director of international students and scholars services, defused the crisis by inviting all interested students inside for an open exchange of views in the Lucas Room. By this strategy she made the international crisis a learning experience—particularly for American students—and prevented violence, even though there were heated verbal exchanges inside the Lucas Room. Until that point, many of the American students had lumped all Middle Eastern students into one ethnic entity.

At least during the Iranian crisis, the American students learned that Iranians considered themselves Persians and not Arabs. Students also saw Religious Studies professor Loy Witherspoon wrestling with his conscience as he declared that he had long considered himself a pacifist but that the hostage-taking created a temptation for vengeance.

Unfortunately, both during the crisis and before and after, too many students, American and international, failed to take advantage of the opportunity to experience the world by socializing with each other. International students tended to stick with their own, and too many Americans were content to allow them to be isolated. Nevertheless, UNC Charlotte, which enrolled the largest population of undergraduate international students in the state, provided the opportunity for a widened cultural experience for any American student who wished to take advantage of the opportunity. As international awareness increased in the business community and in the larger culture, that factor worked in the university's favor.

A similar problem existed in relations between African American and white American students. The problem was a holdover from the civil rights movement. In the early years of that struggle, the quest was for an integrated society. As that goal began to be realized, African American leaders realized they did not want to lose their cultural identity in the process. So they asked for equal access but without the necessity of being blended into white social forms. Those changes in approach played out on university campuses.

Since the early 1970s, the University of North Carolina system had been engaged in a legal dispute with the U.S. Office of Civil Rights and later in federal courts over further desegregation of the system. The complaint was that too few black students were enrolled in the historically white campuses of the UNC system. At the same time, the plaintiffs said they did not want to give up any of the five historically black campuses—more than in any other state. A merger of white and black institutions might have solved part of the problem. Objection to such a merger, however, was and continued to be just as strong from African American citizens as it was from white citizens.

The long legal struggle over further desegregation of the UNC system was resolved by a consent decree in 1981, early in Fretwell's tenure. Reluctance to settle was not resistance to desegregation on the part of UNC General Administration officials but, rather, an unwillingness to accept the loss of control over educational issues that would have resulted had they yielded to the original plan submitted by federal officials. It was stressful to UNC president Bill Friday, who was considered a liberal on social issues, to appear to be obstructing further desegregation. However, he believed that integrity and ultimate authority over the UNC system were at stake.

Although UNC Charlotte was not at the center of the negotiations, there were times when the future of the campus was at risk. At one point, for example, federal negotiators proposed that they arbitrarily assign students to campuses regardless of student choice. This move would have represented a complete break with all national higher education tradition and would have been particularly damaging to a campus like UNC Charlotte, which offered opportunity and hope to students who could not afford to go away from home to college. UNC Charlotte was the only university campus within a ninety-mile radius in a North Carolina region that included nearly five million people.

Vice Chancellor Orr testified for the system during the process. He said that he tried to make two points. The first was that many students served by a campus like UNC Charlotte were place-bound by family and job and could not pick up and move if programs were shifted just to meet federal goals. The second point was that much of the university's strength was in its diversity. Campuses of the system had each evolved with certain strengths, given their history, their location, and the quality of their faculty expertise.

One federal approach would have moved the criminal justice program from UNC Charlotte, in the state's largest city, to N.C. Central University in Durham. One would assume that if any program were needed to relate to the problems of large cities, it would have been criminal justice.

The consent decree that settled the dispute came at a particularly unfortunate moment for UNC Charlotte. At the very time when the Charlotte campus needed new facilities to meet the pressures of explosive enrollment growth, funds from the limited pool available had to be allocated to the historically black campuses. As a result, UNC Charlotte had then and continued to have far fewer square feet of space per student than the historically black campuses—and all of the historically white campuses as well.

Similarly, at a time when UNC Charlotte needed to add programs to meet the demands of a rapidly growing population in the entire Southern Piedmont, many new programs had to be allocated to the historically black campuses, and that delayed UNC Charlotte's reaching a critical mass of program offerings.

Perhaps there was validity in denying new programs to long-established campuses while helping the historically black campuses catch up, but it tended to put the brakes on the legitimate growth needs of a new campus like UNC Charlotte.

Considering the particularly negative impact of the consent decree on UNC Charlotte, it was ironic that it became one of the campuses that took the goals of the consent decree (and the later voluntary continuation of it by the UNC system) most seriously. UNC Charlotte increased its percentage of black students until it had the highest of any historically white campus. By 1995, UNC Charlotte had a total enrollment of 15,895 students; 2,278 students, or 14.3 percent, were African Americans. This total meant that UNC Charlotte served a higher number of African American students than Charlotte's historically black institution, Johnson C. Smith University.

Yet there remained the problem of bringing African American and white students together outside the classroom for cultural understanding. In many cases, African American students had created parallel campus organizations to what they considered white organizations. Like the international students, most African American students moved in their own circles, and most white students were content to let them do so. Even so, relationships between the races at UNC Charlotte were relatively cordial over the years. Most flare-ups of tension stemmed from the occasional appearance of graffiti containing racial or ethnic slurs.

In an effort to expand the students' horizons, UNC Charlotte entered a National Student Exchange Program in which UNC Charlotte students would transfer for a year to another campus somewhere in the country, and students from the other campuses would spend a year in Charlotte.

The UNC Charlotte campus never had a provincial outlook, even though its out-of-state student enrollment was less than 15 percent for most of its history. Because Charlotte was such a magnet for out-of-state employees, many UNC Charlotte students had done much of their growing up in other cities, states, and nations and brought a mix of insights to the institution. By the end of its first fifty years, the university was enrolling the maximum percentage of out-of-state students allowed by the legislature—18 percent.

From the beginning, UNC Charlotte's administrators had recruited faculty and staff from wherever they could find the best candidates, creating a particularly heterogeneous cadre. If a stranger were suddenly dropped into the middle of the campus, it was unlikely that person would know his or her geographic locale. Of course, there were occasional clashes of culture—for example, when a professor from a large northern urban center encountered a student from rural North Carolina. Because of Charlotte's urbanization, that often was the only encounter such professors had with real southern culture. There were also clashes of understanding when a student raised in a strict fundamental religious setting was asked by a professor to challenge or reexamine his or her own beliefs in class. But such clashes occurred at private, religious institutions as well.

Many professors quickly adapted to the local and regional culture. When political science professor Tim Mead, a native of Michigan, arrived from an appointment in the Ford administration in Washington, he jumped right into the culture outside uptown Charlotte. He fished local streams and lakes and attended stock car races—not just the ones at the upscale Charlotte Motor Speedway, but even ones at dirt tracks where the spectators came away covered with the red clay dust thrown up by the racers' tires. For several years Mead, whose expertise was in urban administration, headed the Master of Public Administration program.

Professor Jerry Pyle, an Ohio native and a medical geographer who had an international reputation in his field and had received the First Citizens Bank Scholars Medal, bought a farm near Midland in Cabarrus County and raised sheep.

On the other hand, these and other faculty members were simultanously becoming more sophisticated in the academic arena. In 1979–80, UNC Charlotte had four professors teaching abroad on Fulbright Fellowships—Gary Ferraro (Anthropology) in Swaziland, Eugene Shaffer (Education) in Taiwan, and Phillip Johnson and Arlo Schurle (both of Mathematics) in Liberia.

The increased academic sophistication of individual faculty members translated into more recognition for their departments and colleges. The College of Architecture received its initial national accreditation for a five-year period, a length of time considered unusual for a new school of architecture. The college began bringing in some of the nation's top architects to teach for several weeks, providing an opportunity for students to rub shoulders with the best practitioners available.

The College of Business Administration launched an advisory council, chaired by trustee Thomas M. Belk of the Belk Department Stores. The college also launched a Business Alumni Distinguished Lecture series, which brought some of the nation's leading executives to Charlotte to speak to a combined audience of business alumni and city business leaders. The college's enrollment was now greater than two thousand.

The new master's program in engineering was off to a good beginning, with some thirty graduate students enrolled. The college's total enrollment passed the thousand-student mark.

The College of Education's enrollment was 746, including 439 students at the master's level. It was becoming the program of choice for teachers in the greater Charlotte region who were seeking to return to college for graduate degrees. That meant teachers no longer had to disrupt families to return to graduate school at distant campuses.

A total of 488 students had enrolled in the College of Nursing by the time it began preparations to end a cooperative master's degree program with UNC Chapel Hill and begin its own graduate program.

The comments of a departmental chair, Joseph Spence of Creative Arts, gave some insights into the campus culture at that stage of the university's development. Spence, who came from Bowling Green College in Ohio, said, "I thought I was coming to a laid-back southern campus. But when I got here I found everybody was going ninety miles an hour all the time."

Rapid growth and the university's many transitions had the potential to create an insensitive campus, but attempts were made to prevent this outcome. Instead of leaving students in a state of uncertainty from the time of their admission, usually in early spring, until the beginning of the fall semester, the Academic Affairs and Student Affairs divisions launched a summer orientation program. Having students oriented during the summer made the opening days of the fall semester less frantic. Newly admitted students felt much more at home when they arrived. Gone also were the long lines that had greeted students at the fall semester opening in previous years.

Milestones of institutional maturity were reached when alumnus John L. Fraley Jr. of Cherryville succeeded his father on the UNC Charlotte Board of Trustees and when alumna Terre Thomas Bullock of Shelby was named to the UNC System Board of Governors. Bullock was following in the public service footsteps of her mother, Betty Dorton Thomas of Concord, who served on the Charlotte College and UNC Charlotte Boards of Trustees and in the North Carolina House of Representatives.

Opportunities for students were expanded in 1981, when the administration signed contracts to establish Army and Air Force Reserve Officer Training Corps units on the campus. Army ROTC had been previously available to UNC Charlotte only through a consortium arrangement with Davidson College.

With the addition of apartment-style residence halls, the campus took on

Alumnus John L. Fraley Jr. (pictured here) replaced his father, John L. (Buck) Fraley Sr., on the UNC Charlotte Board of Trustees in 1981. Photo by Sue Johnson.

even more of the flavor of a residential campus. Student intramural sports grew to the point that spaces to conduct their games had become too small.

In the early Fretwell years, a major student event was Jam-Up, an outdoor rock concert. Success killed it. As word spread that it was a fun event, outsiders were attracted in growing numbers. Once the event was invaded by bikers, and Jerry Hudson, director of campus security, feared that he could not contain an eruption of fighting. The university administration had to end the event, because at that time the campus had no secure venue for such a large event—no place where identification could be checked and entrances secured. Students lamented the event's death for several years. Other annual student gatherings included the College of Architecture's cardboard canoe race.

Even with this progress, Fretwell was encountering the difficulties of making do with limited money at UNC Charlotte. In his annual report for 1980–81, he said,

> From the beginning of this institution, there has been a tradition of trying harder but having to "make do" in the face of inadequate resources. This is evident in the accomplishments of UNCC students on statewide examinations and their performance in national competitions of various kinds. It is also evident in the research and publication accomplishments of faculty with extremely limited resources

for these purposes. The athletic accomplishments of this institution are further testimony, as is the expansion of a 100,000-watt FM National Public Radio Station from a modest 10-watt student-run effort.

The student accomplishments to which he referred were these: the campus Model UN delegation had been selected as one of the six top universities in that competition (a tradition that would continue); engineering students had won first place in the Southeast in a paper-writing competition; the delegation to the N.C. student legislature had placed second among large universities in overall performance; student nurses had ranked as the top four-year institution on the state nursing examination; and once again, UNC Charlotte accounting students had taken top place in the UNC system on the CPA examination and had also had the top two individual papers in the state.

Even with the student accomplishments, there was some uncertainty as to how the university appeared to others. There was concern that change had taken place so rapidly that the public view was lagging reality by several years.

Doug Orr's Division of Development and Public Service and its Office of Public Information and Publications assisted with the university's self-examination by helping conduct a focus group examination on the image of the institution, or, as Fretwell expressed it, "applying the mirror test." Some of the suspected misperceptions were identified—that the campus was "way out there" (meaning that many Charlotteans thought it too far from the center of the city to attend its events), that the curriculum was limited, and that the campus was smaller than it really was. Apparently older residents' perceptions of the institution were frozen in time. Some educators contended that awareness of improvements at an institution lagged reality by as much as ten years and that an awareness of a decline in quality lagged by a similar time span. Newcomers to Charlotte had fewer misperceptions and accepted the institution as it was. The focus group results gave some guidance in helping communicate a more accurate picture of the campus, but budget constraints limited such marketing approaches as advertising and direct mail campaigns to overcome the image lag.

Even without full appreciation for what had been accomplished, university leaders continued to make advances in the academic area. These included the installation of a new mainframe computer and the approval of master's degrees in nursing, reading education, and health education. Library book holdings passed the 300,000 mark.

Werntz took several steps to open opportunities for faculty members. For those professors who wanted to explore administrative work to see whether they would like it, he established a Faculty Associates Program. That allowed a professor or two to become a member of his administrative staff for a year, working on special projects. Another advantage of the program was that it allowed women to gain experience in administration to provide them additional opportunity for mobility.

Werntz appointed Professor James Selby, who was visually impaired, as assistant vice chancellor over educational support services, which included special learning assistance programs and disabled-student services.

Werntz made an effort to find ways to provide sabbaticals when there was no specific budget to cover them in the UNC system. He called his approach "reassignment of duties." Under the program, a professor might leave the classroom for a semester to conduct research, work on a book, or carry out a special project. Werntz also took steps to increase the flow of funds into faculty research projects during summer terms. In some situations, this allowed a professor who needed a summer-school teaching salary, but also needed a break from the classroom, a way around the dilemma.

Faculty members also were encouraged when Women's Studies received a $131,965 grant from the National Endowment for the Humanities and when an interdisciplinary gerontology project received a boost with a program development grant from the U.S. Office of Human Development Services and the Administration on Aging.

Graduate work became more formal with the establishment of a Graduate School in 1986, and new master's programs were established in sociology and in computer science. New, more stringent criteria were used for the appointment of professors to the Graduate School faculty.

An anticipated working relationship with IBM followed construction of the firm's 2.5-million-foot facility and the employment of five thousand people. This relationship began to come to fruition when the university began offering courses in statistics and other subjects for the company's middle managers.

The university experienced an extended and troubled national search for dean of the College of Arts and Sciences following the retirement of Sherman Burson. Several outsiders were considered. The offer was made to one who at first accepted it and then declined. A short time later, he indicated that he had changed his mind and wanted the position after all. But the administration and the committee said no. The campus then turned to an experienced insider and in 1985 appointed Schley Lyons, a longtime chair of the Political Science Department, a local political commentator, and, at UNC Charlotte, the founder of one of the nation's most successful Robert A. Taft Institute of Government programs, which educate schoolteachers about the political process.

Lyons was a former Shepherd College football player who was still an avid tennis player and ballroom dancer despite some knee damage from his football years. He entertained and amazed faculty and staff with his dancing at the annual gala celebrating the presentation of the NationsBank Award for Excellence in Teaching. Lyons was a native of Maryland, having grown up in the narrow strip of land between Pennsylvania and West Virginia that forms the state's panhandle. With a Ph.D. from American University, Lyons was recognized in the greater community for his establishment of the Leadership Charlotte program and for his astute political commentaries during election campaigns.

Like the search process that ultimately led to the appointment of Lyons, there occasionally were other troublesome times in the academic arena. Once when the faculty grew restive, a meeting of the entire body was called so that faculty members could ask Fretwell and Werntz some pointed questions about troublesome issues. Among those were inadequate budget support for faculty travel and library acquisitions, charges of discrimination in the College of Architecture, and plans to shift the Computer Science Department out of Mathematics to the College of Engineering without what some faculty considered full discussion and review.

Ed Perzel of the History Department, later an associate dean of Arts and Sciences, said that the problems might be perceptions rather than reality but that nevertheless the perceptions were serious. These, he said, were that administrators were arrogant, that they viewed themselves as infallible and created roadblocks rather than assisting faculty efforts, and that they were insensitive. Bob Coleman of engineering added, "What we have here is a failure to communicate."

Fretwell and Werntz assured the faculty that the issues would be addressed. Fretwell said that a governance process that looked good on paper would have to be made to work. Calm was restored. But issues such as the criteria for salary increases, raises, and tenure continued to be troublesome. Those concerns were expressed at a Faculty Council meeting in November 1983. After Werntz had outlined a plan for allocating new departmental positions, including the salary ranges for those positions, Paul Escott, a history professor, asked to speak. He said that he was distressed that some entry-level salaries represented 90 percent of his own salary despite the fact that he was in his tenth year. He lamented what he said was a lack of reward for scholarly research and publishing. (Escott had already earned a reputation for his scholarly activity and later was lured away to Wake Forest University, where he became Reynolds Professor and later dean.) Werntz replied that in recruiting new professors he had to respond to market conditions. He said those conditions required that salaries for new faculty members range from $19,000 in some fields to twice that in others. Even so, Escott received one of the university's largest salary increases the following year. And after resolving those issues, Fretwell and Werntz restored calm in the academic division.

In the area of student affairs, UNC Charlotte launched an "emerging leaders" program, a type of training that was later to become very popular on many campuses. Student affairs administrators had found that the university lacked programs for training students to become leaders, and they responded to fill the vacuum. One student who completed the program, D. J. Miller, was selected as one of fifty students from 1,150 applicants to participate in Leadership America, a national training program for college students. The program even appealed to at least one international student, Betty Valladares of Venezuela. Unlike those international students who kept apart from U.S. students, she became involved in student life. Later she earned a master's degree and taught at Central Piedmont Community College.

A challenge for one student affairs program occurred in 1980, when leaders of Venture, an outdoor experience program, invited members of the executive staff and the deans to participate in a canoe trip down the Rocky River in Stanly County. Venture had been launched by Orr during the Colvard administration with a grant from the Wallace Foundation. Venture used the principles of the Outward Bound program to teach self-reliance and team-building. In fact, the UNC Charlotte program was the first program ever spun off from Outward Bound.

The purpose of the Rocky River trip was twofold: to demonstrate the program and its value in confidence-building and to show the group two natural areas held by the university.

Normally, the Rocky River lived up to its name—rocky—and was too shallow for good rafting or canoeing. However, the trip took place in April, when heavy rains had filled the river. The outing began at the UNC Charlotte Wildlife Preserve, near Locust, on property donated by Dr. and Mrs. George Leiby.

Now, on most occasions it might have been a good thing for a chancellor to keep his attorney close by. But it wasn't such a good idea to put Bill Steimer in the same canoe with E. K. Fretwell that day. It was before Steimer had lost a great deal of weight with a rigid diet. And with his height, Fretwell carried some weight as well. When the canoe expedition hit some rapids near the end of the run, the Fretwell-Steimer canoe flipped. Steimer came up under the canoe and feared he might drown there. But he and Fretwell righted their craft and bailed out the water, and the procession continued downriver.

Most other members of the group—except for Doug Orr, who maneuvered his canoe like a Native American in a birchbark craft—were more or less soaked. The April breeze had a cooling effect. The most chilling factor, however, was that the finale of the expedition was a meeting with a Davidson College and State of North Carolina delegation that had gathered for a dedication ceremony at the top of Morgan's Bluff. That was the natural area with some rare plant specimens that had been acquired jointly by the two institutions through the efforts of biologists Jim Matthews of UNC Charlotte and

E. K. Fretwell, Jr. (left) and William M. Steimer steady their canoe after it overturns in Rocky River. Photo by Ken Sanford.

Tom Daggy of Davidson. The Davidson and state government group was warm and dry and comfortable. The UNC Charlotte group was wet, cold, and miserable.

Strangely, neither Fretwell nor Steimer moved to revise the Venture program because of the perceived risks. Both, however, grew tired of the kidding about the great underwater river run and the Rocky River Snorkeling Award that was presented them. The citation said, "While distinguished officials from the State of North Carolina and Davidson College observed from the higher elevations of Morgan's Bluff a few hundred yards downstream, the Fretwell/Steimer canoe elected to negotiate this last set of rapids underwater. Eager to view the unique rock formations at the bottom of the stream, these two brave canoeing pioneers ignored personal safety to undertake a unique perspective of Rocky River."

Fretwell explained that he was indeed experienced in canoes, but in the still waters of upstate New York lakes.

His experience in building a campus in the City of Buffalo stood him in better stead. Physical plant improvements at UNC Charlotte early in Fretwell's tenure included the new Reese Administration Building, the Ida

UNC President William Friday speaks at the dedication in 1982 of the business administration classroom building named for him and his wife, Ida. Photo by Sue Johnson.

and William Friday Business Administration Building, a new cafeteria to serve students in residence halls on the northeast side of the campus, and completion of additional residence halls in that area of the campus. The Friday building was an interesting project, because faculty input into its design led to a very practical building that was built quickly—in only thirteen months. Its spartan exterior design, however, had to be revisited in 1994, with the construction of a third-floor addition.

For an institution so relatively young, another significant project was taking place: the construction of the Dalton Special Collections Room of the Atkins Library. The collections of two men—Harry Dalton and Harry Golden—were crucial to that development.

Harry Golden, the internationally known editor of *The Carolina Israelite* and best-selling author of such books as *Only in America* and *For Two Cents Plain*, gave the library his collection of personal papers. That helped launch the library's emphasis, under the leadership of Robin Brabham, on the papers and manuscripts of residents of the greater Charlotte area.

Dalton was a businessman and a collector of books and art, many of which he contributed to UNC Charlotte. He had also helped launch the library's rare book collection with a cash donation of $25,000 back in 1971. Dalton and his wife, Mary, also gave funds toward construction of the Dalton

Room. A carefully designed room-within-a-room on the library's tenth floor, it was the site of the first meeting of the UNC system's Board of Governors, in 1972.

The design preserved a gallery just outside the rare book room that allowed a 360-degree view of the campus and University City. Visitors were able to walk around the exterior of the Special Collections Room for the view but still were protected from the elements inside the walls of the tenth floor of the Dalton Tower.

In addition to his early gift of $25,000, Dalton also gave a rare first edition of Walt Whitman's "Leaves of Grass." In terms of art, perhaps his best-known donations to the library were two paintings, one by Andrew Wyeth and the other by N. C. Wyeth.

In addition to being a sophisticated collector of paintings and rare books, Dalton was a down-to-earth raconteur who usually entered a room telling a joke—like the one about a rookie cop sent out on the beat. A short time later he called the desk sergeant to report that he had found a body. The sergeant, who had some difficulty with spelling, said he needed some information for a report and asked the rookie where he had found the body. The rookie said he found it on Sycamore Street. "How do you spell that?" the sergeant asked. The rookie began, "S-y-c," whereupon the sergeant said, "I tell you what, just drag the body over to Elm and call me back."

Following her husband's death, Mary Dalton endowed the Colvard Distinguished Professor in Nursing in honor of Chancellor Emeritus and Mrs. Colvard, whose daughter, Linda Opdyke, was one of the first master's degree graduates in nursing.

Others, including English professor Julian Mason and former English instructor Liz Patterson, also became contributors to and advocates for the library's special collections. American literature became one of the collection's features, with the Whitman volume setting the tone. Other features were children's literature, beginning with the purchase of the Evelyn Bottome Lewis Collection, which was strong in nineteenth-century publications.

The official papers of Charlotte's mayors were to become a major focus. The library was designated the repository for those papers, as well as those of other key local officials.

In light of these academic successes, it is appropriate to note that problems still cropped up in the academic arena. When tenure was initially denied to Clyde Appleton, a professor in creative arts, his faculty colleagues protested and finally marched with picket signs around the administration building. Administrators relented, and Appleton was given tenure. That incident caused the university no adverse impact in the greater community. In fact, after being asked to assess UNC Charlotte's image in the community, Joe Martin—an NCNB official and brother of Governor Jim Martin—said,

"When I saw faculty carrying picket signs, I thought, 'Now there's a real university.'"

Then a professor in architecture who was denied tenure charged anti-Semitism. The resulting hearings were somewhat divisive, but the charges were not upheld following a review headed by Professor Robert Mundt. Overall, there was cohesion and a continuing sense of mission on the campus.

One of the best indications that UNC Charlotte faculty and staff members had become confident of the university's academic stature was their willingness to depart from tradition. Instead of honoring just the rich and famous with honorary degrees at commencement, in 1982 they chose to honor a modest African American woman, Miss Anita Stroud. She lived in a housing project and had devoted her life to serving children who lived there with after-school and summer camp programs. On her own, she taught the children valuable lessons of life in addition to helping them with their learning skills. However, the commencement speaker that same year—Congressman (later Senator) Paul Simon of Illinois—was in the usual tradition of the prominent state or national figure.

Following a year of applying the "mirror test," Fretwell said in his annual report that he found much with which to be pleased but many things left to be done. After reciting the accomplishments of the year, he listed the shortcomings: relatively poor standing in terms of state appropriations per student and square footage of space per student. He also noted the high percentage of UNC Charlotte students in upper-division and graduate work without any budget recognition of the fact that it cost more to teach juniors and seniors than freshmen and sophomores.

Fretwell, like Colvard before him, was told by officials in the UNC General Administration not to make "invidious comparisons" to other campuses of the system. But how else could the point be made that UNC Charlotte was being shortchanged? Failure to find a sympathetic hearing on such issues may have contributed to UNC Charlotte's becoming the most entrepreneurial university within the UNC system.

CHAPTER 8

The University as Entrepreneur

ONE OF the most significant developments in the early Fretwell administration was that of University City, which included four component parts: the university, University Hospital, University Research Park, and University Place. The following story of those developments shows how they turned Charlotte's historic growth patterns around.

Starved as UNC Charlotte was for operating monies, staff, space, and equipment, its faculty and staff had to concoct other means of developing resources. Their inventive efforts created within the university an aggressive, entrepreneurial thrust that became a hallmark of the institution.

Vice Chancellor Doug Orr said that it was significant that Fretwell, despite his interest in higher education at the national level and his upbringing as the son of a Columbia University professor and his own personal commitment to the academic enterprise, understood the necessity for UNC Charlotte's off-campus involvement in economic development. Basically he facilitated the university's public service role in developing University City, Orr said, and "charged Jim [Clay] and me to make it happen." Orr believed that the green light given by Fretwell was essential to University City's development.

With IBM's development of a 2.5-million-square-foot facility on its fourteen hundred acres, University Research Park was at the same time becoming a "blue chip" park. IBM had the name quality to serve as a magnet for attracting other major firms. That power was to attract big-name corporations, including AT&T; the *Wall Street Journal*; Duke Power; Verbatim (at first a subsidiary of Kodak and later of Mitsubishi); EDS (the company founded by H. Ross Perot and later sold to General Motors); Bell South; Michelin Aircraft Tire; HBO and Company; the Electrical Power Research Institute (EPRI), affiliated in Charlotte with J. A. Jones; Sandoz Chemicals; Allstate Insurance;

197

and Collins & Aikman. Later would come Wachovia Bank, First Union Bank, Tennessee Eastman, and others.

In fact, these developments were among the most significant accomplishments of UNC Charlotte in its entire fifty-year history, and they were among the most significant developments in the history of Charlotte and Mecklenburg County as well. Charlotteans may not have realized the importance of the development of University Research Park. As Charlotte moved toward status as the second- or third-largest banking center in the nation, it also risked for putting all its eggs in one economic basket. The research park, with its focus on technology, communications, and data processing, accomplished an important diversification of the city's economy. Otherwise, a single major corporate takeover of one of the city's major banks, with a relocation of headquarters, could have represented a major disruption of the city's economy.

To understand why the development of University City had such a significant impact on Charlotte and Mecklenburg County and the surrounding region requires a reexamination of issues discussed earlier, particularly the geographical location of the university. Those involved with bringing a university to the Charlotte region believed that a university community would quickly unfold around the new campus. That did not happen automatically. The inertia, even antipathy, concerning development north of Independence Boulevard was pervasive in the 1960s and into the 1970s. Even in the 1980s, a real estate executive said development might happen in twenty or thirty years but maybe not in his lifetime. He acknowledged that real estate personnel did not recommend northeast Charlotte to potential clients. And as noted, the City-County Planning Commission had zoned the campus area to protect it from unwanted development, perhaps damping enthusiasm for commercial projects anywhere nearby.

Soon after the campus was placed at the site between US 29 and NC 49, the Crosland Company had created the College Downs residential development directly across from the university, but little other residential development had taken place. Faculty members and staff recruited early in campus history settled in some modest developments close to the campus—Hidden Valley, Hampshire Hills, and Shannon Park. As they were promoted and their salaries increased, they often looked to move up in their housing. Unfortunately, until the 1980s, there were no upscale developments near the university, so faculty members usually moved to southeast Charlotte and commuted twelve to fifteen miles to the campus.

Indeed, the university was faced with a chicken-and-egg dilemma. Residential developers said they didn't want to create new neighborhoods, because the area lacked amenities like hospitals, shopping centers, restaurants, libraries, churches, and other ingredients of a true community. Developers of shopping centers and some of the other amenities said they didn't want to risk coming into the community because it lacked residential areas—a real catch-22 situation.

Crosland owned the land on which the planning commission had sketched a "town center" on N.C. 49 across from the campus some years earlier, but apparently the development of College Downs was all the risk the company wanted to take given the uncertainties that prevailed.

Almost as important to real estate development as location was timing. As Fretwell arrived, community leaders had joined university leadership in worrying about the future of Charlotte-Mecklenburg development. Residential development was hot in only one corridor of Charlotte—the southeast. In fact, development was plunging headlong toward the South Carolina state line, taking the tax base with it. Had the trend not been arrested, sooner or later uptown Charlotte would have become essentially the northern edge of the City of Charlotte.

One factor that could open the northeast for development was the provision of city water and sewer service. Development along the southeast corridor was aided by the fact that sewer lines followed the county's creeks flowing outward in that direction. On the other hand, the University City area lay north of a ridge over which sewage wouldn't flow but would have had to be pumped. The solution was to build the Mallard Creek treatment facility on a northward-flowing stream.

The community's leadership also tried to impose some disincentives to rapid growth in the southeast by slowing the provision of roads, schools, and water and sewer service there. Years later the community was still trying to overcome some of the fallout from those decisions, because development continued despite the disincentives. As a result, more schools had to be built, and widening the overcrowded, two-lane Providence, Sardis, and Park Roads became more difficult and more expensive.

Even after water and sewer services were provided in the northeast there would remain the deeply ingrained tradition of directing all new home buyers toward the southeast. Might the solution be to create a magnet in the northeast to pull development in that direction rather than try to discourage it in the southeast? Yes, that became the answer.

It appeared that only intervention by government and private enterprise could help balance the community's growth. By 1981, the Planning Commission had created a 1995 Comprehensive Plan, which identified several urban nodes that could develop into miniature downtowns with most of the amenities of a center city—jobs, shopping, health services, schools, libraries, hotels, transportation transfer points, and other services. SouthPark was already developing into one, and the University City area showed the promise of becoming another.

Another good fortune of timing was that by the early 1980s the UNC Charlotte Foundation had developed into something of an entrepreneurial organization to benefit the university. For example, it had bought, held, and sold land. And among its board members were some of the community's most astute business leaders.

At the campus itself, Jim Clay, as director of the Urban Institute, had begun to devote a great deal of his attention to creating a plan for University City and a town center. In fact, the creation of University Place proceeded simultaneously on two tracks. Clay and Orr headed the planning track. Leo Ells, Bill Britt, C. C. Cameron, David Taylor, and other officers of the UNC Charlotte Foundation were working on the project's financing and political aspects at the same time.

Early in the planning, Clay and Orr determined that the best site for a metro town center in the northeast would be on some 250 acres of land that was at the time part of the campus and bounded by Interstate 85, Harris Boulevard, and US 29, with a nine-hole golf course on the northern boundary.

The fact that UNC Charlotte (and thus the State of North Carolina) owned the land also made it clear that it would be difficult to transfer to the private sector for development. It was also certain that the university itself could not get into land development. Attention focused on the nonprofit UNC Charlotte Foundation. But the foundation's board concluded that even it needed an arms-length relationship to real estate development to prevent jeopardizing its tax-exempt status. So the foundation spun off University Metro Town Center Endowment, Inc., headed by the late Robert Lassiter, a Charlotte attorney. C. D. Spangler Jr., then a Charlotte businessman and later to become president of the UNC system, was on an advisory committee to suggest how the foundation might develop the new town. A preliminary master plan for developing the new center was prepared by J. N. Pease Associates.

Another key player was David Taylor, a retired Celanese Corp. executive who had become chair of the UNC Charlotte Foundation Board and the University Research Park Board. As chair of both of these key organizations, he was able to keep them focused on a single goal in developing the center that was to become University Place. In fact, it was Taylor who gave the new development its name.

Another person who played a key role was Chancellor Emeritus Colvard, who had earlier helped create University Research Park.

As the tract of UNC Charlotte land came clearly into focus as the preferred location for the town center, the formidable task of converting state land into private land loomed. At that point, Leo Ells, vice chancellor for business affairs, played one of his most significant roles at the university. Ells was an administrator with a gruff exterior—a retired Army lieutenant colonel who, some said, managed by intimidation. In many ways his authoritarian style did not mesh well with the traditional university leadership style, and in the later years it wore thin.

But this was his finest hour, and Ells excelled in clearing the way for the creation of what was to become University Place. A very complex land swap was required, because the university couldn't arbitrarily just give up a piece of itself. The land swap agreement had the UNC Charlotte Foundation purchasing an equivalent 250 acres of land on the east side of the campus, with most of it east of Mallard Creek Church Road.

When that property was in hand, Ells led the way as UNC Charlotte went to the governor and the Council of State for approval to swap the 250 acres desired for the town center for the 250 acres east of the campus. It helped that C. C. Cameron, the governor's chief financial officer, was on the Council of State at the time, and thus approval was gained.

Of all the major developments undertaken in Charlotte-Mecklenburg, this one had perhaps the most unanimity of all community interests. Credit for real vision and creativity, however, must be given to the Charlotte-Mecklenburg Hospital Authority; to its president, Harry Nurkin; and to its board chair, Stuart Dickson, a UNC Charlotte trustee, for taking some risk in creating University Hospital. Nurkin said it was part of a master plan called "Focus on Excellence." He envisioned a comprehensive, unified system of health care with Carolinas Medical Center as the hub and facilities like University Hospital as part of the spokes. Indeed, his vision had been realized by the mid-1990s, as Carolinas Medical Center entered into operating agreements with a number of hospitals in surrounding counties and acquired Mercy Hospital.

Before the construction of University Hospital, the authority for some time had been considering a suburban hospital, though it was mostly looking at other sectors of the community. University activism on the issue perhaps caused the authority to move more quickly than it otherwise might have. University and foundation leaders entered into negotiations with a private developer, Hospital Corporation of America, for a facility on the site of the old County Home property. That tract had been retained by Mecklenburg County when five hundred acres were donated to UNC Charlotte. Those discussions caused the hospital authority to move quickly to participate. When the hospital authority entered into negotiations, the private hospital corporation withdrew.

The hospital authority broke ground for University Memorial Hospital (later known as University Hospital) on June 13, 1983. The architectural firm of Freeman-White Associates used for its design a patient-oriented snowflake layout to put all services as close as possible to hospital beds.

Some outraged critics complained that the hospital authority was wasting money putting a hospital where nobody lived and was at the least building it well ahead of need. Indeed, the critics appeared to be correct during the first few years of the hospital's operation: it had to be subsidized. But hospital administrators soon learned that as long as uptown medical groups were serving the medical office complex a day a week or so, those doctors wouldn't admit patients to University Hospital; instead they would choose the hospitals closer to their homes. When University Hospital began recruiting new physicians to build their practices in northeast Mecklenburg, the situation turned around quickly, and the medical office complex had to build additions—a total of five by 1995. University Hospital set a trend for other hospitals, as Mercy followed with Mercy South in Pineville and Presbyterian followed with a hospital in Matthews.

At first Charlotte-Mecklenburg School System authorities lent moral support to the development of northeast Mecklenburg but did not act quickly enough in a concrete way when the residential breakthrough came. When Mallard Creek Elementary School opened, a dozen or so mobile classrooms were required immediately, and supply still had not caught up with demand in the area by 1995, although other schools were being constructed or planned.

Those joining in support of the effort to create the new metro town included the City of Charlotte, Mecklenburg County, the Charlotte-Mecklenburg Planning Commission, the Charlotte-Mecklenburg Schools, the Charlotte-Mecklenburg Hospital Authority, the University Research Park Board, the UNC Charlotte Foundation, the news media, and, of course, UNC Charlotte. There was relatively little neighborhood opposition. All this support made it easier for the State of North Carolina to add its own support.

With land in hand, planning of a specific town core began in earnest. Clay and Orr called upon faculty expertise as planning moved forward. There were ten task forces relating to various aspects of the planning. They tackled such topics as transportation, the arts, retailing, and other subjects. For example, the task force led by Professors Dennis Lord of Geography and Christie Paksoy of Marketing studied the feasibility of a regional shopping center as part of the plan. From the beginning, the dream of most of the planners was that the new town would include a large regional shopping center in the one-million-square-foot range.

In light of the power center that ultimately replaced the planned enclosed mall, it was interesting to read Lord and Paksoy's original report. It said, "Other alternatives may also exist to the large regional mall itself. These might include a smaller center and/or something other than an enclosed mall, including a facility with a different tenant mix than is common in regional malls."

Leadership in the entire project came from the top. Chancellor Fretwell took an active role. Part of the planning process included a 1982 symposium to which some of the nation's leading "new town" developers were invited—among them James Rouse, creator of the new town of Columbia, Maryland, and of Charlottetown, Charlotte's first enclosed mall, later known as Midtown Square, and David Carley of the Carley Capital Group of Madison, Wisconsin, who would ultimately be selected to develop University Place. As part of the process, Clay, Orr, and sometimes Fretwell began visiting "new towns" all over the United States and around the world. In the United States they visited Columbia, Maryland; Reston, Virginia; and Irvine, California. Abroad they visited new towns in England, Scotland, Belgium, Germany, and the Netherlands. From each location they picked up ideas they believed would work in Charlotte. For example, they concluded early on that water would be an essential ingredient of a new town. "Water is magic," Orr said. From the waterfront of Geneva, Switzerland, they adapted the large fountain in the lake to the smaller version later seen at University Place. From Las Ramblas in Barcelona, Spain, they adapted the pedestrian walkway that later ran alongside the Shoppes at University Place from US 29 down to and across the lake.

Clay and Orr made an ideal team. Along with Al Stuart, they had established themselves as first-rate scholars in their field with the *Metrolina Atlas*, followed by the *North Carolina Atlas* and an atlas of the South, called *Land of the South*. On a personal level, the two could kid each other and enjoy their differences. Orr kidded Clay about being the urban expert who had come down out of the hills of Crum, West Virginia. Clay kidded Orr about having grown up in an exclusive country club setting in Greensboro but trying to show that he was just one of the guys by playing in a folk music band and hiking and rafting in the mountains. Mostly, however, they had an ability to bounce ideas off each other and come to agreement on those that were most important. To convert their ideas into a concrete plan, they employed the architectural firm of Wallace, Roberts and Todd.

By far the most controversial aspects of the plan were that the mixed-use development would turn its back on the adjacent major highways and focus on the central lake and that residential components would be blended with commercial in close proximity. As a result, when the plan went out for solicitation of a developer, many local and regional developers discarded all its visionary aspects and suggested scraping the site off, filling the ravine that ultimately was to become the lake, and creating a standard strip shopping center. Such a center would have failed to create a magnet to attract major development to University City.

It took visionaries to understand the University Place dream, and two such visionaries were found in the Carley brothers, David and James, who were selected to develop the project. Perhaps it was because David Carley, as an academician himself (political scientist), could communicate well with Clay and Orr. Carley also knew something about the political process, having been a strong contender for governor of Wisconsin. At any rate, Carley was stimulated by the visionary plan and agreed to develop it along its basic concepts rather than throwing the whole thing out. This was consistent with Carley's reputation for accepting high-risk projects with public value for social good.

The Carleys soon found that they needed more from Jim Clay than just his advisory assistance. So Clay was given a two-year leave of absence by UNC Charlotte to become a vice president for the developer and to continue seeing that University Place lived up to the planners' vision.

UNC Charlotte had more of a stake in University Place than just the creation of a town core and a magnet for appropriate development in the area. Carley had agreed to pay $8 million to the UNC Charlotte Foundation for development rights. Then the foundation and the university fell into good luck. The Carleys offered instead to pay $4 million immediately, with the assumption that the foundation could invest it and come out with the equivalent of the $8 million in the eight to ten years over which the $8 million would have been paid. There was grousing on campus that the firm had reneged and that the university was losing out on the deal. Later events, however, would prove acceptance of the $4 million to be a good deal. Because of a restructuring of the national tax laws on real estate development and overcommitments to major projects elsewhere in the nation, the Carley firm went bankrupt. Had UNC Charlotte's foundation not taken the $4 million up front, it might have received only pennies on the dollar.

The City of Charlotte also suffered from the Carley fall. The firm was the developer of the imaginative CityFair project uptown. Because of the Carley bankruptcy, disruption of traffic flow to that in-town shopping mall, the closing of the Belk and Ivey's department stores and, finally, disruption caused by the construction of the NationsBank tower, the center failed and was not revived until 1994, when the Keith Corp. purchased it.

With all the planning required, it took until March 1984 for construction to begin on University Place and until September 1985 for the grand opening. That grand opening was more than just the opening of the center itself, with its mixed-use combination of stores, offices, hotels, theaters, restaurants, banks, apartments, condominiums, and patio homes. At last it attracted residential developers to the area, followed by office developers and more commercial developers. University Place was a major magnet.

An interesting response to the beginning of the University Place development was that the John Crosland Company's shopping center unit regained interest in the area. In fact, the company launched the long-dormant shopping center on the original site of a planned town center on NC 49 across from the campus. A race developed to sign tenants for that development, in competition with University Place. Crosland was able to get the center on

University Place (aerial view) became a catalyst for the development of University City and Northeast Mecklenburg County.

NC 49 up and opened well before University Place opened. This created a bit of resentment on the part of university planners, who had waited in vain for Crosland to move over the years. But that was the free enterprise system at work, and later events were to show that the market had room for many entrepreneurs.

University Place was clearly the catalyst that set off the explosion of development in northeast Mecklenburg County. Finally, city and county growth became balanced, with the exception of slow development in the northwest. In addition to the magnet for growth created by University Place and University City, growth began to explode in the Lake Norman area. With University City, this created a double magnet to the north and northeast. At times more building permits were issued for these areas than for the southeast, historically the hot growth area.

It became clear to developers and would-be residents alike that highway access was a major attraction for the north and northeast. In the University City area there were four four-lane highways running north and south—NC 49, US 29, Interstate 85, and Interstate 77—and there was Harris Boulevard, with plans for widening to four lanes (finally realized in 1995). Meanwhile, the southeast had to make do with clogged two-lane roads until construction began on the Outer Belt in the late 1980s and early 1990s.

Soon there was a proliferation of middle-income residential neighborhoods and even upscale neighborhoods in University City. University

Research Park helped fuel the movement by selling property for nearby developments at cost. The area gained its own strong momentum and boasted such upscale developments as Sweetwater and Davis Lake. It also boasted one of the most successful new concepts in the region—Highland Creek, a master-planned public golf course community that offered many amenities and a wide range of home prices and featured the participation of multiple builders.

As consolidations of America's huge corporations took place, with the attendant downsizing and right-sizing, it became clear that new job creation and entrepreneurial activity would slow in those organizations and would more likely occur in small start-up companies and spinoff small businesses. For that reason it was decided that University Research Park ought to acknowledge that new direction. This resulted in the creation in 1986 of a business incubator center. Orr and Jon Benson, director of the center, went to Ben Craig, First Union Bank executive, and asked him to head its board and make it a success. Orr said that Craig gave the center instant credibility. When he died prematurely, the board named it the Ben Craig Business Incubator Center. Along with the incubator came the Small Business and Technology Development Center, a state entity. The incubator center's first home was in a former church educational building on North Tryon Street. Later, with the help of the UNC Charlotte Foundation, the center was provided with a modern new facility in University Research Park.

Using the support of the Ben Craig Center, small start-up businesses could get advice and consulting help, without which many new businesses failed. Some of Charlotte's leading businesspeople volunteered to serve on strong three-person advisory boards for infant firms in the center. As the center became a success under the direction of political scientist Benson, an extension was later created in Aachen, Germany, to allow U.S. companies to explore the feasibility of locating in Europe. The research park facility also took in some foreign firms that wanted to explore the possibility of locating in the United States. Another experiment was to allow firms that needed to be in larger facilities than the incubator building provided to establish an associate status that would offer access to the consulting and advising services.

For several years after University City's grand opening, its success created an unusual opportunity for national and international visibility for UNC Charlotte. Reporters came from newspapers in Atlanta, Tulsa, Kansas City, and New York City, as well as newspapers in North Carolina. Then the story was picked up abroad, in newspapers in Germany and other nations. With the initiation of the Council for International Visitors, a unit of International House, additional opportunities for visibility were opened. The U.S. State Department identified developing leaders of nations around the world and, through private contractors such as the Council for International Visitors, showed them creative examples of public-private partnerships and technological developments.

Many of these international visitors were directed to Charlotte. Official visitor delegations from fifty nations of the world came to see what UNC Charlotte and the greater Charlotte business community had accomplished. From some of the State Department escorts it was learned that University City was a good site to illustrate how the United States was dealing with technology transfer and university-business partnerships. They found it easy to see the picture in Charlotte because the components of University City—university, research park, medical complex, and University Place—were contiguous.

University City was compact enough that visitors could easily grasp what had taken place. Just a visit to the tenth floor of the Dalton Tower of the library allowed the visitor to see the proximity of university, hospital, town center, and research park, all of which were connected in a symbiotic relationship. Even if the university were failing to make its case for equitable state funding, it was succeeding beyond measure in becoming an indispensable asset to its community and region, providing the Charlotte area with a major economic engine.

Jim Clay (left) and Doug Orr (right) celebrate with developer David Carley at the University Place dedication in 1985.

CHAPTER 9

Adapting to Charlotte's Pace

THE EXPLOSIVE economic development and population growth of the City of Charlotte, which occurred simultaneously with UNC Charlotte's expansion into a significant state university, helped the campus to establish its unique identity within the UNC system. By the mid-1980s, city and campus were being discovered nationally. UNC Charlotte was providing evidence that it would move nearer the top of the pyramid of higher education institutions in North Carolina.

This didn't mean that UNC Charlotte was no longer struggling for the basic resources it needed for its expansion of facilities and programs. When the legislature established the powers of the Board of Governors of the UNC system, it withheld the power to allocate new buildings to the various campuses. Every two years the Board of Governors presented a priority list of proposed new facilities, but the legislature tended to treat that list only as a point of departure. Thus, critical needs were sometimes overlooked by the legislature. Insufficient consideration was given to existing space per student, or the lack thereof, on the campuses. Often there was a tendency to spread buildings around regardless of need. Sometimes a new physical education facility might be funded while an urgently needed classroom or library was left unfunded. The result was that some campuses were overly blessed with space, while others were severely cramped.

When this disparity was pointed out privately to a visiting legislator from the Piedmont Triad area on the biennial Advisory Budget Commission tour, he responded disdainfully, "Well, there's a solution. You guys can just quit growing and someday you'll catch up." His position was reminiscent of earlier attitudes denying equity for Charlotte and the need to provide for students in the growing Southern Piedmont.

Nevertheless, one significant way in which UNC Charlotte distanced itself from some of the other UNC campuses was simply through its location.

By 1983, the Charlotte Metropolitan Statistical Area had passed the one million mark in population, ranking it as one of the nation's major cities. UNC Charlotte and its home city were, indeed, growing up together.

UNC Charlotte's geographers had understood the true size of Charlotte and its region for some time. They had described it as a "dispersed urban region." By that they meant that the Charlotte region was larger than it appeared because it was made up of a central city—Charlotte—and a number of outlying cities, with greenspace between each component. This misled casual observers into assuming that the region was much smaller than its numbers indicated.

Charlotte, the center city, was growing as well. Until the mid-1980s, many Charlotteans denied their city's size. There seemed to be a nostalgia for the small southern city they once knew. If one pointed out that Charlotte was passing cities like Buffalo, Miami, Cincinnati, Oakland, Pittsburgh, and, finally, Atlanta, they would say, "But that's city-limits population. Look at the metro area." Indeed, the lineup of cities did sometimes change when one looked at metro area as opposed to city-limits population. But by 1995, Charlotte and the Charlotte MSA were both about thirty-third largest in the nation in their respective rankings. Charlotte had reached a city-limits population of 440,000, and the metro area had reached 1.3 million. One-fifth of the state's population lived in Mecklenburg and the surrounding fourteen counties. Even more impressive was the population of the urban region within a hundred-mile radius of Charlotte: it was 5.5 million, exceeding the population of all but fourteen states.

Thus the region could no longer be denied, and Charlotte was becoming known to the point that the city could attract the NBA Charlotte Hornets and the NFL Carolina Panthers, although they weren't easy sales. A writer in Phoenix had suggested, in response to George Shinn's bid for an NBA team, that the only franchise Charlotte could obtain would be one with golden arches.

Charlotte/Douglas International Airport had become one of the top two hubs for USAir. It was the nation's twelfth busiest airport in terms of aircraft takeoffs and landings and the twentieth busiest in terms of passengers passing through the terminal.

In the business arena, the city was becoming the second or third biggest banking center in the nation and was in the top ten cities as a wholesale center.

By any measure, Charlotte had moved into the big leagues of cities, and that fact made its university different as well. Students were beginning to select UNC Charlotte primarily because of the campus location among plentiful jobs and big-city attractions.

In the fall of 1982, UNC Charlotte passed the enrollment milestone of

10,000, and by 1983 it had reached 10,347, placing it fourth in the UNC system in terms of numbers of students, behind only N.C. State, UNC Chapel Hill, and East Carolina and ahead of Appalachian State and UNC Greensboro.

Campuses in the UNC system were funded through an enrollment-driven formula. However, the enrollment-increase funding formula, which was calculated as a percentage of the existing appropriations base, tended to disadvantage campuses like UNC Charlotte that had lagged behind in appropriations per student. Thus the shortfall in public funding continued to plague UNC Charlotte administrators. The campus had engaged in private fund-raising going back to Charlotte College days, but it had never conducted a major capital campaign of the type that had become common at major universities. It would have helped to have held such a campaign earlier, but better late than never, because UNC Charlotte first had to break the ice in the Charlotte community.

Part of the ice to be broken was a view held by several corporate leaders that they only gave to private fund-raising campaigns. There was even implied criticism of UNC Charlotte as a state-supported campus for trying to tap private resources. Many of the critics likely had already given to N.C. State and UNC Chapel Hill campaigns when approached by their supporters but saw no illogic in their positions. The truth was that Charlotteans were displayed prominently in honor rolls of major donors at those institutions as well as private ones like Duke, Davidson, and Wake Forest.

It was difficult to get across the message that UNC Charlotte was state-assisted, not state-supported. In the year of the campaign, for example, legislative appropriations made up less than half the budget, at 49.31 percent. And by the early 1980s, the state was beginning to assist its private campuses through grants to in-state students.

For a first major campaign ever, the "Campaign for Excellence" was fairly successful, due in large measure to cochairs Thomas M. Belk, who was also chair of the Board of Trustees, and C. C. (Cliff) Cameron, the trustees' former chair. Both had a lot of I.O.U.'s out with corporate leaders whose campaigns they had supported. The two also got strong lay support from David Taylor, chair of the UNC Charlotte Foundation. The campaign was staffed by Vice Chancellor for Development William Britt and Director of Development Harry Creemers and Alumni Director Susan Piscitelli. Fund-raising counsel was provided by Howard Covington of Ketchum.

History department chair Ed Perzel led the campus drive in raising $277,100 from 454 pledges by faculty and staff members. Alumnus and UNC Charlotte trustee John Fraley Jr. helped raise $350,000 in the alumni portion of the campaign. In fact, the alumni portion of the campaign was considered one of its most significant features, because it moved the university's graduates further toward the traditional alumni role of providing major institutional support. The total of $6 million raised in the Campaign for Excellence may not have looked impressive by existing standards for major universities, but it was a good start for UNC Charlotte and prepared the way for the later Silver Anniversary Campaign.

Success in private fund-raising came during one of the historic and periodic years of state belt-tightening caused by shortfalls against projected revenue collections. The university did, however, get funding for a physical sciences building during 1982–83. When the building was completed two years later, the Departments of Chemistry and Physics were able to occupy a long-anticipated and well-equipped 100,000-square-foot building. By comparison, the Kennedy Building—the place from which they moved—seemed tiny.

There was also progress in athletics: women's teams accepted a higher challenge in 1982, moving up to NCAA Division I status. By not launching a football team, the university was able to allocate more resources to women's sports, moving them toward equity. Also, the university helped move men's soccer, launched in 1976, toward a more visible status, and in 1983, the team won the Sunbelt Conference title.

In academic affairs, the College of Business Administration achieved a significant milestone—accreditation of the undergraduate programs by the American Assembly of Collegiate Schools of Business (AACSB), a distinction achieved by only a select group of business schools. A few years later the college would achieve that organization's approval for the M.B.A. program, even more essential for distinction in a competitive world of graduate business education, and a relatively new accreditation for its accounting program.

Another effort that afforded the business college considerable visibility was the launching of the UNCC–First Union Economic Forecast project. Economist John Connaughton constructed the first model for tracking and predicting North Carolina's gross state product (GSP), and his quarterly forecast attracted considerable media attention over the following years. Later, First Union withdrew as a partner as it became a more regional and national bank, and Connaughton supported the forecast through multiple subscribers.

As in the economy, there were a few rough spots in the academic arena. After a period of some administrative turmoil, Louise Schlachter left the deanship of nursing and returned to the classroom in 1983. When she did so, some faculty members said the college had become fractured among those dedicated supporters of the original dean, Edith Brocker; those who supported former dean Marinell Jernigan; those committed to outgoing dean Schlachter; and those who would support anybody else. The change in the deanship paved the way for a more tranquil period in the college, particularly a transition period under Acting Dean Pauline Mayo. Despite the period of unrest, the college still managed to accomplish its mission of teaching and service. And after the smooth transitional period led by Mayo, the college found a new dean and strong nursing educator and scholar in Dr. Nancy Langston, who had been associate dean of undergraduate programs at the University of Nebraska. She quickly consolidated her leadership and moved the college forward.

Following a study concerned with bringing the creative arts program back into the academic mainstream rather than continuing it as an "open school" program, two departments were created—performing arts, headed by Jack Beasley, and visual arts, headed by Donald Byrum. Later the creative arts would be organized as dance and theater, headed by Sybil Huskey; music, headed by Doug Bish; and art, headed by Sally Kovach. Although the units were moving toward more traditional approaches to instruction, the early history of a more free-wheeling approach to instruction occasionally caused philosophical rifts within the departments.

As somewhat contentious issues were being settled in the 1980s, faculty members were continuing their scholarly output and gaining recognition. The History Department was particularly active. Both Professors Paul Escott and David Goldfield were twice awarded the Mayflower Cup Award for the best work of nonfiction in North Carolina. Likewise, historian Carol Haber won the Valley Forge Honor Certificate of Excellence for her book *Beyond Sixty-Five: The Dilemma of Old Age in America's Past*. Harold Josephson was editing a major reference work, a biographical dictionary of modern peace leaders.

Women's issues were beginning to move to the forefront of campus consciousness. A Women's Studies Program was launched, with Professor Ann Carver as coordinator, and a task force began working on a policy statement dealing with the issue of sexual harassment.

Meanwhile, the Afro-American and African Studies Program was converted into a department (later to be called the Department of African American and African Studies) in spite of some feeling within the UNC General Administration that such departments had seen their peak and were being phased out at many campuses. In some quarters there was a belief that such studies should be housed within existing departments rather than being stand-alone units.

Two people who had played a key role in building the university retired in 1985–86—Sherman Burson as dean of the College of Arts and Sciences, James Kuppers as a professor of chemistry and a former president of the faculty.

Chuck Lynch stepped aside from his interim position as vice chancellor for student affairs as Kathleen Faircloth from the University of Alabama at Birmingham was appointed to the position. One significance to her appointment was that it again diversified the executive staff, which had become all-

Charles F. (Chuck) Lynch became vice chancellor for student affairs in 1987. Photo by Wade Bruton.

male and, with the resignation of Bob Albright to become president of Johnson C. Smith University, all-white.

Faircloth made a major contribution in solving a persistent campus problem. Campus student publications had become very weak—poorly designed, poorly written, and poorly supported. After hearing from consultants, Faircloth brought in Wayne Maikranz as media adviser. He helped students accomplish an immediate turnaround. Thereafter the student publications began winning national awards. A marketing program for student media almost doubled advertising support within one year.

Unfortunately, Faircloth did not enjoy cordial working relationships with her staff, nor with other vice chancellors, and she resigned after a short tenure. In 1986–87, following Faircloth's resignation, Chuck Lynch was finally given the title "vice chancellor for student affairs" without the "interim" attached.

Another major personnel change was the resignation in 1983–84 of Barry Lesley as director of academic grants and contracts to become a vice president of a savings and loan bank after increasing the level of research funding to some $2 million. He was replaced by Lucy Henry, who had been director of grants and contracts at the University of Tennessee at Chattanooga. She picked up where Lesley left off and took the level of grant and contract activity up toward the $10 million mark over the next several years.

The leanness of the university budget again caused a campus unit to behave in an entrepreneurial manner. The staff of the Office of Public Information and Publications had been in conversations with Fretwell about the desirability of distributing a publication to all alumni. Up to this point, the university magazine had been distributed only to a few thousand dues-paying alumni, but the thinking was that the base could not easily be expanded without communicating to a much larger number of alumni. Money, however, was a problem. Fretwell gave his okay to expansion but offered no dollars, creating some frustration.

Suddenly a solution appeared out of the blue. A company called University Network Publishing approached the staff with a proposal that it join with a group of campuses nationwide to publish a magazine. The company would sell the same full-color national advertisements (Kodak, NBC Sports, Vantage cigarettes) that would appear in every participating university's publication. Each campus could plug in its own editorial copy. It was to be a slick four-color magazine, produced monthly. UNC Charlotte would be in good company, too. Other participants included Florida State, the University of Arizona, the University of Northern Arizona, the University of New Mexico, Bradley University, and other major institutions.

The project worked well—for the year that it lasted. Every month UNC Charlotte produced exciting four-color magazines that were distributed to 25,000 alumni, friends, and supporters. Everything about the plan worked—except the sale of national advertising. The agency responsible failed at that task, and with the failure of cash flow, the venture collapsed. However, that one year was long enough to prove the worth of a publication sent to every alumnus plus other supporters and friends of the university. When the magazine venture failed, the Offices of Public Information and Publications, Alumni Affairs, and Development switched to a less expensive tabloid newspaper format on a quarterly basis and continued mailing to the entire list. Development and Alumni Affairs budgets paid for printing and mailing, and Information and Publications supplied most of the writing and design talent.

The expanded publication, in whatever format, helped lift the institution to a higher level of visibility and participation among its alumni and supporters.

In the world of academe, some things take money and others take time. For some four years, the faculty had labored to revamp the curriculum to meet the needs of all graduates and ensure that each student was exposed to a core liberal arts curriculum. Finally, in 1984–85, the task was completed and a program titled "Goals of a UNC Charlotte Education," which established core general education requirements for a baccalaureate degree, was approved. The new program meant that each student would take courses relating to communication and problem-solving skills; the sciences and technology; the arts, literature, and ideas; the values of the individual, society, and culture, and the interrelationships among those aspects of learning. The new requirements included a number of writing-intensive courses to blunt the criticism that too often students could complete their college work without learning to write well. Later critics said the core curriculum plan wasn't very functional, and it may not have been. But those critics weren't present during the four years in which faculty members in many disciplines heatedly debated the value of their offerings and, in the end, compromised and finally found some common ground.

The Council on General Education was established to define the actual degree requirements, ensuring that programs contained the elements of the core curriculum.

A related accomplishment was the adoption of an academic integrity policy to deal with such issues as cheating and plagiarism and other types of misbehavior among students.

By 1985, UNC Charlotte had attained a signal academic achievement for a relatively young university. Programs within all five professional colleges—architecture, business, education, engineering, and nursing—had been given the appropriate national accreditation. Programs in some mature universities continue unaccredited for years.

Another major accomplishment by 1985 was increasing the African American enrollment to 8.9 percent of the student body of 10,842.

Despite these accomplishments, Fretwell and the university faculty continued to seek ways to make the most of resources and to continue the quest for excellence. Like his predecessor Colvard, Fretwell encouraged creative thinking. One of the best examples was his invitation in 1986 to a diverse group of faculty members, under the direction of Professor Bob Mundt of Political Science, to write white papers on the future of the university.

The paper that created the biggest stir with its recommendations was that of Ted Arrington, a professor of political science. Arrington had a way with words that was sometimes startling to administrators. There was the time a newspaper quoted him referring to House Speaker Liston Ramsey as stereotypical of a "fat, beady-eyed politician." Perhaps it was fortunate for UNC Charlotte that Ramsey was shortly thereafter ousted from his leadership position in a coup engineered by a coalition of Republicans and Democrats.

In his white paper, Arrington anticipated the future when he called for new ways of dealing with the General Administration in Chapel Hill and the North Carolina legislature. "Our tactics must include persistent pressure to have the non–Chapel Hill/NCSU point of view represented," Arrington said. In a prophetic statement that would be acted upon some years later, Arrington noted, "Ultimately we want more of our alumni and former employees on the Board [of Governors] and in the General Administration." Later that would extend to getting friends of UNC Charlotte on the board.

What Arrington anticipated for dealing with the legislature wasn't exactly what later developed, but he did anticipate solving the problem through organization. What he suggested was the formation of a UNC Charlotte Political Action Committee (UNCC-PAC). What actually happened later was an even better solution—the creation of the Southern Piedmont Legislative Caucus, an organization of legislators themselves.

An Arrington suggestion that caused some amusement on campus was that the administration come down from the fifth floor of the Reese Building and mix with the faculty, staff, and students. "The placement of the Chancellor and the Vice Chancellor for Academic Affairs on the fifth floor of the Reese Building with the Business office interposed between them and the rest of the campus is a symbolic catastrophe," Arrington said. "It reflects the business corporation mentality. The chair of the board and his president are often isolated from those on the shop floor. Thus a penthouse suite of offices to look over the employees seems natural. But it is counterproductive, especially in the setting of a university," Arrington said. He suggested ground-floor offices near the center of the campus.

Arrington foresaw the future in still another way. He suggested that the chancellor should have the athletic director report to him without an intermediary. "This is to assure that it [athletics] doesn't become malignant or to know exactly whom to blame if it does," Arrington said. Later events across the nation indicated that, indeed, athletics could get out of hand if the chief administrators of universities didn't have direct oversight. For this reason, the UNC Charlotte athletic director would eventually report directly to the chancellor. Thus the blue-sky exercise did bear fruit ultimately, if not immediately.

Even before Arrington's comments on athletics, university administrators had learned that in that area, what goes up can come down. The Lee Rose years and the Final Four trip had taken UNC Charlotte to the summit in terms of visibility and respect in athletics; but the downside was just as far in the opposite direction.

As the successor to Lee Rose and a first-time head coach, Mike Pratt found winning difficult to achieve consistently and resigned after four seasons and a 56–52 won-lost record. He was succeeded by Dr. Hal Wissell, who had been a successful head coach at Florida Southern. Unlike Rose, Wissell was unable to translate success at NCAA Division II into success at Division I in men's basketball. One story, perhaps apocryphal, illustrates the coach's problems. Wissell's rigid coach-in-charge system included his holding up numbered and colored cards to indicate the play to be run. The story goes that the team had a three-on-one fast break going down court and would have scored. Unfortunately, the point guard paused and looked to see which card the coach was holding up, and the opposing team caught up and stopped the play.

Soon a bumper sticker appeared that said, "Blow the Whistle on Wissell." Hal Wissell's teams had continued to lose badly, with won-lost records of

8–20, 9–19, and 5–23. That last year presented the worst record in men's basketball since 1967, when it was 5–17, with a team of nonscholarship athletes. Finally, there was serious dissension between team and coach, even to the point of shouting and shoving matches. UNC Charlotte was not a win-at-all-costs institution, but it was clear that the athletic program was becoming a negative influence. Orr requested and accepted Wissell's resignation.

Orr and Fretwell also concluded that at that stage of development, UNC Charlotte didn't need and couldn't really afford a separate men's basketball coach and athletic director. So Orr also requested and accepted the resignation of Clyde Walker as athletic director.

To replace the two, Orr and Fretwell recruited a person whose name and reputation alone helped cure many of the athletic program's ills—Jeff Mullins, who was named men's basketball head coach and athletic director. Mullins was well known to longtime residents of Charlotte and North Carolina for his career at Duke University, where he made All-America. He went on to the Olympics, where he earned a gold medal on the U.S. team. He then spent ten years with the Golden State Warriors, where five times he was honored as a league All-Star. He led the Warriors to the 1975 NBA championship and to runner-up status in 1976. And like Lee Rose, Mullins was a product of Lexington, Kentucky. He had been highly recruited and had chosen to leave his home state to play at Duke.

Recruiting Mullins as coach was an interesting project. Charlotte friends of his had indicated to UNC Charlotte officials that Mullins had grown restless running his Chevrolet dealership in Apex, even though he was highly successful in that role too. The friends reported that Mullins was interested in getting back into basketball. When Orr first approached Fretwell about the matter, the chancellor is reported to have asked, "You mean you want me to hire an auto dealer as our basketball coach?" But when he heard the full story, Fretwell authorized Orr to explore the possibility.

Mullins agreed to meet Orr at the Blue Mist, a barbecue restaurant in Asheboro that had been a favorite halfway stopping point for Bonnie Cone and other administrators on their way to Raleigh in the days of the quest for university status. After Mullins joined UNC Charlotte, sports columnist Ron Green suggested that if the team were successful, a plaque should be placed in the Blue Mist.

Mullins said later that when he saw Orr driving up in an old green-and-white Dodge Dart, he wondered to himself whether UNC Charlotte would be willing to pay him what he needed to make the move. Actually, Orr probably spent enough on repairs to that old car at Newell Texaco to have bought a new one, and apparently he drove it out of sentiment.

After getting beyond that first impression, Mullins and Orr quickly found grounds for agreement for solving UNC Charlotte's coaching problem and Mullins's itch to return to basketball. In the bargain the university got

Jeff Mullins became the UNC Charlotte men's basketball coach after his successes at Duke, in the NBA, in the Olympics, and in business.

Mullins's wife, Candy, as an irrepressible booster of the university and the team.

Mullins was well received in the community because of the goodwill he brought from his personal athletic accomplishments and his commitment to a high level of integrity. In fact, his program was called "New Attitude" soon after his arrival. Beyond his coaching, Mullins said he wanted to represent the university as well as the team.

Another appointment at the time of the Mullins selection would augur well for the future of athletics. That was the promotion of Assistant Athletic Director Judy Wilkins (later to become Judy Rose when she married Ken). Rose's elevation to associate athletic director was more than just a change in title. It meant that Rose would take on some of the administrative details that would prepare her for her future role as athletic director.

The athletic moves would certainly quiet alumni discontent, which had been calm but persistent in the last few years before the Mullins appointment.

A sign of the maturation of the Alumni Association was the awarding of the first Distinguished Alumnus Award to James G. Babb at the commencement ceremony in 1985. Babb, a graduate of the institution during its two-year status, received his four-year degree at Belmont Abbey College but shared his alumni loyalty with UNC Charlotte. He became head of Charlotte's Jefferson-Pilot Communications, which included WBTV, WBT, and Sunny Radio. He left Charlotte to become head of Outlet Communications in Rhode Island, a company acquired by NBC in 1995.

At that point, UNC Charlotte even had some alumni who had gone on to very unusual jobs. Boone Wayson had become president of the Golden Nugget Casino in Atlantic City, New Jersey. Later he headed his own entertainment company in Annapolis, Maryland, where his brother Ed, also an alumnus, had a law firm. Both became generous alumni donors. Another graduate who found a career with a casino was Kathy Espin, who headed public relations for Caesar's Palace and later the Stardust Resort and Casino in Las Vegas.

Others had achieved public visibility and prominence in more conventional ways. James M. Mead had become a brigadier general in the U.S. Marine Corps and served in Lebanon as commander of the 22nd Amphibious Unit, part of an international force, during a volatile time there. Mike McKay had become a television personality at WBTV.

Ron Alridge had become a television critic for the *Charlotte Observer*, then the *Chicago Tribune*, and later was editor of a media magazine. Ellison Clary served as editor of newspapers in Hickory and Columbus, Georgia, and in public relations for Carolina Power & Light before returning to Charlotte to become a senior vice president in public relations for NationsBank. Garry Ballard, an alumnus, left his position as associate director of public information and publications at UNC Charlotte to become director of public relations at Louisiana State University, and he eventually returned to UNC Charlotte as director of alumni affairs. Larry McAffee became a highly successful cross-country coach at East Mecklenburg High School, leading his teams to several state championships. McAffee also designed one of the Southeast's leading cross-country courses, at McAlpine Park in Charlotte. Ben Chavis had begun his rise to prominence in African American organizations, and the Moody Brothers were becoming known as leading instrumentalists in Nashville.

Alumnus Craig Fincannon's name was often seen, along with his brother's, in the credits at the end of several movies, such as *Nell*, as they achieved success in casting a number of major movies.

Most important, the stage was set for UNC Charlotte to gain national recognition in the academic arena.

CHAPTER 10

The University Wins National Ranking

NATIONAL RECOGNITION for UNC Charlotte came in 1985, in a somewhat surprising fashion. UNC Charlotte was ranked third among comprehensive universities in the South and border states in *U.S. News & World Report's* listing of "The Best Colleges in America." Ranked with UNC Charlotte that year were East Carolina and Appalachian State. Controversy arose from the subjective way in which the rankings were derived that first year: the magazine had asked college presidents to rank the universities and colleges with the best reputations.

Within North Carolina, some said that E. K. Fretwell Jr.'s national stature helped UNC Charlotte achieve its ranking. Perhaps there was some credibility to that position. On the other hand, the first ranking was validated in subsequent years when *U.S. News & World Report* turned to objective as well as subjective methods of evaluating institutions. Fretwell himself issued a disclaimer that while the ranking was appreciated, the university community was aware that ranking institutions was a ticklish endeavor.

Once magazines began such rankings, though, there was no turning back. Even with the rankings, colleges and universities were still chosen for the strangest of reasons. Some students selected a campus on the basis of the institution's athletic prowess. Others decided on the basis of knowing a prominent alumnus. Others selected an institution because it was near the ski slopes or at the seashore or was located in a large city. Still others selected a college because friends or girlfriends or boyfriends were attending it.

It was clear that prospective students and their parents had only a vague notion of institutional quality and breadth of offerings. So the publications that ranked colleges had a very receptive audience. At least they gave parents some criteria on which to evaluate their children's choices.

Later, other publications with other criteria ranked UNC Charlotte, adding some validity to the early rankings. In 1987, *Money* magazine selected

UNC Charlotte as one of the nation's ten best values in higher education. That selection was not made on reputation alone. After UNC Charlotte ranked near the top on some computer models, reporters were sent to Charlotte and the other high-ranking campuses. I escorted the reporter who visited UNC Charlotte around the campus, but he did not allow himself to be steered in any direction. As he spotted a group of students or a professor, he introduced himself and interviewed them. Fortunately, those interviewed said the right things, without any prompting, to benefit UNC Charlotte's final selection. More than one student said to the reporter, "If you are looking for a party school, this isn't it. People come here to get an education." The reporter didn't use that comment, but it may well have influenced UNC Charlotte's selection.

What the September 1987 issue of *Money* did say was very flattering to UNC Charlotte:

> With a venerable, national-calibre public university at Chapel Hill, North Carolina is building another great state institution at Charlotte. True to its mission, UNCC, founded in 1946, is strongest in pre-professional departments such as accounting, architecture, business and engineering, though history also rates a rave. Still, the UNCC curriculum is balanced so that students are liberally exposed to courses other than those required for their majors. . . . Like Chapel Hill, UNCC is affiliated with a research park (2,800 acres) just off campus (with tenants such as AT&T and IBM) that provides a steady local source of jobs for graduates.

The *Money* selection did illustrate that such rankings were fallible, because a few years later, when the magazine broadened its listing to about four hundred best-value institutions, UNC Charlotte wasn't among them.

And one year, for no known reason, UNC Charlotte dropped out of the *U.S. News & World Report* rankings. The examination of data on which the listings were based revealed a substantial omission. The firm that compiled those rankings counted only the endowment held directly by institutions, omitting endowments held by separate foundations. At the time UNC Charlotte held about $16 million directly, while $16 million was held by the foundation, and the total of $32 million was very impressive for a public university. It's not known whether that was a factor, but after it was pointed out to the magazine, UNC Charlotte returned to the rankings.

The year 1987 was also one in which the university received the G. Theodore Mitau Award for Innovation and Change in State Colleges and Universities. This award by the American Association of State Colleges and Universities was in recognition of UNC Charlotte's role in developing University City. E. K. Fretwell Jr. and Doug Orr attended a national meeting of

AASCU to accept the award. The citation noted that by helping create University City, UNC Charlotte provided:

- a boost to the endowment, with the potential for substantial future growth in value;
- a teaching and learning experience for the faculty and students involved;
- employment opportunities for faculty consultants to research park firms, for graduates in the many business enterprises, and also for the student workers;
- a high-quality environment surrounding the campus, entirely compatible with the university;
- the opportunity to demonstrate the university's ability to reach out in service to its surrounding area;
- an opportunity to gain local, national, and international visibility for the university—visitors had come from cities and universities in the United States and from several nations of the world;
- service to the city and state in drawing development to northeastern Charlotte, thus preventing the tax base from slipping over the state line.

The university was on a recognition roll that continued into 1988. That year, Martin Nemko published his book *How to Get an Ivy League Education at a State University*. UNC Charlotte was one of only two North Carolina institutions included. That title was guaranteed to impress parents trying to weigh their budget capabilities against selection of the best possible college or university for their sons and daughters.

During the same year, in a study sponsored by the Council for the Advancement and Support of Education (CASE), Fretwell was selected as one of the hundred most effective college presidents and chancellors in the nation.

Whatever else national recognition provided, it made hard-working faculty, staff, and students feel that their efforts were being noticed. Some students were attracted to the university because of the recognitions—based on anecdotal evidence. A student from Wyoming, for example, indicated that he selected UNC Charlotte after seeing one of the rankings.

Overall, the university's quest for finding its place in the sun continued. Added to that challenge was the uncertainty created by the pending retirement of William Friday after thirty years as president of the UNC system. What would happen to a system so indelibly stamped with the mark of one person? Some of the campuses of the system, including UNC Charlotte, had known no other system president. All the independent campuses merged in 1972 into the sixteen-campus UNC system had known no other chief executive.

CHAPTER 11

After Friday, the Spangler Era

WILLIAM FRIDAY was bringing to a close one of the most distinguished careers in American higher education, having served thirty years as president of the UNC system. It wasn't the end of his service to North Carolina, of course. Friday continued as an active and visible advocate for all the people of the state, particularly the poorest among them, in his role as president of the William R. Kenan Jr. Fund and also as host of the "North Carolina People" program on WUNC Television.

Friday had proved that one of the keys to longevity in a career or in life was simply surviving. He endured some of North Carolina's most contentious issues—the Speaker Ban Law, the dispute with the U.S. Department of Health, Education, and Welfare over how to further desegregate the UNC system, the restructuring of higher education to create a sixteen-campus system, and several crises in athletics programs.

Friday did more than survive, however. He built what came to be considered a model for a state higher education system and one that was studied by many other states. He was known for an ability to disagree without being disagreeable. One of his greatest strengths was his ability to keep the legislature together in support of a high-quality university system. Although he had able support in lobbying from such aides as Rudy Pate, Jay Jenkins, and R. D. McMillan, Friday was usually his own best lobbyist.

In recognition of his three decades of nationally recognized leadership, at its May 1986 commencement UNC Charlotte conferred on Friday the honorary degree of Doctor of Public Service.

The selection of Friday's successor was a pleasant surprise for UNC Charlotte and Charlotteans. C. D. Spangler Jr. was a longtime friend of the institution and of most of its prominent trustees. In fact, his wife, Meredith, had been a UNC Charlotte trustee as well as a UNC Charlotte alumna, having earned a master's degree in education.

C. D. Spangler Jr. (left) became the new UNC President and Thomas I. Storrs (right) became the UNC Charlotte Board of Trustees Chairman in 1985.

Spangler had served on the Charlotte-Mecklenburg Board of Education, where he was known for a no-nonsense approach to board issues. In fact, one of the most vivid memories most Charlotteans had of Spangler was his moving to fire an unpopular school superintendent during a board meeting that was being televised to the community. Indeed, Spangler was perhaps most appreciated in Charlotte for his support of public education. Although he could have sent his daughters to the best private schools in the nation, he chose instead to send them to Charlotte-Mecklenburg public schools.

He then moved on to become chair of the State Board of Education, where he again earned a reputation for insisting on a higher-quality public education. He was nudging the board in that direction even before school improvement became such a hot-button issue.

Spangler also was known in Charlotte as a successful businessman. He had helped his father build a major construction business, and when NCNB acquired a bank the Spanglers owned, he became one of the top stockholders in that up-and-coming bank. An able investor, Spangler served on a number of corporate boards, a practice he continued as president of the UNC system. He earlier served on the UNC Charlotte Foundation board and otherwise exhibited his support for the campus.

Spangler's connections to UNC Charlotte went back a long way. He recalled that he learned how to behave in church as a youngster because he sat with his family in a pew just behind Bonnie Cone at Myers Park Baptist Church. He remembered that his mother told him just to watch Miss Cone and do what she did. He remained an admirer of Bonnie Cone as she set about transforming her college into UNC Charlotte.

For Charlotteans who expected Spangler to give an advantage to UNC Charlotte, however, there would be some disappointment. Spangler was like many public servants of great integrity. When they had a close affiliation, they often leaned over backward to avoid showing favoritism. But Spangler would be fair, would listen to representatives of the campus, and, at the appropriate time, would open a key door to UNC Charlotte—the possibility of offering doctoral work.

In his 1985–86 annual report, Fretwell said of the change in the system's leadership, "The orderly transition from the long, distinguished and essentially unprecedented career of William Friday to the promising new presidency of C. D. Spangler is extremely encouraging to those of us at UNCC. I commend both leaders for their respective accomplishments."

The UNC Charlotte campus was having its own transition at the time, with the election of Thomas I. Storrs, chief executive officer of NCNB (later to become NationsBank), as chair of the Board of Trustees, replacing Thomas M. Belk. Stuart Dickson of the Ruddick Corp. and board chair of the Charlotte-Mecklenburg Hospital Authority became vice chair, and John L. Fraley Jr., secretary.

Storrs came into office with the credentials to understand the academic community, having earned a doctorate himself. Yet at first he didn't fully appreciate UNC Charlotte's dilemma of being last in the system in terms of state appropriations per student and last in terms of classroom and library space per student.

Looking at the way faculty and students performed so successfully, Storrs the fiscal conservative said, "Well, that's good. We are setting an example for the rest of the state as to what can be done with hard work and efficiency. The other campuses ought to be more like us than us like them."

Naturally, Storrs's remarks didn't sit well with members of the UNC Charlotte faculty. But as Storrs learned more about the campus and the system during the next several years, he began to understand that the issue was as much one of equity as it was of efficiency, and gradually he became a strong advocate of fairer treatment of the campus.

Later Storrs would chair a statewide government efficiency study for Governor Jim Martin.

Moreover, the university's leaders had gained additional insights into the power of relationships with the private sector. This understanding was parlayed into two new campus buildings. A building for the College of Architecture was funded by the legislature with strong encouragement from the state's architectural firms and practitioners. It would be difficult to document, but it may have been given a little bit of help through a kinship of House Speaker Liston Ramsey. His first cousin, Bob Ramsey, had a daughter, Dawn, enrolled in the College of Architecture. When Bob Ramsey learned that Liston hadn't supported the building in an earlier session, he paid the lawmaker a visit. Ramsey said to his cousin, "I have never asked any favors of you as long as you have been in the House. But I'm asking you now to support this building, because I know through my daughter how badly it's needed." Who knows whether that plea had an impact, but in the mountains, where both Ramseys grew up, blood was known to be thicker than water.

The new architecture building was named for Thomas I. Storrs following his retirement from the Board of Trustees. Faculty and students had participated in advanced planning for the building. For the first time, the university used a national firm for building design: Gwathmy-Siegle of New York did the major concepts, assisted by the Charlotte firm of FWA Associates.

The second building funded in 1987 was an applied research facility. At the time, the State of North Carolina was recruiting Kodak to locate a major new facility devoted to devices for the optical storage of information on compact disks. State and university officials went to Kodak headquarters and argued that the company should put its facility in University Research Park, since it owned Verbatim, a computer floppy-disk company whose world headquarters was already there. As part of the incentives package, the state offered to build the applied research center on the UNC Charlotte campus and a training facility on the Central Piedmont Community College campus.

Kodak agreed, and both facilities were funded and built. After a major restructuring, however, Kodak's plans changed, and the major operation envisioned had not been built by the mid-1990s. Kodak's Eastman Chemicals subsidiary did later build a small research facility in the park. It could be argued, however, that neither UNC Charlotte, Central Piedmont, nor the state lost in the deal. The applied research facility at UNC Charlotte was to become a major link between the campus and the business community. Central Piedmont immediately put its training facility to good use for other companies. The state thereby was provided additional lures for attracting other companies.

The applied research facility was named for the longtime trustee, foundation chair, and University Research Park board chair C. C. (Cliff) Cameron, who also served as Governor Jim Martin's chief budget officer.

Another development that augured well for the university's future in applied research and its attendant economic development leadership was the approval in the 1986–87 academic year of a cooperative doctoral program in engineering with N.C. State University.

Most of the instruction would be provided by UNC Charlotte faculty on the Charlotte campus, but under the guidance of N.C. State, and with the Ph.D being awarded by N.C. State. That development harkened back to UNC Charlotte's beginnings as the Charlotte Center of UNC, when engineering courses were offered under the supervision of N.C. State. The new relationship helped open the door for UNC Charlotte later to offer its own Ph.D. programs. Johnny Graham was the first recipient of a Ph.D. under this program and later would become a member of the UNC Charlotte engineering faculty.

Another forerunner of doctoral status for UNC Charlotte was a cooperative doctoral program in school administration launched with UNC Chapel Hill.

Fretwell's interest in applying his "mirror test" continued in 1986–87, but with a new wrinkle. Because of the university's progress, he now wanted to know how UNC Charlotte compared at the national level. Under the leadership of Professor Bob Mundt, the campus community evaluated itself in the light of seven national reports on higher education. The findings were that UNC Charlotte was achieving many, but not all, of the national goals. "We will now concentrate on areas where we can develop additional strengths," Fretwell said.

And by 1987, UNC Charlotte's leaders felt that research and scholarly activity were significant enough to be recognized, along with outstanding teaching, with an award. As a result, Graduate School dean Robert Carrubba enlisted the help of a bank to create the First Citizens Bank Scholars Medal.

The first medals and accompanying checks were presented in late spring with a gala reception at the bank in uptown Charlotte. They went to Paul Escott of History (later college dean at Wake Forest University) and Paul Rillema of Chemistry. Escott was a two-time winner of the Mayflower Cup Award for the best work of nonfiction in North Carolina, and Rillema had created a strong team doing research on alternative energy sources.

Enrollment took a surprising jump in 1986–87, to 11,753, an 8.4 percent increase, as compared to the historic average of about 4 percent growth annually. Even with this growth, which could have diluted the percentage of African Americans, that segment of the student body increased from 8.9 to 9.5 percent. Also, despite the high enrollment growth, the average SAT scores went up from 912 to 920. Graduate enrollment increased even more dramatically, by 24 percent—up from 1,487 to 1,837.

The dramatic and unexpected increase in enrollment was well beyond enrollment increase estimates and therefore beyond the budget authorizations. Campuses of the university projected their enrollments for several years out. For some campuses that was not a problem, since their enrollments increased modestly or remained stable. UNC Charlotte had experienced a

Robert Carrubba presents Paul Escott (left) and Paul Rillema (right), as initial First Citizens Bank Scholars Medalists in 1987.

historical average of 4 percent growth, with the early couple of years of 31 percent growth, and then the sudden 8.4 percent jump.

Fretwell and Werntz ordered that enrollment brakes be applied to keep campus growth within budgeted projections. Unfortunately, the brakes worked very well, and this came back to haunt the campus a few years later, when the supply of high school graduates bottomed out, leaving the institution slightly short of its projections.

Managing enrollment at the metropolitan campus was difficult at best. What was certain was that long-term prospects held substantial additional growth, as the children born in the late 1970s and early 1980s graduated from high school. North Carolina's increasing prosperity of the late 1970s and 1980s also suggested a higher college-going rate.

As Fretwell neared the end of his tenure, he decided to restructure his administration once again. He consolidated the Division of Research and Public Service with the Division of Development and named Doug Orr vice chancellor of the combined unit. Bill Britt, who had been vice chancellor for development, returned to his professional field of teacher education as a professor in the College of Education.

When Jim Clay took his leave of absence to direct the construction of University Place, he was replaced as director of the Urban Institute on an interim basis by Mary Dawn Bailey. In 1986–87, a new director was appointed—Professor William J. McCoy, who brought with him new insights and new directions and assured the institute's future.

Activity in private giving had increased substantially. In 1986–87, the family of the late N. K. Dickerson established a distinguished professorship in his name. The estate of the late Nordica Adelaide Jamieson provided $610,000 for a student loan fund, inspired by her admiration for Bonnie Cone. Following the death of Alice Tate, additional funds from her estate came to the university, and around $1 million became available to the university from the bequest of Clara McKay Stone.

David Taylor, the former Celanese executive who had served the university so long and well in development and outreach activities, stepped aside as chair of the UNC Charlotte Foundation board and of the University Research Park Board of Directors. He was named chair emeritus of the foundation. Cliff Cameron succeeded Taylor in both roles.

To honor private citizens who had given substantially of themselves to the university and the community, the Distinguished Service Award was established, and Cameron and Thomas M. Belk were its first recipients at a black-tie gala event in 1987. The Distinguished Service Award was made possible through the support of Cameron Harris, Dale Halton, Felix Sabates, John Fraley Jr., and Gene and Vicky Johnson, who also commissioned a

C.C. (Cliff) Cameron (left) and Thomas M. Belk are the first Distinguished Service Award recipients in 1987. Photo by Al Mahoney.

sculpture of a Charlotte gold miner by Lorenzo Giglieri for the occasion. A miniature casting of the sculpture was given annually to recipients. The bigger-than-life-sized sculpture was placed on campus and became an attraction there.

The university also turned its attention inward and discovered that there was a need to reward and recognize outstanding performance by staff members. Two staff Employee of the Year awards were created, and the first two awards went to Joyce Willis of student records and Craig Bizzell of Financial Services. Other staff members received cash awards for exceptional service.

As for external relations, there was a belief that the university should receive input from a broader spectrum of the region's leadership than the thirteen-person Board of Trustees provided. This resulted in the creation of the Board of Visitors, with John L. (Buck) Fraley as its first chair. Fraley launched the new board in September 1987, with a celebration of the university's outreach efforts and a speech by Governor Jim Martin that traced UNC Charlotte's impact on regional economic development.

Relations with the public and campus morale were enhanced in 1987–88 by Jeff Mullins's most successful season since he took over as men's basketball coach. The team won the Sunbelt Conference regular season title and the Sunbelt Tournament championship with a 22–9 record and advanced to the

Governor James G. Martin (far right) gets Chancellor Fretwell's (center) help as Martin Village campus residential complex is dedicated in 1986. Photo by Al Mahoney.

first round of the NCAA Tournament, the highest accomplishment since the 1975–76 and 1976–77 seasons.

Commencement of 1988 saw the retirement of additional UNC Charlotte pioneers: Robert Rieke, who had written an unconventional early history of the campus and who was serving as university marshal; Julian Mason, who had served as assistant to the chancellor and chair of the English Department; Robert G. Anderson, who had served as first dean of the College of Architecture; William S. Mathis, who had served as dean of the College of Humanities and then returned to teaching music; and Sadie Williamson, who had helped build the strong Accounting Department.

The campus was changing, and by 1987–88 a need was felt to enhance the campus identity to relate better to the new reality of the campus as a major university. Jeff Mullins wanted an identity that linked the campus with Charlotte, saying that the block letters "UNCC" didn't mean anything when his team traveled to play in other regions. Also, Charlotte was moving into the top tier of national cities, and the campus could benefit from identifying with its city.

After a consultant from Georgia Tech visited with university leadership and demonstrated that the campus image was fragmented by the use of various symbols, Orr headed a committee to develop criteria for a single new institutional symbol. Soon there was agreement that the new symbol should tie the campus to two great sources of strength—the UNC system, growing out of the nation's oldest state university, and the up-and-coming major city of Charlotte.

After interviewing several design firms, the committee turned to the firm of Design/Joe Sonderman. Sonderman, while working for Pentes Design, had created the earlier block-letter UNCC logo, which had served the campus well for a number of years.

Sonderman presented several alternatives before the committee focused on the ultimate selection. The resulting new logo was created by linking UNC and Charlotte without a space between the two words and with the "C" in "Charlotte" being larger than the other letters. The word symbol was topped with a stylized crown, representing the university's links to the City of Charlotte, which used another style of crown for its logo. The crown came from Charlotte's historical namesake, Queen Charlotte of the German province of Mecklenburg-Strelitz and wife of King George III of England. The committee pointed out to faculty members that in addition to appearing to be a crown, the design also resembled a lamp of learning and an open book.

At a national conference on campus identity, UNC Charlotte's new logo was well received. When unveiled to the faculty, only one criticism was raised. Professor Tom Walsh, educated in Catholic schools, including Notre Dame

Chapter Eleven

UNC CHARLOTTE

The UNC Charlotte logo represents the university's links to the UNC system, the City of Charlotte, and a dedication to learning.

University, thought that he saw within the logo a cruciform, which he illustrated by covering part of the logo with his hands. His colleagues, however, thought he was straining too hard for the point and endorsed the new symbol. It caught on quickly and was almost universally well received.

The clock was ticking for Fretwell even as the campus polished its identity. As he neared the age of sixty-five, speculation turned to whether Spangler would continue Bill Friday's tradition of requiring chancellors and senior administrators to step aside from their positions at that age. Fretwell was mentally and physically young and maintained a high energy level. His colleagues understood that he wasn't ready to retire. But when Fretwell asked about the matter, Spangler said that he would continue to expect high-level officials to retire at sixty-five.

Once the decision about his retirement was made, Fretwell determined to conduct business as usual in his final year of 1988-89. And it was a very good year. He led the university as if he were not a short-timer.

Even with management controls in place, enrollment increased by 7.8 percent, to a total of 12,970 students. That number included almost two thousand graduate students, which Dean Robert Carrubba said put UNC Charlotte at the average enrollment for graduate schools nationally. Enrollment of African American students reached 1,246, or 9.1 percent.

Enrollment of international students reached 389, or 3 percent of the student body, the largest undergraduate percentage in the UNC system. Even that number didn't tell the entire story. Because Charlotte had become a magnet for internationals relocating with businesses to the area, there was a large enrollment of the children of people who were recent newcomers to the United States. Also, the university had established an English Language Training Institute, which brought as many as two hundred students in to upgrade their English competency. All those factors gave UNC Charlotte a decided cosmopolitan and international flavor.

As Fretwell concluded his ten and a half years, it was clear that he, like Cone and Colvard before him, had left a legacy of accomplishment and progress and had made his mark on UNC Charlotte.

Under his leadership the campus grew from an enrollment of just under 9,000 students to almost 13,000, even with the application of enrollment management controls. The graduate school reached critical mass at the 2,000-student level. Under the leadership of James Lyons and William Heller, work was well under way toward the first doctoral program in educational leadership, although it would later hit a snag because of lack of funding. It was finally approved in 1996.

Planning was also under way for the university's second major fund-raising campaign, scheduled for 1990 to coincide with the school's silver anniversary as a university-level institution.

The number of faculty members had grown to 556 full-time and 216 part-time. Of the full-time faculty, there were now 165 female members. Though not near equity, the female proportion was beginning to grow through the leadership of Fretwell and Werntz in encouraging departments to make a stronger recruiting effort. The number of minority members totaled 60, indicating some progress, but not yet success, particularly in recruiting African American professors.

Fretwell and Werntz had found a partial solution to a nettlesome problem of academia: getting faculty members to cross disciplinary lines to address problems. That solution was to establish academies. The academies addressed issues like the Carolinas, transportation, the environment, and world peace. Faculty from various disciplines crossed departmental lines to work with colleagues from other disciplines to consider the issues. Academies had no powers and no designated budgets. Funds were channeled to them as available. Their great accomplishment was getting faculty members talking to each other across the departmental fences. Because promotion, tenure, salaries, and such issues were not at stake, the academies worked.

With the assistance of Lucy Henry, faculty members had increased the total of academic grants and contracts to $6.1 million, fairly significant for a relatively young, nonflagship campus.

Under the leadership of Norman Schul, the institution increased activity in cooperative programs, in which students alternately worked for companies or organizations for a term and attended class for a term. UNC Charlotte also began to exploit its great advantage in location by placing students from many disciplines in internships. Even English majors, who traditionally had difficulty finding real-world, work-experience opportunities, found internships with businesses, the news media, advertising, and public relations firms.

Experience in cooperative programs and internships began to become much more important to students' job-hunting success as the job market tightened and businesses said they wanted graduates with experience. The large Charlotte metropolitan area provided the needed opportunities.

The athletic program had been restored to health. For the second straight year, the men's basketball team made it to a postseason tournament, this time hosting the University of Connecticut in a first-round NIT game. Fund-raising in athletics was improving.

Under the leadership of Vice Chancellor Leo Ells, UNC Charlotte had probably done more to privatize some of its service units than most universities had. In fact, Jim Crawford, director of auxiliary services, had made national presentations on UNC Charlotte's success with privatization. This included the bookstore, printing services, and food services (a commonly privatized operation). On the other hand, the university had taken over its own vending machines and copying machines and supplied and serviced them. (In 1995, the university again would take over the operation of its bookstore, following a directive from President C. D. Spangler.)

Because of problems caused by his management style, however, Ells was having increasing difficulty working with Fretwell and the vice chancellors. As a result, Ells resigned shortly before the end of Fretwell's term.

The issue of gaining additional legislative and General Administration support remained a thorny one throughout the Fretwell administration. Vice Chancellor Orr and the director of public information urged Fretwell and Werntz to meet with editors and reporters from the *Charlotte Observer* for a candid and in-depth background session on the university's problems.

Some risk was involved. It was feared that if they revealed publicly that the university had some weaknesses, the campus might be perceived as having less quality than it really did. On the other hand, it seemed the university would never overcome its problems unless they were fully understood off campus as well as on. The two university officials very candidly detailed the campus shortcomings, particularly in the area of the shortfall in state funding for support positions and facilities.

Using information and an understanding gained from the session, the editors and reporters from the newspaper were better able to inform the public about the issues. On that base of better understanding, UNC Charlotte officials were able to start building public and political support for more equitable treatment. It would remain for a new chancellor to capitalize on this beginning point.

Fretwell certainly had lived up to expectations in obtaining national and international recognition in the academic arena for UNC Charlotte. The national rankings were evidence, as was the constant flow of high-ranking visitors who wanted to observe the university's success in building University City.

Just as Fretwell had taken some programs begun under the Colvard administration and made them a success, he laid the groundwork for a number of programs that would see success under the next chancellor, such as the Applied Research Center, the Ben Craig Center, and much of University City.

One major accomplishment was setting the stage for UNC Charlotte to become the major facilitator for regionalism for the North and South Carolina cities and counties surrounding Charlotte. Under the leadership of Orr and the Urban Institute, directed by Bill McCoy, UNC Charlotte helped organize workshops and seminars for leaders of the region on such topics as transportation, land use, water resources, education, and other key issues. Fretwell was highly supportive of these efforts, and the momentum carried over and was enhanced under the next administration.

Fretwell had been successful on many fronts, but he wasn't able to be all things to all people. He later acknowledged that perhaps he should have spent more time working with uptown Charlotte leaders, but there were only so many available hours.

As had happened when Fretwell was recruited as chancellor, a consensus began developing as to what qualities were needed in the new chancellor. That consensus was that the new chancellor should establish stronger working relationships with the Charlotte business community, the legislature, and the UNC General Administration and should help overcome the university's inequitable funding for academic support and facilities.

Fretwell clearly was more comfortable negotiating on high-level higher education issues in Washington than in courting legislative support in the back halls of Raleigh. Also, he was recruited to the campus at a time when Bill Friday told his chancellors not to lobby—that he would do it all for them. Spangler was more willing to let his chancellors share some of the lobbying efforts once system priorities had been agreed upon.

There was also some feeling that the next chancellor should have a more decisive management style. Those who felt that way said that Fretwell allowed disagreeing parties, particularly his vice chancellors, to combat each other on an issue until the last one standing won. Many times it was Ells who was still standing. On occasion some people felt that Fretwell should have intervened earlier. Fretwell himself said that if he had it to do over, he would have been firmer in outlining goals and objectives for his administrative staff, working with them to achieve those standards and holding them accountable.

Further, there was an expectation that the new chancellor would do more entertaining and would be a more aggressive fund-raiser, particularly in light of the upcoming Silver Anniversary Campaign.

As he prepared to retire, Fretwell said that one of his wishes remained unfulfilled—"to have greater state support to reinforce and undergird both the quality and growth of university programs."

None of these goals for the new chancellor were meant to take away from the successes of the Fretwell administration. The campus community and the trustees understood that different people bring different talents and that different times call for different strengths.

Fretwell's own wish for the future was to have the institution grow steadily in strength and success of carefully designed programs. He said, "I would like to see expansion at the graduate level in fields related to individual and corporate needs in our multicounty region. This would include doctoral programs started in engineering, education, and possibly business, in ways consistent with available strengths, needs, and resources." He said he would like to see those goals accomplished while maintaining current assets of "good teaching, continuing attention to a well balanced undergraduate program, and commitment to the same measure of human warmth we now have."

In summing up the Fretwell years, *UNC Charlotte Today*, the university alumni publication, recalled what had been said about Fretwell as he prepared to step down at Buffalo State. The *Buffalo Evening News* had said, "Besides accommodating a spectacular growth in student enrollment from 4,500 to about 11,000 at present, the Fretwell administration won a deserved reputation for its commitment to urban-related programs and its invigoration of instruction in career preparation." The UNC Charlotte article noted that if the quote were changed to read "spectacular growth from 8,705 to 13,000," it would also be a fitting statement for his Charlotte career.

In looking back on Charlotte and UNC Charlotte growing up together, Fretwell said in the university magazine, "It is doubly exciting when both the university and the city take off together. It's like a good love affair."

In assessing his own career, Fretwell thanked others, saying, "I admire the hard work the faculty and staff have done—often without the ideal amount of backup support to enhance both academic progress and outreach to the community." Faculty and staff members reciprocated by giving him a "Fretwell Farewell Roast" on May 7, 1989. Actually, it was more of a love feast than a roast, but even his children got in some good-natured digs.

So a still-vigorous Fretwell came to the close of his tenure as UNC Charlotte chancellor. Like Colvard, he had still more to give in public service and continued his higher education career. He did that in a very challenging role as interim president of the University of Massachusetts system, which was undergoing a great deal of difficulty at the time Fretwell was requested to step in. There were other major assignments as well. He worked with the North Carolina community college system in assessing its future, and he consulted with a number of colleges and university systems. Close by, these included Coastal Carolina and Winthrop University in South Carolina. Others were as far away as California, Oregon, and Texas. In addition, he wrote books on leadership in higher education.

Fretwell's contribution was recognized by UNC Charlotte's trustees when they established merit scholarships in his name and, in 1995, when they named the arts and sciences building, the largest classroom complex on campus, in his honor. The Fretwell Building is an especially appropriate tribute to a man who put UNC Charlotte on the national and international higher education maps.

CHAPTER 12

Woodward Comes to Bolster Support

JAMES H. WOODWARD fit the profile of the chancellor needed by UNC Charlotte at the time he was recruited to succeed E. K. Fretwell Jr. Of course, search committees always described a person who could walk on water. But if the job description were peeled back to its basics, it was clear that Woodward was a good match of leader and institution. More than that, he was willing to carry out the mission outlined by the search committee and the UNC Charlotte Trustees.

There were two great expectations for the new chancellor—that he would at last end the inequity of funding from the legislature and that he would dramatically increase the level of private support. Perhaps there was another, more subtle expectation of Woodward as well—that he would exercise a more decisive management style than had been the pattern.

As chair of the Board of Trustees, Thomas I. Storrs had come to understand UNC Charlotte's strengths and shortcomings. So as chair of the search committee, he set out to find a person to meet the university's needs.

It helped that Woodward had been associated for some twenty years with an institution somewhat similar to UNC Charlotte—the University of Alabama–Birmingham (UAB). There was one great dissimilarity—UAB had a medical school, a strong one. Another difference was that UAB was located in the heart of downtown Birmingham, while UNC Charlotte was eight miles from the city center.

Otherwise, both universities were located in large metropolitan areas of southern states, had large commuting populations, and addressed urban problems. Also, like UNC Charlotte, UAB, with the exception of the medical school, had to compete with two flagship campuses in Alabama—the University of Alabama at Tuscaloosa and Auburn University.

Like UNC Charlotte, UAB had gained some national visibility from a successful basketball program. Both institutions had been charter members of

241

James H. Woodward takes the oath of office April 21, 1990, as chancellor from Judge Robert Potter (right) as UNC President C. D. Spangler looks on. Photo by Wade Bruton.

the Sunbelt Conference in earlier years. Because Birmingham was in the heart of football country, there was perhaps more pressure on UAB to begin a program in that sport than there had been on UNC Charlotte. In fact, UAB did launch a football program.

Before coming to UNC Charlotte, Woodward was serving UAB as senior vice president for University College. His responsibility was for the programs other than the medical school. These included schools of business, education, engineering, humanities, natural sciences and mathematics, and behavioral sciences.

As he became a candidate for the UNC Charlotte chancellorship, Woodward also was a strong candidate for a similar position at the University of Central Florida at Orlando. He made his candidacy there a learning experience, because that campus was somewhat similar to both UAB and UNC Charlotte. Like UNC Charlotte, it had a successful research park and was located in a fast-growing urban area. Thus Woodward brought to his position a significant understanding of the developing metropolitan university.

The UNC Charlotte search process unfolded smoothly until its latter stages, when the two finalists—Woodward and Ryan Amacher, then a dean at Clemson University—came to campus to make presentations to the faculty and staff.

Professor Loy Witherspoon served a second term as faculty president early in the Woodward administration. Photo by Wade Bruton.

Woodward's presentation went smoothly, but Amacher made an unfortunate misstep during his. He stated strongly that although women's studies and African American studies programs were valid, students shouldn't plan to major in them, because there were limited career opportunities. There may have been truth in what he said, in terms of real-world career opportunities, but the remarks were certainly "politically incorrect" and were misinterpreted.

Professor Loy Witherspoon felt so strongly that such a gaffe made Amacher unsuitable for the chancellorship that he organized opposition and wrote to UNC System president Spangler. Witherspoon was also quoted by the *Charlotte Observer* as to his opposition. The professor later said that Spangler chided him for communicating directly with him at that stage of the process. But it appeared to campus observers after the public flap that Amacher would not be selected by Spangler.

After his role in the selection process, Witherspoon decided that he would offer himself again as a candidate for president of the faculty, having served a term earlier in the university's history. He won and made it the focus of his term to help bring Woodward and the campus community together, hosting in his own home gatherings of faculty members with Woodward.

Amacher did present strengths in the connections he had built to the Charlotte business community, as well as to business leaders in South Carolina, in his role as dean of business at Clemson.

Woodward, however, also had built strong ties to the business community in Birmingham. In fact, he was scheduled to become chair of the United Way Campaign in Birmingham had he not accepted the UNC Charlotte chancellorship. He was on the Board of Directors of the Birmingham Chamber of Commerce and was a graduate of Leadership Birmingham. He also served as chair of the Alabama Supercomputer Network Authority. After arriving in North Carolina, he continued his commitment to supercomputing, particularly on the board of MCNC.

Another major understanding Woodward brought to Charlotte was that of the future of the urban-oriented university. In fact, in an interview he said that the future American university was the urban-oriented university. He said that such universities were best positioned to address such societal problems as globalization of the economy, the transition to an information-based economy, the aging of the population, and the failure of society to integrate its minorities into the mainstream.

Contrasted with Fretwell's intuitive approach, Woodward brought with him the analytical management approach of the engineer and the M.B.A. graduate. A native of Sanford, Florida, Woodward grew up in Georgia. He earned the bachelor's, master's, and Ph.D. degrees in engineering from Georgia Tech. Later he earned an M.B.A. at UAB after beginning his career there. He served in the U.S. Air Force and became an assistant professor of engineering mechanics in the U.S. Air Force Academy.

He got an early taste of North Carolina higher education when he taught at N.C. State University in 1968–69, but then, in June 1969, he joined UAB as associate professor of engineering. He moved into industry for a time as director of technical development for Rust International in Birmingham, while continuing as an adjunct professor at UAB.

Woodward returned full-time to UAB in 1973 and became assistant vice president for its University College. He was promoted to professor of engineering mechanics, and in September 1978 he was named dean of the School of Engineering. He was promoted to the senior vice presidency of University College in 1984, a position he retained until coming to Charlotte in 1989.

At UAB, Woodward had been through some exercises that would benefit him as he faced challenges at UNC Charlotte. He had helped revise the core curriculum there, had participated in a $55 million capital campaign, had helped organize the graduate program and expansion of the library, had helped secure stronger legislative support, and had helped internationalize the institution. Many of these issues UNC Charlotte also had experienced to some extent already or was preparing to undertake.

After two Presbyterian chancellors, in Woodward UNC Charlotte got a Methodist. Like his predecessors, Woodward was a Rotarian. In fact, following Bonnie Cone's admission to the Charlotte Rotary Club when it began to accept women, all four chief executives were Rotarians.

As he arrived in Charlotte, Woodward had at least one misgiving. The UNC Charlotte trustees had decided not to build the chancellor's residence in

Colvard Park, an upscale development in University City, even though the university had purchased lots there.

Facing the critical challenge of a major fund-raising drive, the trustees decided instead that the chancellor's residence should be located in a new, exclusive, gated development, called Morrocroft, at SouthPark. When asked why, board chair Tom Storrs replied, "Well, it's like Willie Sutton said when asked why he robbed banks—'because that's where the money is.'" Storrs's idea was that the chancellor should live near the people he would be cultivating for major gifts in the upcoming campaign.

Some UNC Charlotte faculty members felt that the decision was a denial of what they had done in making the University City area a viable upscale community and a denial of their success in balancing growth in Mecklenburg County. The UNC Charlotte trustees, however, responded that their reason for choosing the SouthPark area was that they were seriously committed to raising private funds for the university. As a gesture of good faith, they passed a resolution stating that at some future date, a new chancellor's residence would be built on the UNC Charlotte campus.

Woodward had been in higher education long enough to know that some of the most heated controversies in academe are over the building or remodeling of the homes of chancellors and presidents. Fortunately, Woodward's fears were not borne out, and when the residence was completed, the controversy ended. Apparently the trustees' resolution defused it. Moreover, the location provided just what Storrs had hoped: a springboard for entertaining prospective donors and supporters of the university.

Under Storrs's leadership, several friends of the university contributed funds that, when added to the proceeds of the sale of the former chancellor's residence, made construction of the new one possible. Sara Bissell, who had been a UNC Charlotte trustee, decorated the downstairs, the public portion of the house, with furnishings and art.

With the new residence, the Woodwards were prepared to do what had been difficult for previous chancellors—entertain in an elegant way, befitting the status of their guests. Colvard and Fretwell had lived in a very attractive and comfortable chancellor's residence adjacent to the Charlotte Country Club in the Plaza-Midwood section of Charlotte. However, that home wasn't large enough or designed to accommodate large numbers of guests. At one event, when guests filled the house and spilled out onto the lawn, rain began to fall, and the outdoor guests had to huddle under the eaves. Afterward, tents were used to host large receptions there.

The layout of the residence at Morrocroft was similar to that of the North Carolina governor's mansion, but on a smaller scale, with a grand hall and public rooms opening off it, so that guests could enter, be greeted, then flow into the parlor, living room, and dining rooms, and even the breakfast room.

Jane Watson, a former journalist who had experience in special events at UNC Chapel Hill, was employed as assistant to the chancellor to help with entertaining.

The upstairs of the chancellor's home was private to the Woodwards, and they furnished it to suit their own lifestyle. Jim and Martha Woodward performed their role of host and hostess with warmth and grace. When summer came, Martha Woodward enjoyed a well-earned break at a home the couple built at Seven Devils near Boone. That home had a commanding view of several mountain ranges, including Mt. Rogers in Virginia, and allowed the Woodwards to entertain children and grandchildren in comfort and privacy. Jim Woodward had a shop there so he could pursue his woodworking hobby.

The Woodwards were indeed homefolk, but they were also able to adapt to working closely with Charlotte's movers and shakers without difficulty. The CEOs of its two megabanks were Hugh McColl, from a small South Carolina town, and Ed Crutchfield, from a small North Carolina town. Even though the Belks were in their second generation as a wealthy family, they easily mixed with the rank-and-file citizens of the community. Their father, William Henry Belk, had taught them the value of hard work and that they shouldn't get above their raising. Publisher Rolfe Neill of the *Charlotte Observer* had grown up in small towns of North Carolina and other southern states. Many of the other leaders were comfortable mixing with people of all social and economic levels.

Charlotte also was a city that opened its doors to newcomers. Unlike some southern cities, such as Richmond, Charleston, New Orleans, or even Winston-Salem, where one had to be born there to be accepted, Charlotte had welcomed all to the task of community-building. Chancellors had been among those warmly welcomed.

Another perk of the chancellorship was a country club membership, which had also been enjoyed by the two previous chancellors. Membership allowed them to meet the community leaders. Woodward's membership was at Quail Hollow Country Club. Actually, that membership gave him more of a problem early in his chancellorship than did the location of the chancellor's residence. Lack of integration of Charlotte's country clubs became an issue shortly after Woodward arrived. Some of the faculty and staff, particularly members of the African American community and the Religious Studies Department, called on Woodward to resign from the club.

He explained that resigning would be a disadvantage to the university, and not so much to him personally, given the major fund-raising campaign at hand and his need to cultivate prospective donors there. Besides, he said, he was working within the organization to diversify the membership. Fortunately, that diversification was accomplished, and the pressure abated.

Unlike Colvard and Fretwell, Woodward hadn't had to deal much with the challenge of snowstorms, but he found himself dealing with a more serious storm shortly after his taking over the chancellorship on July 1, 1989.

Hurricane Hugo was being followed, as such storms usually are, by UNC Charlotte administrators, who watched its course on the evening television news in late September. But even as the storm headed for Charleston and on a path that appeared to take it toward Charlotte, there was the reassurance that all that Charlotte usually got from such storms were some heavy rains and some gusts of wind.

On the afternoon of September 21, 1989, weathercasters began sounding more of an alarm. There would be really high winds and heavy rains even in Charlotte, they warned. Late in the afternoon, state emergency officials sent an urgent warning that Charlotte could get a serious blow from the storm and suggested that campus officials take precautions. Woodward called the executive staff into a quick conference. "Has a hurricane ever come overland without weakening?" he asked. He was told that Hurricane Hazel back in the 1950s had moved overland from the North Carolina coast with severe damage as far inland as Raleigh. Woodward then asked that emergency precautions be taken. Physical plant staff tightened things down as best they could in the short time available.

The storm struck early in the morning hours of September 22, still packing hurricane-force winds. Weathercasters called it a two-hundred-year storm. It shut Charlotte down totally for a day or two. Individuals were incapacitated for up to three weeks by loss of electric power, telephones, and—for those who lived outside city water service and were dependent on their electric pumps—water.

The city's abundant tree cover, its pride and joy, became an enemy as huge and ancient oaks and maples came crashing down and smashing homes. Even the city's skyscrapers were damaged by high winds and flying debris. Much of the power distribution system and the telephone system had to be rebuilt through the heroic efforts of emergency crews, many from outside the state. City streets were patrolled by military troops, who moved vehicles through busy intersections that lacked working traffic lights.

Fortunately, UNC Charlotte suffered only slight damage. The fact that the central campus had few large trees spared buildings from serious destruction. Power was restored fairly quickly. There was isolated damage. A large awning had been installed at the new Prospector Cafeteria the very day before the storm hit. High winds took the awning and its metal supports and used them to smash the cafeteria's glass panes.

The campus had to adjust to the fact that for a few days, faculty, staff, and students couldn't get there from their homes, and business slowed considerably. Many faculty and staff members who had no hot water at home came to the campus to shave and shower. But other institutions, Queens College in particular, had to be closed for a time as repairs were made.

A damaging blow was struck to the Van Landingham Glen and Susie Harwood Gardens at UNC Charlotte. The canopy of magnificent oaks and shagbark hickories was ripped apart. Many plants that preferred shade would suffer in coming months. The garden had to adjust to new conditions, with more full sun in many areas.

For the first time, the International Festival had to be canceled, mostly because the staff that normally set up tents, stages, and other infrastructure for the event was diverted to storm cleanup. Also, there was concern that few Charlotteans could get out of their neighborhoods and out to the campus.

At first it was frustrating to see that Charlotte had suffered such a heavy blow without the nation's knowing about it. If news stories mentioned Charlotte at all, it was at the end of a story dealing mostly with Charleston and coastal South Carolina. But as time passed, it became clear that the downplaying of the damage to Charlotte was a blessing. The public got the mistaken impression that Charleston had been destroyed, and as a result business and tourism suffered for some time thereafter. But as soon as power was restored and windows replaced, much of Charlotte's business community was back up to speed. Businesspeople and visitors never really stopped coming to the city. And for the most part, Hugo was the stormiest part of Woodward's first months on campus.

The tradition of strong trustee boards continued for Woodward as Ed Crutchfield, CEO of First Union Corporation; Hugh McColl, CEO of NCNB (soon to become NationsBank); and Martha Melvin, first mayor of the town of Harrisburg, joined the board. After a short time, McColl resigned because he also was on the Queens College Board and was elected its chair. He believed that he didn't have time to serve well in both capacities.

During McColl's relatively brief tenure on the board, an interesting phenomenon was observed. McColl, of course, had a reputation as a tough CEO, with vestiges of his Marine training still present. President Spangler had requested that formal photographs be taken of each of the boards of trustees of campuses of the UNC system. At a UNC Charlotte trustee meeting, I was lining up the members for the portrait. I had a place in mind for each one and asked McColl to step into his spot.

McColl said he would prefer to stand beside another trustee and moved to that spot, and I quickly adjusted. But campus photographer Wade Bruton was new to the campus and to Charlotte, having just arrived from a newspaper in Aberdeen. He didn't know McColl or any other trustee. When he arrived on the scene and saw the lineup, he tugged gently at McColl and asked him to move to the assigned place. McColl complied.

McColl's departure from the board didn't mean the end of NationsBank's long-term commitment to helping build UNC Charlotte. One of the top executives of the bank, James Thompson, replaced McColl and also would play perhaps the key role in the upcoming major fund-raising campaign for the university.

Thomas Storrs, a former CEO of NationsBank, left the UNC Charlotte trustee chair generally regarded as one of the institution's ablest board chairs ever. His service was recognized through the 1990 Distinguished Service Award. He was replaced as chair by Russell M. Robinson II, one of North Carolina's leading attorneys and a lifelong friend of President C. D. Spangler.

Shortly after Woodward took office, other changes took place on the Board of Trustees. William R. Holland, chief executive of United Dominion Industries, which had recently moved its headquarters to Charlotte, was added, and longtime trustees R. Stuart Dickson and W. Duke Kimbrell completed their terms. Two other outstanding trustees were added—former North Carolina lieutenant governor Robert Jordan and Dr. Carlton Sears, a former Celanese executive and, at the time, chief executive of Kenmure Enterprises in Flat Rock. Michael Wilson, a strong student government leader, was the student representative on the board as Woodward began his duties.

While in his first year, Woodward performed the expected task of assessing the institution. The job was made easier by a confluence of events. He arrived as UNC Charlotte was preparing to celebrate the institution's twenty-fifth anniversary as a campus of the UNC system. Planning had already begun for the institution's largest private fund-raising campaign. Planning also began shortly for Woodward's installation as chancellor. As the university community simultaneously looked at its past and toward its future, Woodward was able to gain a quick perspective of the campus.

And during his first year, the door was opened by President Spangler and the Board of Governors of the UNC system for a study of UNC Charlotte's mission and goals.

In his first annual report Woodward said, "What I found during all these exercises is a solid University without serious flaws, but one that has yet to realize its full potential and one that perhaps has yet to come to terms with the rapid changes in society and the expansion of Charlotte from its city limits to a multi-county region, crossing city, county and even state boundaries."

The formal celebration of the twenty-fifth anniversary was an unusual—perhaps unique—event for a university: essentially all of its history was present at one time and place in the form of former and present chief executives of the campus and the UNC system. They were President Emeritus Friday and then current President Spangler of the UNC system; Vice Chancellor Emerita Cone; and Chancellors Emeritus Colvard and Fretwell and then current Chancellor James H. Woodward. At that point, UNC Charlotte was forty-four years old as an institution and twenty-five years old as a campus of the UNC system.

As part of the twenty-fifth anniversary celebration, Bonnie Cone reenacted the ringing of the bell that twenty-five years earlier had rung out success in creating the fourth campus of the University of North Carolina.

At his installation, Woodward sought to place UNC Charlotte in context within higher education and the history of the state. He also attempted to describe and characterize the university by rejecting the various descriptive labels that had been attached to it. He said that none of the terms, such as urban, metropolitan, commuter, nontraditional, or regional university, was broad enough to describe UNC Charlotte, although each term might cover an aspect of it.

To an extent, he said, UNC Charlotte had become a research university because of increasing activity in that arena. Although he acknowledged the undergraduate, teaching role of the institution as a most important responsibility, he said that the campus was also a graduate institution, with an enrollment of more than two thousand such students.

In giving his own description, Woodward said, "We are first and foremost a campus of The University of North Carolina placed here to conduct teaching, research, and service programs most reflective of the needs of this region which can reasonably be met by a university. This means we must serve traditional students and non-traditional students; and we must offer a broad range of undergraduate programs and graduate programs. We must do our work on campus and off campus." He added, "We are perhaps the most complex of universities. We are the traditional, residential campus plus more. And we must become even more complex as we move into the next century."

In his installation address, Woodward sought to identify the characteristics of the university's service area that would determine the future nature of the institution. These included a growing regionalism, an aging population, a minority population that was not yet adequately served, a growing international community, public schools with unsolved problems similar to those elsewhere in the country, a business community that was part of the international business climate, a community with workforce needs for continuing education, and a community with a concern for the quality of life.

To address those concerns, Woodward described the kind of campus UNC Charlotte should become: a microcosm of the greater society, with all its diversity; a place that attracts the most capable and creative people with a wide range of views as faculty members; a place with faculty of high standards; a place with faculty who are scholars but also devoted teachers; a place that attracts outstanding students from throughout the state, nation, and world; and a place with a curriculum that assures that graduates are prepared to lead productive and full lives as individuals, members of society, and citizens of the country and, indeed, of the world.

Among other things, Woodward said that he expected further growth in enrollment and programs, an expansion and enhancement of research activities, stronger support of public education, strengthened ties with community colleges, a broader array of graduate programs reflecting the high-growth sectors of the economy, broadened outreach to serve the region, greatly expanded international programs, and expanded service to students where they live and work and to those with family and work responsibilities.

To an extent Woodward was expanding on continuing themes at UNC Charlotte—commitment to undergraduate education with expanding graduate opportunities, university services for the region, university leadership of regional development, and an expanding research component. Those activities were initiated under Colvard and Fretwell. Woodward bought into the University City concept and the Urban Institute's leadership role in external relationships. On the other hand, Woodward urged speedier development of some aspects of the university's mission. He was not going to be content to wait for an indeterminate period for the development of Ph.D. programs, for example. Woodward said, "We are in a region which by any measure is one of the more dynamic in the country. Its aspirations are second to none and its cohesiveness of purpose must surely be unique in the United States."

But there was little time to reflect or even to plan. Woodward had to get on with the immediate tasks at hand. He made two early administrative appointments: he named Harry H. (Hap) Arnold as vice chancellor for business affairs and James E. Dixon III as executive assistant to the chancellor, Arnold's former position.

In appointing Dixon, an African American attorney, Woodward restored to the executive staff of the administration some of the diversity that was lost earlier when vice chancellors Robert Albright and Kathy Faircloth left. Dixon held a law degree from Notre Dame University and came to UNC Charlotte from the law school of the University of Florida, where he was an assistant to the dean. Arnold, who had served as staff liaison to the Chancellor Search Committee, replaced Olen Smith, who had been acting vice chancellor for business affairs following the resignation of Leo Ells. Smith was named associate vice chancellor for business affairs to coordinate strategic planning. Smith and Arnold, who had worked together as officers in the Navy some years earlier, continued to make a strong team. Smith had worked in business affairs at The College of Charleston before coming to UNC Charlotte.

At the faculty level, African Americans and women were gaining academic recognition. Business professor Stella Nkomo received a Rockefeller Foundation grant to study the role of black women in American corporations and was named a winner of the NationsBank Award for Excellence in Teaching, along with Anita Moss, an English professor and authority on children's literature. Nkomo's husband, Mokubung Nkomo, associate professor of human services, gained his own recognition when he received a Fulbright grant to return to the University of Witwatersrand in South Africa, an institution he could not have attended as a student when he was growing up there. His return as a professor was made possible by the abolition of apartheid.

Two African American professors led programs to assist students of their race, one at the entering-student level and the other at the pre-graduate-school level. Professor Herman Thomas of the Department of Religious Studies was appointed to head a program called University Transitional Opportunities Program (UTOP), which brings entering students to the campus in the summer before their freshman year to give them some counseling, tutoring, and social activities to help get them off to a good start. Professor Sandra Govan of the English Department was appointed to head the McNair program. Named for Ronald McNair, an African American astronaut who died in the explosion of the space shuttle Challenger, the program provided enrichment and preparation opportunities for African American college students to encourage them to attend graduate schools.

In the field of science, Banita White Brown, a relatively new African American chemistry professor, received a Presidential Young Investigator Award from the National Science Foundation—one of the most prestigious grants a young faculty member in the sciences can receive. And Lisa-Noelle Hjellming, a white female engineering professor who later left the university, also became a Presidential Young Investigator.

One of the greatest advances for women was in athletics: Judy Rose became athletic director on July 1, 1990, and at the time she was only the third female athletic director at an NCAA Division I university. A graduate of Winthrop University and the University of Tennessee, Rose began her career at UNC Charlotte in 1975, as women's basketball and tennis coach.

Rose's opportunity was provided by a controversy that erupted at N.C. State University over the athletic program under basketball coach Jim Valvano. An investigation found that part of the problem there was that Valvano simultaneously held positions as men's basketball coach and athletic director. Jeff Mullins and coaches at some other UNC system institutions, including coaching legend Bighouse Gaines at Winston-Salem State University, held similar joint positions, although no problems had arisen.

To solve the N.C. State problem, the UNC Board of Governors determined that no coach in the UNC system could also simultaneously hold the athletic director position. That action almost created a serious crisis at UNC Charlotte.

Mullins at first was prepared to challenge the decision because the dual positions were part of the contract that UNC Charlotte had signed with him. It was about to become a dilemma for board chair Russell Robinson as well. He was a close friend of Spangler, but he also was a Duke University alumnus and an admirer and friend of Mullins.

But Mullins decided to give up the athletic director's position and not challenge the breach of contract. Rose was promoted from assistant director, and Mullins was given the additional title of associate vice chancellor for public service. Some speculated that Rose would have the title of athletic director in name only, but she proved them wrong as she immediately took a firm hold on the Athletic Department reins.

Statewide recognition was provided to a female professor as Dr. Jonnie H. McLeod of Human Services won the Governor's Award for Excellence in 1989 as an outstanding employee of the State of North Carolina. In addition to her work in the Department of Human Services, McLeod was active in the community and throughout the state in such programs as drug education and sex education and improving health conditions for pregnant women and their babies. When she retired from UNC Charlotte in 1993, her husband, Dr. Leslie McLeod, joked that it was the only job she ever had that paid her anything.

Many other faculty members were succeeding. Irvin Tucker of Economics won the Leavey Award for Excellence in Private Enterprise Education, presented by the Freedoms Foundation. He also won a first prize presented by the National Federation of Independent Business Foundation. Both awards were for his work in educating school children about economics.

In 1990, Professor Jim Clay also won the Governor's Award for Excellence for his work in building University Place and University City, for his leadership in publishing atlases for Metrolina, North Carolina, and the South, and for his outstanding teaching. Later winners of the award would be Professor Herbert Hechenbleikner, for his continued work on the Botanical Gardens even after his retirement, and James Matthews of Biology for his work in preserving natural areas and rare plant species in the region.

The faculty pattern of success was being repeated by UNC Charlotte alumni. Dr. Ron Caldwell, an African American physician from Asheville, was presented the Distinguished Alumnus Award for his professional and community service. Sue Becht became one of the top female executives at Duke Power Company; she was appointed treasurer and later would be promoted to controller. And Hulene Hill Foster became the first female partner in a Big Eight accounting firm in Charlotte.

Karen Popp, an alumna and former student body president, joined the prestigious firm of Sullivan and Cromwell in New York City, then was appointed an assistant U.S. attorney in New York City, and then transferred to the Justice Department in Washington, D.C. Chet Snow Jr. was succeeding as head of his real estate firm and was elected to leadership positions in his profession at the state level. Gene Johnson was an adventuresome business entrepreneur. Mary Ann Rouse became vice president for financial services of Carolinas Medical Center. Robert Hensley, a history graduate and a successful Raleigh attorney, was elected to the North Carolina House of Representatives for Wake County. R. William McCanless had become senior vice president of administration for Food Lion, Inc.

Les Bowen, an English graduate, began his newspaper career on the student newspaper, reported sports for the *Charlotte Observer*, and later covered national sports for the *Philadelphia Daily News*. Ann Owens, who returned to college as an adult in the Theater Department, was busy acting and appeared in the movie *The Prince of Tides*, based on Pat Conroy's best-selling novel. Ron Lunsford, an English Department alumnus, became the first graduate to return as a department chair. After leaving UNC Charlotte, he had earned a Ph.D. from Florida State University and had risen to the rank of professor at Clemson University before becoming chair of English at Southwest Missouri State University.

Among the most visible alumni were the Moody Brothers, Carlton and David, both graduates in history. They won the International Country Music Award in 1987 and 1988 and were Grammy Award nominees as well. They made a number of appearances on television, including the Grand Ole Opry, the Nashville Network, and the Public Broadcasting System. They also made campaign appearances with President George Bush. The brothers were recognized as Distinguished Alumni at the 1990 UNC Charlotte Commencement.

At about the time the Moodys were being recognized, Fariba G. Homesley was being named National Outstanding Cooperative Education Student of the Year by the National Cooperative Education Association—a recognition of the strength of the university's co-op program under the leadership of Professor Norman Schul. As a student in the co-op program working at IBM, Homesley had developed software that was soon in use by thousands of the company's employees.

Many of those alumni would play a major role in the university's Silver Anniversary Campaign, the most challenging fund-raising effort ever. In preparing for the campaign, UNC Charlotte Foundation leaders and community supporters decided on an unusual and somewhat controversial tack, given the ambitious goal anticipated.

They employed outside fund-raising counsel in the feasibility phase of the campaign but decided to conduct the actual fund-raising themselves without a professional fund-raising organization. Their reasoning was that most of them had worked together on other major Charlotte campaigns and knew exactly what to do.

John Stedman, former president of Republic Bank and a veteran of a number of successful Charlotte campaigns, was elected president of the UNC

Charlotte Foundation and thus manager of the campaign. Campus staff support was provided by Doug Orr, vice chancellor for development; Harry Creemers, director of development, and members of the development, alumni, and public relations staffs.

A key factor in the success of the Silver Anniversary Campaign was the appointment of James W. Thompson, then vice chair of NCNB Corporation (later NationsBank), as the campaign's chair. That appointment brought with it the support and prestige of the bank and opened doors for campaign solicitors.

Thompson had strong support from a steering committee, which included Harry H. Arnold, UNC Charlotte vice chancellor; James G. Babb of Jefferson-Pilot Communications; William M. Barnhardt of Southern Webbing Mills, Inc.; Thomas M. Belk of Belk Stores Services; H. C. Bissell of The Bissell Companies, Inc.; C. C. (Cliff) Cameron, then assistant to Gov. James G. Martin; M. Douglas Crisp of First Union National Bank; Edward Crutchfield Jr. of First Union Corp.; R. Stuart Dickson of Ruddick Corp.; Hugh M. Durden of Wachovia Bank and Trust Co.; John C. Fennebresque, then of Moore and Van Allen; Newton O. Fowler of Philip Morris, Inc.; William C. Friday, former UNC president; John R. Georgius of First Union Corp.; Seddon (Rusty) Goode Jr. of University Research Park; Cameron M. Harris of Cameron M. Harris Co.; Donald F. Hatley, an alumnus from Duke Power Co.; Edwin L. Jones Jr., retired from J. A. Jones Corp.; W. Duke Kimbrell of Parkdale Mills; Joseph P. Lacher of Southern Bell Telephone Co.; James R. Leavelle of NCNB Corp.; John D. Lewis of Arthur Andersen & Co.; Hugh L. McColl Jr. of NCNB Corp.; Rolfe Neill of the *Charlotte Observer*; Russell M. Robinson II of Robinson, Bradshaw and Hinson; Albert F. Sloan of Lance, Inc.; J. William Southerland of Blythe Industries; Thomas I. Storrs, retired CEO of NCNB; and James H. Woodward, UNC Charlotte chancellor.

In addition, there was an impressive campaign advisory board and strong volunteers at almost every campaign position. In fact, the campaign enlisted three hundred volunteers and received support from 5,900 individuals, corporations, and foundations.

University administrators and the campaign leadership determined that a major focus would be on raising funds to endow distinguished professorships for the university. That decision would help lead to the success of the campaign. The North Carolina General Assembly had created a built-in incentive for the professorships. If a donor gave $333,000, the state would add $167,000 to create a $500,000 endowment. Or if the donor provided $666,000, the state would contribute additional funds to create a $1 million endowment. Soon Charlotte area donors were responding to the challenge of creating those distinguished professorships.

The campaign got a boost from very visible kickoffs. UNC President

C. D. Spangler gave a pep talk to help volunteers launch the campaign. H. Ross Perot, who became a 1992 presidential candidate, gave the keynote address for the public portion of the campaign. A major precampaign gift just before the public launching was also a boost. The Alex Hemby Foundation pledged $333,000, which with state matching would provide a half-million-dollar endowment for the Torrence E. Hemby Distinguished Professorship in Banking.

Another major ingredient of the winning campaign was the success of on-campus fund-raising. That success could be traced to the enthusiasm of Hap Arnold, as Family Division chair, and of the campus cochairs, Dean Nancy Langston of Nursing and Professor John Lincourt of Philosophy. With a goal of $1 million, which at first was thought to be ambitious, the campus community raised $2 million in pledges.

The campaign leadership said that it became much easier to raise funds from corporations, foundations, and individuals when they could report the enthusiasm and commitment on campus.

At the victory celebration, on March 18, 1991, campaign chair James Thompson unveiled a large poster with "$30,876,614" emblazoned across it as balloons burst, showering confetti on the celebrating campaign workers. That total was almost twice the goal of $16 million. With additional funds pledged after the official end of the campaign, a total of more than $32 million was reported, doubling the original goal.

Silver Anniversary Chairman James Thompson celebrates the official end of the campaign with a total of $30,876,614 in funds pledged. Photo by Wade Bruton.

The campaign success lifted UNC Charlotte over several hurdles. One was alumni participation. This time the Alumni Association played an even bigger role in the campaign's success than in the Campaign for Excellence. Some pledges from alumni such as Cameron M. Harris were among the largest in the campaign.

Another hurdle overcome was getting major Charlotte donors to understand that they could contribute to a state-assisted university like UNC Charlotte rather than just private institutions.

A final hurdle was raising really significant money for UNC Charlotte. The Silver Anniversary Campaign total was one of the largest ever pledged in a Charlotte fund-raising drive.

When the distinguished professorships were all filled with first-rate scholars, the campaign was expected to lift UNC Charlotte to a higher level of academic attainment. With the supplements to state salaries provided by the endowments, the university was able to recruit nationwide and worldwide for the best scholars available.

The presence on campus of Professor Robert Hocken was evidence of the impact a distinguished professorship could make. He was recruited to UNC Charlotte to fill the Norvin Kennedy Dickerson Jr. Distinguished Professor of Precision Engineering position. It was given by the family of the late vice chair of the Board of Trustees.

Hocken, a Ph.D. graduate of State University of New York at Stony Brook,

Professor Robert Hocken (left) discusses his work in precision engineering with Governor Jim Hunt. Photo by Wade Bruton.

had been chief of the Precision Engineering Division of the National Bureau of Standards and was a recipient of the Presidential Executive Award for 1987.

He found a home in UNC Charlotte's Cameron Applied Research Center and put together a team to conduct research on precision engineering. He captured the Charlotte community's attention with his scientific sparkle and his ability to translate the most complex physics into something that is simple and exciting. Whereas scientists had once only known that atoms existed and had just recently been able to see them with precise instruments, Hocken and his team were among the first in the world to be able to actually pick atoms up and move them.

Although those experiments might have seemed somewhat exotic, Hocken and his team were involved in the very serious business of precisely measuring new manufacturing devices that needed tolerances of just a few atoms' width. Even the manipulating of atoms had a serious purpose. Hocken and his colleagues believed that an atomic-level computer chip could be created, resulting in the storage of huge amounts of information in very small spaces.

Hocken's presence attracted other scientists and graduate students as well. Soon he was mentoring a doctoral student from France, along with American graduate students. Hocken was joined by David Trumper, who was named a Presidential Young Investigator and created excitement with his experiments, magnetically levitating a steel ball and steel beams. He left the campus to teach at his alma mater, MIT, after a stint at UNC Charlotte. The strength of Hocken's program would later help make the case for Ph.D. programs in engineering.

In fact, Hocken's presence helped to attract another distinguished professor when United Dominion Industries decided to pay off a Silver Anniversary Pledge early. Dr. Steven Patterson, holder of a Ph.D. from Cal Tech, had been working on the Star Wars national defense project, particularly the Bright Pebbles portion of it. He came to UNC Charlotte as the United Dominion Industries Professor of Precision Engineering.

UNC Charlotte had established a few distinguished professorships well before the Silver Anniversary Campaign. David Goldfield, historian of the urban South, held the Robert Lee Bailey Professorship of History, the first distinguished professorship established at UNC Charlotte. It was provided by Sanford V. Davenport and his wife, Mildred, and named for her brother, who was killed in World War II. Davenport approached an infant UNC Charlotte in 1965, after first making an offer to another institution with his idea for a professorship. His offer was accepted by Bonnie Cone.

Ed Nicollian had joined the university in 1983 as Distinguished Professor of Electrical Engineering and Engineering Science after a productive research career at Bell Labs. He helped UNC Charlotte move into research in microelectronics before his death in 1995. He was replaced in that distinguished professorship by Raphael Tsu, another former Bell Labs researcher and former head of amorphous silicon research at the Solar Energy Research Institute.

Donna Gabbacia held the Charles H. Stone Professorship in American History. Thomas H. Stevenson held the Charles Cullen Professorship of Marketing, provided through a campaign by members of the Charlotte Sales and Marketing Executives to honor the memory of Cullen, nationally known as a motivational speaker. Cullen's widow, Sarah, worked for the UNC Charlotte Foundation for a number of years.

Mario Azevedo held the Frank Porter Graham Professorship of African American and African Studies, established by Alice Tate and held earlier by Bertha Maxwell-Roddey.

Others who had held distinguished professorships were Edward Walls, the Rush S. Dickson Professor of Finance; Elinor Brooks Caddell, the A. Sue Kerley Professor of Nursing; Philip Hildreth, the Distinguished Professor of Biology; and Douglas Powers, M.D., the Distinguished Professor of Human Services.

After Knight-Ridder Company contributed funds for the Knight Distinguished Professorship of Public Policy, it was filled by John W. (Jack) Sommer, a native of Oregon and an official in the Bush administration. He immediately launched a series of lectures and forums on matters of public policy in the Charlotte region.

When the medical community contributed funds from the Metrolina Medical Foundation to establish a distinguished professorship of public policy on health, William P. Brandon was recruited to fill that position.

Together Sommer and Brandon, along with K. David Patterson, special assistant to the vice chancellor, established Policy House, an organization to help the region address issues of public concern, such as health care.

Earlier, Carlos Bell had held the Celanese Professorship. Bell was a somewhat confrontational professor who did research on the potential threat of earthquakes to nuclear power facilities and who had once worked for Oak Ridge Laboratories. He managed to embroil himself in controversy at Oak Ridge and at UNC Charlotte to the point that his professorship was removed, leading faculty wags to note that he was the only professor whose "chair" had been pulled from under him. Bell left UNC Charlotte to teach at the University of Nevada at Las Vegas and then went to work for the U.S. government at Johnston Atoll in the Pacific, a facility for disposing of the military's stockpile of poison gases.

Later, another controversy would result in a professor's losing his distinguished professorship and UNC Charlotte's receiving media attention from all over the world, including China. Alice Tate had endowed the Rabbi Isaac

Swift Distinguished Professorship in Judaic Studies. It was filled by Tzvee Zahavy, a professor from the University of Minnesota with outstanding credentials. He was to teach courses in Judaic studies for the Department of Religious Studies and to lecture and work in the community toward better understanding of religious issues, particularly those involving the Jewish faith.

The states of Minnesota and North Carolina are quite a few miles apart, even by air, but the academic community in a particular discipline is fairly compact, particularly when its members attend national conferences. At one such conference a few months after Zahavy began teaching, a UNC Charlotte professor of religious studies was telling a professor from the University of Minnesota how much it meant to have his "former colleague" in the department in Charlotte. "What do you mean?" the Minnesota professor asked. "He's still teaching for us."

An investigation revealed that, indeed, Zahavy had not resigned his Minnesota post when he accepted the UNC Charlotte distinguished professorship. He had arranged his teaching schedule so that he could commute by air and teach part of the week in Charlotte and part of the week in Minnesota.

When Chancellor Woodward learned of that, he asked for and received Zahavy's resignation. The University of Minnesota, which was under some pressure about faculty teaching loads anyway, dismissed the professor as well. Zahavy sued for reinstatement at Minnesota.

That Swift Professorship was later held by Richard A. Cohen, who came to UNC Charlotte from the University of Alabama and performed his duties in the way that had been anticipated when the position was established.

One of the most heartwarming stories to come out of the creation of distinguished professorships was that of University of North Carolina president C. D. Spangler's gift in honor of his lifelong friend Russell M. Robinson II.

Since Robinson was chair of the UNC Charlotte Board of Trustees, Spangler wanted to surprise him and announce his gift during a trustee meeting. He came to the campus and requested the privilege of addressing the board. Robinson yielded the floor, and Spangler announced that since his good friend was such a fan of and student of Shakespeare, he was contributing funds to establish the Russell M. Robinson II Distinguished Professorship of Shakespeare. Afterward, Spangler announced that he would contribute a like amount to the other fifteen campuses of the UNC system so that they could qualify for the state matching funds and create their own distinguished professorships.

A worldwide search led to the appointment of Dennis Kay as the distinguished professor of Shakespeare. A lecture presented by the professor in early 1995 drew a full house to the recital hall of Rowe Building, which seated four hundred, an impressive turnout to hear an English literature lecture.

Trustee Chairman Russell M. Robinson II (left) gives friend, UNC President C. D. Spangler Jr., a UNC Charlotte baseball cap in 1990. Photo by Wade Bruton.

Thus the choice of using most of the funds from the Silver Anniversary Campaign to establish distinguished professorships quickly made a positive impact. The campaign helped in other areas as well. The C. C. Cameron Scholarship Fund was increased with a half-million-dollar gift from the First Union Corporation's foundation. That allowed the university to recognize students with leadership potential by awarding a Cameron Scholarship for Merit, which included funds for studying abroad.

The Sandoz Foundation contributed $100,000 for scholarships in chemistry. IBM contributed an equipment grant valued at half a million dollars to support education and research in Engineering and Computer Science.

The overall effect of the contributions was to provide a boost for the entire campus, but the funds raised were not distributed to every department or to every individual faculty member. Therefore, sometimes it was hard to convince a young assistant professor that the campaign helped the entire campus when he or she was in one of the disciplines that did not receive designated funds from the fund-raising effort.

Woodward also discovered that some faculty members weren't happy with the quality of assistance they received from academic support units.

The most important relationship at the administrative level was that between the chancellor and the vice chancellor for academic affairs. For

Woodward to be able to devote time to the many off-campus demands of his position, he had to have a comfortable feeling about the direction of the academic program and confidence in its leadership.

Whereas the balance between Fretwell's intuitive style and Werntz's analytical approach had worked very well, Woodward's own analytical approach was somewhat different because of his engineering and MBA backgrounds. As a result, the Werntz style didn't mesh as well with Woodward's expectations. Woodward was also pressing for a more user-friendly approach in the Division of Academic Affairs, particularly among support units.

Woodward had his own ideas about how to carry out the tasks of chief academic administrator, because he had done that at UAB. When it appeared Woodward wanted major changes made in the way academic affairs was administered, Werntz quietly resigned effective in June 1991 and planned to return to teaching in physics. As he prepared to do so, however, he received an offer to become an educational consultant to the University of the United Arab Emirates, which he accepted.

A search committee recommended Philip L. Dubois, an academic administrator from the University of California–Davis, to replace Werntz. Dubois fit the mold of the academic administrator Woodward was seeking, a person to whom he could entrust the day-to-day management of the teaching and research functions—Mr. Inside—while Woodward worked to strengthen support from the community, the General Administration of the UNC system, and the legislature—Mr. Outside.

Beyond that, however, Dubois was also a person who enjoyed the university's social and outreach aspects. He bought a home at SouthPark, and he and his wife, Lisa, were comfortable working the crowds who were entertained at the chancellor's residence. Lisa Dubois was an attorney who had practiced in Sacramento and had served on the staff of the Speaker of the House in California.

The California-Davis campus was substantially larger than UNC Charlotte. The College of Letters and Sciences alone, which Dubois served as executive associate dean, had an enrollment of 13,000 full-time equivalent students. The Davis campus was also a major research university in the California system. This experience prepared Dubois to assist Woodward in the quest for doctoral status for UNC Charlotte.

As a political scientist, Dubois provided a counterpoint to Woodward's engineering background, but one that was different from what Werntz provided Fretwell. Dubois proved to be an entertaining speaker with a talent for clever phrasing and comic relief.

With political scientists holding a number of key university positions, tongues wagged in a good-natured way. Those political scientists included Schley Lyons, dean of the College of Arts and Sciences, the largest college on

Philip Dubois was named vice chancellor for academic affairs in 1991 and given the additional title of provost in 1994. Photo by Wade Bruton.

campus; Bill McCoy, director of the Urban Institute and associate vice chancellor for extended academic programs; Terrel Rhodes, associate vice chancellor for undergraduate programs; Ted Arrington and later Roger Brown, chairs of the Political Science Department; and Bob Mundt, a former chair of the department who served as interim chair of Criminal Justice and interim dean of the College of Education.

The kidding aside, Dubois dedicated himself to academic progress for the entire campus and with some success.

Enrollment continued to grow and by fall 1991 had reached another historic plateau, passing the 15,000-student mark to reach a total of 15,058. The "baby bust" had arrived, however, and enrollment growth would slow for the next few years until the children from the "echo baby boom" would start turning eighteen, around 1996. Woodward predicted that UNC Charlotte would continue its historical pattern of about 4 percent growth annually.

UNC Charlotte was continuing to move ahead in the academic arena. National recognition came in the form of a step up in the national organizations to which the university belonged. UNC Charlotte had been a member of the American Association of State Colleges and Universities. Its membership included a wide range of institutions, from very small, undergraduate institutions to relatively large universities. But it wasn't the premiere organization for universities like UNC Charlotte. So in 1993 UNC Charlotte applied

Associate Vice Chancellor and Director of the Urban Institute William J. McCoy helped lead UNC Charlotte efforts in regionalism. Photo by Wade Bruton.

to and was admitted to the National Association of State Universities and Land Grant Colleges, signifying a move upward in status.

The outreach thrust for the university, following the successful effort to build University Place and University City, turned toward regionalism. Movement in that direction occurred even while Jim Clay was giving most of his attention to the former projects, but the effort was accelerated under the leadership of Professor William J. McCoy as director of the Urban Institute.

Cities and counties of the region—and even the states of North and South Carolina—began looking to UNC Charlotte and the Urban Institute as a resource for assessing and managing development of the greater Charlotte region. A Carolinas Issues Academy was formed to study issues the region was facing, and under its leadership, the university hosted well-attended conferences on regional transportation, the Catawba River basin, education, and other issues that had an impact on almost all the counties.

But the most dramatic presentation that demonstrated the "we're all in this together" concept was a slide show created by Michael Gallis of Architecture. His presentation showed how the Southern Piedmont had changed from the days of sail-powered boats, to the agricultural era, to the steam engine and the Industrial Revolution, and finally to the electronic and information age.

He also showed a dramatic graphic image of the region. It showed Charlotte at the center, surrounded by ring cities, beginning with the close-in towns of Mecklenburg County. More significantly, the design showed the twenty-miles-out cities—Concord, Kannapolis, Gastonia, Rock Hill, and Monroe—with the arteries that linked them to the center city. No one could have drawn a more perfect model for a region, Gallis told his audiences. Suddenly leaders and citizens of Charlotte and the region saw themselves in the context of a city-state.

Geographers Clay, Orr, and Stuart had long since described the area as a dispersed urban region, going back to the publication of the *Metrolina Atlas*. But Gallis was able to transfer that concept to graphic images that seemed to fire the imaginations of those who had missed the earlier messages.

As word got out about the presentation, Gallis and McCoy began taking it on the road. Gallis and Orr even took the presentation to the North and South Carolina congressional delegations in Washington. And Gallis showed it to members of the North Carolina General Assembly when they visited Charlotte. McCoy and Gallis went out so often with their show that colleagues suggested the creation of a bumper sticker: "Honk If You've Seen the Gallis Slide Show."

All of this activity reinforced UNC Charlotte's role as a catalyst and resource for studying and acting on regional problems and strengthened the university's claim to a strong outreach mission.

CHAPTER 13

Opening the Door to Doctoral Programs

CHANCELLOR JIM WOODWARD learned after arriving on campus that doctoral status for UNC Charlotte, which had seemed such a certainty when it became the fourth campus of the University of North Carolina in 1965, had become a more distant dream after the restructuring of 1972. In seeking to prevent all sixteen UNC institutions from becoming doctoral campuses, the state had blocked the way for the one campus which, by any impartial measurement, should have had such programs.

In fact, under the rules of the game that existed in 1990, UNC Charlotte was not even allowed to present evidence that it should have certain doctoral programs, because its mission statement did not include them. Clearly, the mission statement would have to be revised.

Supporters of other campuses had suspicions that as a Charlottean, C. D. Spangler would show favoritism toward UNC Charlotte when he became president. He had not done so. In 1990, UNC Charlotte still had the lowest appropriation per student and the least amount of classroom and library space per student in the system.

What Spangler did do was the greatest favor he could have done. He opened the door for a change of mission for UNC Charlotte and other campuses. In March 1990, he asked each campus to review its assigned mission and propose changes if it wished to do so. He noted that much had changed in higher education and in North Carolina since the last review of missions of the sixteen campuses when restructuring took place in 1972. Apparently Spangler needed to satisfy himself that the campuses were performing their appropriate roles. Some had grown dramatically since 1972, and others were very much the same institutions they were at that time. For example, UNC Charlotte's setting had changed dramatically as the metropolitan area moved into the top ranks of American cities.

Woodward and the faculty, staff, trustees, and supporters of UNC Charlotte seized the opportunity. Leading the charge was Woodward himself. His arguments would echo those of W. A. Kennedy in the early 1950s. Whereas Kennedy had called for a state-supported institution to serve the most "undercolleged" city of its size in the nation, Woodward called for doctoral programs for the largest city in the nation without such programs.

The *Charlotte Observer* called for a change in mission for UNC Charlotte in an editorial published December 9, 1990. It said, "Outsiders are struck by this region's paucity of opportunities for advanced education. . . . Helping UNC Charlotte become the major research university the region needs should be a top priority for citizens of this region."

One of the strongest arguments UNC Charlotte made was a state map showing the Southern Piedmont region, with a single state-supported university campus pinpointed in the center of a large piece of the state's geography. That campus was UNC Charlotte. When population rather than physical geography was considered, the argument became even stronger.

Woodward pointed out that Mecklenburg and Wake Counties alone provided for about one-third of the state's growth during the 1980s. He noted that according to the 1990 census, Charlotte was the state's largest city and the nation's thirty-fifth largest and the heart of what at the time was the nation's thirty-fourth largest metropolitan statistical area. Later, of course, Charlotte and the region moved even higher in the rankings.

Pointing to an international presence in North Carolina, Woodward said that of the foreign-based companies that had placed their U.S. headquarters in North Carolina, 49 percent had located them in Charlotte, with Greensboro and Raleigh following at 19 and 12 percent respectively. In the latest year for which the data were available, 1989, Woodward noted that the trend had accelerated. Of twenty-four foreign-based companies establishing U.S. headquarters in North Carolina, nineteen selected Charlotte.

Woodward noted what he called a mismatch between the region's higher education needs and the totality of such services available from all sources, including public and private colleges and community colleges. He cited a study on the Charlotte region's needs conducted by the Urban Land Institute, which had concluded, "Aggressive steps should be taken to upgrade The University of North Carolina at Charlotte into a major urban university with expanded research, technical, and professional curricula and doctoral degree programs." Another report cited was by Dr. Jesse L. White, formerly the executive director of the Southern Growth Policies Board, in which he pointed to the absence of a major research university as a weakness of the City of Charlotte.

Woodward contended that weaknesses that hindered the City of Charlotte and the region's economic development also hindered the state by discouraging potential growth in resources and revenues.

The chancellor commissioned his own study of the nation's hundred largest metropolitan areas. He found that Charlotte indeed was the largest MSA without either a public or private university that offered doctoral work. Further, he found that only five of the hundred MSAs, including Charlotte, were located more than ninety miles from the nearest institution where doctoral work was available. The four others were all smaller MSAs than Charlotte.

Since he had studied Orlando closely as a candidate for the head of the University of Central Florida campus, Woodward noted that the Florida institution had pulled ahead in terms of enrollment and doctoral programs despite the fact that the two metropolitan areas shared many other similarities. He went on to report that Florida had also adopted a plan to add doctoral programs in fifteen disciplines by 1995 at Florida International University and Florida Atlantic University even though the University of Miami, a private doctoral-level university, was located in their region of the state. Ironically, a few years earlier, when the Orlando campus was seeking its place in the sun, a reporter from the *Orlando Sentinel* had interviewed UNC System president Friday and UNC Charlotte officials about how the Charlotte campus had forged ahead.

The findings of the studies concerning whether UNC Charlotte should have an expanded mission were presented in a substantial published report titled "UNC Charlotte and Its Region: Partners for the Advancement of North Carolina." The report said, "When viewed in isolation or when compared with other large regions in the United States, the Charlotte region is seen to be inadequately served by higher education. The lack of a major research university is a great impediment to the continued development of the region and, therefore, to the future well-being of all of North Carolina."

Woodward's appeal wasn't just a modest one to allow some doctoral programs on the Charlotte campus; rather, he asked that the university "be formally identified as the state's next major research university and that the leadership of this campus be charged with developing a plan for achieving that goal over a period of time consistent with the state's and university's fiscal capabilities."

The UNC Charlotte proposal for a change in mission outlined a plan to add doctoral programs first in educational leadership, engineering, computer science, and mathematics and then in selected areas of business administration, education, the humanities, the natural sciences, and the social and behavioral sciences. The proposal also asked for the definition of the boundaries of the campus to be changed to include the entire metropolitan region, permitting the university to take instruction, research, and service to a number of off-campus centers operated by the university, with the first to be located in uptown Charlotte.

A further request was that the university be allowed to expand programs in the health professions, visual and performing arts, and international studies; the interdisciplinary programs, such as liberal studies, women's studies, gerontology, biotechnology, environmental studies, and transportation studies; and computer technology and computational sciences.

Additional financial resources were requested to allow enrollments to continue to grow by 4 percent a year; to decrease the full-time-equivalent funding ratio and thereby increase the average faculty salary; to expand support staff in all areas of the university; to expand library and computational resources; and to provide additional space for instruction, for research, and for the library and other basic support functions.

The report made a point that Tom Storrs had made some years previously—that being able to accomplish so much so efficiently is a matter in which to take pride and to seek to continue. But it warned, "While the campus achieved much under the conditions maintained during its first 25 years, any significant next steps in the further development of the campus await fundamental changes in the role of UNC Charlotte within North Carolina higher education."

Woodward didn't just let the initial report speak for itself. He displayed his ability to carry out one of the mandates he was given—to build wide regional support for UNC Charlotte. He traveled the region seeking endorsements from such diverse organizations as the Charlotte City Council and the Pineville Town Council in Mecklenburg County. Outside Mecklenburg County, he garnered endorsements from organizations in Anson County to the east, Cleveland County to the west, Rowan County to the north, and all counties in between. Moreover, endorsements came from individual citizens and from companies ranging from IBM to Romanoff International, Inc. Those expressions of support were bound in a book called *Enhanced Mission for UNC Charlotte: A Regional Imperative*.

After the UNC Charlotte proposal for a change in mission was submitted to President Spangler, he determined that he needed to have outside educational consultants evaluate it and the proposals of the other fifteen campuses of the system. Those consultants were R. W. Fleming, president emeritus of the University of Michigan; Norman C. Francis, president of Xavier University of Louisiana; Billy J. Franklin, former president of Lamar University and later of Bill Franklin & Associates; and Bryce Jordan, president emeritus of the Pennsylvania State University. The committee of consultants made its report to Spangler on November 8, 1991.

For UNC Charlotte, the consultants did not grant every wish in terms of the recommendations, but what they did endorse represented a historic breakthrough for the university and the Charlotte region and the most significant event since Charlotte College became the fourth campus in 1965.

The major breakthrough came in endorsement of the first doctoral programs, which were anticipated with the creation of the university but delayed by institutional rivalries, funding considerations for historically African American institutions, and growing competition for scarce dollars both within and without the higher education establishment.

The consultants supported the Ed.D. in educational leadership, once some system and local campus issues were resolved, and three new Ph.D. programs. They suggested that UNC Charlotte work with the General Administration to prioritize and select three programs from among the seven requested. Consequently, UNC Charlotte selected electrical engineering, mechanical engineering, and applied mathematics. The consultants endorsed master's degree programs, planning for which had already been approved, in statistics, applied physics, and liberal studies, but it failed to recommend other requested master's degree programs because of the scarcity of funding.

Because of Charlotte's emergence as a major health-care center, the consultants endorsed adding programs in health-care fields. They gave qualified endorsement to regional centers away from the campus but raised questions about the needed resources.

No change in classification of UNC Charlotte was recommended, but the consultants did say, "Assuming that these programs are advanced to the planning level, and then to implementation, reclassification to Doctoral-Granting University II should eventually follow."

One other major aspect of the consultants' report was their acknowledgement of the significant role UNC Charlotte played in the university system. The report said, "Situated as it is in North Carolina's largest city, and in one of the South's most strategically important areas, UNC Charlotte has in a relatively short time established itself as a key component of The University of North Carolina." The consultants acknowledged the broad geographical service area and the economic development role of the campus, particularly with the growth of University Research Park and the banking industry and the growing presence of national news media, including the NBC Network and Hearst Magazines.

In March 1992, the UNC Board of Governors approved the new UNC Charlotte mission statement, including its first doctoral programs. It was not yet time to celebrate, however. The proposed doctoral programs would have to be submitted to the Board of Governors with detailed implementation plans.

The biggest shock of all came when the General Administration notified the UNC Charlotte administration that the new doctoral degrees could not be implemented—wouldn't even be given final approval—until they received specific funding by the legislature. Was this just a simple matter of asking the legislature for funding to implement the new programs? Not quite. The situation was far more complex and once again tested Jim Woodward's mettle.

When the 1993 General Assembly began considering the budget for the sixteen-campus UNC system, it had before it a request from the General Administration in priority order. Unfortunately, the Board of Governors, looking at an entire system's budget needs, didn't place the new Ph.D. programs in the level of one-through-four priority usually necessary to get funding. The new programs came in at tenth priority. Historically the legislature didn't fund that far down on the list. But Woodward and Ed Kizer, vice chancellor for development and university relations, devised a winning strategy. When new mission statements were approved in spring 1992, new doctoral programs in engineering were also authorized for North Carolina A&T State University, a historically African American campus of the system.

UNC Charlotte had something else going for it. By now Woodward and Kizer had cultivated a great deal of support for the campus in the greater Charlotte region. In fact, those supporters were part of a group called the Southern Piedmont Legislative Caucus, which had finally realized that it had clout in terms of numbers of legislators, if only it could get those legislators working together.

When the members of the caucus joined with African American supporters of N.C. A&T, they created a formidable force. Under the leadership of state senator Aaron Plyler of Union County and state representative James Black of Matthews, they were able to get the legislature to reach down and cover the tenth priority, which provided funding for Ph.D. programs at both institutions—UNC Charlotte and N.C. A&T. It was quite an accomplishment for a campus that earlier couldn't get attention for its funding plight. The result was an increase of $706,000 to support the initiation of the three doctoral programs.

That wasn't all. Earlier, UNC Charlotte had been acknowledged by the General Administration as one of the high-growth campuses where funding for support positions lagged. Those dollars previously had not been appropriated. But UNC Charlotte actually was given some catchup funding in the 1993 legislative session.

With the appropriation for doctoral programs in hand, Woodward could go back to the UNC Board of Governors and request formal and final approval of the Ph.D. degrees. Approval was given, at last, on October 8, 1993, and the campus celebrated. There was a huge arch of green and white balloons and another ringing of the campus bell that had been rung to celebrate university status—this time by Chancellor Emeritus Fretwell and Vice Chancellor Emerita Cone. Woodward was in Boone for the Board of Governors meeting at which the action was taken and relayed the message of approval by telephone to Vice Chancellor Dubois, who set the celebration in motion. Original faculty members of UNC Charlotte were honored at the event. Classes in the Ph.D. degree programs began without fanfare in January 1994.

Chancellor Emeritus E. K. Fretwell Jr. (left) and Vice Chancellor Emerita Bonnie Cone celebrate approval of Ph.D.'s in 1993. Photo by Wade Bruton.

Following up on another aspect of expansion of mission authorized by the Board of Governors, a UNC Charlotte task force began studying ways in which the university could respond to needs for higher education offerings in health-care fields.

Although the quest for the Ph.D. degree programs and other aspects of an expanded mission required a great deal of attention, otherwise the university's life proceeded as usual. The legislature did begin allowing the university a little more discretion in how it managed its budgets: it implemented a flexibility plan that allowed some shifting from one budget line to the other and some carryover of unspent funds from one budget year to the next after certain conditions were met.

CHAPTER 14

An Infusion of New Blood

EVEN BEFORE the Ph.D. degree issue was settled, other challenges arose. Primarily they related to retirements and resignations to accept key positions elsewhere and the resulting searches for replacements.

Douglas M. Orr Jr., who had contributed in many ways to building UNC Charlotte, resigned effective July 1, 1991, to accept the presidency of Warren Wilson College. Orr had served as a professor of geography; assistant to Chancellor Colvard; vice chancellor for student affairs; vice chancellor for research and public service; and vice chancellor for development and public service, a position in which he had helped conduct the Silver Anniversary Campaign. In addition, in his years as a professor he had won the NCNB Award for Excellence in Teaching. And he, along with Professor Jim Clay, was one of the key "architects" of University Place and University City. As a scholar, he helped produce the *Metrolina Atlas*, the *North Carolina Atlas*, and *Land of the South*, and when he left Charlotte he was working on a new *North Carolina Atlas*.

Friends felt that the Warren Wilson position was tailor-made for Orr. The mountain campus in Asheville emphasized student work and service programs and was a center for folk culture studies and outdoor experiential learning and environmental studies. As a folk musician, Orr performed in Charlotte in a band called Maggie's Fancy. He had also helped launch UNC Charlotte's Venture program.

Bill McCoy was named interim vice chancellor to replace Orr during the search for a successor.

Even before Orr's departure, Chancellor Jim Woodward had begun restructuring his division, toward a more traditional university advancement mode. At many universities that typical structure included a development office, an alumni office, and an office of public relations. Woodward noted that the division previously had evolved to a structure that included certain units because of Orr's unique set of talents and abilities. After Orr's departure, Woodward completed the process of establishing that more typical Division of Development and University Relations.

R. Edward Kizer Jr., who had been president and chief executive officer of United Carolina Bank of South Carolina, was named to replace Orr in August 1992. Kizer, like Orr, was a Davidson graduate and had begun his career in Charlotte with the bank that was to become NationsBank. He worked his way up the ranks in banks across North Carolina, from his hometown of Asheboro to Wilmington and Whiteville and finally to the South Carolina position. During those years he had been involved in major public issues in the communities in which he lived.

Kizer joined Woodward in filling another gap in UNC Charlotte support. Woodward discovered upon his arrival that the Charlotte region had only one member on the UNC Board of Governors. The two mobilized a campaign that led to the addition of six new members: former governor James G. Martin, C. C. (Cliff) Cameron, and Derick Close of Charlotte; Helen Rhyne Marvin and former state senator Marshall Rauch of Gastonia; and former lieutenant governor H. Patrick Taylor of Wadesboro.

Kizer's acquaintances with business and political leaders in Charlotte and across North Carolina were assets as he assisted Woodward in building political and financial support bases. Moreover, his background was useful in a community where banking was the dominant industry.

Other personnel changes were taking place as well. Robert Carrubba resigned as dean of graduate studies to become vice chancellor for academic affairs at the University of Wisconsin–Oshkosh. Nursing Dean Nancy Langston resigned to become dean of Virginia Commonwealth University School of Nursing, a position where she would be affiliated with a medical school. Although these key resignations represented losses, it was a tribute to UNC Charlotte that those involved were moving to higher positions.

There were also retirements of people who had contributed to the development of UNC Charlotte over a number of years. Thomas Turner left large vacancies in two capacities. He had helped build the Accounting Department into one of the best in the state as measured by the success of its graduates. Even the first class of four graduates produced Gary Baucom, president of Ralph Squires Construction Company, and John McArthur, head of his own accounting firm, both of whom had served as president of the Alumni Association. Hulene Hill, a Raleigh accountant, was one of the most successful early female accounting graduates.

Two more recent graduates—Mary Ann Rouse, vice president for financial services of Carolinas Medical Center, and Gail Chapman, a senior manager with Ernst & Young—also served as presidents of the Alumni Association. During Turner's tenure, accounting graduates were medalists on the state CPA examination (i.e., they finished first, second, or third) nineteen times. That tradition was to continue. In 1995, Jeremy Abig, a graduate who had begun working for NationsBank, placed first in the state on the CPA examination, among 676 candidates taking it for the first time.

The other gap left by Turner was the chair of the Faculty Athletic Committee, which he had held since the university joined NCAA Division I in 1970. Turner helped to found the Sunbelt Conference and served as its first president. David Goldfield, the Robert Lee Bailey Professor of History, replaced Turner as chair of the Faculty Athletic Committee.

Professor Louis Diamant, who had come to Charlotte College in 1963 in a three-piece suit and with close-cropped hair, retired in 1991, with long hair, jogging shorts, and sneakers. Muscles rippled over his well-conditioned body, belying his age. His friends joked that he had discovered the "fountain of youth." Diamant had served earlier as chair of the Department of Psychology before returning to the classroom and an active career as a scholar; in the year before his retirement he published two books and had two others in progress.

Another key figure who retired in 1991 was Allan Palmer, who had come to UNC Charlotte in 1968. He served as the first dean of the Belk College of Business Administration before returning to the classroom, and later he served as chair of the Marketing Department. He had also developed and taught a well-respected course in business ethics.

Others who retired were Douglas Powers, Charles Christie, Mary Harper, and Nelson Nunnally. Powers, a physician and distinguished professor in Education, continued his own learning by earning master's degrees in education, human development and learning, and English, and he went on to write scholarly papers on English literature. He also won awards for his woodblock prints. Christie had taught some of the university's first engineering technology courses after arriving in 1971, following a twenty-year career as an engineer. Harper joined the university in 1971 and served as associate professor of English. Nunnally had come to the university in 1974 and had served as chair of Geography and Earth Sciences.

In 1992, the university lost four veteran faculty members—Victor Pollak, Susan Cernyak-Spatz, Gerda Zimmermann, and Jack Beasley—to retirement, although some continued to teach part-time. Three of them were natives of Austria and Germany. Pollak came to UNC Charlotte in 1968 to head the Physics Department and returned to full-time teaching in 1976. Cernyak-Spatz taught German but may have been as well known as a Holocaust survivor who lectured on her experiences at the Nazi death camp at Auschwitz. Zimmermann came to the United States to study under Martha Graham after a dance career in Germany and then taught dance at UNC Charlotte for eighteen years. For eleven of his twenty years, beginning in 1972, Beasley served as chair of the Theater Department and acted in a number of campus and community productions as well. He continued his theater work in the community following his retirement.

Dean H. William Heller of the College of Education, who helped build credibility for his programs during a time of national challenge to teacher education, resigned after thirteen years to become dean and executive officer of the St. Petersburg campus of the University of South Florida.

Richard Neel, dean of the Belk College of Business Administration for fifteen years, returned to teaching and other academic assignments. One of Neel's most outstanding accomplishments was getting the programs of his college, including the M.B.A. and accounting programs, approved by the nation's top accrediting body for schools of business, the American Assembly of Collegiate Schools of Business. He also saw the college grow in enrollment from 1,783 undergraduates to 2,628 and from 187 M.B.A. students to 443. He saw the addition of a master's degree in economics in 1990, which then enrolled eleven students. He saw his faculty grow from forty-three to ninety-one.

Another administrator who retired in 1992 was Harold S. Clarke, assistant vice chancellor for academic affairs and, earlier, dean of admissions and registration. He had served for twenty-three years.

Of course, retirements, resignations, and rotating department chairs opened the door for new blood in faculty and administrative positions. Sue Bishop, who had been professor of psychiatric/mental health nursing and assistant dean for graduate studies at the University of South Florida, was named dean of the College of Nursing, replacing Barbara Carper, who served as interim dean following the departure of Nancy Langston. Bishop led her college in developing two new graduate specialty concentrations—community health nursing (supported by a $531,000 federal grant) and family nurse practitioner.

Richard Schroeder replaced Thomas Turner as chair of Accounting, and James Weekly replaced Allan Palmer as chair of Marketing. Other new chairs were Paul Foos in Psychology, Ronald Lunsford in English, and Gyorgy Revesz in Computer Science.

The creative arts got an infusion of new blood with the appointments of Doug Bish, an enthusiastic and energetic musician, as head of Music; Sally Kovach, a well-trained art educator, as head of Visual Arts; and hometown girl Sybil Huskey, who had made good elsewhere as a dancer and dance instructor, as chair of Dance and Theater.

Paul C. Friday, with an international reputation in criminal justice research, became chair of the Criminal Justice Department, and Jeffrey Meyer, an authority on Eastern religions, was selected from within to be chair of the Department of Religious Studies.

Activities in the Cameron Applied Research Center got a boost from the appointment of Harry Leamy, a materials scientist with more than fifteen years' experience with AT&T Bell Laboratories, as the center's first director. The center itself was dedicated on September 25, 1991, at a gala celebration attended by Governor James G. Martin, UNC President C. D. Spangler Jr., and BellSouth President John Clendenin.

Vice Chancellor Philip Dubois conducted a major reorganization of the Division of Academic Affairs in the 1991–92 academic year. He placed his administrative and support functions under six associate vice chancellors. One objective, he indicated, was to reduce the number of heads of the many units reporting directly to him.

The new associate vice chancellors and the activities for which they had responsibility were: Barbara Goodnight (who held the title of "senior associate vice chancellor"), Academic Personnel, Planning, and Budget; Terrel Rhodes, Undergraduate Programs; Denise Trauth, Graduate Programs; William J. McCoy, Extended Academic Programs (he also continued as director of the Urban Institute); Ray Frankle, Library and Information Services; and Harold Josephson, International Programs.

Denise Trauth was recruited from Bowling Green State University, where she was assistant dean of the graduate college, to head the graduate program. She replaced K. David Patterson, who served as interim dean after the departure of Robert Carrubba. The other associate vice chancellors were selected from within. Trauth used her skills of communication (her academic specialty), her warm personality, and her knowledge and assertiveness to become perhaps one of the strongest graduate leaders to that date.

Two unquestionably strong new deans were recruited to help build their colleges. Edward M. Mazze, a former dean of Temple University's School of Business and Management who had also taught at Virginia Tech and been in private business, was named dean of the Belk College of Business Administration. John M. (Jack) Nagle was named dean of the College of Education. He had been dean of the School of Education at the College of William and Mary.

Mazze quickly moved to involve the Belk College with the region's business leaders and to create a higher profile with the public. He visited editors and reporters of the area's business publications and invited them to the campus to tour the facilities and to be exposed to the expertise of his faculty. Mazze led his college in establishing new programs—the Center for Banking Studies, the Business Honors Program, and a master of science in economics with a concentration in finance. An MBA Plus program, which offered a certificate for study beyond the M.B.A., was also launched.

As he had at William and Mary, Nagle also quickly encouraged his faculty members to become engaged with the educational community of the region. In an editorial column in the *Charlotte Observer* of September 23, 1995, Tom

Bradbury noted how well the College of Education had carried out a mandate from the UNC Board of Governors to provide service to the public schools. He said that the college faculty had reported 13,918 hours of service to schools during the previous year, including 4,312 hours contributed by faculty of other colleges at the university.

These outreach efforts, combined with many others undertaken under Woodward's leadership, greatly strengthened the university's involvement with the Charlotte community and the surrounding metropolitan region. Using the region as a laboratory for teaching and research, UNC Charlotte was at the same time providing a public service that often was unavailable from any other source. From the College of Architecture to the Urban Institute, UNC Charlotte was working hand-in-glove to lift the region as well as build the institution.

Before Paul Escott's departure to become Reynolds Professor and ultimately dean of the college at Wake Forest University, he and David Goldfield collaborated on editing a book called *The South for New Southerners*. They also traveled around the region giving lectures, based on the book, on how newcomers could understand the South.

Medical geographer Gerald Pyle coauthored a book titled *The Geography of AIDS*, about the spread of the disease around the world, and produced a book called *Atlas of Disease and Health Care in the United States*. Pyle also published books on the spread of influenza throughout the world and on other health subjects. He brought medical geographers from all over the world to Charlotte for a conference in 1992, and he began work on a national conference of geographers to be held in Charlotte in 1996. For all these efforts, he was given the 1992 First Citizens Bank Scholars Medal.

Philosophy professor John Lincourt had his work in the field of medical ethics recognized when he was named the 1992 Professor of the Year in North Carolina by the Council for the Advancement and Support of Education (CASE). Lincourt had helped area hospitals create ways of dealing with ethical issues related to life and death.

An international scientific story took on a UNC Charlotte angle in 1992. When the producers of the public television series *Nova* presented their program on the Iceman, UNC Charlotte professor Janet Levy of the Department of Sociology, Anthropology, and Social Work was prominently featured. An authority on the anthropology of early Europe, she provided insights into the significance of various aspects of an early European man found frozen in a glacier at the Austrian-Italian border. Because the body was found so intact, along with clothing and hunting equipment and items of food, the discovery shed light on life five thousand years ago in Europe.

In 1992, UNC Charlotte also had a world champion. Professor Ken Chen had come close to winning the grand prize for several years before finally coming in number one in the world in the ancient Oriental game of Go. But Chen wasn't just participating in an extracurricular recreational game. A computer scientist, he was competing by playing the game with his computer program, called "Go Intellect." The game of Go is so complex, with so many more different moves and combinations of moves than chess, that to simulate it with a computer requires that the computer scientist approximate the human brain. So Chen's playing was relevant to the creation of "artificial intelligence," a quest of computer scientists around the world.

Meanwhile, UNC Charlotte's geographers were producing a sequel to their successful *Charlotte Atlas*. Their new one was *Charlotte: An Analytical Atlas of Patterns and Trends*, edited by James W. Clay and Alfred W. Stuart. In it they said of Charlotte, "In the context of the Sunbelt explosion, this particular community seems fully caught up in the momentum of an historic pendulum swing to the South. Indeed, a succession of events as well as locational advantages make Charlotte-Mecklenburg something of a prototype for what has emerged as a 'Southern tilt.'"

Another accomplishment by geographers using the latest technology was a planning document for the City of Concord that was created through the use of a computer-based geographic information system.

The university took advantage of new distance-learning technology to teach courses at off-campus sites in Mecklenburg and Lincoln Counties. The university was already linked around the state by way of a microwave relay television system and the North Carolina Information Highway. Faculty doing research with colleagues in the Research Triangle area often communicated with them by way of the teleconference facilities. But the new technology used fiber-optic telephone lines to transmit television signals to off-campus sites and required less sophisticated technology. The basic requirements were fairly simple: television cameras and monitors at each site.

Maria Domoto gave one of the most impressive displays of that capability through a course in Japanese taught to high school students at three locations in Mecklenburg County. Students could see her as she taught; she could see them too, and they could carry on a conversation as the class proceeded. A male student who met a girl from another high school via the classroom network even asked for and got a date. *The New York Times* sent a feature writer to cover the story as part of a piece on North Carolina's use of distance-learning technology.

The William States Lee College of Engineering moved into the high-tech world in a major way by setting up a system of networked workstations for students, faculty, and staff members, known as Project Mosaic. Under the leadership of Professor Robert Coleman, the college received a National Science Foundation grant and participated with eight other major southeastern universities to restructure engineering education in a program called Southeastern University and College Coalition for Engineering Education, or SUCCEED.

In a less technological way, an innovative new program that caught the public's fancy was one to teach music to infants and very young children. Wendy Hicks Valerio was using the techniques to study the way children learn and respond to music, but parents wanting to give their children a head start responded enthusiastically by enrolling their youngsters. The professor demonstrated that even infants could learn the basics of music by being exposed, in the presence of their parents, to musical sounds and rhythms.

Religious Studies professor James Tabor, a scholar on apocalyptic movements, made national and international news because of his role in the case of the Branch Davidians. Members of that religious sect burned to death when their compound in Waco, Texas, was destroyed in a government attempt to get them to surrender after they had killed four federal agents. Through a Texas radio station, Tabor and a colleague were able to communicate with cult leader David Koresh and were hoping to negotiate his exit from the compound. Koresh even sent Tabor audiotapes of a manuscript about the Seven Seals of the Bible to show that he really was working on a revelation of them before coming out of the compound. Tabor was also trying to get Federal Bureau of Investigation agents to understand the religious-fanatic mentality that was driving Koresh. After his attempts failed and the compound went up in flames, Tabor said in frustration that he was afraid the agents naively thought the "Seven Seals" Koresh referred to were animals. Tabor later wrote a book on cults as a result of his studies and his experience with Koresh. Earlier he had gained national and international attention as one of the American religious studies scholars interpreting the Dead Sea Scrolls.

CHAPTER 15

Footings for New Facilities

WHILE FACULTY members were pursuing their teaching, research, and service, Chancellor Jim Woodward was trying to relieve the university's space crunch. Even with some new facilities that were added late in Fretwell's term of office, Woodward read in a publication called "Facilities Inventory and Utilization Study Fall of 1992" that UNC Charlotte was still at the bottom of the UNC system in terms of academic space and library space per student.

Continuing growth of the student body allowed no catching up, particularly during a construction dearth that started with the 1990 recession. In addition to a lack of academic and library space, UNC Charlotte had a severe shortage of space for student activities, intramurals, and athletic activities. Nor was there any large gathering place. The largest space for events, McKnight Hall in Cone Center, seated only 620. The Belk Gymnasium seated 2,500 or so, but it was in constant use for physical education classes, intramurals, and athletics.

Woodward discovered that some planning for a student activity center had already taken place. He seized on that as an opportunity to gain space even at a time when the state legislature wasn't appropriating tax money for new facilities. The proposal he took to the legislature was that a new UNC Charlotte student activity center be built with increased student fees and with contributions.

Even though some other campuses had sought state appropriations to help build student activity centers, Woodward concluded that it would be better to seek alternate funding for such a facility and go to the legislature for classroom and library buildings instead. He announced a strategy for funding construction projects that would build student housing and parking decks with user charges, athletic facilities with private gifts, student activity space

283

with student fees, and research space increasingly from indirect cost recovery and federal grants.

In the meantime, Jeff Mullins had urged that an on-campus arena be built. He felt that the campus was lacking something in not having its own athletic facility. Students didn't turn out well for basketball games when they had to drive across the city to the new Charlotte Coliseum or even to the closer Independence Arena. Even good crowds of 7,000 to 8,000 rattled around in the 23,000-seat Charlotte Coliseum, and it was difficult to make the place seem like a home court. Mullins fondly recalled the home court atmosphere of Duke's Cameron Indoor Stadium, where he played basketball during his college days. Because members of the Athletic Department would share the facility with student activities, Woodward challenged them to raise a substantial portion of the new facility's cost.

The idea for a student activity center originated at a Division of Student Affairs retreat during 1988–89. Tom Goins was then president of the student body and strongly supported the concept.

Normally, when the General Administration of the UNC system supported proposals to build facilities with nontax revenues, there was little opposition in the legislature. But timing proved troublesome for the UNC Charlotte proposal. It went to the 1993 legislature at a time when student fees had become a hot issue. A former student body president at UNC Chapel Hill, Mark Bibbs, and a member of the Board of Governors, Charles Flack, had mounted strong opposition to any fee increases. Woodward was particularly offended by Bibbs's purporting to speak for UNC Charlotte students, whom he said opposed the new center. Woodward countered that students themselves had proposed the center three years before he arrived. In fact, on January 17, 1989, Doug Orr was quoted in a front-page story in the Charlotte Observer as saying that an arena would likely be part of a planned student activity center.

A proposed student activity center at Appalachian State University had run into trouble because of environmental concerns related to its location. There was also some controversy over a proposed arena at N.C. State University, which would have been built with a combination of state funding, Raleigh city funding, and contributions. Opponents of the N.C. State arena pointed out that UNC Chapel Hill's Dean Smith Center was paid for with contributions only. There were attempts to tar UNC Charlotte's student activity center with all those brushes.

Opponents miscalculated, however, when they implied that the UNC Charlotte center was being built despite student opposition. Woodward was able to demonstrate strong student support for the center, going back several years, to the idea's origin in 1988–89. Derrick Griffith, student president from 1991 to 1993, was able to demonstrate strong current student support for the center. He told legislators that the project had been initiated by students and that students had been involved in all phases of design and development. Later, Griffith's leadership skills were recognized statewide when he was selected president of the UNC Association of Student Governments.

The struggle for approval of the center was a test for UNC Charlotte's newly found base of political support in the Southern Piedmont region, similar to the challenge the group faced in gaining support for Ph.D. programs. As with the Ph.D. issue, strong leadership among regional legislators emerged in the persons of Senator Aaron Plyler of Monroe and Representative Jim Black of Matthews.

Alumni lobbied their legislators. Marshall Rauch of Gastonia earlier had helped steer the project through the Board of Governors. The new clout of the Southern Piedmont Legislative Caucus was becoming evident. By pulling together, the members won approval for the center.

Groundbreaking was largely a student celebration in the fall of 1993. Richard Hudson, then president of the student body, climbed aboard a backhoe to break ground. In addition to remarks from Hudson, there were comments by student body presidents who had supported the center, beginning with Goins and followed by Michael Wilson from 1989–90, Beth Hamman from 1990–91, and Griffith. Also participating were President Spangler and trustee chair Russell Robinson. Chancellor Woodward thanked Spangler for the support he and the General Administration provided during the quest for funding.

The student activity center was designed to be a multipurpose facility with a food court, weight rooms, training rooms, and meeting rooms. The arena would provide 9,600 seats for basketball and volleyball. It would also serve as the campus auditorium for concerts and large lectures and for commencement, to be held on campus for the first time since the 1960s.

The legislative victory didn't mean that UNC Charlotte was home free in building the arena. There was substantial money to be raised to supplement student fees enough to pay for the $26-million structure.

A longtime friend of the university came through with the first major gift: Dale F. Halton and the Pepsi Cola Foundation committed $1.25 million. Her connection to UNC Charlotte went back to its Charlotte College days, when her grandfather, Henry Fowler, was one of the earliest donors. As a result, the auditorium–playing floor portion of the building was named the Dale F. Halton Arena.

Attention then turned to obtaining the next major gift. That turned out to be the largest in the university's history, valued at around $5 million. It came from the Robert and Mariam Cannon Hayes family of Concord, with additional support from the Cannon Foundation. As a result of their commitment, the UNC Charlotte Trustees named the largest campus facility, at

Construction continues apace in anticipation of the 1996 opening of the Barnhardt Student Activity Center, shown here with playing fields in the background. Photo by Wade Bruton.

200,000 square feet, the James H. Barnhardt Student Activity Center. James H. Barnhardt was the brother-in-law of Robert Hayes. Until his death in 1993, Barnhardt was a Charlotte business and civic leader who developed Barnhardt Manufacturing Company and was a strong supporter of UNC Charlotte and its foundation.

The athletics and intramural programs got another boost in 1994 with the construction of the Wachovia Fieldhouse. Built to provide offices, dressing rooms, restrooms, and concession areas for outdoor athletic activities, the building was provided by way of a major gift from Wachovia Bank and other gifts from a number of donors. Design for the fieldhouse was provided by alumnus Tim Demmitt, a 1980 architecture graduate who had started his own firm in Charlotte. Along with alumnus Dennis Hall, Demmitt also designed an Alumni Room in the Cone Center. Demmitt served as Alumni Association president in 1993–94.

Key leaders of the fund-raising efforts were Judy Rose, Bob Young, and Jeff Mullins, all of athletics. Success in securing funding for the Barnhardt Student Activity Center didn't mean the UNC Charlotte community could relax about the issue of space. Since 1989, when funds for buildings had last been appropriated by the General Assembly, UNC Charlotte had added three thousand students—a good-sized small college. A somewhat similar story was being told systemwide. Enrollment across the UNC system had grown by 16,400 without an additional building being provided. A state tax cut a few years earlier and a recession following 1990 meant that no relief was in sight through appropriated funds. North Carolina had conducted no bond campaign for campus construction since 1976.

Thus, in 1993, the state had one of the lowest levels of bonded debt in the nation and an AAA bond rating. Interest rates were at the lowest point in more than two decades, and construction costs were relatively stable. Harlan Boyles, the somewhat conservative state treasurer, announced that bonds from a statewide campaign could be paid off within anticipated revenues without affecting the tax rate.

So conditions appeared right for a statewide campaign to build campus facilities. The legislature approved $310 million in bond issues for the ballot scheduled for November 2, 1993. For UNC Charlotte the bond issue would provide $22.6 million to construct a 160,000-square-foot classroom for the College of Arts and Sciences and to add a third floor to the Friday Building for the Belk College of Business Administration.

All that remained was for the campuses to organize a full-fledged political campaign and generate a turnout of supporters. That presented a daunting challenge. The campus community at UNC Charlotte had to quickly learn how to conduct a political campaign, working with the other fifteen campuses. Advocates soon learned that the task would not be easy. A no-tax mentality was running strong across the state. In that atmosphere, it was hard to convince voters that a bond issue was the way to go. Thomas I. Storrs, former trustee chair at UNC Charlotte, was named chair for the state campaign and put together a professional team of consultants to assist volunteer campaigners.

Since the previous statewide bond campaign for higher education in 1976, understanding of and support for the role of universities had eroded. Competition for scarce state dollars had brought other needs to the forefront, such as public schools, community colleges, and prisons. When the Research Triangle Park was being launched in the 1950s and 1960s, North Carolinians could see more clearly how universities were helping contribute to the economic boom across the state. With continued success, citizens began taking the universities and their relationship to the economy for granted.

Against that backdrop, UNC Charlotte geared up for the campaign. Betty Chafin Rash, a former member of the Student Affairs staff, was retained as a coordinator and adviser on campaign strategies. She was backed up by alumnus and First Union Bank executive Henry Doss, a veteran strategist in a number of campaigns, who volunteered his services. A steering committee included those two, Ed Kizer, Bill McCoy, Schley Lyons, Ted Arrington, Garry Ballard, and me. From time to time we were joined by others.

Speaking engagements were scheduled at civic clubs in Mecklenburg and throughout the region. Woodward and trustee chair Russell Robinson took all the speeches they could schedule, and other administrators and former governor Jim Martin took what Woodward and Robinson couldn't cover.

UNC Charlotte alumni came through with the maturity of those from more established campuses. They organized and staffed telephone banks, calling fellow alumni in Mecklenburg and the region and sending out mailings. On Election Day, they worked the polls.

Endorsements were sought from news media in the region, with good success. Students and faculty members conducted voter registration campaigns and get-out-the-vote activities. Professor Mike Corwin, a voter registrar, staffed voter registration tables for a number of days.

The staff organization and the campus chapter of the State Employees Association of North Carolina, led by Jim Hoppa and Betty Pennell, respectively, handed out literature and lapel stickers at the Mallard Creek Barbecue. The current faculty president, Mike Pearson, joined former presidents in writing a letter of support.

A sign posted in the Prospector Cafeteria gave the campaign an unexpected boost. It said, "Help! Please do not study at the tables in the Prospector between the hours of 11 A.M. and 2 P.M. We desperately need the space for those who wish to eat lunch. We sincerely appreciate your cooperation." That sign told the story. Space was so cramped on campus that students were using the cafeteria for study space, to the point that diners found it difficult to get a table.

Still, the going was tough in the campaign. With other issues on the ballot in Mecklenburg County—local school bonds and a statewide community college bond issue—the total to be considered locally in the polls was $1 billion.

The bonds were carried statewide—narrowly. It turned out that the issue passed in counties with a university campus and failed in most other counties. There was a bit of finger-pointing: critics said the UNC system had lost touch with the voters.

The counties around Mecklenburg voted against the bonds. Again critics said that UNC Charlotte hadn't done a good job in getting them to understand their stake in the regional campus. On the other hand, most of those counties even voted against their own public school bonds.

Whatever the results, most insiders considered the victory a major cause for celebration, given the antitax and antigovernment mood of the times. But it was also a wake-up call. It was clear that the UNC campuses, including UNC Charlotte, would have to work harder outside the counties in which they were located.

One thing appeared certain about any future statewide bond issue for university facilities. UNC Charlotte was not likely to be shortchanged in such packages, as it sometimes had been in legislative appropriations for buildings. It was clear that the large number of votes in Mecklenburg County and the surrounding region would be necessary to carry a statewide issue.

As short of space as UNC Charlotte had been, success in passing the bond campaign was cause for celebration at an April 20, 1994, groundbreaking ceremony for the new classroom building that the 1993 bond issue had made possible.

Faculty president Mike Pearson donned a hard hat and safety glasses and used a jackhammer to break ground at the site just east of the Friday and Denny Buildings. For a reception following the groundbreaking, Media Services prepared a humorous video in which Pearson was shown, through special effects, using the jackhammer to wreck the bell tower, a nearby Kmart, and Dean Ed Mazze's reserved parking space.

In 1995, UNC Charlotte trustees named the new classroom building for E. K. Fretwell Jr. and his wife Dorrie in recognition of ten years of leadership and commitment to the arts and sciences.

Trustee Chairman Russell Robinson joked that he didn't know how the university would find a way to break ground for the third-floor addition to the Friday Building. Construction was simply begun on top of it. By fall 1995, the Friday Building addition was completed and in use by the Belk College of Business Administration, giving faculty and students of that college much-

Faculty President Michael Pearson breaks ground in 1994 for the Fretwell Building. Photo by Wade Bruton.

needed space for classrooms, seminar rooms, computer laboratories, and faculty and administrative offices.

One bonus of the addition was that it provided an opportunity to add some architectural detail to a building that had been a square box in design. The expanded building presented a new facade, facing into the campus, with tall columns, giving it a much more impressive appearance. The new design was actually suggested by Woodward, who had criticized the spartan design of many of the campus buildings. He was right, of course, but at the time of the original construction, the business faculty had said, "We just want as much functional space as we can get for the dollars and as fast as we can get it." Also, campus administrators had been worn down over the years by lean budgets and by state property control officers, who exercised inordinate control over matters of architectural design.

Another reason the expansion created opportunity for a redesign was that stronger requirements for earthquake protection meant that the building had to be strengthened, and thus additions were required on all four sides. As Woodward had predicted, the new facade of the Friday Building provided a

The addition of a third floor gave the Friday Building of the Belk College of Business Administration a new look in 1995. Photo by Wade Bruton.

better image for the college housed within it—a college that was vital to UNC Charlotte's future in a community driven by business. Associate Dean of Business Richard Conboy (who also serves as the unflappable director of commencements) oversaw construction and negotiated the allocation of space.

Another project, although relatively small compared to the Fretwell Building, was critically important in boosting faculty morale and increasing interchanges among faculty and staff. That was an addition to the Prospector Cafeteria designed to serve as a faculty-staff dining room. It resulted from changes that essentially drove faculty and staff from an older cafeteria in Cone Center. That cafeteria, which was the first one on campus and had served the faculty, staff, and commuting students since 1963, was redesigned in 1989–90 to appeal primarily to students, with an area set aside for their background music and after-hours entertainment.

To replace it and provide service for a larger number of students, faculty, and staff, the Prospector Cafeteria was added to the bookstore building in 1990. No area was set aside for faculty and staff. When the new cafeteria opened, faculty and staff found they were seated among students. Noise prevented conversations from carrying across a table. Professors said it wasn't that they didn't like students; if they didn't, they wouldn't be teaching. But they needed some time apart to spend in conversation with colleagues. As a result, faculty and staff abandoned the cafeteria and found other places to eat.

The faculty president at the time was Paula Goolkasian, a psychology professor and researcher. Her research on how people perceive time differently as a result of using analog versus digital watch faces had been reported in the *New York Times*. Goolkasian took the cafeteria problem to Hap Arnold and Olen Smith, vice chancellors for business affairs during the Woodward administration. Arnold and Smith responded on a temporary basis by having partitions installed to create dedicated space for faculty and staff. During a holiday, they had an acoustical tile ceiling dropped below the original hard concrete ceiling, which had caused the sound to bounce around. That solved the acoustics problem, and faculty and staff returned to the Prospector.

Arnold and Smith also promised more. They said they would seek an addition to the room that would be dedicated to faculty and staff and provide some upscale amenities, like wooden beams and moldings and picture windows. The room would even have a small private dining area. That addition was approved and was paid for out of dining receipts. The resulting room, opened in 1994, was an attractive space and a lunchtime refuge for faculty and staff. It was so welcome that some joked that it ought to be named Paula's Place to recognize Goolkasian's role in making it possible.

In 1995, the space outside the new cafeteria addition and between the McEniry Building and the redesigned Friday Building was landscaped to create an attractive courtyard where tables were placed to encourage outdoor dining in good weather.

Still another project was a boost to the campus aesthetically. Professors Eric Anderson and Michael Gallis submitted a proposal to create a sculpture garden in the space between Storrs Architecture Building and Rowe Arts Building. Woodward approved their idea, and an agreement was reached with the Mint Museum of Art to bring to the campus large pieces of sculpture owned by the Mint. Among them was Sun Target II, a piece that had already been displayed on the campus. The first three pieces were large and were of a geometric-looking, minimalist style. The plan called for adding sculptures of other styles. *Southern Living* magazine noted that the sculpture garden, along with the existing botanical gardens, had the potential to become an attractive amenity for campus visitors.

CHAPTER 16

Out of Controversy, an Uptown Center

WHILE SEEKING solutions to on-campus space problems, Chancellor Jim Woodward also sought off-campus revenue opportunities. This drew him into perhaps the most controversial issue of his tenure, but it ultimately led to a solution to UNC Charlotte's long search for an uptown center.

To understand what happened, one needs to realize that some things about University City had changed since the initial planning. It had been anticipated, for example, that in addition to the shops, the hotel, residential complexes, and other components of University Place, there would be a regional shopping mall, developed by the Hahn Corporation, which had created exciting malls in southern California.

Unfortunately, the Belk organization declined to participate in a regional mall at that location. Earlier it had seemed there was universal agreement in the Charlotte area—by planners, city-county officials, and university leaders—that such a mall would be developed. But without Belk as an anchor, the Hahn Corporation found that it couldn't get the other anchors and tenants needed for such a mall. Essentially, the one decision killed the mall.

University City magazine took the Belk organization to task for its decision. John Belk, in another of his enigmatic quotes to the media, said that his company went where the people were, and that there were no people out there. The fact was that where Belk indicated it wanted to participate in a mall, at the intersection of I-77 and Harris Boulevard, there were then few residents, while the population of University City was more than 50,000. Belk may well have chosen the I-77 site in anticipation of capturing the Lake Norman market as well as University City shoppers. But no matter what the logic, the regional mall was dead at University Place without Belk participation.

Hahn then determined it would build a power center—an upscale one—at the University Place site. Actually, there was a growing trend away from large regional malls anchored by department stores, anyway, and toward power centers, which include large home-improvement or discount retailers as anchors and fewer small retailers than in a mall setting. Even so, other developers continued to see a market for a regional mall in the area, and in 1995, a large mall was announced for an area just north of University City in the Charlotte-Concord corridor, near the Charlotte Motor Speedway. Ultimately there also was so much interest in power centers in the area that city-county planners ended up with four proposals on their desks.

Meanwhile, leaders of the UNC Charlotte Foundation, which had initiated the development of University Place, were wondering how to develop seventeen acres the foundation owned on the northwest side of NC 49 near its intersection with Harris Boulevard. They believed that another revenue stream for the foundation—and thus for the university—could be generated similar to that created by the development of University Place.

Because the Crosland companies had developed much of the retail and residential space in the area, its executives' advice was sought on how best to develop the foundation site. Foundation leaders originally considered construction of apartments, but high-power electric lines overhead seemed to rule out such land use. Crosland's management then proposed that the foundation's land be merged with an additional sixty-three acres the firm would acquire and that a power center be developed.

This meant that two new power centers were proposed for University City. Earlier, another power center had been approved but not developed on property near the intersection of highways US 29 and NC 49. A fourth proposal was submitted that called for a center adjacent to University Place on property then in use for a nine-hole golf course.

This sudden surge of interest in retailing in an area of the county that had been underserved overwhelmed the campus community as well as the University City community. Whereas there had been almost no opposition to previous developments in University City, suddenly there was vocal opposition on campus as well as off. Before Woodward appeared before faculty council to defend the project, some faculty members planned to submit a resolution criticizing the university's role in the Crosland–UNC Charlotte Foundation venture. That was understandable. Faculty members had bought into the earlier administrative position that supported the Northeast District Plan and the designation of University Place as the major retailing center of University City. There also was a fear that too much retailing would eventually result in vacant, deteriorating storefronts.

Woodward later admitted that he should have gone to the campus community earlier in the process to explain what was being proposed. The planning change was being sought through the foundation, but faculty members who had been deeply involved in developing University City believed that they should have been continually informed about the new proposals. Also, faculty members made little distinction between campus and foundation because they were so intertwined. Professor Dick Toenjes of Philosophy sent a memorandum to the faculty council suggesting that it should refuse any funds generated by the proposed power center unless it were shown that there was no ethical conflict. Woodward then wrote a detailed report on the entire matter and presented it to the faculty council.

Substantial neighborhood opposition had also developed against the power center proposal. Those groups also had bought into the earlier University City concepts promulgated by the university. And in rare opposition to the thrust of university development, the *Charlotte Observer* editorially criticized the power center plan.

Many opponents of the proposed Crosland–UNC Charlotte Foundation rezoning were probably comparing that use of the property to no development at all. But in fact, university initiatives were catalysts for all the activity in University City, anyway. Still, opponents envisioned a tree-covered hillside out into the future even though University City was by then exploding in growth, both commercial and residential. It was probably inevitable that the large hillside tract would be developed for something at some point unless it were purchased and developed into a park. Because they envisioned that a natural area would otherwise be maintained, opponents were reluctant to accept Woodward's prediction that a well-planned center would improve the appearance of a major gateway to the campus.

One of the arguments against the power center was that it violated the terms of the Northeast District Plan. Woodward countered that the plan had been changed dramatically anyway, since a major component of it was the regional shopping mall.

Woodward was also concerned by another initiative by the Planning Commission staff that would have made a portion of the university campus useless. Without advance notice, the Planning Commission staff had proposed downzoning to single-family a portion of campus land east of Mallard Creek Church Road. What university anywhere would allow municipal planners to tamper with its ability to develop its own campus for educational purposes? The Charlotte City Council backed off approving the change when the North Carolina attorney general sent word that the state would sue if the recommended downzoning went forward.

The chancellor urged that after the zoning issue for the power center was settled, the Northeast District Plan be revisited. He said that the existing plans did not take into account the university's needs and how the campus interfaced with the surrounding community. He pledged that when a new campus master plan was done, it would take into account the university's relationships with its surrounding community.

Intense lobbying was brought to bear by both sides on the issue of rezoning the Crosland–UNC Charlotte Foundation property. This particularly impacted those city council members who were considered swing votes. Woodward held that nothing extraordinary or unethical was done, but charges were made anyway. Some amendments were made to original plans for the power center, and in the end it was approved.

A major positive result was that the revenue stream from the center helped to make possible one of the university's long-held goals—to create an uptown center. After years of seeking an appropriate and affordable site in the midtown area, the university suddenly had two.

The first would have made an uptown center part of the redevelopment of the old Ivey's department store building at Fifth and Tryon Streets. UNC Charlotte alumnus Jim Gross, a leader in redeveloping stores and factories for close-in residential use, proposed that he include space for the uptown campus in his plans. That appeared to be a viable option, because earlier a UNC Charlotte center had been included as part of the Charlotte-Mecklenburg Schools plan to create an arts magnet school in the building. Opposition to that part of a bond issue had been led by Citizens for Effective Government, headed by UNC Charlotte business professor Frank Barnes, and it was defeated.

Then former trustee Graeme Keith and his son, Greg, proposed to the Charlotte City Council that they be allowed to take over the troubled CityFair development and include an uptown center for the university as an integral part of the revival. When the two plans were compared, the CityFair proposal won out. Its strengths were that it provided adequate parking in an attached deck and proximity to the Charlotte-Mecklenburg Public Library and to such cultural amenities as the Performing Arts Center, Discovery Place, and Spirit Square.

The UNC Charlotte Foundation provided funds for converting the space to classroom and seminar use. The UNC Board of Governors approved the CityFair site as an off-campus center. The importance of that approval was that students taking classes there would pay the same cost for a class as those taking classes on campus. At last UNC Charlotte got its uptown campus, and under the direction of Professor William Seigfried, it opened to good response in January 1995, providing classroom, seminar, and workshop space, with upscale decor, carpeted floors, and padded chairs—comparable to what uptown workers were used to in corporate offices. More than 450 people enrolled in the first semester, and the number grew to more than 500 one year later.

The university played a role in the location of two other facilities in University City, one welcome and the other not so welcome. The welcome one was the Blockbuster Amphitheater, although it didn't totally live up to expectations in terms of cultural presentations. Broadway producer Zev Bufman looked at the site near UNC Charlotte early in his explorations but decided instead to locate the amphitheater on a site overlooking Lake Norman. Adjoining property owners there objected, so the university site became the live option.

Because the university had cooperated with the location of the facility, the company made several commitments—that it would employ UNC Charlotte students to help with productions as well as concessions and parking, that it would allow students in the arts to meet performers in master-class settings, and that each year it would produce a benefit concert or make a contribution to the university.

In the meantime, Bufman received additional financial backing from the Blockbuster company, known best for its video rental stores. After opening, the amphitheater presented many major entertainers and allowed faculty and students access to some, including Liza Minelli and Harry Connick Jr. It also employed students. Most significantly, it provided, either through benefit concerts or direct grants, more than $100,000 to assist the performing and visual arts on campus. When the market was assessed more fully and the Blumenthal Performing Arts Center opened, the company decided not to produce the Broadway plays and classical concerts it first announced for the amphitheater; instead it presented rock, country, and pop music concerts. But even those provided students with nearby entertainment options.

The University City facility that was not so welcome was a waste-to-energy incinerator. Because the city and county governments had helped so much with many aspects of University City development, university administrators did not oppose the construction of the incinerator adjacent to the campus. But the administrators' understanding was that it would be a pilot project, and there was surprise when it turned out to be a full-fledged incinerator. The university entered into an agreement to purchase steam from the facility when needed and when the cost was competitive.

The intense heat with which the garbage was burned was supposed to prevent noxious substances from being emitted from the smokestack. That may have been the case. But what killed the incinerator in 1995 was that new air pollution standards would have required the installation of expensive scrubbers in the incinerator smokestacks, and excessive amounts of lead were being found in the ash trucked to landfills. The incinerator was shut down, but it could reopen if the plant were sold to a private operator.

Although other new amenities were added to the area at great speed, most were welcome. Particularly welcome was a University City branch of the Public Library of Charlotte and Mecklenburg County, adjacent to the campus.

The downsizing of IBM opened the way for some facilities. The corporation sold excess land in University Research Park, keeping only what it needed for its operations. Ground was broken in 1995 for a new branch of the YMCA on the former IBM property at Harris Boulevard and Mallard Creek Road, about four miles west of the university.

In addition, a site for a huge new public school complex based on an "education village" concept was set aside on former IBM property in University Research Park. The school complex would provide for kindergarten through twelfth grade and have a close working relationship with IBM and other organizations in the research park and with UNC Charlotte.

With the continuing leadership of the university and business leaders who comprised the University City Area Council, the dream of a real University City was being realized.

CHAPTER 17

A Breakthrough on the Library

MEANTIME, a campus facilities challenge was becoming more pressing—obtaining adequate library space. The 1992 report of the University of North Carolina Commission on Higher Education Facilities revealed that UNC Charlotte was still last in the UNC system in terms of both classroom space per student and library space per student.

When visitors saw the ten-story library tower, it was sometimes difficult to convince them of the problem. The height made them think there was plenty of space. It was easier to convince them once they went inside the building and could see students sitting in every available space and sometimes standing. The fact that the campus had a large commuting population made the problem more serious. Those students often needed study space between, before, and after classes. National standards suggested providing 2,500 library seats for an enrollment the size of UNC Charlotte's, but the university seated only 700. Those standards did not take into account the fact that the Atkins Library also served as a major regional resource and drew about one-fourth of its users from businesses, colleges, and other organizations.

After the problem of space for students was considered, there was the problem of simply having adequate space for books. Associate Vice Chancellor Ray Frankle estimated that capacity for adding books in the Dalton Tower would be reached by 1996.

Such data should have been sufficient to convince lawmakers of the worth of UNC Charlotte's case for a library addition. In the 1994 session, it did help convince them to appropriate money to plan the expansion.

Funds for planning gave UNC Charlotte hope that it would get an appropriation to construct the addition sometime. But the legislature didn't always respond on a merit basis when it came to giving priority to funding for physical facilities. That meant Chancellor Woodward and Ed Kizer had to go back to square one when the 1995 session began. Woodward understood that without political support, UNC Charlotte's library might have had to yield to another institution's nonacademic facilities in terms of priority.

The 1995 General Assembly was another test of UNC Charlotte's newfound base of political support in the Southern Piedmont Legislative Caucus and a gauge of Woodward's ability to mobilize it when he had a reasonable cause. When the session began, prospects looked uncertain. For the first time in the twentieth century, a Republican majority had been elected in the North Carolina House, and the Democrats held only a slight majority in the Senate. The mood was more toward cutting taxes than responding to funding needs. But as the session wore on, legislators turned more toward providing for constituent needs.

UNC Charlotte had friends in both parties. Democrats Aaron Plyler of Monroe in the Senate and James Black of Matthews in the House made the university's case. They drew solid support from Mecklenburg Democrats Leslie Winner and Fountain Odom in the Senate and Mecklenburg Republican Ed McMahan in the House. Still, funding for the project was iffy until the eleventh hour. At the end it was the firm commitment of House Speaker Harold Brubaker, a Randolph Republican, that probably made the difference. The Atkins Library expansion was assured.

The 110,000-square-foot addition would expand the library from 180,000 square feet to almost 300,000 square feet. With the additional space and renovations, the library could be expanded to 1.3 million or perhaps 1.5 million books, the number needed by a major university.

The awarding of the 1996 Olympic Games to Atlanta deserves some credit for helping provide the campus with a major new outdoor athletic facility. The games offered Charlotte and other southern cities an opportunity to bid for pre-Olympics training sites for foreign teams. Judy Rose and other UNC Charlotte officials worked closely with Mayor Richard Vinroot and other city officials and with Carroll Gray and the Charlotte Chamber of Commerce in proposing ways for the city to participate.

Very early, the goal became to secure the German National Teams because of the quality of their programs and because of the large contingent of German residents and German firms in the Charlotte region. It soon became clear that the city had an abundance of indoor arenas, swimming pools, and other facilities but would be short on appropriate track-and-field facilities. Then the solution appeared: why not build a new complex at UNC Charlotte, since the campus needed facilities anyway? The existing track was not up to standards even for high school and collegiate competition.

Bill Simms, a former track star at Southern California and president of Transamerica Reinsurance Company, which had recently relocated to Charlotte, stepped forward to lead a campaign to raise the needed funds. Irwin Belk, president and chairman of Belk Groups of Stores, and his wife, Carol,

A Breakthrough on the Library | 301

Irwin Belk, lead donor for the track and field facility, celebrates its progress in 1996 with Athletic Director Judy Rose and Athletic Foundation Director Bob Young (left). Photo by Wade Bruton.

made the lead gift of $1 million toward a total of more than $4 million. As a result, the complex carried their names. Other major gifts were made by Transamerica and NationsBank. In addition, Hugh McColl, NationsBank chairman, said his bank would underwrite the cost while the rest of the funds were being raised. He did so that construction could begin in time for the facility to be completed before the arrival of the German team, which agreed to come on the strength of plans for the facility. Alumnus Tim Demmitt's firm of Overcash-Demmitt was selected as architect.

The center provided seating for 4,000 spectators, with the ability to expand temporarily to 20,000. Facilities would accommodate soccer and track-and-field events, such as high jump, long jump, triple jump, water jump, javelin, hammer/discus, shot put, and pole vault. A fieldhouse provided a press box, hospitality skybox, restrooms and concession stands, coaches' offices, and team lockers.

The addition of the Irwin Belk Track-and-Field Center, the Wachovia Fieldhouse, and the James H. Barnhardt Student Activity Center, with its Dale F. Halton Arena, gave UNC Charlotte premier athletic and intramural facilities for almost every sport—except football. As late as 1996, there was still no initiative to launch a football program. The start-up and operating costs and the negative impact on efforts to achieve gender equity in other sports continued to rule football out.

CHAPTER 18

Approaching a Golden Year

During an intense period of activity in acquiring needed facilities, faculty, staff, and students were maintaining their commitment to excellence in the academic arena. That intensity was increased during the year 1996, as UNC Charlotte, looking back to the opening of the Charlotte Center of the University of North Carolina in 1946, began celebrating its fiftieth anniversary as an institution. It would prove to be a golden year.

Symbolic of that commitment was the addition of the title "provost" to that of vice chancellor for academic affairs for Philip L. Dubois. Chancellor Jim Woodward said the title change reflected the true responsibilities of the position. He also noted that other universities were moving in the direction of naming provosts. Most of all, he said, the change reflected Dubois's excellent performance and acknowledged his status as the most senior official on campus next to the chancellor.

Since the days of Bonnie Cone and Charlotte College, the university had established a reputation for excellence in teaching. Under Woodward and Dubois, teaching got even further emphasis. They created the Bonnie E. Cone Distinguished Professorships of Teaching to complement the establishment of twenty other distinguished professorships endowed during the Silver Anniversary Campaign.

The first professorship went to Miriam Leiva of Mathematics, a native of Cuba who came to the United States with her family and attended Guilford College, UNC Chapel Hill, and Union Graduate School. Leiva's expertise was in teaching teachers how better to teach mathematics to schoolchildren, for which she had developed a national reputation. Upon reading of the selection, *Charlotte Observer* columnist Jack Betts said to himself that the story sounded familiar. Indeed, Leiva had been his high school mathematics teacher in Guilford County and even then had the ability to make

Miriam Leiva was named the first Bonnie E. Cone Distinguished Professor of Teaching in 1993. UNC Charlotte Photo.

mathematics understandable. Betts then wrote a tribute entitled "Good morning, Miss Almaguer"—Leiva's maiden name.

The university planned to name five Bonnie Cone Professors. John Lincourt of Philosophy was the second one chosen, Ganesh Mohanty of Engineering the third, and Al Maisto of Psychology the fourth. Dubois also presented to an entire department the university's first Provost Award for Excellence in Teaching. The award went to the Department of Psychology, chaired by Paul Foos. It recognized innovative efforts in teaching, advising, and student-assisted research. It also recognized the fact that Psychology Department graduates consistently finished first in the state on the licensing examination for professional psychologists.

Two more professors received the prestigious Presidential Young Investigator Award of the National Science Foundation—Robert Wilhelm in Mechanical Engineering and Dian Zhou of Electrical Engineering. The two were among only 150 winners nationwide. Earlier UNC Charlotte recipients of the Presidential Young Investigator Award were Lisa-Noelle Hjellming, David Trumper, and Banita White Brown.

Igor Runge of Civil Engineering received the National Academy of Sciences Young Investigator Award, Ganesh Mohanty of Mechanical Engineering the North Carolina Science Star Award, and Stephen Bobbio of Electrical

Engineering the Computer Packaging and Manufacturing Society Best Paper Award.

Judy Aulette of Sociology and John W. (Jack) Sommer, the Knight Distinguished Professor of Public Policy, received Fulbright awards for work abroad.

In high technology, Professor Michael Feldman of Engineering, who was working with researchers at MCNC and other firms in the Research Triangle Park, achieved a breakthrough in transmitting data among several computer chips by using lasers and holograms for connections. The breakthrough was expected to lead to a small and faster link between optical fibers and electronic devices.

Professors continued their scholarly productivity in publishing books. Faculty authors included Carole Haber, chair of History, and Dena Shenk, coordinator of the Gerontology program, both of whom wrote books on aging; Gail Sorenson of Education Administration, who wrote about children with disabilities; Lucinda Grey of English, who published a collection of poems; and Mark West of English, who published a book on the writings of Helen Hunt Jackson.

The story of two veteran professors' scholarship is a heartwarming testimony to the UNC Charlotte work ethic and commitment to continuing learning and scholarly work. Saul Brenner of Political Science won the 1994 First Citizens Bank Scholars Medal for his research on the use of mathematics in understanding why Supreme Court justices made the decisions they did. Although he had received his law degree from Columbia University and his Ph.D. from New York University, Brenner credited his UNC Charlotte colleagues with creating the "graduate school" that allowed him to do his research. He said that research methodology was not a prime consideration during his own graduate school days. Brenner turned to Professors Harold Reiter and William J. Thomas of Mathematics to learn about the mathematical field of "game theory" and to Ted Arrington of Political Science for information on current research techniques in his field. Having arrived at UNC Charlotte in 1965, Brenner was a veteran teacher by the time he hit his stride in research in his specialty. But he became ranked nationally as one of the top scholars in his field.

Edward Menhinick of Biology also arrived at UNC Charlotte in 1965. Just two years later, in 1967, he began a research project on freshwater fish. But not until 1991 was he able to publish his book, *The Freshwater Fishes of North Carolina*. He used the intervening years to search the freshwater streams of the state for the presence of various species. Among his discoveries were that some species had disappeared because of pollution and other impacts of development and change and that some thought to be extinct still existed.

Menhinick also used the many years to search for a publisher and finally found one in the North Carolina Wildlife Resources Commission. Still, he invested his own funds in the project, and his wife and children waded streams with him to help locate fish across the state. He and Brenner are but illustrations of what many professors at UNC Charlotte were willing to do in pursuit of their academic careers.

Another professor recognized for years of almost single-minded devotion to a cause was Samuel D. (Sam) Watson Jr. of the English Department and director of University Writing Programs. Watson was honored with the NationsBank Award for Excellence in Teaching in 1994. In 1973 he and Leon Gatlin of English had brought to the campus the Bay Area Writing Project concept, and they expanded the project's original goal—to teach students to write by having them write—to that of teaching students to *learn* by having them write. Governor Jim Hunt, seeking to build a reputation as an education governor, heard about the project and dropped in by helicopter on July 28, 1982. He sat in on a class being taught to schoolteachers to help them take the concepts back to their classrooms. Afterward he told an aide, "You told me it was good, but not this good."

A further extension of the concepts was a writing retreat at Wildacres near Little Switzerland, provided through the generosity of the Blumenthal family, beginning May 9–12, 1983. At those sessions, the writing concepts were presented to UNC Charlotte faculty colleagues to help them in their classroom teaching. The retreats were held in the spring, immediately after the conclusion of the semester, and had a rejuvenating effect on tired professors. Between sessions, faculty could sit and rock on a patio, looking toward Mount Mitchell, the highest peak in the eastern United States, or they could hike trails up to the Blue Ridge Parkway. It was an idyllic and inspirational setting for improving writing skills. The story of how I. D. Blumenthal, a Jewish businessman, was able to buy the land, earlier owned by a Ku Klux Klan sympathizer, and turn it into an interfaith, interracial retreat center only added to its mystique.

Professor Steve Fishman of Philosophy even found an avocation, writing poetry and fiction, after attending the retreats. His writing later won several awards. Another professor, Sallie Ives of Geography, credited the writing-to-learn approach with helping her to become a good enough teacher to win the NationsBank Award in 1993.

Other faculty members were succeeding in different ways, some by helping their students become winners in national and state competitions. UNC Charlotte's Model United Nations team, led by Professor Cynthia Combs and always a contender in national competition, won the Outstanding Delegation award in 1994. They defeated 150 universities nationwide, despite the fact that just before the conference Combs had been seriously injured in an

Artist Joni Pienkowski used a panel of portraits to capture the many facets of Duke Power's Bill Lee, for whom the Engineering College was named in 1994.

automobile accident. The team was then invited to participate in an international conference at The Hague.

The leadership of Professor Joyce Beggs of the Management Department helped win her and her students the Small Business Administration Award for Best Case in 1994–95. And Howard Godfrey and a team of students placed second in 1994 in a national tax-accounting competition.

The early leadership of Professor Jim Clay and the continuing work of Lecturer Jeff Simpson in teaching cartographic design took UNC Charlotte's student mapmakers to the top in national competition year after year, even against professional mapmakers. This included thirteen first-place awards since 1985. Other awards included best of show and six honorable mentions. Even better, the students brought home more than $5,600 in prize money.

For those outside the campus who assisted in the climb toward excellence, the university also provided recognition. In 1994, the college of engineering was named the "William States Lee College of Engineering," in honor of the then-retiring chief executive officer of Duke Power Company. Over several years, through contributions and pledges, UNC Charlotte had received more than $2 million from the corporation, Lee himself, and alumni working for the company. Duke Power employed more than four hundred UNC Charlotte alumni. Among them were corporate officers, such as vice presidents Sue Becht and Don Hatley. A symposium with leading engineers and educators in November 1994 marked the official dedication of the college and the presentation of a portrait of Lee. The program was attended by Governor James B. Hunt Jr., UNC System president C. D. Spangler Jr., and UNC System president emeritus William C. Friday.

Earlier the Belk College of Business Administration had been named for members of the Belk family and organizations in recognition of more than $2 million in gifts over the years.

Students themselves began turning away from a "me first" attitude and toward service to humanity. A UNC Charlotte student, Kimberly Aiken from South Carolina, won the title of Miss America 1994 and dedicated her reign

Miss America 1994 Kimberly Aiken, a former student, presents a crystal eagle to Chancellor Jim Woodward. Photo by Wade Bruton.

to helping the homeless. During her travels, she stopped off at UNC Charlotte to present her university with a $25,000 Miss America Scholarship. She also brought with her and presented to the university, as a gift from the Miss America organization, a crystal piece by Waterford, a sponsor of the pageant. Aiken also plugged her institution on a couple of national television talk shows. When one of the hosts asked, "So you go to college at North Carolina—a Tar Heel, eh?" she replied, "No, I go to UNC Charlotte. I'm a 49er."

Another student, Melissa Brafford, who became Miss UNC Charlotte 49er, helped start a project in Cabarrus County to use venison contributed by North Carolina hunters to feed local poor people. Still another student who dedicated himself to helping the hungry was Glenn Hutchison, who began a program on campus to collect leftover food from the cafeterias and take it to feed the homeless in Charlotte shelters. Hutchison was a participant in the University Honors Program, led by Professor Al Maisto, and was named to the 1995 All-USA College Academic First Team, sponsored by *USA Today*, in recognition of his accomplishments.

In other fields, alumni were working their way to the top of their organizations. Larry Ferguson, a business alumnus, moved up in his company to become president of First Data Corporation's Health Systems Group, which employed about a thousand people in University Research Park. First Data spun off that subsidiary company, and Ferguson joined another corporation.

For many faculty members who came as pioneers to build UNC Charlotte, the fact that thirty years had passed since the beginning of university status meant they were retiring. Those retiring in 1994 included Karl M. Gabriel of German, who arrived in 1963; Cloyd S. Goodrum Jr. of Mathematics, who began teaching for Charlotte College and returned to UNC Charlotte in 1967; Ben Hall Hackney Jr. of Educational Administration, who came in 1964 and had helped launch graduate programs; Nish Jamgotch of Political Science, who arrived in 1966, a Cold War specialist whose teaching saw the rise and fall of that era; Joseph F. Schell of Computer Science, who came in 1964 and served as chair of Mathematics before moving to Computer Science; Richard A. Underwood of Religious Studies, who joined in 1974 and had served as chair of the department; and Loy Witherspoon of Religious Studies, who joined in 1964, had served as chair of his department (and Philosophy before the two departments were separated), and founded the United Religious Ministry and the Office of Religious Affairs.

Others were Peter Lamal, 1970, of Psychology, who retired early to continue his research; Pauline Mayo, 1976, of Nursing, who had served as interim dean; Dean B. Vollendorf, 1976, of Architecture; and Walter Roth, 1968, and Hazel Wright, 1966, both of Mathematics.

Among those retiring in 1995 was Paul Saman of Foreign Languages, who had fled the Communist regime in Czechoslovakia and arrived in 1963. He had to wait for an early break in the Cold War to verify his Ph.D. credentials from Charles University in Prague. Others were Robert Gibson, who had come in 1965 and had served as chair of the Chemistry Department; William Smith, a Charlotte College graduate, who came to the campus in 1963 to join Engineering; Ed Walls, who had joined the faculty in 1971 and held the Rush Dickson Professorship of Finance; and Edward Willis, who joined Civil Engineering in 1976.

Harry H. (Hap) Arnold, vice chancellor for business affairs, retired in spring 1994, after serving earlier as executive assistant to the chancellor and liaison to the search committee that brought Chancellor Woodward to the campus.

Replacing those retirees were new appointments. Olen Smith, who had served earlier as interim and then as associate vice chancellor, was named vice chancellor for business affairs. Sandra James was named director of development, having served as community relations and major gifts coordinator for the Colorado Public Radio system.

In the area of student records there were difficulty and considerable leadership turnover over the years, perhaps partly because of rapid growth and changes in technology that necessitated more funds than were available. On

Left: Harry H. (Hap) Arnold retired in 1994 as vice chancellor for business affairs. Right: Olen Smith succeeded Hap Arnold in 1994 as vice chancellor for business affairs. Photos by Wade Bruton.

the other hand, admissions, a related area that experienced much turnover at some campuses, experienced stability and made progress under the capable leadership of Kathi Baucom. In fact, more than once Baucom also had to step into the leadership role in the records office during a vacancy there. She was named interim registrar again in 1995, and in 1996 she was given a permanent appointment as registrar.

Three trustees—Eulada Watt, wife of Congressman Mel Watt; Bobby G. Lowery, a Charlotte businessman; and Margaret King, a Republican Party leader—served out their eight-year terms and were replaced by alumna Stephanie Counts, chief executive officer of the YWCA; Ruth Shaw, senior vice president of Duke Power Company and former president of Central Piedmont Community College; and Dorothy (Dee-Dee) Harris of Cameron M. Harris Company and wife of alumnus Cameron Harris.

Although change continued to be the only constant at UNC Charlotte, sometimes it appeared to take a while. The university finally got a major in communications after several task forces over many years had studied the issue. Many students, of course, had prepared themselves for careers in writing and communications even without a major. Alumni such as Toni L. P. Kelner, who had worked on the student newspaper and interned in the Public Information Office, were finding success as writers. She published three novels in the Laura Fleming Mystery series.

Another program that was important in an urban setting and was added in 1994 was the master's degree in liberal studies, which allowed adults who wished to take graduate courses in many fields to apply them toward a master's degree.

After many years of being neighbor to the Charlotte Motor Speedway, the university began to benefit directly from the association. The R. J. Reynolds Tobacco Company's racing division established the Alan Kulwicki Memorial Scholarship in the name of the Winston Cup champion who died in an airplane crash in 1993. More than $100,000 was raised for the fund through the sale of a commemorative poster of the racer, and the university began awarding the scholarship.

Then the Hendrick racing team provided funds to the William States Lee College of Engineering for research on improvements in welding techniques. Children of members of the racing community—including Kelley Earnhardt, daughter of Dale Earnhardt, one of NASCAR's superstars—began enrolling in the university. Driver Michael Waltrip married Elizabeth Frank, a UNC Charlotte alumna. Jeff Gordon, one of the rising stars of the Winston Cup Racing series, married a former student, Brook Sealey. Indirectly, who knows how many inquiries the university received because some of the 160,000 or more race fans who passed the campus twice a year decided to learn more about the institution.

The quest for an expanded mission, which had led to the first Ph.D. programs, also led to the university's offering the master's degree in health

Vice Chancellor Ed Kizer (right) accepts a plaque from Wayne Robertson of the RJR Racing Division commemorating the Kulwicki Scholarship. Photo by Don Hunter.

administration in 1995, under the direction of Professor Carolyn Thompson. With the burgeoning of the health-care industry in Charlotte, the program clearly filled a need.

The efforts of faculty such as Professors John Lincourt and Dick Toenjes and of benefactors such as William Barnhardt Jr. and the Jule Surtman family were rewarded with the establishment of the Center for Professional and Applied Ethics.

UNC Charlotte also survived a threat that would have brought an unwelcome change to its mission. The legislature had seen a need to trim the number of universities offering master's and doctoral degrees in educational administration for principals, superintendents, and other school officials from twelve to seven. It required that each university wishing to offer such programs reapply and justify them.

Under the leadership of Professor James Lyons, chair of the department at UNC Charlotte, and Dean Jack Nagle, a new proposal was submitted and reviewed by consultants. It won a high ranking from the consultants and approval from the Board of Governors as one of the seven authorized. Success also led finally to the establishment of the Ed.D. in education administration at UNC Charlotte after delays relating to funding and restructuring within the UNC system.

With all the rapid growth and change over fifty years, some commitments remained constant—to excellence in teaching and research, to inclusiveness in terms of serving qualified applicants, to outreach to the greater region, to warm human relationships, and to the strength of work ethic needed to build a doctoral-level university.

So, at its golden anniversary, what had UNC Charlotte become? By any measure, it had attained a high level of quality. The *U.S. News & World Report* rankings were one measure. There UNC Charlotte ranked in the top fifteen regional universities in the South for 1996. That publication ranked it one of the South's best buys as well. And in terms of efficiency—the quality of education offered based on a relatively low expenditure per student—UNC Charlotte ranked in the top five. Beginning in 1985, the university had received high marks for quality and value from other publications, including *Barron's 300, Money* magazine, and Martin Nemko's *How to Get an Ivy League Education at a State University*. Consider these quotes from those publications: "North Carolina is building another great state institution at Charlotte" (*Money* magazine); "What makes UNC Charlotte attractive is that, in addition to liberal arts and preprofessional programs, it offers programs specifically designed to groom its top students for leadership. UNC Charlotte's academic program is solid, and at the undergraduate level offers some advantages over august [universities]. . . . Over 90 percent of undergraduate classes are taught by real professors, and, importantly, professors for whom teaching is a high priority" (*How to Get an Ivy League Education at a State University*); "In North Carolina, where Chapel Hill has long been the jewel in the crown, successful restructuring of the state-university system brings the Charlotte campus ... to the forefront" (*U.S. News & World Report*); "[UNC Charlotte's role in developing University Research Park, University Place, and the Ben Craig Business Incubator has provided] an opportunity to gain local, national and international visibility for the university. Visitors have come from cities and universities in the U.S. and from several nations of the world" (from the citation of the Mitau Award, 1987, by the American Association of State Colleges and Universities).

From a July 26, 1988, editorial in the *Charlotte Observer* came this quotation: "In a world economy increasingly driven by information, technology and the ability to apply new ideas to old methods, UNCC has become the key to future economic development in the Charlotte area. At the same time, in an urban center increasingly buffeted by regional currents, it has also become the key for interpreting and redirecting the economic and governmental forces swirling around it."

There were other measures as well. In a report called "Benchmarking University-Industry Technology Transfer in the South," the Southern Technology Council ranked UNC Charlotte one of the top three universities in six of seven categories in 1995. UNC Charlotte ranked first in patents awarded per dollars of research and licenses to start-up companies, second in patent applications per dollars of research and royalty returns on research investments, and third in licenses per dollar of research and licenses to in-state licensees.

As it continued to improve the quality of teaching, UNC Charlotte joined eleven other institutions in participating in a national project of the American Association for Higher Education to find new methods for college teaching.

To provide the growing number of evening students with admissions, business office, financial aid, registration, and other services during evening hours, the university opened an Office of Evening Services.

Student Model UN and cartographic teams consistently ranked among the top university teams in national competition, and accounting graduates consistently scored among the highest in the state on the state C.P.A. examination. *Sanskrit*, the student literary magazine, during seven out of eight years won the Columbia Scholastic Press Association's Gold Crown Award, given to the top three publications in the country. Civil engineering students won first place in the National Timber Bridge Design Competition, and four accounting students finished in the top ten for the second year in a row and placed third in the Arthur Andersen Tax Challenge. Not every program had a competition or a certification examination, but these measurable results indicated that UNC Charlotte students held their own statewide and nationally on almost any measure.

Faculty members consistently made national and international news because of their activities. Consider one brief period in which *Southern Living* magazine featured the UNC Charlotte sculpture garden initiated by Professors Eric Anderson and Michael Gallis; *Parade* magazine, in a cover story on the Branch Davidian tragedy in Waco, Texas, quoted Professor James Tabor; radio stations from Hong Kong to Toronto, Canada, inquired about a book by Professor Miriam Adderholt-Elliott; Dr. Janet Levy, who earlier had appeared on the public television program *Nova*, was interviewed by WGBH Television in Boston for a national PBS special on Levy's mentor, Dr. Patty Jo Watson; and James Werntz, vice chancellor emeritus, was featured in the *Chronicle of Higher Education* in a story about his efforts to assist the United Arab Emirates University.

Other professors whose work was frequently recognized outside the region in media reports were David Goldfield of History, David Hartgen of Transportation Studies, John Connaughton of Economics, Paul Friday of Criminal Justice, William McCoy of the Urban Institute, Schley Lyons of the College of Arts and Sciences, and Ted Arrington of Political Science.

Judy Rose was increasingly winning respect for her administrative skills in athletics. She played a major role in hosting the NCAA Final Four in men's basketball in 1994 and in attracting and hosting the NCAA Final Four in women's basketball in 1996.

Men's basketball coach Melvin Watkins also came into the limelight. After twenty-two years as player and assistant coach, he endured a national search and convinced authorities that he was the choice to succeed his mentor, Jeff Mullins, who retired in 1996. The prospect of playing in a new arena, in a tough new conference, and with a new coach stimulated renewed interest in the men's basketball program.

Several athletic teams were becoming competitive. The men's soccer team was ranked as high as fourth in the nation and competed in the NCAA tournament in recent years, and it was drawing significant crowds. A women's soccer program was added to the sports lineup. The men's basketball team returned to the NCAA playoffs in 1995. The men's baseball team had won the conference championship and reached the NCAA tournament. The women's basketball team was doing well in stronger competition than ever. Women's softball, volleyball, and soccer teams were making steady gains.

Rose stood her ground when U.S. civil rights officials, following an anonymous complaint of discrimination against women's athletic programs, ordered the university to install lights on the women's softball field. It was ironic that such a charge should be made against one of the few female athletic directors in the nation. She and Woodward said it would be ridiculous to pay a much-needed $120,000 to light fields when almost all of the school's softball games were played during the day. Rose also pointed out that only two college softball fields in the entire Southeast were lighted.

The most telling evidence of the university's arrival in athletics was its admission to Conference USA, a new superconference that also included the University of Alabama–Birmingham, Cincinnati, DePaul, Houston, Louisville, Marquette, Memphis, Saint Louis, South Florida, Southern Mississippi, and Tulane. Again, Rose and Woodward enlisted the aid of Charlotte city officials, chamber of commerce officials, and the city's major business leaders in their quest for conference membership. Although some of the institutions in the new conference competed in football, Rose noted that above all, its teams had a rich basketball tradition.

In numbers of students alone, UNC Charlotte had arrived as a major university by its fiftieth birthday. An enrollment of nearly 16,000 students—15,895 by fall 1995, to be precise—placed it in the top 5 percent of universities in the nation in terms of size. In North Carolina, UNC Charlotte was the fourth largest university, following N.C. State, UNC Chapel Hill, and East Carolina.

For 1995, freshman enrollment was up 6.2 percent. That indicated that the enrollment trend was turning upward again, and UNC Charlotte would grow rapidly again as the freshman class moved up through the classes and was joined by transfer students.

African American students, totaling 2,278 or 14.3 percent of the enrollment, gave UNC Charlotte the largest such percentage among the historically white institutions in North Carolina.

As its first fifty years neared an end, the university was also gaining attention through the recognition given to Chancellor Jim Woodward. After giving up the chairmanship of the United Way Campaign in Birmingham to move to Charlotte, Woodward received that honor again: he was named the chair of the Charlotte region's 1996 campaign. A member of the Air University's Board of Visitors for several years, he was named its chair in 1996. He received two prestigious awards: Charlotte's 1995 Excellence in Management Award and the 1995–96 Distinguished Alumnus Award from the National Alumni Society of the University of Alabama at Birmingham. The management award, given by the Charlotte Chamber of Commerce, the Charlotte Rotary Club, and the *Business Journal* had previously been won by such luminaries as Bill Lee of Duke Power and Ed Crutchfield of First Union. Woodward was a rare winner outside the corporate community. Woodward became an alumnus of Alabama-Birmingham when he received his M.B.A. degree there in 1973. His community role included service on the Charlotte Chamber of Commerce's City-County Consolidation Task Force, the Charlotte Mecklenburg Education Forum, the Executive Committee of the University

Edward E. Crutchfield, chairman and chief executive of First Union Corp., continued his bank's long tradition of supporting UNC Charlotte by serving as a member of the university's Board of Trustees. Photo courtesy of First Union Corp.

of the New South, and the Executive Committee of the Arts and Science Council. In those roles he was continuing the tradition of public service established by his predecessors, Cone, Colvard, and Fretwell.

Measured by almost any standard, then, UNC Charlotte had arrived at a golden age by fifty. Indeed, during the commencement ceremony the university awarded its 50,000th degree. UNC Charlotte was no longer an "instant university." The question then was, where to from here?

CHAPTER 19

Urban Wave Brightens Future

TO PARAPHRASE Proverbs, "Where there is no vision, the university perishes." There should have been no worry on that count for UNC Charlotte. Born of a vision by Charlotteans who wanted a university to serve their region's needs and aspirations, UNC Charlotte arrived at age fifty with a renewed concept of a university sufficient in quality and breadth of offerings to serve the city-state that Charlotte and its region had become.

UNC Charlotte had the potential to become a leader in a national movement that would see institutions in metropolitan settings likely to become the next great universities in America. Just as the classic private universities, the early state universities, and the land-grant universities had over time fulfilled their destinies, the post–World War II universities built in the nation's major metropolitan areas were rising to take their place in the national spotlight.

Professor David Goldfield of UNC Charlotte collaborated with Blaine A. Brownell, provost of the University of North Texas, in an essay titled "Metropolitan Universities, an Emerging Model in American Higher Education." In that essay Brownell said that such institutions would be universities in every sense of the word—"open intellectual communit[ies] in which faculty and students share knowledge, pursue truth, hone analytical skills, and provide training in the professions." He added that they were "an integral part of the modern American urban region, with all its complexity, opportunity, conflict and confusion." Looking ahead, Brownell said that the "dynamic tension between institutional purpose and an environment that both impels and hampers it has produced the metropolitan university and also has shaped its options and its future."

Envisioning the metropolitan university, Brownell asked, "[What other institution] has the capacity to interpret one group to another, serve as a neutral site and forum where problems can be discussed and resolved, bring the latest knowledge and technology to bear on the problems of the dispossessed,

Fifty years of UNC Charlotte executive leadership are represented in this 1994 photograph. The leaders are E. K. Fretwell Jr. and Bonnie Cone (front row) and D. W. Colvard and James H. Woodward (back row, left to right). Photo by Wade Bruton.

join the vigor and capacity of business with the compelling needs of the public at large, and, perhaps most importantly, help restore a sense of 'civitas,' of belonging to one polity and community?"

Much of Brownell's description of the metropolitan university could be applied to UNC Charlotte. Moreover, UNC Charlotte had acquired another strength that portended a bright future: the attainment of critical mass in the number of faculty members with research and scholarship skills that commanded regional, national, and international attention. An adequate list would include a large number of the faculty, so the following is just a sampling of the scholars and their areas of expertise: Tanure Ojaide in African poetry, David Walters in community planning, Kingston Heath in architectural preservation, Thomas Reynolds in plant cloning, James Oliver in biotechnology, Stanley Schneider in the study of African bees, Anthony Plath in banking, Thomas Dubois in chemical compounds, Jy Wu in environmental studies, Raphael Tsu in computer chips, Farid Tranjan in technology transfer, Paul Friday and Charles Dean and Richard Lumb in criminal justice research, Kathleen Reichs in forensic anthropology, Eugene Shaffer in teaching methods, Bryan Robinson in counseling, John Connaughton in economic forecasting, Al Stuart in employment projections, Howard Godfrey in accounting, Sam Watson and Leon Gatlin in writing to teach and learn, Cindy Combs in United Nations simulations, Michael Feldman in optical-electronic devices, Anita Moss and Mark West in children's literature, Judith Suther in languages, Boyd Davis in linguistics, Kathleen Yancy in technical writing, John Healey in kinesiology, Owen Furuseth in land-use planning, Wei-Ning Xiang in geographic information systems, Dennis Lord in retail location, David Hartgen in transportation planning, Linda Berne in health promotion, Dan Morrill in historic preservation, David Goldfield in southern cities, Carole Haber in the history of aging, Harold Josephson in international studies, Bil Stahl in technology planning, Stella Nkomo in women as managers, Linda Swayne in the marketing of health services, Miriam Leiva in teaching mathematics to children, Robert Hocken and Steven Patterson in precision engineering, Doug Bish in music, John Lincourt in ethics, Silverio Almeida in identification through optics, Dennis Kay in Shakespeare, Cheryl Brown and Alan Shao in Asian studies, Dena Shenk in gerontology, K. David Patterson and Gerald Pyle in the history and geography of disease epidemics, Jack Sommer and William Brandon in public policy, Saul Brenner and Dennis Dorin in U.S. Supreme Court research, Ted Arrington in politics, George Windholz in Pavlovian studies, Eric Anderson and Rod MacKillop and Martha Strawn in art, James Tabor and Jeffrey Meyer in religious studies, Janet Levy in the anthropology of ancient Europe, and Zbigniew Michalewicz in computer science in evolution computation.

In addition to individual professors, several departments had gained reputations beyond the campus for the strength of their scholarship. These departments built strength in diverse ways. Joseph Quinn, as chair of the Mathematics Department, recruited internationally known mathematicians, many of whom were Soviet Jews fleeing that nation in the years before the demise of the Communist system. Other recognized departments included Geography and Earth Sciences, Psychology, Accounting, Architecture, Biology, Electrical Engineering, Engineering Technology, History, and Political Science. Others were building strengths in specialized areas.

Clark Kerr, former president of the University of California and a noted observer of American higher education, made some predictions about where the outstanding research universities of the future would develop. UNC Charlotte and Charlotte met Kerr's criteria on several counts. Kerr said that great universities were likely to develop in leading centers of the historic professions, including banking. Charlotte's position as the nation's third largest banking center would qualify UNC Charlotte on that point.

Kerr also said such universities would develop in places that were centers of progressive economic activity, including some in the South. Charlotte was certainly one of those centers. The city had already been dubbed one of the nation's economic "hot spots," and a March 1995 issue of *National Geographic* noted that "glittering new bank headquarters proclaim Charlotte's rising rank as a financial powerhouse of national stature." Of the city that for many years was the hub of the nation's gold mining, the *National Geographic* said, "Today's gold sits above ground. Charlotte has surpassed Atlanta as the Wall Street of the South. Its two homegrown banks, First Union and NationsBank, have combined assets of 230 billion dollars—more than the annual gross national product of Sweden."

Still another predictor of university success would be city size, according to Kerr. He said size would be important for the sake of career development opportunities for spouses of faculty members. Charlotte already had become the nation's thirty-third largest city, with a city-limits population of 440,000, and would soon become the thirtieth largest city, through a planned annexation that would move its population toward the half-million mark. Mecklenburg County's population was estimated at 581,466. A Metropolitan Statistical Area population of 1.3 million ranked the city thirty-third largest by that measurement. The urban region population was 5.5 million.

Kerr noted that a university's location in a city that was an airline hub would also be an asset because of the ability of productive faculty members to travel easily. Charlotte was home to a major hub for USAir, with some five hundred flights per day.

Charlotte had some growing to do before reaching another criteria listed by Kerr—a university located in a rich community with a vigorous cultural establishment and in a large, rich state. Charlotte's cultural establishment was developing rapidly, with one of the best rates of per capita giving to the arts in the country. Location in a large, rich state was cited as particularly important for state-supported universities. North Carolina was the tenth largest state, and its economy was growing rapidly, but it still could not be considered rich. Historically, it had given a disproportionate share of its revenues to higher education, but many other claims were being made on state revenues, and the future was not entirely clear.

Still another predictor of success in the Kerr model was location in an area with effective and committed political leadership. That had been true historically in North Carolina, but some uncertainty in the political climate had developed by 1996.

In discussing another measure of potential for future success—location in areas of great physical beauty and good climate—Kerr cited central and western North Carolina by name. The UNC Charlotte campus exemplified the beauty of the Central Piedmont region, with its open fields, streams, and wooded, rolling hills.

Overall, Kerr's predictors seemed to bode well for UNC Charlotte. Its location was indeed a major advantage as its leaders sought to move it into the top ranks of American universities. Kerr, who was a friend of E. K. Fretwell, had visited Charlotte and consulted with the Board of Governors of the UNC system and knew first-hand of UNC Charlotte's potential.

At UNC Charlotte, a vision for the future was committed to writing and graphic illustrations in two major documents: "The Campus Academic Plan—1996–2001," and the Campus Master Plan. Indeed, the title of the Campus Master Plan publication was "Vision." It was clear, however, that the university would have to run just to stay close to where it needed to be to serve the Charlotte city-state in 1996, and it would have to have a major infusion of public and private support if it were to catch up.

On the other hand, the Charlotte region itself was at risk of stalling in its own growth and development if UNC Charlotte did not develop into the major metropolitan university the region needed to move forward and compete globally with city-states that already had such universities in place. Even as Chancellor Jim Woodward was assuming his new duties in 1989, Charlotte Chamber of Commerce executive Carroll Gray was telling him that Charlotte had to have a Ph.D.-granting university if it were to continue to progress. Charlotte gained doctoral degrees in 1994, but by then it was clear that the target had moved—that progress toward research university status was required.

Shortly after his arrival, Chancellor Woodward began proclaiming that UNC Charlotte would have to have better planning if it were to make maximum use of its land and physical plant. He often said in the early days of his administration that the university owned about a thousand acres and that it would still likely have only a thousand acres one hundred years hence, because of the escalation in land costs. For that reason, Woodward said, it was incumbent upon his administration to insure that a plan was devised to make the maximum possible use of that resource. To create such a plan, Woodward appointed a Campus Master Plan Task Force under the leadership of Dean Charles Hight of the College of Architecture. Hight earlier had done some thinking about how the campus ought to develop. After visiting some of the best European universities, he brought back to UNC Charlotte the concept of the campus quadrangle as a guiding design principle.

Hight's planning task force first created a set of visions and values as guiding principles for their work. To help translate the visions and values into a workable plan, the university engaged a design team comprising the Charlotte firm of Lee Nichols Hepler Architecture; the London planning and urban design firm of Edward Cullinan Architects; the landscape design firms of Colejenest of Charlotte and Dan Kiley of Charlotte and Vermont; the transportation planning firm of Barton-Aschman Associates of Washington, D.C.; and the utilities planning firm of McCracken & Lopez.

The resulting plan would create a "City for Learning" for 25,000 students and 1,500 faculty members. Among its concepts were that from its outer edges, the campus's center would be no more than a ten-minute walk. The planners said that by developing protected quadrangles, arcades, and shaded

UNC Charlotte Chancellor James H. Woodward led efforts, completed in 1995, to draft a master plan for expansion. Photo by Wade Bruton.

paths and a denser, more compact and citylike central campus, the university might influence the course of future development in the City of Charlotte itself.

They noted that the City of Charlotte had expanded to the point that the campus had become an integral part of it. Further, UNC Charlotte had taken its place as one of the city's major amenities, along with the airport, the Mint Museum of Art, the Coliseum, the uptown business district, and the Carolina Panthers Stadium. Given its location, the university could become "the most important campus in the University of North Carolina system," the planners believed.

Better connections to the surrounding community were envisioned through the construction of buildings on the campus edges to serve both the community and university. Prospective occupants of those facilities were a performing arts center, a continuing education center, a conference center, research institutes, retail businesses, and recreational facilities.

Redesigned entrances that would be more welcoming were proposed, along with better signage, road systems, and pathways to make the campus more visitor-friendly. Also envisioned was an "elegant" tree-lined inner loop road, with lanes for vehicles, bicycles, and pedestrians.

Enhanced natural areas would require improving the botanical gardens, the ecological reserve, and the links to the Greenway system. Another possible feature would be a lake in the Toby Creek Valley, first envisioned in an Odell Master Plan early in the university's history.

The planners said, "All over the world, there are fine universities, which are intimately meshed with the city which hosts them—Oxford, Harvard and the Sorbonne, for example—and it is towards this goal that The University of North Carolina at Charlotte will move."

Woodward acknowledged the magnitude of the plan's challenge. "We must have three million more square feet of space to accommodate a university of 25,000 students," he said, adding, "We must have space for a wider variety of academic activity and for research leading to doctoral degrees. We must adapt to development that is rapidly filling the rural landscape that once surrounded us. We must find ways to make even better use of the valuable resources that have been entrusted to us." His vision was that UNC Charlotte would be "a model for development through the region, and especially for the surrounding University City area. We want it to be an inviting place, one that inspires creativity, that supports inquiry, that promotes contemplation, the feeds the spirit as well as the mind, and that sets a high standard for the quality of life all around it."

The university's Academic Plan was appropriately drawn for a shorter term than the Campus Master Plan because of the changing needs of society, the community, and the state, as well as the changing availability of resources. In fact, the plan would be revised every two years to relate to the state's budgeting process.

The "Campus Academic Plan, 1996–2001" incorporated the visions of Philip Dubois, provost and vice chancellor for academic affairs; his staff; college deans; department chairs; and faculty members. Among its most important assumptions was that in terms of student enrollment and institutional commitment, UNC Charlotte would continue primarily to be concerned with outstanding undergraduate education, but with gradual and selective increases in the numbers and size of master's and doctoral programs. The plan also anticipated that the university would enroll increasing numbers of older students, females, and underrepresented minority groups.

A commitment was made to respond to the needs of the Charlotte region while aspiring to achieve national and even international standards of excellence in teaching, research, and public service. The plan included a long-term vision statement which said that UNC Charlotte aspired to be "North Carolina's most energetic and responsive University." It would offer educational opportunities for nearly 25,000 students seeking the highest-quality undergraduate and graduate educations. It would also offer continuing personal or professional enrichment in the liberal arts and sciences and selected professions. The plan said that the university would be known especially for the individual commitment of its faculty members to providing educational opportunity and ensuring student learning and success. In addition, it would join with other institutions to address the major educational, economic, social, and cultural needs of the greater Charlotte region.

Improved retention of students was addressed through improved advising and support. A customer-oriented approach was the goal in providing support services, such as admissions, registration, financial aid, the library, and computing services.

The plan also included a commitment to increasing the presence of women and minorities among the faculty. Another commitment was toward improving the way faculty were recognized and rewarded for their contributions to the success of the university and its students.

Several themes for campus development emerged in the plan. These included providing a basic liberal education; serving the region as a major resource on critical issues, such as economic development, crime and violence, transportation, urban planning, and the environment; serving the business community's needs for continuing professional education and applied research; strengthening the preparation and continuing education of teachers; addressing the educational needs of health-care providers; promoting the increasing internationalization of the campus, city, and state; and helping the manufacturing sector improve the quality of products and the efficiency of operations.

In addition to the several new baccalaureate and master's degrees proposed, there would be new doctoral programs in biology, information technology, and public policy, along with continuing development of programs in several other fields. Like the physical plant plan, the academic plan presented the daunting challenge of acquiring sufficient state appropriations.

Beyond the vision for the university represented in the two planning documents, there were individual visions for the future. Just as Addison Reese, who laid the foundation for NationsBank, was one of the pioneering visionaries of UNC Charlotte, Hugh McColl, chair of the bank in 1996, shared his enthusiasm for the university's future. "This is our city's university," he declared. "It was born of local initiative and built through local leadership. It is attended by local sons and daughters, and it has returned the community investment." UNC Charlotte, McColl said, "has responded to our ideas about how to build a great university, is providing well-educated, capable graduates to advance our local economy and is offering abundant opportunities for continuing education that keep our city moving forward."

McColl's own vision had been instrumental in crafting one of the nation's largest banks and in turning the City of Charlotte into one of the nation's most dynamic and attractive cities, with the help of bank-led initia-

Hugh McColl, NationsBank chairman, in 1996 saw Charlotte's future intertwined with UNC Charlotte's. Photo by Wade Bruton.

tives. It was instructive that his vision included UNC Charlotte as well. Moreover, he put action where his words were. His support of UNC Charlotte's fund-raising efforts in the Silver Anniversary Campaign was crucial to the campaign's success. It was his willingness to underwrite the university's track-and-field complex and to make a major contribution toward its construction that made that development feasible.

McColl said that the university shared Charlotte's heritage and tradition of self-determination. "Its future," he said, "is as bright as our city's future: The best of what a 'town-and-gown' relationship can be."

Another visionary was Chancellor Jim Woodward. He suggested an intriguing way to look at the need for UNC Charlotte to develop into a major university for Charlotte. "If you were to remove suddenly all the existing North Carolina universities and the historic circumstances which caused them to be located where they were and start all over again, where would you locate some new ones?" he asked.

Woodward suggested the first three would be placed in the Charlotte region; the Research Triangle area of Raleigh, Durham, and Chapel Hill; and the Piedmont Triad area of Greensboro, Winston-Salem, and High Point. There would be others, but Charlotte clearly would be among the first three established. That conclusion might have become obvious by 1996, but earlier it was not clear to the state's leaders that Charlotte needed a state-supported institution of higher education of any kind.

"You must place major universities in large urban areas," Woodward said. "In those few instances where that is not already the case, there will be growing pressure to develop such universities," he added.

Woodward said that universities exist to serve the public good and that their leaders must be thinking constantly of what higher education needs are likely to be in the future and do their utmost to respond. He said that community needs relate to what universities do in addition to providing graduates for society. He was thinking of the service role of universities and the positive influence they have on the cultural, political, and business sectors of their regions.

Further, he said that the needs of communities are driven by social and economic trends that include the growing international character of business activity; the need for an educated workforce to compete globally; the growing minority population, which historically has not been taken into consideration in economic development; the increasing realization that learning is a lifelong process for professional advancement and personal enhancement, requiring that higher education be provided where people are; the expectation that universities participate more fully through their service roles in responding to community needs, requiring collaborations on research; and the growing urbanization of society.

Then he described the major university he envisioned. It would offer a broad array of undergraduate and master's degree programs in the arts and sciences and certain professional disciplines. It would offer doctoral work in a number of areas that relate to community needs, including liberal arts disciplines, not just professional areas.

That major university would see growth in the student body rise toward 25,000, if the institution responded to needs. It would have all the characteristics of a residential campus, and a large number of young students would have an exciting extracurricular life in addition to academic activities. Increasingly, the university would provide services to a large number of nontraditional students, those whose work and families prevented them from attending full-time. These students would include both young and old. The university would still see as its core purpose the presentation of strong undergraduate academic programs. The university envisioned would more closely reflect the racial and ethnic distribution of the general population, Woodward said.

College athletics would continue to be an integral part of UNC Charlotte, Woodward believed. He said the university would have to compete at the highest level. At the time, he believed that Conference USA, which UNC had recently joined, was at that high level. He said that the university would continue to feel financial and legal pressures for equity between women's and men's athletic activities and that this would mitigate against adding football because of its high cost.

The chancellor's vision was that in ten to fifteen years, UNC Charlotte would be regarded as one of the most beautiful campuses in the nation and as a place to visit when one came to Charlotte. There would be a large main campus plus satellite campuses in population and business centers, similar to the uptown Charlotte campus at CityFair. These would be located near the major traffic arteries that linked the ring cities with uptown Charlotte.

The campus also would be linked, through extensive collaboration, with all other community sectors—business, cultural, and educational, and including both private and public institutions. "We do not want to compete in a harmful way with the private colleges, nor with the cultural agencies, but rather through collaboration to serve the needs," Woodward said. He cited the excellent private colleges in the Charlotte area but noted that they continued to look to the future with their very focused missions. Then he noted Central Piedmont Community College and other outstanding community colleges in surrounding counties, again with focused and limited missions.

Woodward concluded that if the administration of UNC Charlotte did what it should, his institution would emerge as that major university in Charlotte within ten years. "If we do a poor job," he said, "it will still happen but maybe later." Woodward said that if one looked at any parameter and extrapolated ten years into the future, it was clear that a major university would have to be developed in Charlotte. "There is no other alternative to that institution's being UNC Charlotte," Woodward said.

Since the days when UNC Charlotte was launched fifty years earlier, the need for a great university had grown stronger and the expectations much higher. Indeed, the University of North Carolina at Charlotte had moved closer to becoming the institution the community wanted and needed, sometimes by small steps forward and sometimes by leaps and bounds.

And if the past were prologue, UNC Charlotte would become that great university. Already, the vision of Woody Kennedy had become reality. In the late 1940s, he had lamented a low college-going rate by high school graduates in the Charlotte region. Just as he predicted, the presence of a state-supported college or university would dramatically improve that rate. In 1965, only 49.3 percent of Charlotte area high school graduates indicated that they would enroll at an institution of higher education. By 1994, that percentage had climbed to 75.7 percent. By 1996, the university's enrollment was almost 16,000, indicating that a need had been met.

UNC Charlotte was nearing the crest of the wave of the next generation of great universities—the urban or metropolitan universities born after

The 1995 UNC Charlotte Commencement fills the lower tier of the 23,000-seat Charlotte Coliseum. Photo by Wade Bruton.

World War II that had come of age and would address and help solve the problems of American society and provide well-prepared graduates for a new century.

Founded to provide educational opportunities to men and women who otherwise might not have a chance to go to college, UNC Charlotte remains committed to raising the education level of an old, textile-oriented, under-colleged metropolitan region. In reaching out to enrich the quality of life for millions of the region's people through excellence in teaching, market-oriented and applied research, vital public service, and wider economic opportunity, it is more than meeting the expectations of its founders. As long as the torch lighted by Bonnie Cone and her early supporters is kept aflame and passed on to generations of other visionaries, UNC Charlotte has the prospect of becoming the next great North Carolina university.

Appendix

UNC Charlotte Board of Trustees, 1995–96

Mark E. Almond	President of the Student Body	Winston-Salem
Stephanie R. Counts	Chief Executive Officer YWCA of the Central Carolinas	Charlotte
Edward E. Crutchfield Jr.	Chairman and Chief Executive Officer First Union Corporation	Charlotte
James B. Garland	Garland Drum & Hood	Gastonia
Dorothy W. Harris	Harris Land Company	Charlotte
William R. Holland	Chairman and Chief Executive Officer United Dominion Industries	Charlotte
Robert B. Jordan	Jordan Lumber Company	Mt. Gilead
Russell M. Robinson II	Robinson, Bradshaw and Hinson	Charlotte
Carlton A. Sears		Flat Rock
Ruth G. Shaw	Senior Vice President Duke Power Company	Charlotte
Charles M. Shelton	The Shelton Companies	Charlotte
Edward J. Snyder	E. J. Snyder & Co.	Albemarle
James W. Thompson	Vice Chairman NationsBank Corporation	Charlotte

Honorary Trustees: Recognized for Past Service on Board of Trustees

Thomas M. Belk
F. Douglas Biddy
Sara H. Bissell
William E. Bluford
Douglas W. Booth
C. C. (Cliff) Cameron
Kathleen R. (Kat) Crosby
R. Stuart Dickson
John L. (Buck) Fraley

John L. Fraley Jr.
James C. Fry
Elisabeth C. Hair
James A. Hardison Jr.
Howard H. Haworth
Graeme M. Keith
W. Duke Kimbrell
Margaret R. King
John D. Lewis

Hugh L. McColl Jr.
Bobby G. Lowery
Martha H. Melvin
Meredith R. Spangler
Thomas I. Storrs
Eulada P. Watt
Bland W. Worley

Honorary Degree Recipients

1968, Frank Porter Graham, Addison H. Reese
1969, Luther H. Hodges, John Paul Lucas Jr.
1974, Sam J. Ervin Jr.
1977, Harry L. Dalton, Harry L. Golden, Alice Lindsay Tate
1979, Dean W. Colvard, Bonnie E. Cone
1982, Anita Stroud
1983, Charles Clifford (Cliff) Cameron, John L. (Buck) Fraley, John Hope Franklin, Susie Marshall Sharp

1984, William J. Bennett, James J. Harris, Ellen Black Winston
1985, James G. Martin, Loonis R. McGlohon, Edyth F. Winningham
1986, William C. Friday
1987, Thomas M. Belk, Richard H. Hagemeyer, Oliver R. Rowe, Terry Sanford
1988, William States Lee III, W. Ann Reynolds, David Taylor
1989, Dr. David S. Citron, Hugh L. McColl Jr.

1990, R. Stuart Dickson, Dr. Jacob B. Freedland, James B. McMillan
1991, Jack E. Claiborne, Elizabeth S. Randolph
1992, John Cocke, S. Scott Ferebee
1993, W. Duke Kimbrell
1994, George T. Butler
1995, Herman Blumenthal
1996, Mariam Cannon Hayes, Robert G. Hayes

Distinguished Service Award Recipients

1987, Thomas M. Belk, Charles Clifford (Cliff) Cameron
1988, John L. (Buck) Fraley, David Taylor
1989, William States Lee III

1990, Thomas I. Storrs
1991, James W. Thompson
1992, William M. Barnhardt
1993, John Stedman
1994, Bonnie E. Cone

1995, Dr. Jonnie H. McLeod
1996, Edwin L. Jones Jr.

UNC Charlotte Faculty Presidents

1972–74
Robert Williams

1974–75
Edward St. Clair

1975–76
Gerald Stone Jr.

1976–77
Loy Witherspoon

1977–78
Edward Perzel

1978–79
George Rent

1979–80
Robert Mundt

1980–81
James Kuppers

1981–82
Anne Newman

1982–83
Virginia Geurin

1983–84
Theodore Arrington

1984–85
James Selby

1985–86
Robert Coleman

1986–87
Timothy Mead

1987–88
James McGavran Jr.

1988–89
Terrel Rhodes

1989–90
Paula Goolkasian

1990–91
Loy Witherspoon

1991-92
Michael Corwin

1992–93
Albert Maisto

1993–94
Michael Pearson

1994–95
Sallie Ives

1995–96
Rafic Makki

Winners, NationsBank Award for Excellence in Teaching

1968, Seth Ellis

1969, Mary Embry, Roy Moose, Loy Witherspoon

1970, Elinor Caddell, Dan Morrill

1971, William Dailey, Barbara Goodnight, Nish Jamgotch Jr.

1972, Sherman Burson, James Matthews, Thomas C. Turner

1973, Robert Gibson, Douglas Orr Jr.

1974, David Bayer, William McCoy, Lorraine Penninger

1975, Eric Anderson, Marvin Armstrong, James Crosthwaite

1976, Douglas Grimsley, Anne Newman

1977, Boyd Davis, Stephen Fishman

1978, Edward Perzel, James Selby

1979, Robert Conrad, Lyman Johnson

1980, Stephen Jolly, Vera Smith

1981, Michael Corwin, Miriam Leiva

1982, Robert Coleman, Nancy Edwards

1983, Harold Josephson, Louis Trosch

1984, Harry Chernotsky, Edward Malmgren

1985, John Lincourt, Albert Maisto

1986, Edward Hopper, Deborah Langsam

1987, Surasakdi Bhamornsiri

1988, Anita Moss, Stella Nkomo

1989, Dennis Dorin, Harold Reiter

1990, Ira Hutchison

1991, Rajaram Janardhanam

1992, Sallie Ives

1993, Samuel Watson Jr.

1994, Dennis Lord

1995, Ann M. Newman

Winners, First Citizens Bank Scholars Medal

1987, Paul Escott, Paul Rillema

1988, David Goldfield, James Oliver

1989, Bryan Robinson

1990, K. David Patterson

1991, Judith Suther

1992, Gerald Pyle

1993, Thomas Reynolds

1994, Saul Brenner

1995, Farid Tranjan

1996, Zbigniew Michalewicz

Alumni Association Faculty Service Award Recipients

1992, Linda Berne

1993, Loy Witherspoon

1994, James W. Clay, Mary Thomas Burke

1995, Harold Josephson

1996, Daniel L. Morrill, Alfred W. Stuart

Past Presidents of Alumni Association

1963–64
Bill J. Reid, '57

1964–65
Daniel McCaskill, '56

1965–66
Edward J. Silber, '60

1966–67
Steve Mahaley Jr., '52

1967–69
William L. Mills Jr., '48

1969–70
Philip Chadwick, '67

1970–71
Gary Baucom, '67

1971–72
John McArthur Jr., '67

1972–73
Parry Bliss Jr., '68

1973–74
Ellison Clary Jr., '68

1974–75
Danny Phillips, '69

1975–76
John Gaither III, '68

1976–77
Kathryn Ward Davis, '71

1977–78
John Lafferty Jr., '69

1978–79
Eugene Johnson, '73

1979–80
David Taylor, '71

1980–81
Michael Wood, '68

1981–82
Boyd Cauble, '71

1982–83
Terre Thomas Bullock, '77

1983–84
Norman Morrow, '70

1984–85
John Fraley Jr., '77

1985–86
Hulene Hill, '71

1986–87
Frank Jones, '67

1987–88
Donald Hatley, '71

1988–89
Robert Bullock, '75

1989–90
Steve Jester, '77

1990–91
Walter Hall III, '80

1991–92
Mary Ann Rouse, '80

1992–93
Gail Chapman, '83

1993–94
Timothy Demmitt, '80

1994–95
Harry J. Stathopoulos, '84

1995–96
Carol Lesley, '89

Alumni Hall of Fame

Martha B. Alexander, '79, M.H.D.
James Babb Jr., '58, A.A.
Sue A. Becht, '75, B.S.
Wyatt Bell, '51, A.A.
Louise S. Brennan, '70, B.A.
Dr. Ronald Caldwell, '71, B.A.
Jane K. Carrigan, '71, B.A.
Vail Carter, '75, B.A.
Benjamin Chavis, '71, B.A.
Stephanie Counts, '81, M.H.D.
Dr. Nancy B. Davis, '70, B.A.
Sheila B. Dillon, '75, B.S.
William Disher, '57, A.A.
John Fraley Jr., '77, B.A.
Maria H. Hall, '81, M.H.D.
Cameron Harris, '68, B.A.
Donald Hatley, '71, B.S.E.E.
Hulene D. Hill, '71, B.A.
Arthur Jeske, '70, B.S.
John W. Kilgo, '55
Mary Norton Kratt, '92, M.A.
John Lafferty Jr., '69, B.S.
Floyd Lockamy, '73, B.S.
Susan Ludvigson, '73, M.A.
Dr. Steve Mahaley Jr., '52, A.A.
Cedric Maxwell, '80, B.A.
James Mead, '73, M.B.A.
Carlton Moody, '84, B.A.
David Moody, '84, B.A.
Dr. Freda H. Nicholson, '76, M.Ed.
Reece Overcash Jr., '48
Dr. Jesse Register, '68, B.A., M.Ed.
Mary Ann Rouse, '80, B.S.
Rodney T. Smith, '70, B.A.
Chet Snow Jr., '72, B.A.
Dr. Richard Thompson, '74, M.Ed.

Alumni by Choice Award Recipients

1994
  Dale Halton

1995
  Dr. Loy Witherspoon

Student Body Presidents

1946, Ralph (Red) Williams
1947, David Littlejohn
1948, Arthur Drummond
1949, Maurice Hooks
1950, Jim Kilgo
1951, Hugh Adams
1952, Jack Proctor
1953, Arthur Farley
1954, Jerry Martin
1955, Donald Payne
1956, Billy J. Reid
1957, Bill Henson
1958, Richard D. Matthews
1959, Wiley Martin
1960, Ed Phillips
1961, Howard Payne
1962, Bill Ferguson
1963, Beth Groom
1964, Dudney Jarnagan
1965–66, John Scott
1966–67, Gus Psomadakis
1967–68, Tim Britton
1968–69, John Gaither
1969–70, F. N. (Bud) Stewart
1970-71, Alan Hickok
1971–72, Stan Patterson
1972–73, Roland Gentry
1973–74, Richard Butterfield
1974–75, Edward Hendricks
1975–76, Jamie Stemple
1976–77, Ricky Pharr
1977–78, Chase Idol
1978–79, Larry Springs
1979–80, Karen Popp
1980–81, Ron Olson
1981–82, Polly Purgason
1982–83, Jan Hobbs Turpin
1983–84, Rick DeRhodes
1984–85, Elliott Bryant
1985–86, Joey Preston
1986–87, Mark Major
1987–88, Jody Jessup
1988–89, Tom Goins
1989–90, Michael Wilson
1990–91, Beth Hamman
1991–93, Derrick Griffith
1993–94, Richard Hudson
1994–95, Demond Martin
1995–96, Mark E. Almond

UNC Charlotte All-Americans

Markita Aldridge, Women's Basketball, First Team, Freshman (1992), Preseason, Third Team (1995)

Joey Anderson, Baseball, Freshman Team (1993)

Paula Bennett, Women's Basketball, First Team (1980), Honorable Mention (1982)

Craig Brown, Soccer, First Team, GTE Academic (1985)

Jon Busch, Soccer, Freshman Team (1994)

Paul Carpenter, Golf, Honorable Mention (1995–96)

Mac Cozier, Soccer, First Team (1994)

Tim Collie, Baseball, Third Team (1995)

Andre Davis, Men's Basketball, Fifth Team, Freshman (1992)

Charlita Davis, Women's Basketball, Honorable Mention (1993)

Byron Dinkins, Men's Basketball, Honorable Mention (1987, 1988)

Gabe Garcia, Soccer, Second Team (1991)

Pam Gorham, Women's Basketball, Honorable Mention (1991)

Cynthia Higgins, Cross Country, First Team, GTE Academic (1992, 1993)

Celena Illuzzi, Cross Country, First Team, GTE Academic (1993, 1994, 1995)

Katie Kerin, Cross Country, First Team, GTE Academic District (1992, 1993)

Molly Kerin, Cross Country, First Team (1994, 1995) and Track and Field, First Team, 5000 Meters (1995)

Chad Kinch, Men's Basketball, First Team, Freshman (1976), Third Team (1977), Honorable Mention (1978, 1979)

Bobby Kummer, Men's Basketball, First Team, GTE Academic District (1994, 1995)

Jarvis Lang, Men's Basketball, First Team, Freshman, (1991), Honorable Mention (1993, 1994, 1995)

Julia (Candy) Lucas, Women's Basketball, Honorable Mention (1985)

Christopher Mark, Tennis, First Team, GTE Academic (1992, 1993)

Cedric Maxwell, Men's Basketball, First Team (1977)

Bo Robinson, Baseball, Freshman Team (1995)

Randy Sheen, Soccer, Honorable Mention (1994)

Barry Shifflett, Baseball, First Team, Freshman (1983), Second Team (1986)

Steve Waggoner, Baseball, First Team, GTE Academic (1986), Second Team GTE Academic (1987)

Patricia Walker, Women's Basketball, Honorable Mention (1982)

Henry Williams, Men's Basketball, First Team, Freshman (1989), Honorable Mention (1989, 1990, 1991, 1992)

Kristin Wilson, Women's Basketball, Honorable Mention (1986, 1987)

UNC Charlotte Staff Employees of the Year

1986, Craig Bizzell, Joyce Willis

1987, Kenneth Burrows, James Houston Jr., Gladie Reid

1988, George Hahn Jr., Calvin Miller, R. B. (Sam) Simono

1989, Arthur (Rock) Rollins, Marian Beane

1990, Kenneth (Ken) Sanford, Dale Trembley

1991, Kathi Baucom, Judith Freed

1992, Rose-Marie Walley, Wayne Maikranz

1993, T. L. Smith, Terrie Houck

1994, Betty Pennell, Diane Aldridge

1995, Craig Fulton, Christine Morrison

Bibliography

Manuscripts and Archives

Special Collections, J. Murrey Atkins Library, University of North Carolina at Charlotte.
Woodford Armstrong Kennedy Papers, J. Murrey Atkins Library, University of North Carolina at Charlotte.
Charlotte News
Charlotte Observer

Extensive Interviews

Arnold, Harry H. Former vice chancellor for business affairs, University of North Carolina at Charlotte.
Colvard, Dean Wallace. Chancellor emeritus, University of North Carolina at Charlotte.
Cone, Bonnie Ethel. Vice chancellor emerita, University of North Carolina at Charlotte.
Fretwell, E. K., Jr. Chancellor emeritus, University of North Carolina at Charlotte.
Friday, William C. President emeritus, University of North Carolina.
Orr, Douglas M., Jr. Former vice chancellor for development and public service, University of North Carolina at Charlotte, and president, Warren Wilson College.
Woodward, James H. Chancellor, University of North Carolina at Charlotte.

Books

Blythe, LeGette, and Charles Raven Brockmann. *Hornet's Nest: The Story of Charlotte and Mecklenburg County.* Charlotte: Public Library of Charlotte and Mecklenburg County, 1961.

Claiborne, Jack. *The Charlotte Observer: Its Time and Place, 1869–1986*. Chapel Hill: University of North Carolina Press, 1986.

Clay, James W., and Douglas M. Orr Jr. *Metrolina Atlas*. Chapel Hill: University of North Carolina Press, 1972.

Coffin, Alex. *Brookshire & Belk: Businessmen in City Hall*. Charlotte: University of North Carolina at Charlotte, 1994.

Colvard, Dean W., Douglas M. Orr Jr., and Mary Dawn Bailey. *University Research Park: The First Twenty Years*. Charlotte: Urban Institute, University of North Carolina at Charlotte, 1988.

King, Arnold K. *The Multicampus University of North Carolina Comes of Age, 1956–1986*. Chapel Hill: University of North Carolina, 1987.

Larrabee, Charles X. *Many Missions: Research Triangle Institute's First 31 Years*. Research Triangle Park: Research Triangle Institute, 1991.

Lefler, Hugh Talmage, and Albert Ray Newsome. *North Carolina: The History of a Southern State*. Chapel Hill: University of North Carolina Press, 1954.

Link, William A. *William Friday: Power, Purpose, and American Higher Education*. Chapel Hill: University of North Carolina Press, 1995.

Mitchell, Memory F., ed. *Messages, Addresses, and Public Papers of Terry Sanford, Governor of North Carolina, 1961–1965*. Raleigh: Division of Archives and History, 1966.

———, ed. *Messages, Addresses, and Papers of Daniel Killian Moore, Governor of North Carolina, 1965–1969*. Raleigh: Division of Archives and History, 1971.

———, ed. *Addresses and Public Papers of Robert Walter Scott, Governor of North Carolina, 1969–1973*. Raleigh: Division of Archives and History, 1974.

———, ed. *Addresses and Public Papers of James Baxter Hunt Jr., Governor of North Carolina, Vol. I, 1977–1981*. Raleigh: Division of Archives and History, 1982.

Poff, Jan-Michael, ed. *Addresses and Public Papers of James Grubbs Martin, Governor of North Carolina, Vol. I, 1985–1989*. Raleigh: Division of Archives and History, 1992.

Powell, William S. *The First State University: A Pictorial History of the University of North Carolina*. 3d ed. Chapel Hill: University of North Carolina Press, 1992.

Romine, Dannye. *Mecklenburg: A Bicentennial Story*. Charlotte: Independence Square Associates, 1975.

Timblin, Carol L. *Central Piedmont Community College: The First Thirty Years*. Charlotte: CPCC Foundation, 1995.

Index

A. Sue Kerley Professor of Nursing, 259
Abernathy, George, 28
Abernathy, George R., Jr., 65, 88
Abig, Jeremy, 277
Academies, 235
Accounting competitions, 188, 307, 313
Accounting Department, 128, 276–277
Adair, Mary Jarrett, 140
Adderholt-Elliott, Miriam, 314
African American and African Studies Department, 117, 213
African American community, university relations with, 177
African American faculty, 251–252
African American students
 Carver College for, 31, 38, 45, 50, 57–58
 separate but equal doctrine and, 31
 at UNC Charlotte, 116–118, 127, 182–184, 216, 246, 252, 315
Aiken, Kimberly, 307–308
Air Force ROTC, 186
Aitken, G. Douglas, 46, 57
Alander, Bob, 157
Alan Kulwicki Memorial Scholarship, 311
Albright, Robert, 179, 181–182, 214, 251
Alridge, Ron, 220
Alexander, Hezekiah, 4
Alex Hemby Foundation, 256
All-Americans, 334
Allstate Insurance, 123
Almeida, Silverio, 319
Alumni
 achievements of, 220, 253–254, 308–309
 giving by, 211–212
 publications for, 215

Alumni Association, 130, 163, 219–220, 257, 276, 287
 past presidents of, 332
Alumni Association Faculty Service Award, 332
Alumni by Choice Award, 333
Alumni Hall of Fame, 333
Amacher, Ryan, 242–243
American Association of Junior Colleges, 30, 34
American Association of State Colleges and Universities, 169, 222–223, 263
American Council on Education, 169
American Credit Foundation, 97
Anderson, D. B., 109
Anderson, Eric, 292, 314, 319
Anderson, Robert, 109, 163, 233
Angel, Ken, 155
Antonelli, George, 113–114
Appalachian State College/University, 44, 121, 131
Appleton, Clyde, 194
Archie, William C., 69
Army ROTC, 186
Arnold, Harry H., 251, 255, 256, 292, 310
Arrington, Ted, 142, 216–217, 263, 288, 305, 314, 319
Art department, 110
Arthur Andersen Tax Challenge, 313
Athletics. *See also specific sports*
 at Charlotte Center, 26–28, 112
 at UNC Charlotte
  in Colvard era, 112–114, 152–161
  facilities for, 284–287
  in Fretwell era, 212, 217–219, 232–233, 236

Athletics
  at UNC Charlotte *(cont'd)*
    future of, 326–327
    in Woodward era, 252–253, 277, 284–287, 300–301, 314–315
Atkins, J. Murrey, 10–11, 28–29, 33, 35, 45, 48, 49, 54, 56–57, 67
Atkins, J. Murrey, Jr., 10
Atkins, Judith, 10
Atkins, Judith Woods, 10
Atkins, Katharine, 10
Atkins Library, 174
  in Colvard era, 52, 99–100, 152
  Dalton Special Collections Room of, 193–194
  Dalton Tower of, 118–119, 132, 194
  in Fretwell era, 174, 180, 193
  funding for, 174
  online services at, 152, 180
  in Woodward era, 299–301
Atlas of Disease and Health Care in the United States (Pyle), 280
Aulette, Judy, 305
Auto racing, 311
Avery, Waightstill, 4
Azevedo, Mario, 259

Babb, James G., 18, 220, 255
Baber, Brycie, 57
Backman, Earl, 144–145, 162
Bailey, Mary Dawn, 231
Bailey Professorship of History, 258, 277
Ball, Bob, 155
Ballard, Garry, 220, 288
Barden, Larry, 162
Barkley, Brock, 31
Barnard, Bascomb Weaver, 56, 97
Barnard Building, 51, 52
Barnes, Frank, 296
Barnett, Ross, 92
Barnette, Newton H., 102, 108, 111, 129, 163
Barnhardt, William H., 57
Barnhardt, William M., 165, 255, 312
Barnhardt Student Activity Center, 284–287, 301
Baseball, at Charlotte Center, 27–28
Basinger, Ben, 113
Basketball
  at Charlotte Center, 27–28, 112
  at Charlotte College, 112
  at UNC Charlotte, 156–158
    arena for, 284–286
    in Colvard era, 112, 152–161

  in Fretwell era, 178, 212, 217–219, 232–233, 236
  national exposure from, 157–158, 160
  in Woodward era, 284–285, 314
Batchelor, Kenneth, 67, 80, 81, 107
Batte, P. H., 29
Baucom, Gary, 128, 130, 276
Baucom, Kathi, 310
Baxter, Herbert, 29
Beane, Marian, 144, 182
Beasley, Jack, 213, 277–278
Beatty, Roy, 154
Beaty, E. A., 48, 58, 67
Becht, Sue, 253, 307
Beggs, Joyce, 307
Belk, Carol, 300–301
Belk, Henry, Jr., 29
Belk, Irwin, 76–77, 78, 89, 138, 300–301
Belk, John M., 57, 293
Belk, Thomas M., 20, 43, 48, 52, 56, 67, 139, 140, 185–186, 211, 231, 246, 255
Belk, William Henry, 98, 246
Belk Bell Tower, 52, 97–99
Belk College of Business Administration. *See* College of Business Administration
Belk gymnasium, 118
Belk Track and Field Center, 301
Bell, Carlos, 259
Bell, Wyatt, 18
Belmont Abbey College, 106
Ben Craig Center, 206, 236
Benson, Jon, 206
Berea College, 89, 90–91
Bernard, Charles, 11–13, 15, 21, 25, 26
Berne, Linda, 319
Betts, Jack, 303–304
Bibbs, Mark, 284
Biddy, F. Douglas, 140
Billups, Bill, 124
Bish, Doug, 213, 278, 319
Bishop, Sue, 278
Bissell, H. C., 255
Bissell, Sara, 245
Bizzell, Craig, 232
Black, James, 272, 285, 300
Blackmun, Robert, 180
Blacks. *See under* African American
Blackwell, Carol, 28
Blockbuster Amphitheater, 296–297
Bloody Friday, 178
Blue, Robert Earl, III, 153
Bluford, William, 140
Blumenthal, I. D., 306

Index | 341

Blythe, LeGette, 49
Board of Governors, of UNC, 136, 138–140, 216, 276
Board of Trustees
　of Charlotte College, 48, 63–64, 67, 139
　of UNC, 62, 70–76, 94, 135
　of UNC Charlotte. *See* University of North Carolina at Charlotte, Board of Trustees
Board of Visitors, 232
Bobbio, Stephen, 304–305
Bogue, Jesse P., 29, 34–35
Boney, Leslie, 101, 119
Bonnie E. Cone Distinguished Professorships for Teaching, 17, 303–304
Bonnie E. Cone University Center, 52, 96, 146
Bonnie's Boys, 17–18
Bookout, Joe, 35
Bostian, Carey, 41
Bowen, Les, 254
Bowers, Dick, 160
Bowles, Joe, 154
Boyd, Ty, 166
Boykin, Joseph, 102, 132, 152
Boyles, Harlan, 287
Brabham, Robin, 193
Bradbury, Tom, 94
Bradford, Isabell, 22
Brafford, Melissa, 308
Branch Davidians, 282, 314
Brandon, William, 259, 319
Brenner, Saul, 305, 319
Brevard College, 91
Britt, William M., 107, 179, 200, 211, 230
Broadrick, George, 79–80, 125
Brocker, Edith, 102, 109, 144, 212
Brookshire, Stan, 95
Brown, Banita White, 252, 304
Brown, Cheryl, 319
Brown, Edward H., 31
Brown, Roger, 263
Brownell, Blaine A., 317–318
Brown v. Board of Education, 31
Brubaker, Harold, 300
Bruton, Wade, 248
Bryant, Victor, 134
Bubas, Vic, 160
Buffett, Jimmy, 143
Bufman, Zev, 297
Bullock, Terre Thomas, 186
Burgess, Jimmy, 23
Burgess, Nancy, 23

Burgess, O. Ned, Jr., 22–23
Burson, Sherman, 65, 102, 117, 149, 168, 178, 189, 213
Bush, Fowler, 113
Bush, George, 254
Butterfield, Richard B., 140
Butz, Earl, 143
Byers, J. W., 11
Byrum, Donald, 213

Caddell, Elinor Brooks, 259
Caldwell, Henry, 155
Caldwell, Jesse B., 67
Caldwell, Ron, 118, 253
Cameron, C. C. (Cliff), 138, 139, 140, 163–164, 167, 168, 177, 200, 211, 231, 255, 276
Cameron Applied Research Center, 228, 237, 258, 278–279
Cameron Scholarship, 261
Campaign for Excellence, 211–212
Campbell University, 177
Campus Academic Plan, 321
Campus Master Plan, 321
Cannon, Alf, 166
Cannon, James G., 56
Cannon Foundation, 285–287
Carley, David, 203–204, 207
Carley, James, 203–204
Carlisle School, 20
Carlyle, Irving, 62
Carlyle Commission, 61, 62, 64, 130
Carolinas Issues Academy, 264
Carolina Panthers, 141, 210
Carolinas Medical Center, 70, 201
Carper, Barbara, 278
Carrubba, Robert, 229, 230, 276, 279
Cartographic competitions, 307, 313
Carver, Ann, 213
Carver College, 31, 33, 38, 45, 50, 57. *See also* Mecklenburg College
　merger of with Central Industrial Education Center, 57–58
Case, Everett, 152
Cathey, C. O., 100
Caudill, Rowlett and Scott, 147
C. C. Cameron Scholarship Fund, 261
CCUNC (Charlotte Center), 30
Celanese Professorship, 259
Center for Banking Studies, 279
Center for Professional and Applied Ethics, 312
Central Industrial Education Center, Carver College merger with, 57–58

Central Piedmont Community College, 31, 58, 59, 63, 74, 111, 121, 228, 327
Cernyak-Spatz, Susan, 277
Chapman, Gail, 276
Charles Cullen Professorship of Marketing, 259
Charles H. Stone Professorship in American History, 259
Charlotte
  assets of, 319–320
  as financial center, 128, 198, 320
  growth and development of, 3, 209–210, 264–265, 319–320
    patterns of, 198–199, 264–265
    University City and, 197–207
  historic preservation in, 162
  Hurricane Hugo and, 247–248
  lack of educational opportunities in, 8–9, 35–39, 74–75
  medical school for, 70
  political climate in, 3
  in postwar era, 2, 6–8
  in Revolutionary War, 4
  UNC Charlotte involvement in, 3, 141–142, 161–163, 177–178, 181, 237, 264–265, 280
Charlotte: An Analytical Atlas of Patterns and Trends (Clay & Stuart), 281
Charlotte Area Educational Consortium, 126, 148
Charlotte Center, 9–13, 15–31, 26
  academic quality of, 24
  administration of, 15, 21
  Advisory Committee of, 28–29
  athletics at, 26–28, 112
  becomes Charlotte College, 29–31
  birth of, 9–13
  Charlotte Central High School and, 24–25
  Charlotte City Schools and, 30–31
  faculty of, 16, 21–22, 26
  first year of, 21–25
  funding for, 29–30
  known as CCUNC, 30
  opening of, 15, 21–22
  second year of, 25–31
  social life at, 24
  student government at, 23–24
  summer school at, 30
  UNC-Chapel Hill and, 26, 27, 30
Charlotte Central High School
  Charlotte Center at, 24–25
  Charlotte College at, 33–45, 48
Charlotte Chamber of Commerce, 53, 80, 300

Charlotte College and, 38–39, 48
University Research Park and, 122
Charlotte City Schools
  administration of Carver College by, 31
  administration of Charlotte Center by, 30–31
Charlotte Clippers, 6–7, 27
Charlotte College, 33–59
  accreditation of, 34–35, 48
  administration of, 49, 51–52, 58, 65, 75
  assets of, 75
  birth of, 33–35
  Board of Trustees of, 48, 67, 139
    resolution for university status, 63–64
  campus of
    architecture of, 51–52, 66
    building program at, 51–52, 54–55, 57, 58, 67
    growth of, 67, 69
    site selection for, 45–47
  at Charlotte Central High School, 24, 33–45
  community support for, 44
  curriculum at, 52, 66
  enrollment at, 44, 52, 53, 58, 65
  executive board of, 35
  faculty of, 49–50, 65–66, 75
  foundation for, 56–57, 75
  4-year status for
    achievement of, 61–83
    campaign for, 37, 39, 41, 42, 53–54, 58–59
    Carlyle Commission and, 62–63, 64
  funding for, 35–45, 48, 49, 50
  growth of, 44–45, 58–59
  mission statement of, 50, 64–65
  North Carolina State engineering division at, 56
  transition of to UNC Charlotte, 81–83
  university status for
    achievement of, 76–83
    campaign for, 67–76
    King report on, 70–76
    legislative approval for, 76–80
    State Board of Higher Education approval for, 76
    UNC Board of Trustees approval for, 76
  W. A. Kennedy and, 33, 35–47
Charlotte College Center. *See* Charlotte Center
Charlotte College Foundation, 56–57, 75
Charlotte Community College System, 33, 63
Charlotte/Douglas International Airport, 210

Index

Charlotte Engineers Club, 56
Charlotte Female Academy, 5
Charlotte Hornets (baseball), 6
Charlotte Hornets (basketball), 141, 210
Charlotte Male Academy, 5
Charlotte-Mecklenburg School System, 202
Charlotte Motor Speedway, 311
Charlotte Observer, 73, 74, 77, 94, 236, 268, 313
Chase, John B., Jr., 108–109, 163
Chavis, Ben, 116–118, 220
Chemistry Department, building for, 212
Chen, Ken, 280–281
Cheng Liu, 173
Cherry, R. Gregg, 9
Chi Phi, 129
Christie, Charles, 277
Ciochon, Russell, 173
CityFair, 204
    off-campus center at, 53, 151–152, 296–298
Civil rights movement, 116–118
Claiborne, Jack, 7, 53
Clark, James H., 67
Clarke, Harold, 179–180, 278
Clary, Ellison, 220
Clay, James W., 141, 142, 144, 174, 181, 230, 253, 264, 265, 275, 281, 307
    University Place and, 200, 203, 204, 207
Clemson University, 154–155
Clendenin, John, 279
Close, Derick, 276
Cockshutt, Rod, 142
Coggins, Danny, 112
Cohen, Richard A., 260
Coker College, 17, 20–21
Coleman, Robert, 190, 281
College of Architecture, 108, 109, 151, 161, 187, 216, 227–228
College of Arts and Sciences, 178, 189
College of Business Administration, 108, 110–111, 161, 185–186, 212, 216, 278, 279, 289–290, 307
    master of management degree of, 110–111
    M.B.A. program of, 212, 278
College of Education, 108–109, 110, 186, 216, 279
College of Engineering, 108, 110, 128, 151, 178, 186, 216, 228–229, 281, 307, 311
    doctoral program of, 228–229
    naming of, 307
College of Human Development and Learning, 110
College of Humanities, 109, 178

College of Nursing, 102, 108, 109, 144, 146, 151, 161, 174, 186, 212–213, 216, 278
College of Science and Mathematics, 109, 178, 319
College of Social and Behavioral Sciences, 109, 178
College(s) of UNC Charlotte
    establishment of, 108
    restructuring of, 178
Collins & Aikins, 123
Collyar, Carol, 171
Coltrane, David S., 39, 42, 43
Columbia Scholastic Press Association Golden Crown Award, 313
Colvard, Dean Wallace, 72, 85, 88, 90, 149, 170, 194, 249, 318
    administrative experience of, 91–93
    education of, 89–91
    family and childhood of, 90
    illness of, 115–116
    at Mississippi State, 91–92, 93, 96
    at N.C. State, 91, 93
    receives honorary degree, 175
    at UNC Charlotte
        administration of
            from 1965–1970, 95–133
            from 1970–1978, 133–166
        as athletic booster, 152–161
        builds faculty and staff of, 100–103, 107–108, 114–115
        goals of, 107
        legacy of, 165–166
        management techniques of, 144, 145–146
        receives Hugh McEniry award, 148
        retirement of, 164–166
        selection of as chancellor, 92–93
    University City and, 200
    University Research Park and, 122–124
    Urban Institute and, 129
Colvard, Martha, 91, 93, 115–116, 165, 175, 194
Colvard, Mary Elizabeth Shepherd, 90
Colvard Building, 52
Colvard Scholarships for Merit, 165
Combs, Cynthia, 306–307, 318
Communications major, 310
Community College Act of 1957, 48
Community colleges, 10, 33, 63. *See also specific colleges*
    UNC Charlotte and, 111
Conant, James B., 169
Cone, Addie Lavinia Harter, 20
Cone, Bonnie E., 7, 12, 15, 16, 33, 53, 54, 82,

Cone, Bonnie E., *(cont'd)*
   115–116, 178, 218, 227, 231, 244, 249, 250,
     258, 272, 273, 318, 328
  attends American Association of Junior
    Colleges meeting, 34
  Bonnie's Boys and, 17–18
  on Carlyle Commission, 62, 63
  at Charlotte Center, 16–31
    as director, 25–31
    as teacher, 15–16, 21–22
  at Charlotte College, 34, 35, 38, 47–48
    as administrator, 49, 51–52, 58, 65
    as president, 58, 66, 72
    as teacher, 49
  education of, 17, 20–21
  family and childhood of, 16–17, 20
  as founder of UNC Charlotte, 61
  influence of, 17–19
  as lobbyist for UNC Charlotte, 78–79
  personality and demeanor of, 17, 20
  receives honorary degree, 175
  receives Hugh McEniry award, 148
  receives UNC Charlotte Distinguished
    Service Award, 19
  as teacher, 16–19, 21–22
  at UNC Charlotte
    as Acting Chancellor, 77, 83, 86
    as administrator, 85, 87, 89, 93–95, 111,
      115, 117
    as liaison officer, 146
    retirement of, 146
    as vice chancellor, 94–95, 107, 108
  work ethic of, 66, 115
Cone, Charles Jefferson, 20
Cone Center, 52, 96, 97, 146
Cone Distinguished Professorships of
  Teaching, 17, 303–304
Conference USA, 315, 326–327
Connaughton, John, 212, 314, 318
Conroy, Pat, 254
Consolidated University of North Carolina,
  10, 62, 134, 135
Co-op program, 235–236, 254
Corwin, Mike, 288
Council on General Education, 216
Counts, Stephanie, 117, 310
Covington, Howard, 211
Craig, Ben, 206
Cramer, J. Scott, 57
Crawford, Jim, 236
Creative arts departments, 110, 213
Creemers, Harry, 211, 255
Criminal justice program, 111, 183, 318
Crisp, M. Douglas, 255

Crosby, Kathleen, 177
Crosland, John, 204–205, 294–295
Crowe, Earl, 28
Crowell, Frank H., 139, 140
Crutchfield, Ed, 7, 119, 246, 248, 255, 315,
  316
Cullen, Charles, 259
Cullen, Sarah, 259
Cullen Professorship of Marketing, 259
Cummings, Humphrey, 118

Daggy, Tom, 162, 192
Dale F. Halton Arena, 285, 301
Dalton, Harry, 95, 193–194
Dalton, Mary, 193, 194
Dalton Special Collections Room, 193–194
Dalton Tower, 118–119, 132, 138, 194
Davenport, Mildred, 258
Davenport, Sanford V., 258
Davidson College, 5, 22, 27, 28, 36, 74, 99,
  122–123, 126, 162, 175, 176, 191–192
Davie, William Richardson, 4
Davis, Boyd, 319
Davis, Kit Ward, 163, 176
Davis, Walter, 155
Davis, William A., Jr., 143
Day, Norris, 153
Dean, Charles, 318
Delaney, John H., 67
Demmitt, Tim, 287, 301
Demonstrations
  faculty, 194–195
  student, 116, 127
Denny, Mary, 12, 15, 21, 25, 26, 49, 53, 111
Denny Building, 51, 52, 97
Departments. *See under specific academic*
  discipline
Deremer, Arthur, 27
Desegregation
  at Mississippi State University, 92
  of Quail Hollow Country Club, 246
  at University of North Carolina, 182–184
Diamant, Louis, 102, 277
Dickerson, Norvin Kennedy, 139, 140, 231,
  257
Dickerson Distinguished Professor of
  Precision Engineering, 257
Dickey, Frank Graves, 149–150, 155
Dickey, James, 89
Dickson, R. Stuart, 201, 249, 255
Dickson Foundation, 97
Dickson Professor of Finance, 259
Disher, Bill, 17–18
Distance learning, 281

Distinguished professorships, 255, 257–261.
    See also specific professorships
Distinguished Service Award, 231–232, 330
Division of Academic Affairs, 179–180
Division of Research and Public Service, 180–181
Dixon, James E., III, 251
Dobson, Rick, 153
Doctoral programs
    at regional universities, 132
    at UNC Charlotte, 132, 228–229, 235, 267–273, 279, 312, 324
Dole, Robert, 143
Domoto, Maria, 281
Dorin, Dennis, 319
Dormitories. *See* Residence halls
Dorton, J. S., 140
Doss, Henry, 288
Dubois, Lisa, 262
Dubois, Philip L., 262–263, 272, 279, 303, 323
Dubois, Thomas, 318
Duke, James B., 37
Duke Power Company, 88, 307
Duke University, 18, 25, 47, 61
Duncan, Edwin, Sr., 139
Durden, Hugh M., 255

Earnhardt, Dale, 311
Earnhardt, Kelley, 311
East Carolina College/University, 44, 131, 145, 155
Ecumenical ministry, 130
Edelman, Irving, 112
Eisenhower, Dwight D., 68, 169
Elizabeth City State College/University, 44, 121, 132, 137
Elizabeth College, 5
Ellis, Seth, 65, 109–110
Ells, Leo, 179, 200–201, 236
Emergency college system, 9–10
Employee of the Year Award, 232, 335
Engelhardt, Leggett, and Cornell, 51, 52
Engineering technology program, 111
English, Mildred, 35, 102, 113
English Language Training Institute, 234–235
Enhanced Mission for UNC Charlotte: A Regional Imperative, 270
Ervin, Sam, Jr., 150
Escott, Paul, 173, 213, 229, 230, 280
Espin, Kathy, 220
Evening Program Information Center, 174
Evening programs, 174

Everett, George, 29
Evett, Jack, 173

Faculty Associates Program, 188
Faculty Athletic Committee, 277
Faircloth, Kathleen, 213–214, 251
Fayetteville State College/University, 9, 44, 132
Feldman, Michael, 305, 318–319
Fennebresque, John C., 255
Ferguson, Larry, 308–309
Ferraro, Gary, 173, 185
Ficklen, Mrs. J. B., 29
Fincannon, Craig, 220
First Citizens Bank Scholars Medal, 229, 230, 332
First Data Corporation, 308–309
First Union Bank, 163, 164, 315–316
Fishman, Steve, 306
Flack, Charles, 284
Fleming, R. W., 270
Foos, Paul, 278, 304
Football
    at Charlotte Center, 27–28
    at UNC Charlotte, 112, 178, 301
Foreign students, 182
49ers. *See* Athletics
Foscue, Henry, 89
Foster, Bill, 152–153, 161
Foster, Hulene Hill, 253, 276
Foulkes, Fred, 147
Fowler, Henry, 285
Fowler, Newton O., 255
Fox, Eugenia, 21
Fraley, John L. (Buck), 19, 67, 68, 140, 177, 232
Fraley, John L., Jr., 19, 140, 186, 187, 211, 231
Francis, Norman C., 270
Frank, Elizabeth, 311
Frankle, Raymond, 180, 279
Franklin, Billy J., 270
Frank Porter Graham Professorship of African American and African Studies, 99, 259
Fraternities, 129
Freshwater Fishes of North Carolina (Menhinick), 305–306
Fretwell, Dorrie, 170
Fretwell, E. K., Jr., 10, 155, 167–239, 215, 216, 218, 222, 230, 232, 236, 249, 272, 273, 318, 320
    achievements of, 235–239
    administration of, 167–239
    background and experience of, 168–170

Fretwell, E. K., Jr., *(cont'd)*
   desegregation order and, 183–184
   elected chancellor, 168
   goals of, 171–172, 238
   installation of, 172–173
   management style of, 237–238
   mirror test and, 188, 229
   national reputation of, 221, 223
   oversees restructuring, 178–182, 230
   personal characteristics of, 170–171
   post-UNC Charlotte career of, 238–239
   retirement of, 234
   Rocky River canoe trip and, 191–192
   staff appointments of, 178–182
   University City and, 197–207
Fretwell, E. K., Sr., 10, 170
Fretwell Building, 239, 290, 291
Friday, Paul C., 278, 314, 318
Friday, William C., 10, 33, 62, 64, 131, 137, 172, 234, 249, 255, 307
   achievements of, 225
   background of, 68
   as president of UNC, 138, 149, 172, 183
   receives Hugh McEniry award, 148
   retirement of, 223, 225
   seeks Colvard as chancellor, 85, 86, 91–93
   supports UNC Charlotte, 68–70, 78, 101–102, 119–120
   UNC restructuring and, 135–137
Friday Business Administration Building, 193, 289–291
Fulbright Fellowships, 185
Fuller, Buckminster, 87
Furuseth, Owen, 319

G. Theodore Mitau Award for Innovation and Change in State Colleges and Universities, 222–223
Gabbacia, Donna, 259
Gabriel, Karl M., 309
Gaffney High School, 17
Gaines, Bighouse, 252
Gallis, Michael, 264, 292, 314
Galvin, Hoyt, 42, 46, 47
Gardens and landscaping, 103–105, 106
Gardner, Max O., 83
Garibaldi, Linn D., 48, 67
Garinger, Elmer H., 10–13, 15, 17, 25, 28, 29, 31, 37, 49, 170
Garinger High School, 48
Gaston Community College, 75, 111
Gatewood, Maud, 86
Gatlin, Leon, 306, 318
Gentry, Roland, 139

Geography Department, 141–142, 181
The Geography of AIDS (Pyle), 280
Georgius, John R., 255
GI Bill, 7–8
Gibson, Robert, 100, 309
Giglieri, Lorenzo, 232
Gilchrist, C. W., 57
Giles, Ed C., 49
Gillett, Rupert, 49
Gilmour, Monroe, 95
Glenn, James H., 29, 35
Godfrey, Howard, 307, 318
Goins, Tom, 284, 285
Golden, Harry, 50, 127, 193
Golden Crown Award, 313
Goldfield, David, 113, 213, 258, 277, 280, 314, 317, 319
Goldwater, Barry, 127
Goode, Rusty, 122, 123, 255
Goodknight, Barbara, 179, 180, 182, 279
Goodrum, Cloyd S., Jr., 309
Goolkasian, Paula, 292
Gordemer, Barry, 176
Gordon, Jeff, 311
Govan, Sandra, 252
Governor's Commission on Veterans Education, 9
Governor's Commission on Education Beyond High School. *See* Carlyle Commission
Graduate programs, 128
   in Colvard era, 128, 136, 141, 146, 148
   in Fretwell era, 174, 189, 228–229, 235
   future directions for, 324
   in Woodward era, 267–273, 279, 310–312, 324
Graham, Frank Porter, 33, 36–37, 127, 134
Graham, Johnny, 229
Graham, Billy, 7
Graham Professorship of African American and African Studies, 99, 259
Grant, Daniel R., 87
Gray, Carroll, 300, 321
Gray, Gordon, 68, 93
Gray, Robert Waters, 174
Great Decisions Program, 162
Green, Ron, 160, 218
Gregory, Dick, 143
Grey, Lucinda, 305
Griffin, C. Frank, 67
Griffith, Brodie, 82
Griffith, Derrick, 284–285
Grogan, Robert, 102
Gross, Jim, 296

Gruber, Jeff, 155
Grumman, Russell M., 9
Gwaltney, Bob, 156

Haber, Carole, 213, 305, 319
Hackney, Ben, 111, 113, 309
Hahn Corporation, 293
Hair, Liz, 177
Hall, Dennis, 287
Hall, John O. P., 88
Halton, Dale F., 231, 285
Halton Arena, 285, 301
Hamman, Beth, 285
Hardison, James A., Jr., 139, 140
Harper, Mary, 277
Harrelson, J. W., 38, 43
Harris, Cameron M., 19, 231, 255, 257, 310
Harris, Dorothy (Dee-Dee), 310
Harris, James J., 19, 29, 57
Harris, Ken, 18
Harris, W. T., 123, 125
Hartgen, David, 314, 319
Hatfield, Mark, 150
Hatley, Donald F., 255, 307
Hauersperger, Dick, 125, 165
Haus, Loren, 124
Hayes, Mariam Cannon, 285–287
Hayes, Robert, 285–287
Heald, James E., 114
Healey, John, 319
Health administration, master's degree in, 311–312
Heath, Jon, 153
Heath, Kingston, 318
Heaton, George, 35
Hechenbleikner, Herbert, 21, 22, 47–48, 103–106, 253
Heller, H. William, 163, 235, 278
Hemby Distinguished Professorship in Banking, 256
Hemby Foundation, 256
Henderson, D. E., 29
Henry, Lucy, 235, 214
Hensley, Robert, 254
Highsmith, J. Henry, 30, 34, 35
Hight, Charles, 163, 321
Hildreth, Philip, 109, 149, 178, 259
Hill, Hulene, 253, 276
Hillman, James E., 9, 25, 30, 34
Hirschel, David, 174
History Department, 213
Hjellming, Lisa-Noelle, 252, 304
Hobson, George, 43
Hocken, Robert, 257–258, 319

Hodges, Luther, 33, 41, 43
Holland, William R., 249
Holshouser, James, 142
Holt, Thomas, 99
Homesley, Fariba G., 254
Honorary degrees, 127, 150, 163, 330
Hoppa, Jim, 288
Hopper, Ed, 96, 331
Hostetter, John, 127
How to Get an Ivy League Education at a State University (Nemko), 223, 312–313
Hoyle, Frances, 21
Hoyle, Hughes, Jr., 49
Hubbard, Phil, 158
Hudson, Jerry, 187
Hudson, Richard, 285
Hugh McEniry Award, 148
Hull, Raymond, 143
Hunt, Earl G., Jr., 82
Hunt, James B., Jr., 91, 144, 171, 257, 306
Huntley, Ben, 46, 47
Hurley, Lane, 112
Hurricane Hugo, 247–248
Huskey, Sybil, 213, 278
Hutchison, Frank, 95–96
Hutchison, Glenn, 308

IBM, 189, 197, 297
Ida and William Friday Business Administration Building, 193, 289–291
Inaba, Jean, 176
Ingalls, Gerald, 174
Institute for Urban Studies and Community Service. *See* Urban Institute
Institute of Government (UNC Chapel Hill), 150
International Festival, 144–145
International students, 182
Internships, student, 235–236, 254
Iranian students, 182
Irwin, Robert, 4
Irwin Belk Track and Field Center, 301
Ives, Sallie, 306

Jackson, Dot, 143
James, Sandra, 309
James H. Barnhardt Student Activity Center, 301
Jamgotch, Nish, 309
Jamieson, Nordica Adelaide, 231
Jam-Up, 187
Jenkins, Jay, 225
Jenkins, Leo, 61, 145
Jernigan, Marinell, 144, 163, 212

J. N. Pease Associates, 123
Johnson, Amos N., 139
Johnson, Cecil, 30
Johnson, Gene, 231, 254
Johnson, Phillip, 185
Johnson C. Smith University, 5, 74, 140, 182
Johnson, Vicky, 231
Jones, Arthur H., 48, 53
Jones, Bob, 70–71
Jones, Edwin, 165, 255
Jones, J. A, 43
Jordan, B. Everett, 97
Jordan, Bryce, 270
Jordan, Robert, 249
Josephson, Harold, 213, 279, 319
Joyner, Felix, 120, 147

Kahn, Herman, 87
Kaplan, Sis, 154
Kaplan, Stan, 154
Kappa Alpha Psi, 129
Kappa Sigma, 129
Kay, Dennis, 260, 319
Keast, William, 147
Keen, Sam, 150
Keith, Graeme, 296
Keith, Greg, 296
Keith, Larry, 154
Kelner, Toni L., 310
Kennedy, W. A. (Woody), 36, 327
    Charlotte College and, 53
      in fundraising, 33, 35–45
      in site selection, 45–47
    death of, 55
Kennedy Building, 52, 55, 118, 212
Kerr, Clark, 319–320
Kilgo, Jimmy, 19
Kilgo, John, 19, 154
Kimbrell, W. Duke, 249, 255
Kinch, Chad, 158–159
King, Arnold K., 70–76, 81, 86, 89, 96
King, Kevin, 155
King, Laura, 171
King, Margaret, 140, 310
King Building, 51, 52, 70, 96
King report, 70–76
Kissinger, Henry, 87, 127
Kizer, R. Edward, 272, 276, 284, 288, 299, 311
Knight Distinguished Professorship of
    Public Policy, 259
Kodak, 228
Koresh, David, 282
Kovach, Sally, 213, 278
Kuester, Clarence O., 6, 29

Kuhn, Maggie, 87
Kulwicki Memorial Scholarship, 311
Kuppers, James, 65, 213
Kuralt, Charles, 7, 87, 143

Lacher, Joseph P., 255
Lake View High School, 17
Lamal, Peter, 309
Land of the South, 275
Langdale, Noah, 87, 88
Langston, Nancy, 213, 256, 276, 278
Lassiter, Robert, 56, 200
Lawrimore, Earl (Buck), 175
Law school, request for, 177
Leamy, Harry, 279
Leath, Thomas H., 89, 139, 140
Leavelle, James R., 255
Lee, Bill, 307, 315
Lee College of Engineering, 307
Leggett, Stanton, 46
Leiby, Mr. and Mrs. George, 191
Leiva, Miriam, 303, 304, 319
Lesley, Barry, 214
Levy, Janet, 280, 314, 319
Lewis, John D., 255
Liberal studies, master's degree in, 310–311
Liberty Hall Academy, 4
Library. *See* Atkins Library
Lightfoot, Gordon, 143
Limestone College, 21
Lincourt, John, 256, 280, 304, 312, 319
Link, William A., 131, 137
Little, Lee & Associates, 98
Littlejohn, David, 35, 49
Lockhart, Thomas, 99
Lord, Dennis, 202, 319
Lowery, Bobby G., 310
Lucas, John Paul, 35, 48, 57, 58, 67, 82, 123
Lumb, Richard, 318
Lunsford, Ronald, 254, 278
Lupo, W. S., 45
Lynch, Charles F. (Chuck), 163, 181, 213, 214
Lyons, James, 235, 312
Lyons, Schley, 142, 189, 262–263, 288, 314

Mabry, Earleen, 124, 127
MacFayden, Alex, 79
MacKay, Donald, 102
MacKillop, Rod, 319
Macy, Pierre, 54
Macy Building, 51, 52, 55
Mahaley, Steve, 18
Maikranz, Wayne, 214
Maisto, Al, 304, 308

Index | 349

Mallard Creek Elementary School, 202
Manning, Norm, 172
Martin, Hoyle, 143
Martin, James G., 124, 194, 227, 228, 232, 276, 279, 285
Martin, Joe, 194–195
Martin, Steve, 143
Marvin, Helen Rhyne, 276
Mary Reynolds Babcock Foundation, 114
Mason, Julian, 100, 144, 194, 233
Massey, Lew, 155
Master's degree programs
  at regional universities, 132
  at UNC Charlotte
    in Colvard era, 128, 141, 146, 148
    in Fretwell era, 174, 189, 235, 239
    future of, 324
    in Woodward era, 310–312
Mathematics Department, 109, 178, 319
Mathis, William S., 109, 110, 233
Matthews, Jim, 113, 162, 191, 253
Maxwell, Bertha, 99
Maxwell, Cedric, 155, 156, 157, 158, 159, 160
Maxwell-Roddy, Bertha, 259
Maynard, Reid, 94
Mayo, Pauline, 212–213, 309
Mazze, Edward M., 279, 289
McAffee, Larry, 220
McArthur, John, 276
McCanless, R. William, 254
McCartey, G. S., 40
McCarthy, Belinda, 173
McColl, Hugh, 7, 246, 248–249, 255, 301, 323–324, 325
McColl High School, 17
McCoy, S. J., 65
McCoy, William J., 161, 231, 236, 263, 264, 275, 279, 288, 314
McCraw, Carl G., 57
McDuffie, Jim, 154
McEniry, Hugh, 100–101, 107, 126, 148
McEniry, Mary, 148
McEniry Award, 148
McGovern, George, 143
McGuire, Al, 159
McIntosh, C. E., 10, 11, 13, 26, 27–27, 30
McIntyre, William E., 125, 165
McKay, Mike, 220
McKinney, Bones, 153
McKnight, C. A. (Pete), 21, 55, 58, 64, 67, 89, 160
McKnight, Thomas, 89
McLendon, L. P., 53
McLeod, Johnnie H., 253
McLeod, Leslie, 253
McMahan, Ed, 300
McMillan, Alex, 7
McMillan, Dorothy Schoenith, 104
McMillan, R. D., 80, 225
McMillan, Thomas, 104
McMillan Greenhouse, 104
McNair, Ronald, 252
McRae, John A., 48, 55
Mead, James M., 220
Mead, Tim, 185
Mecklenburg College, 31
Mecklenburg County. *See also* Charlotte
  growth of, 3
  political isolation of, 3
Medical school, for Charlotte, 70
Mellichamp, Larry, 106, 162
Melvin, Martha, 248
Menhinick, Edward, 305–306
Meredith College, 47
Merritt, Kathy, 176
Metrolina Atlas, 141–142, 275
Meyer, Jeffrey, 278, 319
Michalewicz, Zbigniew, 319
Miller, Paul A., 114, 144, 149
Mills, William L., Jr., 18
Mitau Award for Innovation and Change in State Colleges and Universities, 222–223
Mitchell Community College, 111
Mobley, Charlotte, 29, 35
Model United Nations team, 188, 306–307, 313
Moelchert, Louis W., Jr., 143–144
Mohanty, Ganesh, 304
Molinaro, Leo, 87
Money, UNC Charlotte ranking in, 221–223
Monroe, Andy, 40
Moody, Carlton, 220, 254
Moody, David, 220, 254
Moody Brothers, 220, 254
Moore, Dan K., 78–79, 82–83, 94, 97, 101, 127
Morrill, Dan, 65, 127, 162, 319
Morrison, Cameron, 19, 29, 43
Morrocroft, 245
Moss, Anita, 252, 319
Mullins, Candy, 219
Mullins, Jeff, 218, 219, 232, 233, 252–253, 284, 287, 314
Mundt, Robert, 195, 216, 229, 263
Murphy, Harvey, 102, 112–113, 153

Nader, Ralph, 87
Nagle, John M., 279, 312
NASCAR, 311
National Association of State Universities and Land Grant Colleges, 264
National Student Exchange Program, 184
National Timber Bridge Design Competition, 313
NationsBank, 139, 163, 248, 249, 323
NationsBank Award for Excellence in Teaching, 139, 306, 331
Nattress, John A., 49
NCNB, 139, 163
Neel, Richard, 163, 278
Neill, Rolfe, 246, 255
Nemko, Martin, 223, 312
Newspaper
　alumni, 215
　student, 214
Nicollian, Ed, 258–259
NIT Tournament
　in 1975–1976 season, 156–158
Nixon, David, 65, 102, 180
Nixon, Richard M., 150
Nkomo, Mokubung, 252
Nkomo, Stella, 251–252, 319
North Carolina Agricultural and Technical College/University, 9, 131, 272
North Carolina Association of Colleges and Universities, 148
North Carolina Atlas (Clay, Orr & Stuart), 142, 275
North Carolina Board of Higher Education, 64, 69, 76, 134
North Carolina Central College/University, 132, 183
North Carolina College Centers. *See also* Charlotte Center
　closure of, 30–31
　establishment of, 9–10
　second-year status of, 29
North Carolina College Conference, 9, 12, 29, 30
North Carolina Medical College, 5
North Carolina School of the Arts, 132
North Carolina State College, in Consolidated University of North Carolina, 134
North Carolina State Legislature, 216–217
　appropriations for Charlotte College, 35–45, 48, 49, 50
　appropriations for UNC Charlotte
　　in Colvard era, 101–102, 118, 157–158
　　in Fretwell era, 174, 195, 209–210, 211, 216–217, 236
　　in Woodward era, 272–273, 288–289
　approves Charlotte branch, 76–80
　approves doctoral programs, 268–273
　confers 4-year status on Charlotte College, 37, 39, 41, 42, 53–54, 58–59, 61–83
North Carolina State University, 44, 47, 120, 211
　basketball at, 152
　birth of, 5
　Charlotte Division of, 56
　D. W. Colvard at, 91
　joint engineering doctoral program with, 228–229
　in NIT tournament, 156–157
　School of Design, 108
Norvin Kennedy Dickerson Jr. Distinguished Professor of Precision Engineering, 257
Nunnally, Nelson, 277
Nursing program, 102, 108, 109, 144, 146, 151, 161, 174, 186, 212–213, 216, 278

OASES, 174
Odell, Gouldie, 52
Odell and Associates, 51, 52, 57, 98, 103
Odom, Fountain, 300
Office of Public Information and Publications, 188
Ojaide, Tanure, 318
Oliver, James, 173, 318
Orr, Douglas M., Jr., 96, 107–108, 113, 141, 142–143, 144, 146, 149, 155, 160, 161, 165, 179
　achievements of, 275
　basketball and, 218–219
　Gallis slide show and, 265
　radio station and, 175
　resignation of, 275
　Silver Anniversary Campaign and, 255
　student activity center and, 284
　University City and, 197, 200, 203, 206, 207
　Venture program and, 191–192
　as vice chancellor of Division of Research and Public Service, 181, 183, 188, 230, 233
Osman, John, 88
Otts, John, 29
Outward Bound, 142–143
Overcash, Reece, 17, 18
Owen, Larry, 144
Owens, Ann, 254

Paksoy, Christie, 202
Palmer, Allan V., 108, 163, 277

Pate, Rudy, 115–116, 225
Pathways Program, 174
Patrons of Excellence, 96–97, 165
Patterson, K. David, 259, 279, 319
Patterson, Liz, 194
Patterson, Steven, 258, 319
Payne, Eugene, 73, 74
Peace College, 40
Pearce, Don, 155
Pearson, Mike, 288, 289, 290
Pembroke State College/University, 44, 121, 132
Pennell, Betty, 288
Pentes, Jack, 121
Perel, Bill, 65
Performing Arts Department, 213
Perot, H. Ross, 197, 256
Perreault, Quentin, 130
Perzel, Ed, 113, 127, 211
Ph.D. programs. *See* Doctoral programs
Phillips, Charles W., 11
Phillips, Dwight L., 57, 130
Physics Department, building for, 212
Piedmont Urban Conference, 88
Pierson, W. W., 51
Piscitelli, Susan, 163, 211
Pittman, Robert (Bo), 175
Plath, Anthony, 318
Plyler, Aaron, 272, 285, 300
Policy House, 259
Politics. *See also* North Carolina State Legislature
　state, 3
Pollak, Victor, 277
Popp, Karen, 177, 253
Potter, Robert D., 49, 242
Powers, Douglas, 259, 277
Pratt, Mike, 161, 217
Presbyterian College, 52
Presidential Young Investigator Award, 304
Pressly, William C., 40
Preyer, Richardson, 78, 127
Price, Reynolds, 140
Prince, Cecil, 48, 55, 94
Prince, Elizabeth, 94
Project Mosaic, 281–282
Prospector Cafeteria, 291–292
Provost, office of, 149
Psychology Department, 304
Publications, 188
　alumni, 215
　student, 214
Public relations, 188
Puette, Mrs. Ross (Lucille), 21, 49

Pullen, Stanhope, 5
Pully, Harold, 118
Purks, Harris, 41
Pyle, Gerald, 185, 280, 319

Quail Hollow Country Club, 246
Queens College (private), 5, 47, 74, 166, 248
　UNCC Charlotte off-campus center at, 151
Queens College (public), 4–5
Queen's Museum, 4
Quinn, Joseph, 319

Rabbi Isaac Swift Distinguished Professorship in Judaic Studies, 99, 259–260
Radio station (WFAE-FM), 175–177
Ramsey, Bob, 228
Ramsey, D. Hiden, 39
Ramsey, Dawn, 228
Ramsey, Liston, 216, 228
Rankin, Ed, 40, 101
Rash, Betty Chafin, 162, 288
Rash, Dennis, 157, 162
Rathbun, Bob, 154
Rauch, Marshall, 276, 285
Reddy, T. J., 118
Reese, Addison H., 48, 51, 54, 56, 57, 58, 67, 80, 82, 122, 127, 138, 139, 163
Reese Administration Building, 52, 163, 192–193
Reeves Brothers, 123
Regional universities, 131–132
Reichs, Kathleen, 318
Reid, Billy J., 49–50
Reimer, Bob, 113
Reiter, Harold, 305
Religious life, student, 129–130
Religious Studies Department, 246
Research and Public Service Division, 180–181
Research Triangle Park, 41, 122
Residence halls, 186–187
　air-conditioning for, 119
　co-educational, 119
　construction of, 106, 119, 146, 193
　funding for, 106, 119
Revesz, Gyorgy, 278
Reynolds, Charles, 53–54
Reynolds, Thomas, 318
Rhodes, Terrel, 263, 279
Rieke, Robert, 102, 233
Rillema, Paul, 229, 230
Ritchie, Fiona, 176

R.J. Reynolds Tobacco Company, 311
Robbins, John, 113, 114, 127
Robert A. Taft Institute, 142, 189
Robert Lee Bailey Professorship of History, 258, 277
Robertson, Wayne, 311
Robinson, Bryan, 318
Robinson, Cotton, 145
Robinson, Jay, 145, 176
Robinson, Joe, 57
Robinson, Russell M., II, 7, 249, 253, 255, 260, 261, 285, 288
Rocky River Venture trip, 191–192
Romine, Benjamin, 144
Rose, Judy Wilkins, 161, 219, 252, 287, 300, 301, 314–315
Rose, Lee, 155–156, 158, 160, 161, 218
Ross, George, 40
ROTC, 186
Roth, Jennifer, 175, 176
Roth, Walter, 309
Rouse, James W., 87, 88, 203
Rouse, Mary Ann, 254, 276
Rowan, Carl, 87
Rowan-Cabarrus Community College, 111
Rowe, Oliver R., 47, 48, 49, 51, 56, 57, 58, 67
Rowe Arts Building, 118, 292
Ruggles, Edward, 11
Runge, Igor, 304
Rupp, Adolph, 155, 156, 158
Rush S. Dickson Professor of Finance, 259
Russell M. Robinson II Distinguished Professorship of Shakespeare, 260

Sabates, Felix, 231
St. Andrew's Presbyterian College, 52
Saman, Paul, 309
Sanford, Terry, 33, 61–62
Sanger, Paul, 29
Sanskrit, 313
Sarow, Roger, 177
Savage, Donald, 173
Sawyer, Annie Lee, 25
Schell, Joseph F., 102, 178–179, 309
Schlachter, Louise, 163, 212
Schlechta, Joseph, 65
Schneider, Stanley, 318
Schroeder, Richard, 278
Schul, Norman W., 109, 141, 150, 235, 254
Schurle, Arlo, 185
Science division, 109, 178, 319
Scott, Ralph, 133, 134
Scott, Robert W., 91, 98, 133–134, 135–137, 138

Scott, W. Kerr, 35, 37, 133, 134
Sculpture garden, 292, 314
Sealey, Brook, 311
Sears, Carlton, 249
Seigfried, William, 296
Segregation, 31. *See also* African American
Selby, James, 189
Separate but equal doctrine, 31
Serling, Rod, 150
Sewell, Elizabeth, 87, 143
Shaffer, Eugene, 185, 318
Shao, Alan, 319
Shaw, Ruth, 310
Shenk, Dena, 305, 319
Shinn, George, 210
Shipman, Sheldon, 155
Shoemaker, James D. (Bill), 144
Silver Anniversary Campaign, 237, 254–257, 324
Simms, Bill, 300
Simon, Paul, 195
Simono, Sam, 113, 143
Simpson, Jackie, 163
Simpson, Lee, 307
Sims, Juanita, 66, 80, 113, 139
Sloan, Albert F., 255
Sloan, Norman, 156
Small Business Association Award, 307
Smith, Olen, 251, 292, 309, 310
Smith, R. T., 148
Smith, Sheldon P., 43, 48, 67
Smith, William, 309
Smith Building, 52
Snow, Chet, 253–254
Snyder, Robert, 163, 178–179
Soccer, 212
Sommer, John W., 259, 305, 319
Sonderman, Joe, 121, 233
Sorenson, Gail, 305
Sororities, 129
Southeastern University and College Coalition for Engineering Education (SUCCEED), 282
Southerland, J. William, 255
Southern Association of Colleges and Secondary Schools, 48
Southern Association of Junior Colleges, 49
Southern Piedmont Legislative Caucus, 272, 285, 300
SouthPark, 245
Spangler, C. D., Jr., 7, 164, 200, 236, 248, 249, 261, 279, 285, 307
asks for revised mission statements, 267
background of, 226–227

Index | 353

Spangler, C. D., Jr., *(cont'd)*
   named president of UNC, 225, 226
   in selection of Woodward as chancellor, 242, 243
   Silver Anniversary Campaign and, 255
   University City and, 200
Spangler, Meredith, 164, 225
Spangler, Patrick R., 139
Spence, Joseph, 186
Spitzer, Dwayne, 124
Sports. *See* Athletics
Staff Employee of the Year Award, 232, 335
Stahl, Bil, 180, 319
Stanly Community College, 111
State Community College Act of 1963, 58
Stavrakas, Nick, 112
Stedman, John B., 139, 254–255
Steimer, William, 145, 191, 192
Stevenson, Thomas H., 259
Stewart, Bud, 148
Stone, Mrs. Charles H. (Clara), 97, 231
Stone Professorship in American History, 259
Storrs, Thomas I., 164, 177–178, 226, 227, 241, 245, 249, 255, 270, 288
Storrs Architecture Building, 228, 292
Strawn, Martha, 319
Stribling, Paul, 176
Stroud, Anita, 195
Stuart, Alfred W., 142, 203, 281, 318
Student activity center, 284–287, 301
Student body presidents, 333
Student demonstrations, 116, 127
Student publications, 214
Styron, William, 18
Sunbelt Conference, 160, 277
Surtman, Jule, 100, 312
Susie Harwood Gardens, 103, 248
Suther, Judith, 319
Swayne, Linda, 319
Sweet, Mrs. Gordon, 50
Swift Distinguished Professorship in Judaic Studies, 99, 259–260

Tabor, James, 282, 314, 319
Taft Institute, 142, 189
Tate, Alice, 98–99, 231, 259–260
Tate Culbertson Scholarships, 99
Taylor, David, 200, 211, 231
Taylor, H. Patrick, 41, 276
Taylor, Robert L., 48, 67
Tenure disputes, 194–195
Thomas, Betty Dorton, 67, 139–140, 186
Thomas, Herman, 252

Thomas, Jay, 154
Thomas, William J., 305
Thomas I. Storrs Building, 228
Thompson, Carolyn, 312
Thompson, James, 249, 255, 256
Thorpe, Marion, 137
Toenjes, Dick, 295, 312
Torrence E. Hemby Distinguished Professorship in Banking, 256
Tranjan, Farid, 318
Trauth, Denise, 279
Trumper, David, 258, 304
Tsu, Raphael, 259, 318
Tucker, Irvin, 253
Turner, E. Daymond, 132
Turner, Frank, 51
Turner, Tom, 113, 128, 160, 276
Tuttle, Arthur, 68

Udall, Morris K., 150
Umstead, William B, 40
UNCC-First Union Economic Forecast, 212
Underwood, Richard A., 309
United Religious Ministry, 130
University City, 197–207. *See also* University Hospital; University Place; University Research Park
   Blockbuster Amphitheater of, 297
   growth and development of, 3, 124–126, 165, 293–298
   mall at, 293–294
   power centers at, 293–296
   waste-to-energy incinerator at, 297
University Forum, 87–88
University Hospital, 201–202. *See also* University City
University Metro Town Center Endowment, Inc., 200
University Network Publishing, 215
University of Alabama-Birmingham, 241–242
University of North Carolina
   administrative headquarters of, 120
   Board of Governors of, 136, 138–140, 216, 276
   Board of Trustees of, 135
      approves Charlotte campus, 76
      authorizes Charlotte campus study, 70–76
      elects Colvard chancellor, 94
      executive committee of, 135
   desegregation of, 182–184
   doctoral programs of, 136
   expansion of, 130–132, 134–135

University of North Carolina (cont'd)
  General Administration of, 216–217
  historically black colleges of, 183–184
  restructuring of, 135–137
University of North Carolina Advisory
  Council, 68–69
University of North Carolina at Asheville,
  130–131, 134
University of North Carolina at Chapel Hill,
  4, 8, 9, 44, 211
  Charlotte College Center and, 26, 27, 30
  in Consolidated University of North
    Carolina, 134
  as flagship campus, 120, 135
University of North Carolina at Charlotte
  academic achievements of, 188, 312–313
  academic deans of, 108
  academic organization of
    in Colvard era, 107–112
    in Fretwell era, 178–182
    in Woodward era, 275–276, 279
  academic planning for, 147, 323–324
  academic standards for, 215–216, 263–264
  academies at, 235
  accreditation of, 151, 216
  administration of
    in Colvard era, 107–112, 143–145,
      148–150, 163
    in early years, 85–86
    in Fretwell era, 178–182, 213–215,
      216–217, 230–231, 235–239
    in Woodward era, 251, 262–263,
      275–276, 279, 303, 309–310
  Alumni Association of, 130, 163, 219–220,
    257, 276, 287, 332
  athletics at. See Athletics
  becomes residential school, 106, 119, 132
  benefits of university system membership
    for, 120–121
  birth of, 67–83
  Board of Trustees of, 329–330
    in Colvard era, 139–140, 163–164
    in Fretwell era, 186
    honorary members of, 330
    in Woodward era, 241, 244–245,
      248–249, 310
  Board of Visitors of, 232
  building programs of
    in Colvard era, 106, 118–120, 146–147
    in Fretwell era, 192–193, 212, 227–228
    in Woodward era, 283–292, 299–301,
      321–323
  campus of
    in early years, 95–96, 103–105, 118–120

    master plan for, 321–323
  chancellor's residence for, 245–246
  colleges of, 108–112
  in Colvard era, 85–166
  community colleges and, 111
  constitution of, 129
  cultural activities at, 87–88, 143, 144–145,
    185–187
  curriculum at, 128, 215–216, 310–311
  desegregation and, 182–184
  developmental planning for
    in Colvard era, 103, 114, 146–147
    in Woodward era, 249–251, 321–323
  diversity at, 182–185
  endowment of, 222, 255
  enrollment at
    in Colvard era, 126, 132, 143, 147–148,
      165
    in early years, 89
    in Fretwell era, 174, 210–211, 216,
      229–230, 234, 235
    in Woodward era, 263, 315
  as entrepreneur, 111, 181, 197–207, 215
  evening programs at, 174
  faculty of
    in Colvard era, 88, 102–103, 115, 128,
      143–145, 161–163
    distinguished professorships for, 255,
      257–261
    endowment for, 255, 257
    in Fretwell era, 173–174, 185, 188–190,
      194–195, 213, 215–216, 235
    presidents of, 331
    in Woodward era, 251–252, 276–282,
      303–307, 309, 314, 318–319
  50th anniversary of, 303, 312–313
  in Fretwell era, 167–239
  funding for
    in Colvard era, 101–102, 118, 157–158
    in Fretwell era, 174, 195, 209–210, 211,
      216–217, 236
    in Woodward era, 272–273, 288–289
  fundraising for, 97–99, 211–212, 237, 245,
    254–257
  future directions for, 319–328
  gifts to, 97–100, 106
  graduate programs at
    in Colvard era, 128, 136, 141, 146, 148
    in Fretwell era, 174, 189, 228–229, 235
    future directions for, 324
    in Woodward era, 267–273, 279,
      310–312, 324
  honorary degrees granted by, 127, 150,
    163, 195, 330

Index | 355

University of North Carolina at Charlotte (cont'd)
   increasing sophistication of, 185–188
   innovation at, 110
   international programs at, 162
   international visitors to, 206–207
   internship program at, 235–236, 254
   land acquisition for, 106
   logo of, 121–122, 233–234
   media coverage of, 126–127, 173, 206–207
   mission statement of, 148, 267–271
   national reputation of, 221–223, 236–237, 263–264, 312–313
   off-campus centers of, 281
      at CityFair, 53, 151–152, 296–298
      at Queens College, 151
   privatization at, 236
   public perceptions of, 188, 236, 288
   radio station of, 175–177
   regional impact of, 3, 141–142, 161–163, 177–178, 181, 237, 264–265, 280
   research funding and facilities at, 214, 228, 235, 318–320
   restructuring of
      in Colvard era, 107–112
      in Fretwell era, 178–182, 230–231
      in Woodward era, 275–276
   school colors of, 86
   seal of, 86
   self-evaluation of, 188, 229, 249
   site of, 45–47
      development around, 198–207, 209–210. *See also* University Place
      selection of, 45–47
   student achievements at, 188, 306–307, 313–314
   student life at
      in Colvard era, 119, 129–130
      in Fretwell era, 182, 185–187, 190–191
   summer orientation at, 186
   10th anniversary of, 150–151
   town-gown relations and, 161–163
   transfer students at, 111
   25th anniversary of, 249–250
   UNC Board of Governors/General Administration and, 216–217
   as urban-oriented institution, 88, 95, 107, 209–211, 244, 317–328
   water and sewer service for, 124–125
   in Woodward era, 241–327
   work ethic at, 114–115
University of North Carolina at Charlotte Foundation, 96, 130, 139, 146, 255, 294
   University City and, 200

University of North Carolina at Charlotte Institute for Urban Studies and Community Service. *See* Urban Institute
University of North Carolina at Greensboro, 8, 134
University of North Carolina at Wilmington, 130–131, 134
University of North Carolina Press, 141
University of North Carolina Woman's College, 8, 44, 47
University Place, 88, 125, 144, 293. *See also* University City
   development of, 200–205, 293–298
University Research Park, 122–124, 165–166, 197–207. *See also* University City
   Ben Craig Center of, 206, 236
Uptown campus at CityFair, 53, 151–152, 296–298
Urban Institute, 128–129, 141–142, 162, 165, 181, 200, 230–231
   Bill McCoy and, 161–162
   directors of
      James L. Cox as, 150
      James W. Clay as, 181
Urban Land Institute, 268
U.S. News and World Report, UNC Charlotte ranking in, 221, 222, 312

Vairo, Phillip, 108
Valerio, Wendy Hicks, 282
Valvano, Jim, 252
Van Landingham, Ralph, 103–104
Van Landingham Glen, 103, 248
Vann, Ann, 50
Vaughan, Silas M., 107, 144
Velikovsky, Immanuel, 150
Venture program, 142, 191–192
Vice chancellors, organization of, 107–108
Vietnam War protests, 127
Vinroot, Richard, 300
Visual Arts Department, 213
Vogler, James, 76, 78–79
Vollendorf, Dean B., 309

Wachovia Fieldhouse, 287, 301
Wahab, James, 100
Wake Forest University, 47
Walker, Clyde, 161, 218
Wallace, George, 65
Wallace, Robert, 65, 102
Walls, Edward L., 162, 259, 309
Walsh, Tom, 233–234
Walters, David, 318
Waltrip, Michael, 311

Warren, Harold, 171
Warren, Lindsay, Jr., 135
Warren Committee, 135, 136
Warren Wilson College, 275
Watkins, Melvin, 155, 314
Watkins, Thomas, Sr., 48, 67
Watson, Jane, 246
Watson, Patty Jo, 314
Watson, Samuel D., Jr., 306, 318
Watt, Eulada, 310
Watt, Mel, 310
Wayne, Burt, 113
Wayson, Boone, 220
Wayson, Ed, 220
Wentz, C. H., 67
Werntz, James H., 179, 188–189, 230, 235, 236, 262, 314
West, Cameron, 137
West, Mark, 305, 319
Western Carolina College/University, 44, 121, 145, 148–149
Western College, 4
WFAE-FM, 175–177
Wheatley, Phillis, 144
Wheelock, John G., 50
Whelchel, Chester, 29
White, Jesse L., 268
White, Thomas J., 77
Whitley, Phil, 40
Wigginton, Eliot, 143
Wildacres retreat, 306
Wilhelm, Robert, 304
Wilkins, Judy. *See* Rose, Judy Wilkins
Williams, Robin, 143
Williams, Scotty, 113
Williamson, Sadie, 233
Willis, Edward, 309
Willis, Joyce, 232
Wilmington College, 34
Wilson, Elise, 89
Wilson, J. W., 29
Wilson, Michael, 249, 285
Windholz, George, 96, 319
Winner, Leslie, 300
Winningham, Edyth, 26, 87
Winningham Building, 51, 52
Winston-Salem State College/University, 132
Winthrop College, 20

Wise, Louis, 92
Wissell, Hal, 217–218
Witherspoon, Loy, 80, 99, 102, 118, 130, 144, 182, 243, 309
Woman's College of Greensboro, 8, 44, 47
  in Consolidated University of North Carolina, 134
Women's Studies Program, 213
Woods, Marian, 27, 28
Woodward, James H., 308, 314, 315, 318, 322
  achievements of, 315–316
  administration of, 241–327
  Atkins Library addition and, 299–301
  background of, 243
  building program and, 283–292
  community involvement of, 246
  goals of, 250–251
  honors awarded to, 315
  Hurricane Hugo and, 247–248
  installation of, 250–251
  lobbies for doctoral programs, 268–273
  management style of, 244, 262
  mission statement revision and, 267–271
  national reputation of, 315–316
  residences of, 245–246
  selection of as chancellor, 241–243, 309
  Silver Anniversary Campaign and, 255–257
  staff of, 251, 262–263, 275–276
  at University of Alabama-Birmingham, 241–242
  Uptown Center and, 293–298
  as visionary, 325–327
World War II veterans, educational needs of, 7–10, 8–9
Wright, Hazel, 309
Wu, Jy, 318

Xiang, Wei-Ning, 319

Yancy, Kathleen, 319
Young, Bob, 287, 301
Young, Dick, 29, 35

Z. Smith Reynolds Foundation, 114
Zahavy, Tzvee, 260
Zhou, Dian, 304
Zimmermann, Gerda, 277

9 781469 668543

www.ingramcontent.com/pod-product-compliance
Lightning Source LLC
Chambersburg PA
CBHW031131160426
43193CB00008B/105